KU-520-700

SOCIAL IDENTITY AT WORK

SOCIAL IDENTITY
AT WORK
Developing Theory
for Organizational Practice

Edited by
S. Alexander Haslam
Daan van Knippenberg
Michael J. Platow, and
Naomi Ellemers

LIVERPOOL
JOHN MOORES UNIVERSITY
AVRIL ROBARTS LRC
TITHEBARN STREET
LIVERPOOL L2 2ER
TEL. 0151 231 4022

PSYCHOLOGY PRESS
New York and Hove

Published in 2003 by
Psychology Press, LTD.
29 West 35th Street
New York, NY 10001
www.psypress.com

Published in Great Britain by
Psychology Press, LTD.
27 Church Road
Hove, East Sussex
BN3 2FA

Copyright © 2003 by Taylor & Francis Books, Inc.

Psychology Press, LTD., is an imprint of the Taylor & Francis Group.
Printed in the United States of America on acid-free paper.

Cover Design: Pearl Chang
Cover photo: Corbis

All rights reserved. No part of this book may be reprinted or reproduced or utilized in any
form or by any electronic, mechanical, or other means, now known or hereafter invented,
including photocopying and recording, or in any information storage or retrieval system,
without permission in writing from the publishers.

10 9 8 7 6 5 4 3 2 1

Library of Congress Cataloging-in-Publication Data

Social identity at work : developing theory for organizational practice / edited by
S. Alexander Haslam . . . [et al.]
    p. cm.
    "The formal proposal for this book was developed at the 12th General Meeting of the
European Association of Social Psychology in Oxford, 199' –P..
    Includes bibliographical references and index.
    ISBN 1-84169-035-X
    1. Industrial sociology. 2. Group identity. 3. Organizational behavior.
4. Communication in organizations. 5. Teams in the workplace. 6. Industrial
Management—Psychological aspects. I. Haslam, S. Alexander
HD6952 .S624 2003
302.3—dc21

2002068203

This book is dedicated to the memory
of our friend and colleague

Jan Bruins

1961–1998

Contents

About the Editors

S. Alexander Haslam is professor of social and organizational psychology at the University of Exeter, UK. His research examines social identity and self-categorization processes in groups and organizations. Formerly an associate editor of the *British Journal of Social Psychology*, he is currently Editor of the *European Journal of Social Psychology* and serves on the editorial board of several international journals. His most recent book is *Psychology in Organizations: The Social Identity Approach* (2001).

Michael J. Platow is a senior lecturer in the School of Psychological Science at La Trobe University, Australia. His research uses social identity and self-categorization principles to study the social psychology of distributive and procedural justice, leadership, trust, social influence, and the self. Some lessons from this work are applied in his recent book *Giving Professional Presentations in the Behavioral Sciences* (2002).

Daan van Knippenberg is professor of organizational behavior at the Rotterdam School of Management, Erasmus University Rotterdam, The Netherlands. His research is in the area of group processes (leadership, influence, diversity, decision making, performance) and organizational identifications. Together with Michael Hogg he edited *Identity, Leadership, and Power* (forthcoming) and a special issue of *Group Processes and Intergroup Relations*, on social identity processes in organizations.

Naomi Ellemers is professor of social and organizational psychology at the University of Leiden, the Netherlands. Her research addresses theoretical developments in the social identity tradition, as well as the application of social identity theory to organizational problems. She is a former associate editor of the *British Journal of Social Psychology*, and a current associate editor of the *Journal of Personality and Social Psychology*. She is a coeditor of previous books on stereotyping (1997) and on social identity theory (1999).

Contributors

Sebastian Bachmann, University of Kansas, USA
Nyla R. Branscombe, University of Kansas, USA
Rachael Eggins, The Australian National University
Naomi Ellemers, University of Leiden, The Netherlands
S. Alexander Haslam, University of Exeter, UK
Yuen Huo, University of California, Los Angeles, USA
Michael A. Hogg, University of Queensland, Australia
Martin Lea, University of Manchester, UK
Robin Martin, University of Queensland, Australia
Mark Nolan, The Australian National University
Michael J. Platow, La Trobe University, Australia
Tom Postmes, University of Exeter, UK
Anthony Pratkanis, University of California, Santa Cruz, USA
Katherine Reynolds, The Australian National University
Paul Rogers, University of Manchester, UK
Tara Samuels, San Jose State University, USA
Heather J. Smith, Sonoma State University, USA
Michael T. Schmitt, Dartmouth College, USA
Russell Spears, University of Amsterdam, The Netherlands
Deborah Terry, University of Queensland, Australia
Marlene Turner, San Jose State University, USA
Tom Tyler, New York University, USA
Daan van Knippenberg, Erasmus University, The Netherlands
Esther van Leeuwen, Free University of Amsterdam, The Netherlands
Juergen Wegge, University of Dortmund, Germany
Michael Wenzel, The Australian National University

Corrections

Preface and Acknowledgments

*T*he formal proposal for this book was developed at the 12th General Meeting of the European Association of Social Psychology in Oxford, 1999. Our goal in developing the proposal was to respond to three distinct trends. First, it was very clear that social identity research was generating more interest within social psychology than it had ever done before. So, where once social identity researchers had been something of a marginal group at social psychology conferences, their work was now center stage and very much in the ascendancy. Where once social identity principles had been investigated only by small groups of researchers and reported only in select texts and journals, they had now broken through into mainstream (i.e., North American) texts and journals, and were embraced by an ever-expanding and ever more disparate band of researchers.

Second, and partly as a result of this, the social identity approach was starting to receive much more attention from researchers outside social psychology. Illustrative of these developments, interest was beginning to be expressed by political scientists, sociologists, historians, geographers—even theologians. Most obviously, though, social identity and self-categorization theories were coming to the attention of academics in organizational psychology programs and business schools who were using them to improve understanding of the group processes that lay at the heart of almost all the issues in which they were interested. Significantly, too, this was a direction in which our own work and that of many of our colleagues was moving—primarily because organizations provide a natural and powerful context in which to explore social identity processes at work. This is for the simple reason that organizations *are* groups, and the group memberships they provide have a distinct impact on people's behavior. As a result, issues of group identity prove central to leadership, motivation, communication, decision making, negotiation, diversity, culture, productivity, teamwork, indeed, to just about every substantial organizational topic.

Third, however, it was apparent that while the above two developments were generally very positive, they were not without their perils. Along these lines, John Turner who had originally developed social identity theory with Henri Tajfel, sounded warnings that some core ideas were being diluted and distorted in the social identity goldrush (Turner, 1999; for more detail see chapter 1, this volume). He explicitly rejected the view that the theory should be embraced as a form of dogma, but nonetheless urged against development as a form of asset stripping whereby rich theoretical analysis (which, amongst other things, requires the specification of content and context in order to have any predictive value) is reduced to a set of impoverished one-factor dictates.

As we saw it, then, there was a clear need for a volume that showcased exciting developments in social identity work as it was being conducted in the organizational domain, but which reflected and held faith with a deep understanding of the tradition from that that work emerged. Our strategy for achieving this was quite simple: We solicited contributions from colleagues around the world who had a strong grounding in social identity and self-categorization theories but who, like us, had been elaborating upon these in the process of attempting to shed light on key organizational issues. The result, we feel, is a compelling and timely text that points to a powerful synergy between theory and practice: On the one hand, theory serves as a tool with which to develop applied and practical understanding; on the other hand, the attempt to address novel organizational problems provides a basis for teasing out and refining theory.

In elegant temporal symmetry, the completed manuscript was delivered to the publishers at the 22nd General Meeting of the European Association of Social Psychology in San Sebastian, 2002. In helping us to achieve this goal we would like to thank Paul Dukes and Pat Connolly at Psychology Press, as well as our many friends and colleagues around the world who have provided input and guidance.

Of course, between these two scientific meetings, we have been working with other social identities than the one that made this volume possible. Most notably, three of the editors had children (Alexander to Daan and Barbara, Ethan to Michael and Diana; Nathaniel to Naomi and Dick) while Alex moved from Australia to England with Cath. Although these events did not necessarily facilitate the completion of this volume, they do remind us that social identities have many different forms and that their creative potential is not only a source of change but also of peculiar joy.

Alex Haslam, Daan van Knippenberg, Michael Platow, and Naomi Ellemers
San Sebastian, June, 2002

PART I

INTRODUCTION

1

Social Identity at Work
Developments, Debates, Directions

NAOMI ELLEMERS
University of Leiden
S. ALEXANDER HASLAM
University of Exeter
MICHAEL J. PLATOW
LaTrobe University
DAAN VAN KNIPPENBERG
Erasmus University Rotterdam

Recent years have witnessed a surge of interest in using the social–psychological insights provided by social identity theory (and its extension, self-categorization theory) to analyze issues and problems that arise in work settings. This is evident simply in the sheer number of publications devoted to such endeavors, as summarized in special issues of journals from social psychology and the organizational sciences (*Academy of Management Review*, Albert, Ashforth, & Dutton, 2000; *Group Processes and Intergroup Relations*, van Knippenberg & Hogg, 2001), recent monographs (Haslam, 2001; Tyler & Blader, 2000), and edited volumes (Hogg & Terry, 2001; Polzer, in press; van Knippenberg & Hogg, in press; the present volume). This development reflects the growing realization among research psychologists, as well as those who actually work with people in organizations, that work behavior is to an important extent determined by people's membership in social groups, and hence that work-related issues can often be best understood with reference to intragroup processes and intergroup relations.

Whereas previous work in this area has mainly tried to illustrate the feasibility of such an approach and to demonstrate the usefulness of social identity as a construct that helps us understand social behavior in work settings, the present volume builds on these initial efforts in order to take a somewhat different perspective. Now that it has become more common to use a social identity framework to analyze organizational problems, it is important to take a closer look at the implications of doing this. This is because, in our view, further scientific progress in this particular area of research is only possible if we develop a more refined notion of the status and characteristics of social identity theory as an analytical tool and explicitly consider the implications of applying insights from this theoretical perspective to organizational problems.

Accordingly, the aim of this chapter is to provide a general introduction to social identity theory and its relation to work and organizational psychology, as a means of outlining the broader theoretical background that constitutes the frame of reference for the different chapters in this volume. In doing this, we will focus on (1) explaining key theoretical concepts and their relationship to previous work; (2) discussing some complex issues that have been subject to different insights and scientific debate; and (3) outlining the likely directions for future theory development and its application in work organizations.

THE ADVANTAGES AND DISADVANTAGES OF A "GRAND THEORY"

A well-known assumption in the philosophy of science is that creative ideas and novel hypotheses more easily emerge when insights from different areas of research are combined. Indeed, on occasion, the expectation that multidisciplinary research should be particularly innovative is even institutionalized (e.g., in the criteria that are used by research funding bodies to judge applications). In principle, it can be argued that insights from neighboring fields of science introduce alternative theoretical perspectives and raise additional questions that help to broaden intellectual input and increase the relevance of output. However, as we know from research on the effects of diversity in work teams, heterogeneity of insights only stimulates divergent thinking and creativity when the recipients of different viewpoints are in a position to benefit from the exchange process (e.g., De Dreu & West, 2001). Unfortunately, this means that, just as the boundary conditions for reaping the benefits from diversity in the workplace are not always met, so too exchange of scientific perspectives and insights often bears less fruit than expected. For this reason, it is important to be aware of potential problems in applying a particular theoretical perspective to work that has been done in a different tradition, as a lack of awareness of theoretical specificities may impede rather than promote constructive development.

Social identity theory is one of the few "grand theories" in social psychology. In contrast to so-called single-hypothesis theories, the theory is complex, multifaceted, and dynamic. Indeed, in different periods, different aspects of the social identity process have been the focus of attention, and parts of the theory have developed at different points in time (Turner, 1999). In the case of social identity theory, this meant that in addition to original formulations in the late 1970s (Tajfel, 1974, 1975, 1978c; Tajfel & Turner, 1979) the theory was elaborated within the broader theoretical framework of self-categorization theory in the 1980s (Turner, 1982, 1985, 1987; Turner, Hogg, Oakes, Reicher, & Wetherell, 1987). As a result, more than 20 years of research have contributed to important elaborations of the theory and its implications and these have yielded more precise specifications of the psychological processes involved (Turner, 1999).

One obvious advantage of such a grand theory is that it can be applied to many different problems, including more complex real life situations, such as interethnic conflict (Hewstone & Brown, 1986), political activism (Simon, Loewy et al., 1998), union participation (Kelly & Kelly, 1994), and workplace behavior (e.g., Ellemers, de Gilder, & van den Heuvel, 1998; Haslam, Powell, & Turner, 2000; van Knippenberg, van Knippenberg, Monden, & de Lima, 2002). Indeed, social identity theory has inspired a substantial body of experimental work intended to specify particular psychological processes as well as providing an analytical framework that can been used to understand, intervene in, and perhaps even resolve a variety of social and organizational problems (for illustrative overviews, see Augoustinos & Reynolds, 2001; Ellemers, Spears, & Doosje, 1999; Haslam, 2001).

However, the broadness, complexity, and dynamic nature of the theory also has important drawbacks. First, social identity theory has been the focus of considerable confusion and sometimes heated debate (a recent exchange can be found in the *British Journal of Social Psychology*, e.g., McGarty, 2001). This has led some to doubt the usefulness of the theory because they maintain that hypotheses as well as counterhypotheses happily coexist. Indeed, one of its distinctive features is that, rather than providing simple truths, social identity theory emphasizes the *contingencies* inherent in many social processes, causing people to adapt their perceptions and behavior to the opportunities and restrictions inherent in the situation at hand (Turner, 1999). Second, some have failed to take into account that social identity theory is still developing, and rely on specific theoretical "interpretations" to represent (and sometimes misrepresent) established theory (e.g., Jost & Elsbach, 2001, pp. 182–186). We feel that such readings do not always do justice to the theory because they fail to take into account nuances, specifications, and developments (McGarty, 2001; Turner, 1999). At the same time, we also recognize that it may seem difficult to keep abreast of current developments, especially for those who follow the theory "from a distance," which may complicate use of the theory in a multidisciplinary analysis.

In this chapter we aim to elucidate some aspects of social identity theory that can easily go unnoticed by those who have been educated in a different tradition, have been working with other theoretical frameworks, or have been following the scientific debate in journals. In doing this, we observe that there are not only empirical and theoretical, but also political dimensions of social identity theory, and argue that this has important implications for the resulting view of behavioral processes in organizations. In the remainder of this chapter we will therefore elaborate the different dimensions of social identity theory, address the consequences of adopting a particular interpretation of the theory, and specify how the contributions in the present volume relate to this discussion.

THE INITIAL STATEMENT OF SOCIAL IDENTITY THEORY

We will begin our argument by going back in time in order to trace how current insights in social identity theory have developed from initial statements, and analyze how particular research findings, theoretical views, and specific publications have crucially impacted upon this development as well as the resulting notion of what social identity theory actually stands for.

Social identity theory was initially formulated to account for the unexpected finding that people tend to display intergroup discrimination in so-called minimal groups (Tajfel, Flament, Billig, & Bundy, 1971). Specifically, in an experimental situation that excluded the operation of conflicting interests, people tended to allocate more resources to an anonymous ingroup member than to an out-group member, even when they were randomly assigned to one of two groups, did not even know who their fellow in-group members or out-group members were, and were aware that they could not personally benefit from their discriminatory behavior. This turned out to be a rather robust phenomenon, as these results were replicated in a number of follow-up studies where different variations of this paradigm were investigated in order to exclude various alternative explanations (see Diehl, 1990, for an overview). These initial findings prompted Tajfel to develop the original foundations of social identity theory, connecting three social–psychological processes, namely:

Social categorization—the tendency for people to perceive themselves and others in terms of particular social categories, instead of as separate individuals;

Social comparison—the tendency to assess the relative worth of groups as well as individuals by comparing them on relevant dimensions with other groups; and

Social identification—the notion that people do not generally relate to social situations as detached observers, but, instead, their own identity is typically implicated in their perceptions of, and responses to, the social situation.

In his initial writings about the theory, Tajfel (1974, 1975, 1978) elaborated on these processes and the way they interact with each other, to develop the notion that—in contrast to situations that are purely defined at the individual level and involve interpersonal behavior—there is also a class of situations where people primarily define themselves and others at the group level, and interact with each other in terms of their group membership. In doing this, Tajfel heavily relied on his observations of real life phenomena, such as interethnic conflict and struggles of underprivileged social groups, in order to develop his argument and illustrate the resulting phenomena.

These initial arguments culminated in the seminal chapter with John Turner (Tajfel & Turner, 1979; later slightly updated and retitled in Tajfel & Turner, 1986). This is usually seen as *the* formulation of social identity theory and summarizes its main propositions and hypotheses. An important part of the 1979 chapter is devoted to explaining the plight of members of underprivileged social groups, and specifying the different responses they are likely to display in an attempt to cope with the situation they face. Departing from the assumption that inclusion in a group that fares negatively compared to relevant other groups necessarily challenges one's social identity, Tajfel and Turner argue that different cognitive and behavioral strategies are available to individual group members, depending on the psychological and sociostructural conditions (level of commitment to the group, stability and legitimacy of existing intergroup relations, permeability of group boundaries).

Individual group members may resolve identity threat by distancing the self from the group in question, and moving into another group. This strategy, which is referred to as *individual mobility*, tends to be used by those with relatively low levels of commitment to the group (e.g., Ellemers, Spears, & Doosje, 1997), and when group boundaries are permeable (e.g., Ellemers, Wilke, & van Knippenberg, 1993). At the group level, an unfavorable intergroup comparison may be addressed by trying to improve the in-group's standing through *social competition* with the goal of social change. Such a group-level strategy is most likely to occur when people are more closely tied to the group either for psychological reasons (high commitment) or for practical reasons (impermeable boundaries), and when current intergroup relations seem unstable or illegitimate (e.g., Ellemers, van Knippenberg, & Wilke, 1990). Alternatively, when stable or legitimate intergroup differences provide little scope for achieving social change (and leaving the group is not a feasible option) group members may try to enhance the image of their group at a cognitive level. Such *social creativity* strategies include redefining the value of characteristic group traits (e.g., Ellemers, van Rijswijk, Roefs, & Simons, 1997), introducing alternative dimensions of intergroup comparison (Lemaine, 1974; Mummendey & Schreiber, 1983; Mummendey & Simon, 1989), or alternative comparison groups (e.g., Spears & Manstead, 1989), among others (see also van Knippenberg & Ellemers, 1990; Galinsky, Hugenberg, Groom, & Bodenhausen, in press).

FURTHER DEVELOPMENTS

Interdependence and Bias

Despite this explicit theoretical consideration of the different strategies that group members may employ to maintain or enhance their social identity, in the 1970s and early 1980s research effort and scientific debate were directed mainly at establishing the psychological process responsible for the occurrence of *ingroup favoritism* in the minimal group paradigm. As an alternative to the contention that ingroup favoritism was motivated by a desire to enhance one's social identity, some researchers argued that perceived interdependence between group members would provide them with an important instrumental reason for displaying such behavior (Bornstein et al., 1983; Rabbie, Schot, & Visser, 1989). This inspired a number of empirical tests, which conclusively demonstrated that, while interdependence did elicit biased outcome allocations, in-group favoritism persisted when all individually instrumental reasons for doing so were eliminated (e.g., Diehl, 1990) in a manner consistent with the theoretical ideas originally put forward by Tajfel and Turner (1979).

Self-Esteem

Once it was widely accepted that social identity maintenance and enhancement provided an important basis for the behavior of individuals, further efforts to understand the precise motives underlying displays of intergroup discrimination in minimal groups resulted in the development of the so-called *self-esteem hypothesis* (Hogg & Abrams, 1990). This hypothesis consists of two corollaries. In addition to the notion that inclusion in a positively valued social group contributes to a positive identity and hence may enhance group members' collective self-esteem, Hogg and Abrams (1990) suggested that those with depressed group-based self-esteem should be motivated to enhance it by displaying in-group favoritism. Although this development inspired a substantial amount of empirical work, much of this research suffered from methodological shortcomings that make it difficult to draw unambiguous conclusions (e.g., Long & Spears, 1997). In particular, a key methodological problem arose from the tendency for researchers who were unfamiliar with the social identity tradition to take personal self-esteem as a proxy for collective self-esteem (i.e., esteem derived from one's membership of a relevant group).

Going back, in a way, to the idea of interdependence, the implicit assumption thus remained that people would generally be driven by individually instrumental motives. That is, group situations were simply regarded as interpersonal situations where individual instrumentality (the desire to have high personal self-esteem) is tied to the group's fate, and hence the individual only contributes to the group as a means to advance the self. As a result, what theoretically was supposed to be group-based self-esteem was often assessed with stable and global measures referring to the personal self in empirical research (e.g., after Rosenberg, 1965), while a proper test of the theoretical proposition would require assessing the temporary state of the social self-esteem derived from a particular intergroup comparison (e.g., Crocker & Luhtanen, 1990). Indeed, more recent work that avoids these problems has elucidated more clearly the relationship between individual-level and group-level self-esteem and specified much more convincingly how they are related to displays of in-group favoritism (e.g., Hunter, Platow, Howard, & Stringer, 1996; Long & Spears, 1998; Rubin & Hewstone, 1998).

At the same time, this more sophisticated work makes it clear that there is no simple one-to-one relationship between single motives (such as self-esteem enhancement) and particular behaviors (e.g., intergroup discrimination). Indeed, as was made clear in early formulations of social identity theory, favoring the ingroup is only *one* possible strategy that can be used to enhance or protect one's social identity. Furthermore, there are indications that under some circumstances establishing the in-group as a separate entity may be so important that group members prefer to differentiate the in-group in a *negative* way, rather than perceiving the in-group as positive but indistinct (Mlicki & Ellemers, 1996). This further attests to the notion that *socially* meaningful motives rather than individual instrumentality drive the responses of group members.

Self-Categorization

In the late 1980s and early 1990s, along with the general shift toward the examination of cognitive processes in social psychology, work in the social identity tradition also focused on the development of theory describing the *cognitive aspects* of social categorization, and its consequences for social behavior. As noted above, this resulted in the formulation of self-categorization theory (Turner, 1985; Turner, Hogg et al., 1987; Turner, Oakes, Haslam, & McGarty, 1994), which focused on the implications of cognitive self-categorization for self-perception and social perception (stereotyping). Important components of this theoretical and empirical work were devoted to (1) examining and explaining the context-dependence of particular self-categorizations (e.g., Haslam & Turner, 1992), and (2) demonstrating the manifest expressions of these self-categorization processes in people's perceptions, attitudes, and normative behavior (e.g., Oakes, Haslam, & Turner, 1994; Spears, Oakes, Ellemers & Haslam, 1997; Turner, 1991). Amongst other things, such work examined the crucial role that social self-categorization (i.e., definition of the self in terms of social identity) played in processes of stereotyping, social influence, and coordinated group activity.

LIVERPOOL
JOHN MOORES UNIVERSITY
AVRIL ROBARTS LRC
TEL. 0151 231 4022

Social Creativity

Although from the outset social identity research had been conducted with artificially constructed as well as more naturally occurring social groups, in the late 1990s, more frequent attempts were made to understand the actual problems occurring in real social groups by applying insights from social identity and self-categorization theories. Here investigations of interethnic relations, political groups, and teams in organizations, underlined the notion that rather complex processes are involved when people act in terms of their social identity. For example, as Hinkle and Brown (1990) concluded from a review of empirical studies, there is no simple relationship between group status and ingroup bias. Instead, investigations with natural groups consistently reveal that in more complex settings various alternative strategies are employed in addition to the display of ingroup favoritism on the status-defining dimension. These more socially creative ways of coping with unfavorable intergroup comparisons include introducing alternative domains of comparison (Mummendey & Schreiber, 1983, 1984; Mummendey & Simon, 1989), reevaluating the relative importance of status-defining comparison dimensions (van Knippenberg & van Oers, 1984; Ellemers, van Rijswijk, et al., 1997), redefining and reappropriating the meaning of such dimensions (Galinsky et al., in press), and focusing on comparison with a different group (Spears & Manstead, 1989).

Group Commitment

Work in the late 1990s moved on to look at how, within the same group, responses to social identity threat may differ, depending on the extent to which group members regard their inclusion in this particular group as subjectively important. From this work it became clear that cognitive awareness of being included in a particular group does not automatically elicit group-level responses. Instead, some sense of subjective commitment to the group turned out to be crucial for people to start acting in terms of their group membership (Ellemers, Kortekaas, & Ouwerkerk, 1999). That is, in artificially constructed laboratory groups as well as more natural group settings it was established that only those who identify strongly with the group are inclined to address their group's plight collectively—for example, by engaging in intergroup competition or by displaying social creativity (Kelly & Kelly, 1994; Veenstra & Haslam, 2000). In contrast, low identifiers tend to respond to unfavorable intergroup comparisons by distancing the self from the group, either psychologically (i.e., by emphasizing intragroup differences, Doosje, Ellemers, & Spears, 1995; Spears, Doosje, & Ellemers, 1997), or by actually trying to move into another group (Ellemers, Spears, & Doosje, 1997).

Audience Constraints

Further research, however, revealed that people do not always feel free to express their behavioral preferences, especially when they are under surveillance from in-group members (Reicher & Levine, 1994), and such action implies defecting from the group (see Ellemers, Barreto, & Spears, 1999, for an overview). Thus, for structural reasons, salient motives (e.g., to distance the self from the group) do not always have a parallel in overt action (e.g., refusal to help the group), but may remain hidden from public scrutiny, as they are only expressed in private (Ellemers, van Dyck, Hinkle, & Jacobs, 2000). For instance, while low identifiers may indicate a preference to invest in self-improvement as long as these preferences remain anonymous, they tend to align with the group when they run the risk of being sanctioned by other group members (Barreto & Ellemers, 2000; Reicher & Levine, 1994).

In sum, whereas the general motive underlying group-based behavior might be relatively straightforward and simple, it is clear that this motivation may translate into a variety of behaviors depending on a number of factors. These include (1) individuals' predisposition to define themselves in terms of that group membership; (2) feasibility estimates of different possible strategies, which are determined by characteristics of the intergroup situation (salient comparisons and structural possibilities for change); and (3) considerations of which forms of behavior would be considered acceptable or desirable by others who are in the position to judge it (normative considerations).

As a result, similar motives may manifest themselves in different behaviors and the same behavior may result from diverse motives, with the result that it is not self-evident from isolated observations or single measures what group members are actually trying to achieve and why. Nevertheless, the basic assumption of social identity theory, that people are motivated to act in terms of their group membership for socially meaningful (instead of individually instrumental) reasons, still remains valid. Moreover, empirical research has convincingly demonstrated that each of the three identity management strategies that were originally specified by the theory will be observed, given appropriate circumstances.

While this underlines the general validity of the social identity perspective, and demonstrates its usefulness for analyzing complex social phenomena, at the same time it is clear that a full and proper social identity analysis requires consideration of various psychological and social contextual factors, in order to specify the particular response pattern that is most likely to emerge in any given situation. Indeed, an important challenge for future research is to further refine methods for the empirical assessment of what group members are actually trying to achieve in any given situation, so that these specific goals can be related to the behavioral strategies they employ.

IMPLICATIONS FOR WORK SETTINGS

Starting with the influential publication of Ashforth and Mael (1989), researchers in the area of organizational behavior have picked up on many of the ideas outlined above by using insights from social identity theory to examine specific issues and problems in the workplace. Topics that have been approached from this perspective relate to questions such as: Under what circumstances are individuals willing to exert themselves on behalf of their team or the organization? When will different work groups compete with each other and when will they collaborate? What makes people leave an organization, and how can they be retained?

Application of a Complex Theory

In trying to examine these and similar specific questions, particular constructs, motives, or processes that play a role in social identity theory have often been borrowed by researchers who have primarily been working in another tradition. However, as we indicated above, the broadness of scope and complexity of social identity theory implies that focusing on a single hypothesis or compartmentalizing a particular variable will generally fail to do justice to a full understanding that the theory might provide.

In this way a more narrow research focus can easily lead to misunderstandings or even incorrect assumptions about the theory. One case in point is the notion that unfavorable intergroup comparisons should always promote discriminatory intergroup behavior (e.g., Jost & Elsbach, 2001, pp. 185–188). We have shown above that social identity theory does not lead to this prediction—at least not in any general sense—as people may also use more socially creative strategies, or turn away from the group altogether in order to cope individually with such a situation. In a similar vein, some have incorrectly argued that social identity theory predicts that mere inclusion in a group should always elicit ingroup favoring behavior (e.g., Jost & Elsbach, 2001, pp. 184–185). As a result, the observation that in a range of situations group members fail to display in-group favoritism (e.g., because they do not consider their group membership sufficiently important to engage in a group-level strategy) are, unjustly, taken as evidence against the validity of social identity theory, or at least as demonstrating its limited application to real-life settings (see also van Knippenberg, in press; cf. Hogg & Terry, 2000).

In this way, lack of awareness of social identity theory and its recent elaborations, has hampered (and has the potential to further impede) the development of insight across different domains of psychological research. In particular, some findings that have been obtained in an organizational context have been viewed as providing novel insights that call for theoretical development when they actually replicate previous observations that lie at the heart of the development of social identity theory. For instance, a much-cited study by Elsbach and Kramer (1996) showed that faculty in business schools that performed less well in *Business Week* rankings worked to maintain their sense of valued social identity by emphasizing performance in selective organizational categories that helped to emphasize favorable school performance. However, within social psychology, there is a substantial body of research on multidimensional intergroup comparisons (summarized above), which demonstrates essentially the same phenomenon in a variety of group contexts (e.g. Brown & Wade, 1987; van Knippenberg & van Oers, 1984; see Ellemers & van Knippenberg, 1997, for an overview).

Conceptualization

A slightly different problem that has emerged in applying social identity insights to the organizational domain relates to ambiguity in the exact definition and measurement of central concepts in social identity theory. Because similar concepts and processes are described in the work and organizational literature (albeit from a different theoretical perspective), an important question is how the constructs used in these different research domains relate to each other, and whether or not they can be seen as interchangeable.

The concept of "social identity" in particular has generated a considerable amount of theoretical debate and empirical work. In social psychology, part of the difficulty is that the same term (*social identification*) has been used to refer to both (1) the tendency to perceive the self as a group member (i.e., the *process* of being identified), and (2) the self-image that derives from the group (i.e., the *state* of being identified). Importantly, however, although they may covary, strength of identification can and should be distinguished from the content of the resulting social identity. In an organizational context, this would imply that organizational identification (referring to the ties between the individual and the organization) should be differentiated from organizational identity (the content of the resulting identity).

A first complication is that within the field of organizational behavior there is a strong tradition of thinking in terms of stable individual differences, which (if appropriately measured) can predict a range of relevant behaviors in a variety of settings. When either the strength or content of social identity is viewed in this way, this fails to do justice to the fact that social identity is defined as a dynamic construct that may not only develop and change over time but is also context dependent (e.g., see Haslam et al., 2000; McGarty, 1999). For example, the same person may identify strongly with some parts of the organization (e.g., the work team) but not with other constituencies (e.g., management), so that making a general distinction between high and low identifiers becomes meaningless (Ellemers, de Gilder, & van den Heuvel, 1998; van Knippenberg & van Schie, 2000). Likewise, the social identity derived from a particular group may be positive in one context (e.g., when comparing organizational productivity) but negative in another (e.g., when comparing the quality of leader–member relations), implying that attempting to assess whether the social identity derived from a particular team or organization is globally positive or negative will not help to predict work-related behavior across different contexts.

A second point of debate relates to the nature of identification as either a unidimensional or a multidimensional construct, and the related issue of the difference between commitment and identification. In order, quite reasonably, to underline the added value for the applied literature of the concept of organizational identification relative to the more traditional concept of organizational commitment, Mael and Ashforth (1992) argued that the term *organizational identification* should be reserved to refer to the cognitive–perceptual self-definitional component of group membership, the psychological merging of self and group, while *organizational commitment* be used to refer to the affective ties between the individual and the organization (see also Pratt, 1998; van Knippenberg & Sleebos, 2001). Consistent with this analysis, linked commitment, more closely than identification to attitudes toward the job and the organization, was found to be more predictive of job satisfaction, motivation, and involvement, turnover intentions, and perceived organizational support than identification (Mael & Tetrick, 1992; van Knippenberg & Sleebos, 2001). Identification, however, was found to be more closely aligned with a measure of the degree to which organizational membership was self-referential (van Knippenberg & Sleebos, 2001). In addition, the fact that identification and commitment were empirically distinct (Mael, 1988, in Ashforth & Mael, 1989; Mael & Tetrick, 1992; van Knippenberg & Sleebos, 2001) confirmed that identification and commitment may be viewed as separate constructs.

Others, however, have argued that a conceptualization of identification in cognitive–perceptual terms does not do justice to the original definition of social identity as a multifaceted construct that incorporates cognitive as well as affective components (Ellemers, Kortekaas, & Ouwerkerk, 1999; cf. Karasawa, 1991). Indeed, Tajfel (1978c) classically defined social identity as "the individual's knowledge that he [or she] belongs to certain groups together with some emotional and value significance to him [or her] of the group membership" (p. 31). In a study that attempted to capture this three-component conceptualization of identification, Ellemers, Kortekaas, and Ouwerkerk (1999) conclude that the affective component (labeled "affective commitment" by Ellemers et al.) is the primary predictor of people's tendency to act in terms of their group membership (see also Ouwerkerk, Ellemers, & de Gilder, 1999). Ellemers et al.'s approach would thus favor a conceptualization of the cognitive and the affective component of group membership as aspects of the same construct, identification, and, by implication, would view studies of organizational identification as defined by Ashforth and Mael (1989) and studies of affective organizational commitment (e.g., Meyer & Allen, 1997) as pertaining to different aspects of the same construct.

As van Knippenberg (2002) argues, however, the Ellemers et al. study did not incorporate a measure of identification as defined by Ashforth and Mael (1989) and others (e.g., Pratt, 1998; van Knippenberg & Sleebos, 2001); that is, as a sense of oneness of self and group (i.e., which is not the same as awareness of group membership). And whether or not identification is seen as a unidimensional or a multidimensional construct is ultimately a conceptual issue rather than a measurement issue (i.e., the fact that different questionnaire items measure different things does not make them part of the same construct). The nature of organizational identification and the relationship between organizational identification and organizational commitment thus very much remains an issue of debate.

To conclude, in this section of the chapter we have discussed some of the issues that have emerged in the application of social identity theory to the behavior of people in work settings. On the positive side, it is important to note that there has been some fruitful cross-fertilization, in the sense that this work broadened the scope of researchers educated within a single tradition, resulting in the validation of similar theoretical ideas across different research domains. At the same time, the relatively separate development of two different research areas has also been the cause of confusion and misunderstanding. Indeed, within the organizational sphere, a limited number of publications have come to represent "the social identity approach," when they were never intended to (and hence do not) provide a complete overview of the theory's richness and complexity. This is for the simple reason that, quite rightly, these publications focus on a specific issue or reflect concerns that were pertinent to the authors at a particular point in time (e.g., Ashforth & Mael, 1989; Dutton & Dukerich, 1991; Elsbach & Kramer, 1996). One important conclusion from our current argument is that efforts to tie social identity theory (or self-categorization theory) to issues in work and organizational psychology, should aim to go beyond the application of single hypotheses in order to benefit fully from available theoretical insight.

THE POLITICAL DIMENSION

The foregoing discussion points to theory-related hazards that newcomers to social identity research might encounter. However, beyond this, we now want to raise some political questions that confront researchers who seek to apply these tools in the organizational domain. In fact these issues are pertinent to all organizational research where scientific knowledge is used to address certain problems, rather than others. But given the socially progressive aspirations of social identity theory (e.g., its original aim to understand processes of social change that might counteract social inequality), the concerns we will elaborate on below are particularly relevant for researchers who use this specific theoretical framework.

In his television series on the history of science, the scientist and historian Jacob Bronowski knelt at a pond in the Auschwitz death camp and gathered the silt and ashes from it into his hand. Rhetorically he asked his audience whether the that occurred there atrocities committed there were actually the result of science. He asked, in essence, whether the millions of murders committed there and at other death camps were the end result of the technologies provided by science: the gas, the trains, the ovens, indeed, the *scientific management* needed to ferry people through and kill them with such administrative precision. Brownowski's answer was clear. It was not done by science, "it was done by arrogance" he said, "it was done by dogma" (1974, p. 374).

Why, you may ask, do we raise this image in a book on the psychology of organizational behavior, in a chapter on social identity? It should be clear from the preceding review that the social identity approach is grounded firmly in the methods of science. It is only through formal theory development accompanied by rigorous experimental analysis that the approach has proved successful. And through this method we gain confidence, but never certainty, in the veracity of the knowledge it produces.

But the knowledge generated by science is merely a tool. This knowledge may, in the abstract, be neutral, but its application is not. By necessity, the application is guided by personal and social values, ideologies, and political ambitions. And as Bronowski reminded us, through our dogma and through our arrogance we garner the capacity for evil with each new discovery. This observation is important, because the moment we translate abstract scientific knowledge from the textbook to resolve particular organizational problems, we become political animals. And the science of organizational behavior is far from immune to political use or perhaps even abuse. So, although the chapters in this book are offered as part of a larger body of scientific work, we need to recognize that this science can be used by different parties to acheive various, often conflicting, objectives. For instance, the same scientific principle can be applied either (e.g., by management) with the purpose to consolidate or (e.g., by the union) to change current work practices. With this in mind, it is incumbent upon us to consider, at least briefly, some of the political implications of the social identity approach to organizational behavior (see also Haslam, 2001, chapter 11).

MORE WORK WITHOUT MORE PAY?

One of the most significant and robust empirical findings derived from social identity research is the discovery that heightened organizational identification generally leads to improved task performance and organizational citizenship behaviors (e.g., Ellemers, van Rijswije, Bruins, & de Gilder, 1998; Haslam et al., 2000; James & Greenberg, 1989; Ouwerkerk et al., 1999; Tyler & Blader, 2000; van Knippenberg, 2000a; Worchel, Rothgerber, Day, Hart, & Butemeyer, 1998). From one perspective, this appears to be an excellent outcome: employers able to enhance employees' identification with the organization can reap greater amounts of *happily produced work* from those employees, in the absence of enhanced material compensation. Indeed, along these lines, Huo, Smith, Tyler, and Lind note that procedural fairness has the capacity to enhance social identification and, on this basis, they conclude that organizations can "redirect people's focus away from outcomes to interpersonal, relational concerns allow[ing] authorities to *worry less about providing desired outcomes to group members* and to concentrate more on achieving the greater good and maintaining social stability" (1996, pp. 44–45; emphasis added).

To many managers (including those not interested in the greater good) this may seem like a godsend for the simple reason that it offers the prospect of more work without more pay. And for those skeptical about the applied benefits of theoretical knowledge, social psychology finally appears to have delivered where it really matters: the bottom line.

Unfortunately, though, neither managers nor employees can live on social identity alone. For this reason (and others), in a range of situations, people *are* concerned with material outcomes and they do seek better individual outcomes for themselves. In this regard, it is important to emphasize that what the social identity analysis tells us is that personal outcomes are not the *only* ones people will seek because group-based outcomes also have an important influence on behavior. Indeed, an additional complicating factor here is that material compensation itself often has a group function—serving to communicate identity-based respect and perceived social value as much as to pay the bills (Thierry, 1998).

Of course, attempting to increase social identification with an organization in order to obtain more work without more pay ought to appear risky, even without reading the scientific literature, if only because human behavior is not driven by unitary acontextual motivations (social or otherwise). And, as noted above, the actual scientific insights gained from the social identity analysis of organizational behavior confirm the complexity of human behavior. Indeed, to conclude that increased social identification paves the way to "more work without more pay" is no more than what McGarty (2001) calls "SIT-lite" (p. 175), an instance of abstracting one or two features of the theory *in the absence of the others* to simplify unduly the analysis and human social behavior (see also van Knippenberg & Ellemers, chapter 2, this volume).

Social identity and self-categorization theories tell us that people are as much group members as they are unique individuals, and that these group memberships facilitate coordination, cooperation, and communication. They also make possible the achievement of personal and group goals, and provide valid and important aspects of self-definition. However, in line with our previous argument, what the theories do *not* tell us is that there are simple one-to-one relationships between certain forms of social identification and some criterion variables.

Organizational practitioners should therefore bear in mind that social identity is fluid and varied. People can and do self-categorize with more than one group at a variety of levels of inclusiveness. Changes in the social context, both proximal (e.g., salient frame of reference) and distal (e.g., temporal, historical), affect the salience of different social categories. And a variety of behavioral (e.g., fairness, unfairness) and structural (e.g., status, legitimacy, permeability) factors can and do affect people's identification with the salient social category. Even if there would be no dispute about the desirability of doing so, it could therefore prove rather difficult to implement seemingly simple principles, as when aiming to increase employee productivity by enhancing their organizational identification. To expect employees to develop social identity on the basis of membership of some organization and not, say, on the basis of professional, class, gender, or ethnic grouping is to misunderstand the lessons of social identity theory and research.

TAYLORISM REVISITED?

Nearly a century ago, in writing for an audience of managers, Frederick Taylor (1911) outlined several principles of scientific management, with the goal of increasing organizational productivity, organizational profits, as well as worker salaries. His work, and other explicitly psychological work that followed (e.g., Gilbreth, 1914/1971), relied heavily on job and personnel analyzes to gather data that would allow managers to achieve their desired ends. In light of the continued influence of this approach, and its persistent status as a benchmark for organizational theory (e.g., Haslam, 2001; Parker, 1993; Pruijt, 2000), it seems relevant to examine its relationship to social identity research at both theoretical and practical levels. To illustrate further our general argument about the political dimension of theory application with this specific example, we will now consider whether social identity work goes beyond scientific management and, if so, in what ways.

First, let us recall what Taylor (1911) did. His classic text, *Principles of Scientific Management*, was written for a managerial audience and outlined procedures for job analysis, recruitment, and personnel management. At the cornerstone of this was a recommendation that both workers and work be subjected to systematic analysis with a view to maximizing the ability of one to perform the other. All of this was to be done to enhance productivity *as defined by management*. Indeed, Taylor assumed fundamentally the rightness of managers, both in terms of the privileges they possess and the correctness of their goals. In his words, "the duty of enforcing the adoption of standards and of enforcing this cooperation rests with the *management* alone" (1911, p. 83).

In this way the nature or structure of organizations is never questioned: they are a given, part of the natural order. Nor does his analysis question the social order that gives rise to them. On the contrary, Taylor was an apologist for the social order, and many of his recommendations were informed by a desire to maintain it. His desire to conceal the privileges of the managerial class and to protect them from collective challenge is typified by observations that "it does not do for most men to get rich too fast" (p. 74), that "profit-sharing [is] at best only mildly effective in stimulating men to work hard" (p. 94), and that it is best to deal "with every workman as a separate individual" (p. 69).

Importantly too, despite the fact that Taylor's approach to management was empirical, it did not need to rely on scientific data to gain approval and impact. Instead, much of its appeal was ideological, incorporating as it did a philosophy of conservative individualism that was assumed to be shared with the reader. This analysis took it for granted that the individual was the basic unit of psychological and organizational analysis, and that collective challenges to organizational productivity and practice (e.g., in the form of trade unionism) were both undesirable and irrational.

Furthermore, much of the resilience of Taylorism can be attributed to the resilience of this ideology. For this reason alone, despite its systematic and empirical form, the nature of Taylor's science is questionable if only for its unacknowledged lack of neutrality. So, in the end, his analysis is likely to be accepted not because it reveals organizational truths, but because it enhances profits (Taylor, 1911, p. 9). Moreover, such laws of behavior as Taylor developed were descriptive rather than explanatory, and specific rather than general. It was never Taylor's intention to outline processes or fundamental principles of human (organizational) behavior—not least because he was an engineer rather than a psychologist.

By contrast, the social identity approach to organizational behavior developed from a systematic theory of intergroup relations that explicitly recognizes that group membership has the capacity to transform the psychology of the individual and, in the process, to promote creative forms of behavior and distinctive social and organizational products (Turner, 1991). Moreover, despite the fact that such products are often judged (by members of particular organizational communities) to be undesirable and counterproductive, where error exists, its basis is typically seen to lie in social and organizational reality rather than individual psychology (e.g., Oakes et al., 1994).

In this, the social identity approach addresses a much wider variety of human motivations and human pursuits than does Taylor's, and rejects his assertion that "personal ambition always has been and will remain a more powerful incentive to exertion than a desire for the general welfare" (1911, p. 95). If anything, the social identity analysis is aligned more closely with Kropotkin's (1902/1972) earlier historical study of mutual aid which argues convincingly for people's strong and inherent sociality. Amongst other things, the explanatory scope of this analysis allows us to understand why, on occasion "when workmen are herded together in gangs, each man in the gang becomes far less efficient" (Taylor, p. 72), *as well as* why group members will sometimes join voluntarily in collective action to risk more than they would alone (e.g., Kelly & Kelly, 1994). Moreover, the theory's attention to structural variables (e.g., status and legitimacy) allows us to understand how employer–employee power relations informed Taylor's own theorizing.

This ability to appreciate the interplay between psychological and political aspects of organizational life in fact represents one of the distinct advantages of the social identity approach and one of the features that most markedly distinguishes it from Taylorism (and many other organizational metatheories; Haslam, 2001). Significantly, though, it is worth bearing in mind that this fact does not make the theory's application any less political or any more immune to political and ideological bias than another approach. Also, it does not mean that the theory cannot be translated into regressive forms of organizational management. Indeed, Parker and others note that a sound appreciation of the psychology of social groups is integral to modern forms of *team-Taylorism* in which the exploitative features of the manager–worker relationship have been superseded by potentially more insidious peer relations which encourage team members to colloborate in their own exploitation (Parker, 1993; see also Haslam, 2001; Kelly & Kelly, 1991).

Rather than being inherently progressive, then, the social identity approach merely provides tools that allow issues of politics and ideology to be disentangled from those of psychological process. One of the principal advantages of this is that it should have a *democratizing* impact on organizational science—having the capacity to prove useful not only for managers (who want to bring about change or maintain the status quo) but for all organizational groups.

As we see it, and as many of the contributions in this book attest, helping to translate this democratic vision into organizational practice (e.g., in areas of strategic planning, diversity management, antidiscrimination policy) is one of the key challenges of social identity work. To clarify this point, and explain the overall structure of the book, we can now provide a brief overview of its sections and chapters.

THE STRUCTURE AND CHAPTERS OF THIS BOOK

The contributions to this book bring together researchers who are at the cutting edge of work that is using and developing the insights of the social identity approach in order to improve the understanding and management of key organizational issues. Thus while there is a marked diversity in the content and focus of the chapters, all are informed by an awareness of the distinctive role that groups and group membership play in organizational life, and all point to the need (and opportunity) for organizational analysis to do justice to that role in order to advance both theory and practice.

Importantly, though, largely because the contributors are highly conversant with the basic tenets of social identity and self-categorization theories, the contributions to the book are distinguished by a desire to do more than mechanically apply insights from these social–psychological theories to the organizational domain. Instead, the chapters display a willingness to use theory to tackle a range of the most topical organizational issues in creative and challenging ways. This has two distinct dividends. On the one hand, the book serves to enlarge the debate that surrounds these various topics, and, on the other, engagement with these topics allows the theory itself to be elaborated and developed in interesting and novel ways.

These features are apparent in each of the five sections that follow. Part II contains three chapters that speak to issues of *motivation and performance*. In the first, van Knippenberg and Ellemers integrate and review a large body of research that points to the critical role that identification with a salient group plays in motivating employees to work hard on collective tasks. They point out that, while the organization as a whole can provide the basis for shared social identity at work, more commonly this is associated with more inclusive lower-level units such as workteams or departments. Moreover, in common with other researchers, they note that identification of this form is central to employees' willingness to engage in supracontractual acts of citizenship that are integral to optimal organizational performance. The model they develop points to a range of normative and structural factors that can weaken the link between social identity and group performance. Nonetheless it is apparent that organizational outcomes will typically be compromised *unless* employees define themselves in terms of a work-related group membership that they share with their colleagues.

Some of these ideas about the link between group membership and performance are elaborated in Wegge and Haslam's chapter. This addresses literature and theory in the area of goal-setting—one of the most influences on contemporary organizational practice. Traditionally, work in this area has discussed goal-setting as a strategy targeted at individual employees. However, in this chapter the authors review evidence which indicates that while setting individual goals can improve individual performance, group performance is more likely to be enhanced by group goal-setting because this defines and engages employees at a more appropriate level of self-categorization. As well as this, the authors' research suggests that difficult goals are more likely to be achieved when groups participate in the goal-setting process, as this increases ownership of the goals and increases the likelihood that they will be internalized as self-defining and normative.

The final chapter in this section considers the relationship between organizational diversity and performance, another particularly topical and fertile research area. Previously, researchers have pointed to the fact that, from a social identity perspective, diversity could be considered either detrimental or conducive to group performance because it has the capacity either to undermine a perception of similarity-based shared identity or to provide a multiplicity of nonredundant inputs from which a group can benefit. Van Knippenberg and Haslam attempt to reconcile these potentially contradictory outcomes and to clarify the conditions that lead to them. As part of their analysis, they point out that diversity itself can represent part of the content of social identity, such that group definition itself either is or is not predicated upon an awareness of, and respect for, intragroup difference. Consistent with these ideas, the studies they report confirm that normative beliefs about ingroup composition can moderate the relationship between group structure and group output and help to make sense of a major conundrum in this field.

Part III examines *communication and group decision making*. In the first of the three chapters in this section, Postmes provides an integrated analysis of organizational communication from a social identity perspective. This chapter examines the role that communication plays in mediating between social structure and psychological process, so that, on the one hand, social structure serves to define social identity and, on the other, social identity helps to create social structure. Relating to each component of this dynamic, the chapter outlines the way in which organizational communication can help to define both who we are and who we are not, and how it serves validation and coordination functions that allow for collective self-realization and expression.

In the chapter that follows, Lea, Spears, and Rogers hone in on a particular form of organizational communication, via e-mail or on the Internet. Again, this is highly topical work and a particular brief of this chapter is to challenge some of the myths that have quickly come to characterize popular wisdom in this field—in particular, the assumptions that, compared to more conventional forms of communication, computer-mediated interaction is relatively unaffected by social variables (e.g., power, status, group norms). Contrary to this view, the chapter demonstrates that social identity processes often play a stronger role in electronic than other forms of communication precisely because individuating information about communicators is less accessible. It also shows how sensitivity to this fact—and to the distinctive cognitive and strategic dimensions of social identification—can help to reconcile some of the contradictory findings that emerge across different communicative contexts.

A theme that unifies the chapters in this section relates to the capacity for social identity to provide a platform for distinctive forms of group interaction and action. Importantly, though, it is not necessarily the case that all such action has positive social or organizational consequences. Indeed, in the last chapter in this section, Turner, Pratkanis, and Samuels build on previous work that shows how motivations to maintain social identity can contribute to groupthink (decision making characterized by excessive concurrence seeking). The chapter presents findings from a fascinating organizational case study of the computer memory company Intel. Examination of archival and interview data shows first how a desire to maintain social identity under conditions of threat led company executives into danger, and second, as a corollary, how strategic metamorphosis of that social identity led the company to safety and market dominance.

The chapters in Part IV address issues of *leadership and authority*. The three contributions here challenge traditional approaches to these topics, by pointing to the need for leaders to behave in ways that reinforce a social identity that is shared with their subordinates rather than to manage them using principles of resource-based exchange. In their chapter Hogg and Martin make this point through a detailed critique of leader–member exchange (LMX) theory. This theory asserts that it is the quality of dyadic relations between leaders and followers that are the primary determinant of the character and efficacy of any organizational leadership—with higher quality relations leading to more positive outcomes. The authors suggest that while this may be true in contexts where members of an organization relate to each other primarily in interpersonal terms (i.e., where they do not have a strong sense of shared identity), it is far less true in situations where a shared identity is highly salient and followers expect leaders to embody that identity rather than to relate to people on a personalised basis.

Along related lines, Smith, Huo, and Tyler's chapter reviews evidence from a program of large-scale studies in order to test between models which suggest that employees' behavior is primarily determined by instrumental concerns (e.g., for high pay) and those which suggest the motivational underpinnings of organizational behavior are more relational and identity-based (e.g., derived from being treated with respect). The survey and experimental studies they discuss measure people's perceptions of these two key aspects of authorities' behavior and look at the ability of these to predict both in-role and extrarole organizational behavior. The findings provide compelling evidence for the importance of relational rather than instrumental factors—at least in intragroup settings where the authority in question is perceived to share social identity with the employee.

Elaborating on such points, in their chapter Reynolds and Platow turn the spotlight on the nature of power in organizations and on the consequences of using it in particular ways. The differentiation between power and influence is a central feature of their analysis. In line with self-categorization theory, they argue that while influence is essentially an ingroup process (made possible by shared identity), power is an intergroup phenomenon. For this reason they suggest that reliance on power as a managerial strategy emanates from, and is likely to reinforce, intergroup division and to prove counterproductive. On the other hand, they suggest (and provide evidence) that authentic forms of power sharing can overcome such differences and yield significant organizational dividends.

Part V contains four chapters that examine social identity processes associated with *change and change management*. In the first, Ellemers examines points of contact between the concepts of organizational culture and organizational identity, and goes on to examine how these relate to processes of organizational change. Noting the strong links between these concepts, Ellemers argues that insights from the social identity approach might be used to help understand the dynamics of organizational culture—particularly as they relate to change. Evidence from three organizational case studies bears this out, by showing that employees who identify highly with an organization are likely to feel more threatened by change and to be more resistant to it, but that these responses can be offset to the extent that employees are willing and able to take on a new organizational identity.

The next two chapters provide a social identity perspective on a particularly significant form of change—that of the organizational merger. In their chapter, van Leeuwen and van Knippenberg provide evidence from a series of experimental studies which point to the fact that employees are likely to respond more positively to a merger if they are able to maintain a dual identity with both the premerger and postmerger organizational units. Amongst other things, this is because dual identification protects employees from the identity threat associated with the announcement that a formerly prized identity is to be rendered obsolete. Significantly, though, their research also shows that responses to mergers are conditioned by the perceived fit of the resultant identity and the extent to which it represents a meaningful entity for employees.

The research in Terry's chapter draws primarily on the core hypotheses of social identity theory to examine mergers in organizational contexts. In particular, the chapter focuses on the way in which group status mediates reaction to this form of organizational change. Building on her previous work, the empirical heart of the chapter presents findings from a longitudinal case study of a merger between high and low status metropolitan hospitals. The results underline the important role that perceived status, permeability of group boundaries, and group similarity play in shaping responses to both the other merging group and the change process as a whole.

In the final chapter in this section Eggins, Reynolds, and Haslam present details of an model of organizational planning and development designed to translate social identity and self-categorization principles into effective forms of identity and organizational management. This model, for Actualizing Social and Personal Identity Resources (ASPIRe) builds on the large corpus of research in the social identity tradition, much of which is discussed in other chapters. It suggests that activities such as diversity management and planning are most likely to be effective where organizations go through a process of (1) discovering which social identities are important for their employees; (2) empowering employees to act in terms of those identities; and (3) harnessing those identities within a superordinate organizational identity which accommodates and respects subgroup differences.

The book's final section, *perceiving and responding to inequity*, contains three chapters that focus on issues of justice that lay at the heart of social identity theory's original formulation. The chapter by Platow, Wenzel, and Nolan focuses on two forms of justice—distributive and procedural—and considers the factors which lead people to perceive these and to respond to them in particular ways. A key point here is that, as customarily encountered in organizational (and other) contexts, there is a distinctly intergroup flavor to fairness such that (1) what is perceived as "fair" depends on the meaning for one's in-group of any distribution or procedure, and (2) claims of fairness (or unfairness) have a political dimension in legitimating certain forms of group act. In their contribution, the authors work through these points in order to demonstrate how central a role fairness plays in organizational and social life, and to show how a social identity analysis enriches our understanding of this role.

In the book's penultimate chapter, Schmitt, Ellemers, and Branscombe use hypotheses from social identity theory to provide a systematic and thoroughgoing analysis of gender-based discrimination in the workplace. In keeping with the theory, two key points that inform this analysis are first, evidence that responses and perceptions of gender inequity vary qualitatively as a function of whether perceivers define themselves in individual or group (i.e., gender-based) terms, and, second, evidence that such definition is greatly determined by structural features associated with gender relations in the workplace (e.g., perceived status, permeability, legitimacy). The chapter examines the practical implications of this analysis by identifying ideological and structural features of the work environment that serve to maintain inequality and by pointing to associated changes that might help to promote equality.

Concluding this section, in the book's final chapter Haslam, Branscombe, and Bachmann look at the conditions that lead consumers who receive poor service to react in various ways. Like the previous chapter, the analysis and empirical work here are based on an assertion that forms of behavior are conditioned by consumers' self-categorizations as either individuals or group members, and that this in part reflects features of the organizational structure that confronts them. The chapter discusses ways in which contemporary forms of consumer interaction encourage different types of self-categorization and shows how dysfunctional consumer responses (e.g., rage, sabotage) can arise from violation of the norms and expectations these create.

FINAL COMMENT

We noted above that the chapters of this book are pioneering in two distinct senses. On the one hand, they provide novel perspectives on a wide array of important and highly topical organizational topics. On the other hand, they provide impetus for the refinement and specification of cutting-edge social–psychological theory.

However, in addition to this—and in keeping with the original spirit of social identity theory—the chapters also throw open the door on another key debate by encouraging researchers and practitioners to look *beyond* issues of psychology to reflect on the group-based politics of organizational life with which that psychology interfaces. When we do this we see that the key variables that are addressed by social identity theory are useful in helping us understand not only the facets of organizational life upon which psychologists cast their gaze, but also the practice and interpretative leanings of psychologists themselves.

The result, we hope, is a book which is challenging in the fullest and most positive sense—inviting readers both to engage with a rich seam of academic theory and to help develop and apply it in productive and progressive ways. Happily, too, by building upon a theoretical framework that is shared within a growing community of researchers, the book stands not only as an appreciation of social identity at work but also as its embodiment.

PART II

MOTIVATION AND PERFORMANCE

2

Social Identity and Group Performance
Identification as the Key to Group-Oriented Effort

DAAN van KNIPPENBERG
Erasmus University Rotterdam
NAOMI ELLEMERS
University of Leiden

*F*ormal job requirements may form the basis of work performance in organizations, but only a very narrow basis. As Katz argued, "an organization which depends solely upon its blueprints of prescribed behavior is a very fragile social system" (1964, p. 132). Formal job requirements typically leave employees substantial leeway to do their job in any way between the best possible way and a marginally passing way. Indeed, when people start "working to rule" this usually severely reduces the effectiveness of their efforts. Although the bureaucracy—where people are supposed to work according to an elaborate system of rules and regulations—was designed to organize work more efficiently (Weber, 1947), it is generally acknowledged that such reliance on formal arrangements does not enable workers to deal adequately with the tasks they face in many organizations (Organ, 1988; Roethlisberger & Dickson, 1939).

As a result, as Katz (1964) already argued, organizational performance depends to a large extent on employees' willingness to go beyond formal job prescriptions. This not only implies that they "go the extra mile"on the tasks they are assigned, but also that they take on additional responsibilities if and when this would benefit the organization. Thus, although this may not always be explicitly acknowledged or rewarded (MacKenzie, Podsakoff, & Fetter, 1991), no organization can survive if employees do not engage in spontaneous acts of cooperation, helping, and innovation (Podsakoff, Ahearne, & MacKenzie, 1997). Because an important part of such desired behavior seems difficult, if not impossible, to enforce through formal channels, an important question for the organizational sciences is what motivates employees to exert themselves on the job and beyond. In this chapter, we address this question from the perspective of the social identity approach to organizational behavior outlined in chapter 1 (this volume; see also Haslam, 2001; Hogg & Terry, 2000).

MOTIVATING THE INDIVIDUAL OR MOTIVATING THE GROUP MEMBER?

In recognition of the fact that organizations cannot function properly if they rely solely on the performance prescribed by formal job requirements (cf., Katz, 1964), organizational scientists have proposed a distinction between formal task, or in-role, performance and extra role performance. This extrarole performance is alternatively called organizational citizenship behavior, contextual performance, extra-role behavior, or prosocial organizational behavior (for a discussion of conceptual similarities and differences, see Van Dyne, Cummings, & Parks, 1995; see also Smith, Huo, & Tyler, chapter 9, this volume). In this chapter, we will use the term *organizational citizenship behavior* (OCB; Organ, 1988) because this seems to be the term most often used in the literature to describe the kind of behavior Katz and others alluded to, and may be seen as equivalent to Borman and Motowidlo's (1993) concept of contextual performance (Organ, 1997; Podsakoff, MacKenzie, Paine, & Bachrach, 2000).

In contrast to task performance, OCB, such as helping others, showing initiative, and upholding the reputation of the organization toward outsiders, can only be demonstrated if the situation calls for it. The occurrence of such situations typically is rather unpredictable, and even when it is obvious that they will occur, it may still be difficult to specify in advance which particular behavior will be appropriate. This makes it virtually impossible to incorporate OCB in formal job requirements. As a consequence, although the willingness to engage in OCB may be crucial for organizational success, it cannot easily be included in formal task goals, nor is it possible to motivate employees to engage in OCB through incentives targeted at individual performance. On the contrary, even though individual task performance may be enhanced by goal and incentive systems, to the extent that such systems make self-interested motives salient they may discourage individual workers to invest in OCB (Wright, George, Farnsworth, & McMahan, 1993).

This line of reasoning suggests that a concern with collective goals—to elicit OCB as well as task performance—may benefit organizations more than a focus on more individualistic motivations (cf. theories of transformational vs.

transactional leadership; e.g., Bass, 1985). Nevertheless, there is a long tradition in approaches to work motivation (e.g., Vroom, 1964; see also Lawler, 1973) that takes an instrumental exchange orientation, arguing that individual workers can be motivated to exert themselves on the job and beyond by providing them with concrete individual goals (Locke & Latham, 1990b) and offering them valued outcomes in return for their achievement of these goals. However, as we have argued above, OCB is likely to suffer if employees are involved in their task primarily for selfish motives, such as earning individual incentives and bonuses, or improving their own career opportunities. In fact, it has repeatedly been pointed out that there are limits to the extent to which the provision of desirable rewards induces the intended task behavior (Kerr, 1995; Kohn, 1993; Pearce, 1987).

Instead of asking what motivates individuals to exert themselves on individual tasks, the above argument suggests that we have to consider what motivates individuals to exert themselves *on behalf of the collective*, that is, what motivates *group-oriented* effort. We examine this question from a social identity perspective, arguing that identification with the organization and its goals is an important cause of increased task effort (see also Castells, 1997; Reichheld, 1996). This implies that organizational functioning should benefit more from *motivated group members* than from *motivated individuals*. In the following section, we present key evidence that identification may affect performance because it leads individuals to internalize the collective interest. The remainder of the chapter is devoted to outlining a number of important moderating factors in the relationship between organizational identifications, and task performance and OCB. To conclude, we present a model capturing these moderated relationships between identification and performance on the job.

IDENTIFICATION AND THE COLLECTIVE SELF

As elaborated in chapter 1 (this volume), the social identity approach describes how the strength of an individual's identification with a group reflects the extent to which he or she conceives of the self in terms of that group membership (e.g., by focusing on characteristics shared with other members of his or her group) rather than in terms of more individualized, personal characteristics that differentiate him or her from other individuals (Tajfel & Turner, 1986; Turner, Hogg et al., 1987). Identification thus blurs the distinction between self and group, and turns the group, psychologically, into a part of the self (E. R. Smith & Henry, 1996). This "social" or "collective" self (i.e., "we," as opposed to the "I" of the personal self) lies at the heart of the perceptual, attitudinal, and behavioral effects of group membership. The more one conceives of oneself in terms of one's membership in a group (i.e., the more one identifies with the group), the more likely one is to act in accordance with the social identity implied by the group membership (Turner, Hogg et al., 1987). Organizational or work group identification may thus lead individuals to adopt the organization's or work group's goals and interests as their own (Dutton, Dukerich, & Harquail, 1994). The sense of collective self associated with group identification implies that individuals are primarily concerned with the collective interest, while personal self-interest—at least to the extent that it is incompatible with the collective interest—seems less relevant (Ellemers, Spears, & Doosje, 1997; van Knippenberg, 2000a). Conversely, a focus on individual self-interest may enhance a conception of self in individual terms. Thus, while workers may be motivated to perform well when the personal self is salient, their efforts will primarily be self-directed, instead of focusing on the collective, for instance by engaging in OCB.

Although a number of studies provide evidence in favor of the proposed relationship between identification and efforts on behalf of the collective (e.g., Doosje, Spears, & Ellemers, in press; Mael & Ashforth, 1992; Tyler & Blader, 2000), these studies do not provide evidence that identification motivates group-oriented efforts because it leads group members to experience the collective's interest as the self-interest; however, a recent study by van Leeuwen and van Knippenberg (1999) does so. Van Leeuwen and van Knippenberg studied group performance on a manual task: Putting sheets of paper in envelopes. Group performance was determined by the total number of envelopes filled by the group and, hence, the individual's contribution to the group product was determined by the number of envelopes filled by the individual. Most relevant to the present discussion is the interaction between identification and prosocial versus proself value orientation (an individual difference variable reflecting the extent to which individuals are prone to focus on the personal self-interest alone—proselfs—or on joint interests—prosocials; Messick & McClintock, 1968) tested in their second study. Van Leeuwen and van Knippenberg predicted that identification would motivate group members to exert effort on the group task, but especially for group members who were not dispositionally inclined to take others' or group interests into account (i.e., individuals with proself as compared with prosocial value orientations). Results supported these predictions (see Figure 2.1).

Individual contributions to the group's performance were higher the more group members identified with the group, but this effect was mainly observed for group members with a proself rather than a prosocial orientation. This finding demonstrates that identification may elicit the motivation to exert effort on behalf of the collective because it leads individuals to experience the collective's interests as their self-interest (i.e., their collective self-interest rather than their personal self-interest)—this should affect individuals who dispositionally focus on self-interest more than individuals who dispositionally focus on joint interests. Very similar findings outside of the performance domain were obtained by De Cremer and Van Vugt (1999). In a situation in which

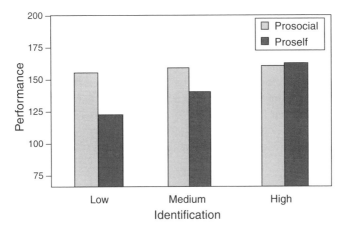

FIGURE 2.1. Individual contributions to the group's performance as a function of group identification and social value orientation. Van Leeuwen and van Knippenberg (1999).

personal self-interest and collective interest were explicitly at odds (a social dilemma), De Cremer and Van Vugt found that identification was more strongly related to contribution to the collective good for individuals with a proself orientation than for individuals with a prosocial orientation. The evidence for the proposed effect of identification is thus consistent over research paradigms.

As an aside, another aspect of the van Leeuwen and van Knippenberg findings is noteworthy. Some researchers have proposed that there are individual differences in the extent to which organizational members are concerned with their own self-interest or the collective interest (e.g., J. A. Wagner, 1995). One may be tempted to argue that an implication of this observation is that management activities targeted at individuals that are dispositionally concerned with their own self-interest need focus on individual-level interests; for instance, through individual incentive schemes. In contrast, the van Knippenberg and van Leeuwen study suggests that social identification can be an effective means of mobilizing individualistically oriented individuals in pursuit of collective goals.

Even though research such as the van Leeuwen and van Knippenberg (1999) study supports the proposition that identification leads individuals to internalize collective interests, and research more generally supports the proposition that identification leads individuals to define the self in collective terms (e.g., Spears, Doosje, & Ellemers, 1997; Simon, Hastedt, & Aufderheide, 1997), there is reason to assume that there is not a simple, direct relationship between identification and performance. The social identity approach suggests two key factors that play a moderating role in the relationship between identification and performance: Social identity salience and group performance goals and norms. In addition, research inside and outside the social identity tradition suggests a third important moderator of the relationship between identification and performance: The extent to which performance is under volitional control (cf. self-efficacy and group efficacy). These three factors are discussed in the following sections. First, however, we address another important qualification where the relationship between identification and performance is concerned: The fact that organizations provide multiple foci of identification and that performance (both from a practitioner's and a researcher's perspective) needs to be related to the appropriate level of identification.

THE MULTIPLE FOCI OF IDENTIFICATION

Studies of organizational identification typically focus on identification with the organization as a whole (e.g., Elsbach, 1999; Mael & Ashforth, 1992; Pratt, 1998), as do studies of the related, but distinct, concept of organizational commitment (e.g., Meyer & Allen, 1997). This may make perfect sense when identification is intended to predict general retention–withdrawal tendencies, which are usually assessed with data on absenteeism, tardiness, or turnover (e.g., Meyer & Allen, 1997). However, it is important to keep in mind that employees can consider themselves in terms of multiple overlapping or cross-cutting group memberships (e.g., their work group, the junior staff, female employees) within the organization (Reichers, 1985), and accordingly may have *multiple foci* of identification (Ashforth & Mael, 1989; van Knippenberg & van Schie, 2000). Thus, at the level of the predictor variable, more conceptual precision may be required to properly assess the hypothesized relationship between identification on the one hand, and work performance on the other.

It is important to acknowledge these multiple (potential) identifications. First, especially in large or multinational organizations, employees' own work group or department is likely to be the primary focus of identification for most employees (van Knippenberg & van Schie, 2000; cf. Ellemers, de Gilder, & Van den Heuvel, 1998; Moreland & Levine, 2001). The work group is where organizational life takes place for most employees and day-to-day employee functioning is more likely to be determined by features of their work group than by organizational membership (see also Kramer, 1991a). Second, work group goals, norms, and interests need not converge with organizational goals, norms, and interests (Haslam, 2001; Reichers, 1985; van Knippenberg, 2000a). As a result, behavior induced by work group identification (e.g., covering up for lack of knowledge of one's colleagues) does not necessarily serve the goals of the organization as a whole (which may aim to eliminate knowledge differences among employees through additional training).

The importance of distinguishing between different foci of identification is illustrated by Ellemers et al. (1998). Ellemers et al. distinguished between commitment to the organization, to one's work team, and to one's own career, as possible predictors of a range of work-related behaviors—note that although identification and commitment should not be equated (Ashforth & Mael, 1989; Pratt, 1998; van Knippenberg & Sleebos, 2001), we may assume that what holds for the different foci of commitment also holds for the different foci of identification. They assessed the three different forms of commitment, and then examined respondents' work-related behavior one year later. Results revealed that commitment to the organization was related to the likelihood that workers had attempted to find a job elsewhere, which is consistent with previous findings on organizational commitment. However, the willingness to work overtime in order to help colleagues at work (a form of OCB) only depended on team-oriented commitment. Finally, career-oriented commitment predicted the desire to focus on one's own work and take additional training, instead of spending time to help others. Thus, the predictive value of work-related commitment to the behavior that workers displayed depended on the *match* between the focus of commitment and the goal of the specific behavior (see also Becker & Billings, 1993; Zaccaro & Dobbins, 1989).

These findings demonstrate that it is important to realize that group-oriented efforts may be displayed at the organization level; for example, by representing the organization favorably to outsiders (i.e., *loyalty*; Van Dyne, Graham, & Dienisch, 1994), but also at the interpersonal or work group level, for instance by interpersonal helping behavior (i.e., *altruism*, Organ, 1988) (L. J. Williams & Anderson, 1991). An important conclusion of our discussion thus far is therefore that performance enhancement at the organizational and the work group level is likely to be contingent on different identifications.

SOCIAL IDENTITY SALIENCE

Whereas the argument about the correspondence between performance and the focus of identification advanced in the previous section may not be specific to the social identity approach (and indeed not to the study of the determinants of performance; cf. Fishbein & Ajzen, 1975), the social identity approach highlights two factors that may be proposed to moderate the strength of the relationship between identification and performance. The first of these is the extent to which social identity is *salient*.

Studies of the related concept of organizational commitment (Meyer & Allen, 1984; Mowday, Porter, & Steers, 1982) typically focus on the psychological link between the individual and the organization as something that should exert a relatively stable and constant influence on organizational attitudes and behavior. The social identity approach, in contrast, highlights the fact that the influence of organizational identifications is context dependent (Haslam, Powell, & Turner, 2000; Hogg & Terry, 2000; van Knippenberg,

2000a). Even though identification itself is seen as a relatively stable concept (albeit subject to change over time), the social identity approach proposes that identification with a group only affects behavior to the extent that the group membership is salient. The fact that an individual identifies with a group does not mean that this group membership is always salient in the individual's mind, or forms a relevant behavioral guideline. Although identification itself may contribute to social identity salience (i.e., group membership is more likely to be salient for individuals who identify strongly with the group), contextual factors affect salience as well. The prospect of a merger may for instance render organizational identity salient (cf. van Leeuwen, van Knippenberg, & Ellemers, 2001a, 2001b), while conflict or competition between work groups may render work group identity salient and distract attention from the common organizational identity (e.g., Kramer, 1991a, 1991b). On the other hand, the threat of individual layoff may render personal identity salient (for a more elaborate discussion of the salience of social identities in organizations, see Haslam, 2001; Hogg & Terry, 2000).

Group membership only affects attitudes and behavior to the extent that the group membership is salient (Turner et al., 1987). Social identity salience is thus an important precondition for the effects of identification to occur (i.e., salience "triggers" identification effects). We may therefore expect that identification is mainly related to the willingness to exert effort on behalf of the collective when social identity is salient (van Knippenberg, 2000a). Although, to our knowledge, no study has directly tested the interaction between identification and identity salience implied by this proposition, there is experimental evidence relating task performance to social identity salience per se. Participants in a study by James and Greenberg (1989) worked on an anagram task while the salience of their organizational membership was manipulated by presenting half of the participants with cues that rendered their university membership salient, whereas the other half received cues unrelated to university membership. In addition, they were told that the performance of members from their university would be compared to the performance of another university (Experiment 1). In Experiment 2, James and Greenberg also manipulated whether or not such intergroup comparison was to be expected. As predicted, in both studies participants in the salient social identity condition solved more anagrams than participants in the condition where social identity was not made salient, but only when intergroup comparison was implied (similar results were shown by Worchel, Rothgerber, Day, Hart, & Butemeyer, 1998). These findings provide an important demonstration of the role social identity salience plays in triggering the effects of psychological group membership (i.e., identification), which in turn elicits group-oriented behavior.

The social identity approach thus suggests that attempts to mobilize group-oriented efforts by fostering identification may in itself not be enough. Such attempts should also focus on rendering social identity salient, for instance by a focus on group goals (see chapter 3, this volume), group-based work, group-based incentive systems, and leadership that concentrates attention on the collective identity in question (cf. Bass, 1985; De Cremer & van Knippenberg, in press; Shamir, House, & Arthur, 1993).

GROUP NORMS AND GROUP GOALS

The James and Greenberg (1989) findings also allude to another key factor highlighted by the social identity approach as a moderator of the effects of identification, namely the extent to which high performance is seen as important to the group (or as a group goal, or as group normative). Presumably, a salient social identity was only associated with increased performance in the James and Greenberg study when intergroup competition was implied (see also Worchel et al., 1998), because only then was it perceived to serve a function for the group; for example, because it was instrumental in allowing the ingroup to be favorably compared to another group. More generally, we would predict that identification will only result in a motivation to perform well (be it on the task or in terms of OCB) when high performance is seen as a collective goal, is a group norm, or is in some other way important to the group.

A key proposition in the social identity approach is that identification with a group leads individuals to internalize group norms and attitudes (e.g., Abrams & Hogg, 1990; Turner, 1991; Turner et al., 1987; van Knippenberg, 2000b). As a result, adoption of group norms, and hence their influence on group member attitudes and behavior should increase the more group members identify with the group. Although it has long been recognized that work group norms may exert an important influence on group member behavior (e.g., Feldman, 1984; Hackman & Morris, 1975; Roethlisberger & Dickson, 1939), the social identity approach deviates in this respect from much of the earlier work on group norms. Whereas group norms are traditionally conceptualized as an "external" influence on the individual (Deutsch & Gerard, 1955), group norms are conceptualized in the social identity approach as standards that are internalized through identification and thus mainly affect group member attitudes and behavior *to the extent that individuals identify with the group*. At the same time, it is made clear that the *content* of group norms determines the nature of the resulting behavior (Doosje, Ellemers, & Spears, 1999; Ellemers, in press). In terms of our present argument, this implies that identification should only lead to increased performance if high performance is seen as a group goal or as group normative (Haslam, 2001; van Knippenberg, 2000a). However, increased identification may just as well undermine performance when group norms favor low performance (e.g., in the context of hostile management–employee relationships).

The opposing effects that group norms may have were demonstrated experimentally in a study by Barreto and Ellemers (2000), who induced different group norms, and investigated how this affected the behavior of high and low identifiers in problem-solving groups. Regardless of the content of the group norm, high identifiers always indicated a greater willingness than low identifiers to improve their group's standing. Of most interest to our present argument is the finding that the *behavioral strategy* group members adopted to achieve this goal depended on what they thought was normative for the group. High identifiers were likely to work with the group when this was what the group norm prescribed. However, when the group norm encouraged group members to work individually, high identifiers opted relatively more frequently to work individually. Low identifiers, by contrast, were less inclined to follow the group norm: they generally worked for their own individual improvement, and were only willing to go along with the norm to work for the group when they were held publicly accountable for their behavior. The results of this study clearly show that, even though high identifiers may generally be more motivated than low identifiers to work at group goals, the nature of their effort depends on the content of salient group norms (see also Barreto, 2000).

Although not designed from a social identity perspective, a study by Podsakoff, MacKenzie, and Ahearne (1997) shows that similar results may be obtained in organizational settings. In a study of work crews in a paper mill, Podsakoff et al. studied the relationship between group cohesiveness and group performance. Group cohesiveness (a group-level variable) arguably is a group-level proxy for identification (an individual-level variable; cf. Hogg, 1993). Podsakoff et al. argued that the relationship between cohesiveness and performance should be contingent on the group's acceptance of performance goals. If the group accepted the performance goals, cohesiveness should be positively related to group performance, whereas cohesiveness should be unrelated to performance, or even have negative performance effects, when the group does not accept performance goals. Indeed, results showed that group cohesiveness and group goal acceptance showed the hypothesized interaction in predicting task performance. When seen as a test of the relationship between identification, group goals/norms, and performance, these findings also yield clear support for our proposition regarding group goals/norms as a moderator of the identification–performance relationship (for a similar study—with similar results—focusing on norms rather than goals, see Langfred, 1998).

Evidence from the laboratory and the field thus converges on the conclusion that the effects of identification on group performance are contingent on group performance goals and norms. Because standards are not necessarily particularly high, clear, or salient—especially for OCB—this suggests that it is important to take group goals and norms into account when considering the identification–performance relationship. Moreover, even if group or organizational norms or goals are clearly defined, it may still be the case that different performance standards are salient at different organizational levels. For instance, top management may emphasize output *quantity* as a goal for the organization as a whole, while informal work group norms perhaps mainly promote professional performance *quality*. Because it cannot be assumed that all work groups or organizations have similar (high performance) goals, it is important to specify that identification is only expected to enhance work-related effort when this is prescribed by group and organizational goals and norms.

EFFICACY AND BEHAVIORAL CONTROL

Research on self-efficacy (Bandura, 1986) and group efficacy (Bandura, 1986; Guzzo, Yost, Campbell, & Shea, 1993) has shown that individuals are more likely to engage in tasks or behaviors that they expect to be able to perform successfully (either individually or as a group). Moreover, research on the attitude–behavior relationship has demonstrated that for attitudes to translate into behavior, the behavior needs to be perceived to be under volitional control (Ajzen, 1991). In the same vein, the earliest formulations of social identity theory (Tajfel, 1974; Tajfel & Turner, 1979) emphasized that for group members to strive at position improvement it is crucial that they see *scope* for such improvement in the current situation. Indeed, it has been empirically demonstrated that people tend to accept an inferior group performance when this appears to be a legitimate or stable reflection of their group's relative competence (Ellemers, Wilke, & van Knippenberg, 1993), and only attempt to advance their group's standing when position improvement seems feasible. We may therefore propose that an identification-induced motivation to perform well only results in actual attempts to perform well to the extent that high performance is perceived to be under volitional control.

A first implication of this proposition is that identification should be more strongly related to OCB than to task performance, because OCB by its very definition is more discretionary (Organ, 1988) than task performance, which is subject to formal job descriptions, rules, regulations, and sanctioning systems. Although studies of the relationship between identification and performance are yet too small in number to substantiate this proposition, research on organizational commitment does corroborate this point. Meta-analyses suggest that the relationship between commitment and OCB is far more reliable (Organ & Ryan, 1995; Podsakoff et al., 2000) than the relationship between commitment and task performance (Mathieu & Zajac, 1990; see also Ellemers, van Rijswijk, Bruins et al., 1998). Both OCB and task performance may, however, vary in the extent to which they are (perceived to be) under volitional control, and our proposition regarding the moderating role of efficacy–behavioral control should apply to both OCB and task performance.

A clear demonstration of the effects of group efficacy is found in the work of Ouwerkerk and colleagues (see Ouwerkerk, Ellemers, & de Gilder,

1999, for an overview). Ouwerkerk et al. examined how knowledge about performance development over time and differential prospects for future performance improvement affected group members' level of ambition as well as the amount of effort actually invested to improve their group's performance. Specifically, research participants were asked to work on a collective task, and received feedback about their group's performance relative to another group present in the experimental situation, during four consecutive rounds of the task. The (bogus) feedback about the development of their group's relative performance either induced the impression that intergroup performance differences were stable, or that they were subject to change. The results of two studies showed that when another group had shown a better performance than one's own group, this increased collective performance goals for those who identified strongly with their group, but only when they had been led to believe that current performance differences were unstable (Ouwerkerk, Ellemers, Smith, & van Knippenberg, in press). A further study confirmed that, when their group's performance was inferior, group members actually displayed greater performance improvement when (1) they identified strongly with the group, and (2) when performance improvement seemed realistically possible (Ouwerkerk, de Gilder, & de Vries, 1999; for similar findings regarding the moderating role of efficacy concerns, see Pillege & Holtz, 1997).

IDENTIFICATION AND PERFORMANCE: A MODERATED MODEL

The propositions we developed regarding the relationship between identification and collective performance are summarized in a model (adapted from van Knippenberg, 2000a), that focuses on the psychological process involved, and points out relevant moderators at each stage of this process (see Figure 2.2). The model proposes that group identification results in the willingness to exert effort on behalf of the group, but only in situations where this group membership is salient. The willingness to exert effort on behalf of the group in turn increases the motivation to perform well (on the task or in terms of OCB), provided that high performance is a group goal or norm. Finally, for the motivation to perform well to translate into actual performance, it is necessary that the intended performance is perceived as being under volitional control of the person or group in question. Thus, although identification is the key to group-oriented effort, the relationship between the two is not a straightforward or simple one. Instead, other additional conditions have to be met to be able to actually turn the key and unlock the desired performance.

In this chapter, we argued that because organizations depend not only on the task performance of their members, but also on their OCB for effective functioning, organizations may greatly benefit from work motivations rooted in a concern for the collective and should therefore not only rely on work

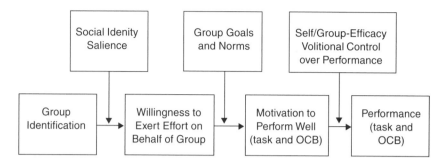

FIGURE 2.2. A social identity model of group performance. Adapted from van Knippenberg, 2001a.

motivations based on more personal, self-interested motives (see also Tyler & Blader, 2000). Our analysis suggests that identification is a key factor in determining the willingness to exert effort on behalf of the collective, and thus should be considered as an important causal factor for organizational success. This argues in favor of group-based structuring of tasks and incentives, and identity-based appeals to employee motivation.

At first sight this conclusion would seem to be somewhat at odds with the fact that groups are often faulted for suboptimal productivity (i.e., compared to individualized performance; Karau & Williams, 1993; Steiner, 1972). Our analysis suggests that this is not because groups are inherently "bad," and group processes inevitably lead to production losses. Instead, we have argued that groups may not fullfil their performance potential for a number of reasons: Identification may be low, the group may not be salient as a meaningful entity in the social situation, group norms may not favor the production standards that are endorsed by the organization, or achieving the desired performance may not seem feasible to the individuals or groups concerned. Group-based work thus not only calls for managerial practice that fosters a climate that is conducive to group and organizational identification but also requires conditions that lead group members to consider themselves in terms of that identity, that foster acceptance of organizational performance goals (cf. Podsakoff et al., 1997; see also chapter 4, this volume), and make the actual achievement of these goals seem realistically feasible.

CONCLUSION: IDENTIFICATION IS A VALUABLE ASSET, NOT A MANAGEMENT TOOL

Despite our focus on identification as a key factor in optimizing collective performance, we would by no means advocate fostering identification as a

LIVERPOOL JOHN MOORES UNIVERSITY
LEARNING SERVICES

blanket strategy to achieve performance improvement. First, of course, as we have tried to demonstrate, this is because a number of additional conditions have to be met before increased identification translates in performance improvement. Second, this is because one can definitely identify too much. When people overly identify with a group or organization, this may cause people to hold on to the current situation instead of adapting to altered circumstances (cf. van Knippenberg & van Leeuwen, 2001; chapters 11 and 12, this volume), or it may breed a highly homogeneous organization with a culture that stresses conformity, at the expense of organizational decision making and innovation, and thus ultimately at the expense of organizational effectiveness (see chapter 7, this volume). Third, identification may create the preconditions for the group-oriented efforts that effective organizational functioning depends on, but identification does not replace other necessary ingredients in the employee–organization relationship such as the need to pay people fairly (cf. Folger & Cropanzano, 1998). Identification should therefore be seen as something that induces group-oriented concerns to *complement* self-interested concerns rather than to replace self-interested concerns.

Moreover, extreme levels of identification may be dysfunctional for the individual employees involved, in the sense that they are driven to invest in their work to the extent that they are likely to become ill or experience burnout (cf. Maslach, Schaufeli, & Leiter, 2001). Pratt (2000), for example, describes the case of the socialization of medical residents, where new members in the organization are subjected to a culture in which organizational identification and the job are expected to take priority over all else, at the exclusion of all else. Such a strong focus on identification and performance is intended to yield highly committed organization members, but does so at potentially severe costs (e.g., at the expense of their marriages or other social relations). Indeed, in the long run, employees who are required to neglect the interests and duties linked to other identities (e.g., their family identity) in favor of organizational goals and interests, are likely to become less balanced and emotionally stable workers and hence may become less productive (cf. Haslam, 2001).

In sum then, overly high identification is not only undesirable from the perspective of the employees, but also from the perspective of organizational effectiveness and performance. Our analysis therefore suggests that member identification is necessary (albeit not sufficient) for organizational functioning, but at the same time more identification is not necessarily better. Managerial attempts to build identification (cf. Pratt, 2000) should therefore only be undertaken when the focus of the identity is in line with the performance in question, and when it is clear that additional conditions that are required for optimal performance have been met.

LIVERPOOL JOHN MOORES UNIVERSITY
LEARNING SERVICES

3

Group Goal Setting, Social Identity, and Self-Categorization
Engaging the Collective Self to Enhance Group Performance and Organizational Outcomes

JÜRGEN WEGGE
University of Dortmund
S. ALEXANDER HASLAM
University of Exeter

*S*trategies to encourage teamwork in the workplace have become very popular in light of evidence that teams are often associated with the most creative and energetic forms of organizational activity. At the same time, though, since the pioneering work of Taylor (1911), many organizational practitioners have counseled against allowing collectives too loose a rein in organizations on the basis of evidence that groups can often produce *less* than the sum of their individual parts. Consistent with these conflicting perspectives and advice, employees who work in groups appear to show both *impaired* and *enhanced* motivation and performance relative to those who work alone. In this chapter, we attempt to explain how this variation can be understood within an integrated theoretical framework and to demonstrate that the group processes responsible for variable outcomes are not inherently problematic but actually confer organizational advantage.

A large body of research confirms the efficacy of *goal setting* as a performance enhancement strategy (after Locke & Latham, 1990b). In line with this work, we propose that the direction and the magnitude of changes in effort and performance are strongly affected by the specific nature of individual and group goals that are salient in any organizational setting. At the same time, though, we argue that the impact of these goals is itself a function of the context-dependent salience of employees' personal or shared social identities. More specifically, in concert with specific moderator variables (e.g., group status, group composition, and perceived threat), we propose that goals *interact* with self-categorization processes to determine whether motivation losses (e.g., soldiering, sucker effects, free riding, social anxiety) or motivation gains (e.g., social compensation, social laboring) emerge in a given work context.

To support this basic view, we discuss findings from a number of our recent studies. On the basis of these, we argue that a sound explanation of the robust phenomena reported in goal-setting research is best reached through theoretical *integration* of goal-setting theory and the social identity approach. In particular, on the basis of insights from self-categorization theory (Turner, 1985; Turner, Oakes, Haslam, & McGarty, 1994), we argue that goal-setting theory can be enriched by an awareness of the role that *self-processes* play in mediating between individual and collective goals and organizational performance. We also show that the social identity approach gains predictive power by taking account of the various self-regulatory mechanisms that are usually linked to the activation of goals. In our view, the marriage of goal setting and social identity approaches is therefore very fruitful—primarily because it offers a new analytic framework and new tools for researchers and practitioners who are interested in understanding (and improving) the performance of groups in organizations.

INDIVIDUAL GOALS, GROUP GOALS, AND GROUP PERFORMANCE

There are literally hundreds of studies that demonstrate a reliable impact of goals (intentions) on human behavior (Boekaerts, Pintrich, & Zeidner, 2000). Based on this evidence it is widely acknowledged that goals are an immediate and powerful regulator of activity in the workplace (and outside it). Consistent with this basic idea, goal-setting research examines which aspects of goals are most important for predicting and obtaining improvements in task performance (Locke & Latham, 1990b). The current evidence on this question is conclusive. It has consistently been found that *specific* and *difficult* performance goals result in higher individual performance than easy goals or nonspecific goal instructions (e.g., to "do your best"; DYB). When the preconditions for this effect are favorable (e.g., given low to medium task complexity, high goal commitment, and feedback during task performance), striving for challenging goals leads to an increase in *individual* performance in the range of 8 to 16% (this reflects effect sizes ranging from $.42 < d < .80$; Locke & Latham, 1990b, p. 30).

Moreover, the evidence accumulated in recent years has shown that at least four mediating mechanisms underlie this effect. Difficult and specific individual goals motivate people (1) to exert more effort (e.g., to work faster or harder) during task performance; (2) to continue working on the task until the performance goal is reached (persistence); (3) to direct their actions and attention to behavior and outcomes that are relevant for goal attainment; and (4) to use or develop appropriate task strategies and plans (Locke & Latham, 1990b; for a more detailed account of these mechanisms see Locke, 2000; Wegge, 2001b).

The effects of goal setting have usually been examined in studies of individual performance (Locke & Latham, 1990b). As a result, there are far fewer studies analyzing the impact of *group goals* (an intention shared by members of a group) on group performance. Nevertheless, there is now considerable evidence that goal setting also works at the group level (Durham, Locke, Poon, & McLeod, 2000; Guzzo & Dickson, 1996; Knight, Durham, Locke, in press; Ludwig & Geller, 1997; O'Leary-Kelly, Martocchio, & Frink, 1994; Wegge, 2000; Weldon and Weingart, 1993; Widmeyer & Ducharme, 1997). In a meta-analysis covering 26 effect sizes derived from 10 studies conducted between 1978 and 1991, and comprising data from 163 groups and 1684 individuals, O'Leary-Kelly et al. (1994) found that the performance of groups striving for a specific, difficult group goal was almost one standard deviation higher (d = .92) than the performance of groups that did not have clear goals.

Illustrative of such research, Wegge and Kleinbeck (1996) conducted an experiment designed to analyze the effects of group goal setting on the performance of 27 three-person groups. These groups differed in the extent to which they contained dispositionally anxious people and each had to solve three different group tasks that differed in complexity and requirements for interdependence: an anagram task (complex, medium interdependence), a brainstorming task (easy, low interdependence) and a motor coordination task (easy, high interdependence). Consistent with the tenets of goal-setting theory (Locke & Latham, 1990b), it was found that—compared to "do your best" conditions—striving for specific, difficult group goals (assigned or participatively set) led to much improved group performance especially for the two relatively easy tasks. Relevant means are presented in Table 3.1. From this it can be seen that, while group goal setting did not help teams solve complex problems faster, it was very effective in improving their idea generation and motor coordination.

Moreover, even though participative group goals did *not* improve overall group performance more than assigned group goals, this study suggested that participation can be superior in particular conditions. Specifically, it was observed that groups composed of dispositionally anxious individuals improved their performance in the brainstorming task much more under participative goal conditions (M = +13.0 ideas) than under assigned goal conditions (M =

TABLE 3.1. Group performance as a function of goal setting
(from Wegge & Kleinbeck, 1996).

	DYB	Assigned group goals	Participative group goals
Brainstorming (no. of ideas)	−5.0	+11.7	+12.4
Motor coordination (no. of hits)	+0.0	+5.8	+7.1
Anagram task (solution time in seconds)	−99.3	−110.0	−90.6

Note: All means are relative to a baseline phase in which groups were provided with DYB instructions.

+8.4 ideas). However, for groups with nonanxious members, both methods of group goal setting worked equally well ($M = +10.4$ for participative and $M = +10.8$ for assigned group goals). As it is well known that anxiety (evaluation apprehension) can hinder performance in group brainstorming (Camacho & Paulus, 1995; Paulus, Larey, Putman, Leggett, & Roland, 1996), this finding suggests that participation can have the additional advantage of *reducing* the negative effects of anxiety. Participation in group goal setting should therefore be particularly useful in improving the performance of (dispositionally or situationally) anxious groups performing tasks in which collective performance is easily undermined by arousal of anxiety (Wegge, 2001b).

Of course, anyone who is interested in improving group performance can make use of the knowledge accumulated in goal-setting research. Other things being equal, interventions that lead to the setting of specific, difficult group goals and that increase the commitment and conformity of group members to those goals will tend to enhance group performance. Moreover, in anxious or threatened groups, strong commitment to group goals might be best achieved by using participative group goal-setting techniques.

PREVIOUS EXPLANATIONS OF GROUP GOAL-SETTING EFFECTS

The efficacy of group goal setting procedures is impressive. But what mediating mechanisms underlie the overall group goal-setting (GGS) effect? Several answers to this question have been proposed. Most commonly, though, it is suggested that the processes responsible for GGS-effects are essentially identical to those mechanisms (e.g., increased effort and persistence) that are responsible for the individual goal-setting effect (IGS; Durham et al., 2000; Locke & Latham, 1990b; Knight et al., in press). This proposition might appear plausible because individual performance is obviously a critical ingredient of team performance. Moreover, evidence suggests that team members often set individual goals on the basis of group goals (Widmeyer & Durchame, 1997), so that individual goals and corresponding (individual) mechanisms might mediate the effect of group goals. There are, however, at least three lines of evidence which suggest that the GGS-effect is not routinely identical to the IGS-effect.

First, the individual goals of (one or more) group members are sometimes in conflict with group goals (Goethals & Darley, 1987; Hinsz, 1995; Mitchell & Silver, 1990; Tjosvold, 1998). If such goal conflicts become important, deviant group members will often be renounced by the group so that they receive less support and resources and, as a result, are unable to perform optimally. In addition, severe goal conflicts can lead to the dissolution of the group. Conflicts between individual and group goals can also contribute to motivation losses (e.g., sucker effects; N. L. Kerr, 1983) and motivation gains (e.g., social compensation effects; Karau & Williams, 1997; Williams & Karau, 1991) in groups. In all such cases it is apparent that the performance of the group is very different from that of (some or all) individual group members.

Second, previous research has found that a combination of individual and group goals can enhance group performance *more* than having merely individual *or* group goals. Matsui, Kakuyama, and Onglatco (1987) found that dyads working with both a team goal and an individual goal identified more targets in a perceptual speed task than individuals working with only an individual goal. These authors argue that this finding might be due to increased goal difficulty because dyads set more difficult team goals than the sum of their own (also self-set) individual goals. Moreover, commitment to individual goals was higher if both kinds of goals were present. Unfortunately, Matsui et al. did not analyze the impact of team goals without individual goals. Thus, it is not clear what performance level would have been observed with a group goal alone. More recently, however, Crown and Rosse (1995) found that teams striving for shared goals in combination with corresponding (group-relevant) individual goals outperformed teams striving for team goals of comparable difficulty. Based on these findings, Crown and Rosse propose that the combination of both types of goals improves individual effort and also establishes a special kind of group performance orientation that promotes group goal commitment and organic cooperative strategies.

Third, explaining the GGS-effect requires researchers to extend the list of possible mediator variables since group work itself can arouse specific (social) emotions such as evaluation apprehension or fear of social rejection that, if present, can have a strong impact on performance (Wegge, in press-a). As already illustrated above (participative) group goal setting can help to overcome the performance inhibiting effects of negative emotional states (it might also intensify positive emotions like group pride but this is another story). In the same vein, group work usually involves additional processes such as communication, coordination, and collaborative planning that are not necessarily involved in individual performance (e.g., Moreland, Argote, & Krishnan, 1996; Weick & Roberts, 1993). In line with this view, Weldon and Weingart (1993) developed a model that incorporates not only individual processes but also several group processes. Their model points to the importance of three group-level mechanisms: (1) *group planning* (e.g., talking about who should do what, when, and where in the team); (2) *cooperation within the team* (e.g., listening to others' ideas, helping teammates do their work); and (3) *morale building communication* (e.g., statements that build a sense of efficacy or that stimulate supportive emotions and enthusiasm in achieving the group goal). It is suggested that these processes facilitate team performance by increasing, amongst other things, the quality of group plans and the expectancy of success. Yet while there is some evidence showing that the GGS-effect is indeed mediated by task-specific group planning (e.g., Durham et al., 2000; Knight et al., in press; Weingart, 1992; Weldon, Jehn, & Pradhan, 1991), the empirical evidence for the two other specific group mechanisms is weak. To date, only a few group goal studies have examined these variables (Weldon & Weingart, 1993; Widmeyer & Ducharme, 1997) and their findings are mixed.

EXTENDING PREVIOUS MODELS OF GROUP GOAL SETTING: GOAL SETTING AND SELF-CATEGORIZATION

Consistent with the approach of Weldon and Weingart (1993), we assume that several group-specific mechanisms are responsible for GGS-effects. Indeed, we propose that those motivational phenomena usually discussed in social psychology texts under the heading of "motivation losses" (e.g., sucker effects, social loafing; see Karau & Williams, 1993) and "motivation gains" (e.g., social compensation, social facilitation; see Hertel, 2000) can also determine the ultimate outcome of collaborative goal setting. Group goal setting, if it is well done, promotes motivation gains and prevents motivation losses in groups (Haslam, 2001; Wegge, 2001c; Wegge & Haslam, n.d.). Moreover, we believe that a better explanation of goals' impact on group performance can be provided by drawing on insights from *self-categorization theory* (Turner, 1982, 1985; Turner, Hogg et al., 1987)—in particular those that relate to the analysis of *social identity salience* (i.e., the process through which a group comes to define a person's sense of *self*; Oakes, 1987; Oakes, Haslam, & Turner, 1994; Turner, 1985; Turner, Oakes et al., 1994). Recent findings that speak to the importance of these self-categorization processes in explaining group performance are discussed in the next section.

At this point, the most fundamental question to address is how individual and group goals are linked to the salience of group members' shared social identity as (potential) group members. Here we suggest that there is generally some *congruence* between the nature of activated goals and the nature of self-categorization. To date, very little research has examined the relationship between the content of activated goals and social identity salience. However, it follows from self-categorization theory's argument that category salience is interactively determined by category fit and accessibility (Oakes, 1987; Oakes, Turner, & Haslam, 1991) that one way in which current goals can impact on self-categorization is by increasing the relative accessibility of a particular self-category (i.e., a perceiver's readiness to use the category as a basis for self-definition).

Preliminary empirical evidence (Haslam, Veenstra, & Wegge, 2001; Wegge, 2000, 2001c; see below) supports this basic notion and speaks to the model presented in Figure 3.1. If individual goals are all that is activated in a given situation, workers should be inclined to define themselves in terms of their personal identities (i.e., as individuals) as the setting of such goals acknowledges and instantiates the individual self ("I" or "me") as a fundamental organizational unit. This is especially true if individual goals are specific (e.g., "I intend to achieve an A in this test"). If individual goals are more vague (e.g., "I will do my best in this task"), self-categorization is less well-defined and increases the possibility of movement toward a social level of self-categorization (i.e., definition of the self as "we" or "us").

On the other hand, the setting of group goals makes social identities more

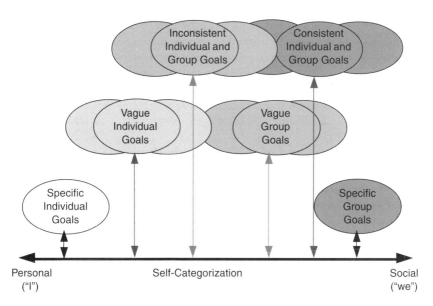

FIGURE 3.1. Typical relationships between goals and level of self-categorization. *Note:* Darker vertical arrows are indicative of more direct (and more clearly defined) relationships between goals and self-categorization.

accessible and encourages depersonalization of the self (i.e., self-stereotyped perception of the self as interchangeable with other group members; Turner, 1982). Group goals should also make social identities more fitting because they provide a sense of common fate and purpose (cf. Campbell's 1958, analysis of entitativity) that metacontrastively increases the categorical definition of the ingroup (Haslam & Turner, 1992; Turner, 1985). This should be particularly true when group goals are set *competitively* so that different groups vie to outperform each other (cf. Worchel, Rothgerber, Day, Hart, & Butemeyer, 1998). Such practice is commonly encouraged in contemporary organizations through the use of "league tables" which serve as a basis for rewarding superior team performance (e.g., Ghoshal & Bartlett, 1997; Parker & Slaughter, 1988).

When group goal setting of this form occurs, individuals are encouraged to seek out and behave in line with those norms that define the group in context. However, social identity salience can still be reduced if the behavior that is (or becomes) prototypical for a group is incongruent with salient individual goals or values (e.g., if a team of salespeople has to travel extensively to promote a product, but a team member needs to stay at home to look after a sick relative). For this reason, many models of leadership and management (in particular House's, 1971, path–goal theory) suggest that a key role of managers is to ensure there is alignment between lower-level individual and higher-level group and organizational goals (in this example, the manager might identify a role for the representative which allows them to defer travel or work from home). This sort of combination of (group-relevant) individual goals and group goals can improve performance and be associated with a cooperative collective orientation in many task contexts—especially if the group has an organic social identity that allows for internal differentiation (Crown & Rosse, 1995; Haslam, 2001, p. 255; Moreland et al., 1996). However, striving solely for specific group goals (e.g., "as a team, we will try to sell 20 cars today") should generally lead most reliably to self-categorization in terms of social identity.

In order to prevent misunderstanding, we should add at this point that there is *no simple causal link* between the activation of goals and social identity salience since both variables are dynamic and context-sensitive (Fielding & Hogg, 2000; Haslam, Powell, & Turner, 2001; van Knippenberg, 2000; Wegge, 2001; see chapter 1, this volume). Moreover, it is worth emphasizing that the salience of group goals does not guarantee superior group performance. One reason for this is that a bunch of loosely connected individuals striving for *challenging* individual goals would be expected to outperform a well-established group striving for a very *easy* group goal on an additive group task (e.g., door-to-door selling). More importantly, however, group performance is not a linear function of social identity salience because—depending on the goals that are prototypical for the group in a particular context and the *content* of its identity—strong identification with a particular group can lead to both output losses (e.g., as a result of soldiering; Taylor, 1911) and output gains (e.g., as a result of social laboring; Ouwerkerk, Ellemers, & de Gilder, 1999). The following section elaborates on these points by summarizing our analysis of the relationship between self-categorization and group performance.

SOCIAL IDENTITY SALIENCE, GOAL SETTING, AND IMPROVEMENT IN GROUP PERFORMANCE

Having noted that there is generally a correspondence between the nature of goals that are orienting behavior in any given context (i.e., individual vs. group) and the level of workers' self-categorization (personal vs. social), the next question is, How does this fact help us understand the relationship between goals and performance? The short answer to this question rests on an assertion that the previously demonstrated capacity for goals to impact positively on performance derives from the goals' capacity to *focus and channel* self-relevant exertion. In effect, goals serve as a lens which concentrates the energies of the self and thereby increases its impact on selected aspects of one's own behavior or the work environment—a point that is schematically illustrated in Figure 3.2.

Importantly too, like goals, the self can be defined in either individual- or group-based terms. When individual goals are set they focus and give meaning to personal identity and serve as a basis for organizing and coordinating (potentially) disparate individual behaviors. When group goals are set they help to direct and give meaning to a shared social identity which is used as a framework for coordinating and organizing the behavior of (potentially) disparate individuals. One of the best examples of this point is provided by Weick

FIGURE 3.2. Schematic illustration of the role that goals play in focusing self-exertion. *Note:* Goals can direct either individual or group behavior. Individual goals serve to focus and coordinate the disparate activities of the individual by giving meaning to personal identity; group goals do the same for the disparate individuals that the goals help to define in terms of a shared social identity.

and Roberts's (1993) study of the way in which the challenging goal of landing planes on an aircraft carrier helped create a theory of the collective self (an organic social identity) which then served as a basis for a very large number of people to engage in a multitude of complex and interdependent tasks.

For this reason we would suggest that goals only ever inform and direct social behavior to the extent that they are internalized as an aspect of the personal or social self. Indeed, in line with self-categorization theory (e.g., Turner et al., 1994), we would broadly define a goal as *a desired state or outcome that is perceived to be prototypical for a salient self-category*. Amongst other things, what this means is that when the self is defined in terms of personal identity the goals that individuals tend to generate and the goals to which they respond most vigorously are those that promote their personal interests. In contrast, when people define themselves in terms of a social identity that is shared with other members of a salient ingroup, they should tend to identify and respond to goals that advance that group as a whole. In a context in which individuals respond to group goals and define themselves in terms of a shared social identity, those individuals should also be motivated to coordinate their goal-setting activity with other members of their ingroup and should respond best to goals that have emerged from this collaborative process. This is because, following Turner's (1991) analysis of social influence, under these conditions other ingroup members will be perceived to be qualified to inform the individual about self-relevant features of the social world—indeed, their input will be sought out for this purpose. As argued by Haslam (2001), social identity salience therefore creates the motivation for effective organizational communication, planning, and team building of the form discussed by Weldon and Weingart (1993).

Further support for these arguments emerges from a recent study conducted by Wegge (2000, 2001c) that examined the efficacy of group goal setting as well as the benefits that might accrue from making that process participative. In this study, four-person groups completed three-phase brainstorming tasks in which they had to identify uses for common objects. The first phase of brainstorming trial was a practice trial, and in the second phase groups were instructed to "do your best" (DYB) in order to establish a baseline for group performance. For groups in a control (DYB) condition, this instruction was then repeated in the third phase of the study. However, different instructions for this third phase were provided in each of three other conditions. Groups in a participative group goal condition (PG) were asked to determine a specific and challenging group goal through group discussion. For this purpose, each group member first suggested an appropriate group goal and these suggestions were then discussed until group consensus was reached. In another condition, all group members had to determine individual goals in combination with group goals (PG+IG). After group goals had been established, the experimenter explained that individual goal setting usually supports group goal setting and, therefore, in this condition individual goals were set that were in line with the overall group goal. Finally, in an assigned group goal condition (AG) a "tell and sell" strategy was used to set group goals that matched those generated in the two participative group goal conditions. Therefore, goal difficulty was held constant across the three conditions in which specific group goals were set.

Confirming the well-established utility of group goal setting as a productivity enhancement strategy, in phase 3 of the study there was more improvement in performance in the three conditions that involved goal setting than in the control condition (Ms = +11.0, +5.8 respectively). Consistent with our argument that group goal setting should generally serve to increase social identity salience, responses on relevant process measures (after Luhtanen & Crocker, 1992) also indicated that individuals were significantly more likely to define themselves in group-based terms in the three goal-setting conditions than in the control condition (Ms = 1.1, 1.4, respectively, on scales ranging from 0 to 4). The study also demonstrated the utility of participative group goal-setting strategies, although there was no overall difference across the three goal-setting conditions in either performance improvement (Ms: AG = +11.6, PG = +11.8, PG+IG = +9.7) or social identification (Ms: AG = 1.4, PG = 1.4, PG+IG = 1.3). However, as in Wegge and Kleinbeck's (1996) study, it was again observed that for groups containing anxious members, participation in group goal setting enhanced performance (M = +12.7) more than merely assigning group goals (M=+9.2). Unexpectedly though, for nonanxious groups, the opposite pattern was observed (participative goals: M=+10.4; assigned goals: M = +15.6). For this reason, the anxiety or confidence of group members seems to be an important moderator variable that deserves more attention in future research (Wegge, in press-b).

SOCIAL IDENTITY SALIENCE AND THE POTENTIAL FOR GROUP GOAL SETTING TO INDUCE UNDERPERFORMANCE

Goal-setting research has identified several mechanisms that help us understand why individual goal setting has such a reliable and strong impact on individual performance (e.g., Locke & Latham, 1990b; Wegge, 2001b). Following the above analysis, the fact that social identity-based *group* goal setting brings into play additional processes of social influence, cooperation and organic coordination also helps us understand why this can lead to even more positive outcomes (e.g., O'Leary-Kelly, 1994; Wegge, 2000). Importantly, though, reviews of the general group performance literature tend to reveal that the actual performance of groups is often much lower than the aggregate capacity of individual members. To explain underperformance in groups (beyond that which results from mechanical coordination losses), several researchers argue that (self-managed) group work—in particular, participative decision making and group goal setting—brings about motivation losses because groups decide to strive for very easy or counterproductive goals. Consistent with this thesis, previous research on the effects of participation has revealed that, across all available studies, the impact of participation on performance and satisfaction is neither strong nor consistent (Locke, Alavi, & Wagner, 1997).

As Wegge (2000, 2001c) argues, some of this apparent variation appears to result from methodological problems which undermine the validity of studies that seek to test the efficacy of participative group goal setting (e.g., failure to distinguish between involvement that is substantial or insubstantial, short-term or long-term, authentic or cosmetic). However, there is little doubt that collectives sometimes appear to underachieve in organizations. Indeed, as Haslam (2001) argues, this derives partly from the ability of groups to stimulate and foster processes of organizational *change* (cf. Reicher, 1982) that can also serve to question established ways of operationalizing and demonstrating productivity. As Taylor (1911) found in his pioneering studies at the Bethlehem Steel plant, while individuals will typically go along with manager-defined organizational goals when they are individualized and isolated, they are much more inclined to question those goals when they perceive themselves to be part of a meaningful workgroup (Wallace, 1998; see also Haslam's, 2001, reinterpretation of studies by Paulus and Dzindolet, 1993). Moreover, as studies of collective protest show (e.g., Kelly, 1993; Tougas & Veilleux, 1988; Wright, Taylor, & Moghaddam, 1990), this is especially true when the goals promoted by management can be construed as unreasonable or unfair.

The double-edged problem for those who would encourage group goal setting in organizations is therefore that unless they are set effectively by management, the goals that groups establish for themselves can end up departing (in form and content) from those against which performance has previously been measured. Yet if goals *are* set by management, groups may resile from them altogether. As a result, along lines alluded to in this chapter's introduction, many organizational theorists counsel against participative group activities, opting instead for a "safety-first," individualized approach in the spirit of classical Taylorism. However, this strategy involves sacrificing all the potential motivational benefits that can flow from (participative) group goal setting. In addition, Haslam (2001) argues against this strategy because groups need to be recognized and harnessed as a source of creativity that give vitality to organizations and that help to ensure a critical rather than a compliant culture. A similar argument also underpins the ASPIRe model of organizational planning, negotiation, and development (see Eggins et al., chapter 14, this volume; Haslam, Eggins, & Reynolds, in press; Reynolds, Eggins, & Haslam, 2001).

In order to test the validity of these arguments, Haslam, Veenstra, & Wegge (2001, experiment 2) conducted a study modeled on Wegge's earlier (2001c) experiment, in which small groups of four or five students in an organizational psychology course worked on brainstorming tasks to devise novel uses for everyday objects. In order to ascertain a baseline for productivity, in phase 1 of the study all groups were instructed to "do your best" to identify as many uses as possible for a broom in a 5-minute period. In subsequent phases, they had to do the same for a kitchen knife and a bicycle tire, but here the groups were assigned to one of five independent conditions. In a control condition, the groups were simply asked to continue to "do your best." In the four other conditions the groups were asked to reach either moderately or very difficult goals and these goals were either set by the group itself or by the experimenter. Experimenter-set goals were presented as targets for improvement that the course instructor thought were achievable and appropriate on the basis previous research (though here the experimenter did not employ the vigorous "tell and sell" approach used in Wegge's, 2001c, assigned goal condition). Self-set goals gave groups this same information but asked them to reflect on it and determine for themselves a goal that they thought was achievable and appropriate. Moderately difficult goals suggested that groups should improve on their phase 1 performance by generating 20% more uses for objects in phase 2 and 40% more in phase 3. Very difficult goals suggested that performance should improve by 40% in phase 2 and 80% in phase 3.

Consistent with Wegge's (2000, 2001c) previous work and points made above, responses on measures of social identification (Doosje, Ellemers, & Spears, 1995) again showed that this was higher in the four conditions that involved group goal setting than in the control condition (Ms = 5.0, 5.4, respectively, on scales ranging from 1 to 7). The results on measures of group performance are presented in Figure 3.3, which plots improvement from the phase 1 baseline in phases 2 and 3 for all five conditions.

Again confirming the ability of group goal setting to increase productivity, from this graph it can be seen that while overall performance in the control condition declined across the final two phases of the study, the four conditions involving various forms of group goal setting (and increases in social identity salience) led to improved performance. In addition, though, across the four goal-setting conditions, the extent of improvement varied interactively as a function of level of participation, task difficulty, and phase. This arose from the fact that while goal setting was generally associated with increases in performance, group productivity actually varied substantially across conditions in the final phase of the study. It was particularly low where the very difficult goal of achieving an 80% improvement in performance had been set by the experimenter.

This pattern is consistent with the general theoretical framework provided by self-categorization theory in suggesting that it is engagement of the self that is responsible for the efficacy of goal setting. In those conditions where goals had been set by groups themselves and hence had been internalized as

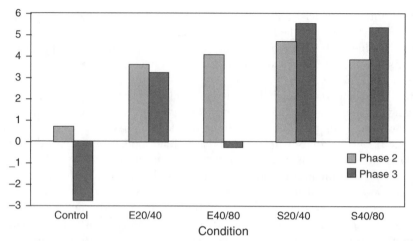

FIGURE 3.3. Improvement in performance (relative to phase 1 baseline) as a function of goal source and goal difficulty. From Haslam, Veenstra, & Wegge, 2001.
Note: E = Experimenter-set goal
S = Self-set goal
20/40 = moderately hard goals (to improve by 20% in phase 2 and 40% in phase 3)
40/80 = very hard goals (to improve 40% in phase 2 and 80% in phase 3)

self-relevant and self-defining, performance was commensurate with attainment of those goals. However, this was less true where the goals had been externally set, and much less true when the difficulty of an experimenter-set goal made it easy to interpret the goal as explicitly non-self-defining (e.g., as the imposition of a malevolent supervisor). Indeed, when the experimenter asked them to almost double their output it would appear that participants collectively rejected this goal as a valid behavioral guide (along lines observed in previous research by Paulus and Dzindolet, 1993; Wallace, 1999).

At a practical level, these results confirm the value of group goal setting as a procedure for focusing the energies of group members and enhancing group productivity (cf. O'Leary-Kelly, 1994; Wegge, 2001c). At the same time, though, they point to the fact that goals do not have a universal, context-independent impact. Instead their impact is mediated by engagement of the self. To the extent that workers define themselves in terms of a given shared social identity, they should be willing to accept goals determined by other representative (prototypical) members of that group (e.g., leaders, supervisors; see Haslam & Platow, 2001a, 2001b). However, to the extent that the apparent unreasonableness of a goal allows for its source to be *recategorized* as unrepresentative of the self, the goal will not be internalized as a basis for action. This recategorization process explains why the setting of goals that appear unattainable does not usually help improve productivity, and why imposing unreasonable group goals can also backfire (as it did in the present study).

Moreover, as suggested by Wegge's (e.g., 2001c) previous research, the negative feelings of anxiety induced by nonparticipative goal-setting procedures can contribute to underperformance, even if these goals are accepted.

CONCLUSION

In contemporary organizational and management textbooks, goal setting is commonly heralded as an organizational practice that is distinguished from many others by (1) having a sound theoretical basis and (2) actually working (Wegge, 2001a). Indeed, a number of commentators have suggested that this combination of features makes the practice of goal setting almost unique. Whether or not this is the case, it is certainly true that the clarity with which the process has been explicated and justified, and the evidence of its general robustness have given it pride of place in the organizational practitioner's arsenal of tools. Our own goal in this chapter has not been to question these conclusions or the practice itself. We come to praise goal setting not to bury it. Nonetheless, we suggest that there are important ways in which both the theory and practice of setting goals can be extended.

At a theoretical level, we have attempted to show how our understanding of the processes through which goal setting achieves its impact can be enhanced by integrating previous insights with ideas from self-categorization theory concerning the role that self-processes play in mediating between goals and outcomes (e.g., Turner, Oakes et al., 1994). In particular, we have suggested that goals (especially specific ones) serve both to define the self at a particular level of self-categorization (personal or social) and to focus and concentrate self-exertion at that level. This means that personal goals are internalized as aspects of the personal self and generally encourage and promote activities that advance the perceived interests of the individual. However, at a higher level of abstraction, group goals articulate and make salient a shared social identity and provide a focus for the coordination and planning of members' activities in a way that enhances their shared collective interests. Thus, individual goals, group goals, personal identity salience, social identity salience, specific emotions, and the content of emergent self-categories operate *in concert* to determine whether (and which) motivation losses and motivation gains emerge in a given work context (Wegge, 2001c; Wegge & Haslam, n.d.). Moreover, as summarized above, the available evidence indicates that (participative) group goal-setting techniques in combination with interventions that foster social identity salience are the best basis for promoting motivation gains and preventing motivation losses in (anxious) teams.

Yet, these points notwithstanding, at a practical level, researchers have generally been unwilling to advocate group work and group goal setting (especially of the participative variety) as a widespread organizational practice.

This reluctance stems from evidence that groups often fail to achieve their expected productivity and that participative group endeavors can precipitate underperformance and unwanted social change. Although there is empirical support for this thesis, we would argue that management practices that focus on establishing individual goals are limited by virtue of their inherent conservativeness. These limitations are perhaps most clear if we reflect upon the *actual content* of goals and are prepared to acknowledge that while the goals that are usually set by those who occupy offices of power in organizations (e.g., managers, supervisors, shareholders) will often be worthwhile and valid, they also have the potential to be misguided and regressive. In simple terms, some goals are good and some are bad. The danger, then, is that when they are inappropriate in some (perhaps unforeseeable) way, the culture of acquiescence that is promoted by individual goal setting provides little foothold for processes of change that might contribute to social and organizational correction. Our advocacy of participative group goal-setting processes is based on evidence that groups can serve this corrective and progressive role while at the same time channeling employees' energies in ways that contribute to clear increases in (collectively self-valued) productivity.

As we have argued elsewhere (e.g., Haslam, 2001, pp. 298–312), strategies of this form are no guarantee of progress. However, in the spirit of organic pluralism, they help to protect organizations and society from the perils of an imperialistically singular set of goals which, at a macrolevel, encourage compliance, torpor, and stagnation. In Western countries, this has been apparent for the last 20 or so years in a political and organizational landscape that is characterized by a relentless drive for efficiency as measured by the financial bottom line—a drive that largely precludes alternative metrics and alternative goals. However, other ways of measuring human achievement are available (e.g., Kleinbeck & Fuhrmann, 2000) and other goals *do* exist. So discovering and striving for these would seem to be an important way for organizations (and society) to promote creativity, vitality, and sustainable growth.

Group goal setting has the potential to help in this process (in a way that individual goal setting cannot) because it provides individuals with the power, resources, and focus that they need in order to challenge, and move beyond, received and conventional wisdom. This is especially true if the technique of (participative) group goal setting is married with other interventions (e.g., benchmarking with regard to superordinate objectives) that promote self-categorization at a collective level (Eggins, Haslam, & Reynolds, in press; see also chapter 14, this volume).

Indeed, taking these arguments further still, we would suggest that social and organizational breakthroughs that are customarily celebrated as triumphs of the individual are often preceded by the internalization of group goals that have been developed collaboratively in the context of higher-order objectives and identities. This claim is consistent, for example, with Kuhn's (1962) observation that scientists are more likely to make ground-breaking discoveries when there is a war to be won.

Despite the relatively low billing it receives, it thus appears that group goal setting is fundamental to most forms of organizational progress. The social identity approach helps us to understand why this is the case and provides a framework for a range of future projects. The lessons of this chapter suggest that the success of those projects is likely to depend, at least in part, on their capacity to provide goals that we and others can embrace as our own. That capacity, we believe, is substantial.

4

Realizing the Diversity Dividend
Exploring the Subtle Interplay between Identity, Ideology, and Reality

DAAN van KNIPPENBERG
Erasmus University Rotterdam
S. ALEXANDER HASLAM
University of Exeter

*D*iversity is a fact of organizational life. Most work groups and most organizations are composed of people with different demographic characteristics, attitudes, norms, values, knowledge, expertise, and so on. Moreover, evidence suggests that organizations are becoming increasingly diverse (e.g., Jackson, 1992; Williams & O'Reilly, 1998). Amongst other things this trend is suggested by evidence that a growing number of women are joining the labor market, that societies are becoming more ethnically diverse, that traditional professional boundaries are breaking down, and that multi-disciplinary work teams are increasingly popular. One consequence of this is that now, more than ever before, managers and organizational scientists are seeking answers to questions about diversity: What does it mean? What does it lead to? What are its benefits? How can we realize them?

Studies of the effects of diversity on individual-level (e.g., commitment, satisfaction, turnover) and group-level outcomes (e.g., performance, cohesiveness) yield a complex picture. Often, diversity appears to have negative effects. Less often, but often enough to hint at diversity's potential benefits, diversity is found to have a positive effect. These apparently contradictory findings raise three obvious questions: What underlies the negative effects of diversity? What underlies the positive effects of diversity? And, perhaps most important, what determines whether diversity has negative or positive effects?

In this chapter, we analyze the effects of diversity from the perspective of the social identity approach outlined in chapter 1 (this volume), and discuss how the approach helps us answer these three questions. First, however, we briefly review the main findings from research in organizational diversity. A comprehensive review of diversity studies would go beyond the scope of this chapter, and recent reviews are available elsewhere (e.g., Guzzo & Dickson, 1996; Milliken & Martins, 1996; Williams & O'Reilly, 1998). Accordingly, in the following section, we focus on the main findings of diversity research and outline the main points of contention that emerge from these.

A BRIEF REVIEW OF DIVERSITY EFFECTS

The study of diversity is the study of group composition: How do similarities and dissimilarities between group members affect group members' responses to each other and to the world at large, as well as the overall functioning of the group? This issue can be studied either at the individual level (e.g., How does being similar or different to the rest of the group affect the individual?; e.g., Tsui, Egan, & O'Reilly, 1992) or at the group level (e.g., How do groups that are relatively homogeneous differ in their functioning from those that are relatively heterogeneous?; e.g., Watson, Kumar, & Michaelsen, 1993). The group composition variables of interest may be readily observable (and consensually agreed upon) demographic characteristics such as sex, ethnicity, or age, or less readily discerned (and more negotiable) characteristics such as expertise, knowledge, intelligence, experience, attitudes, norms, or values. Similarities and differences on all these dimensions may affect the way people view their group and the people in it, and the way they interact within the group and the organizational environment as a whole.

Perhaps the most consistent finding in diversity research is that dissimilarity to fellow work group members (at the individual level) and work group heterogeneity (at the group level) tend to be associated with less positive affective and evaluative responses, including lower commitment (e.g., Riordan & Shore, 1997) and higher turnover (e.g., Wagner, Pfeffer, & O'Reilly, 1984). For performance measures, findings seem to be more mixed, with diversity sometimes being associated with superior performance (e.g., Bantel & Jackson, 1989) and sometimes with inferior performance (e.g., Pelled, 1996). The negative effects of diversity also appear to be more common when this is observed on demographic dimensions such as ethnicity than when it is identified on more idiosyncratic dimensions such as experience or functional specialization. In addition, and more relevant than it may at first appear, results tend to be rather inconsistent in that composition variables, which are found to have an effect in some studies, are often unrelated to outcome variables in others, and composition variables that are found to have negative effects in one study may well be associated with positive effects in another (for a review that confirms these observations, see Williams & O'Reilly, 1998).

The negative effects of diversity are typically interpreted within a social categorization (or similarity/attraction) framework, whereas the positive effects of diversity are usually explained from an information/decision making perspective (Williams & O'Reilly, 1998). The social categorization interpretation reflects the most common application of the social identity approach in this area. More specifically, based on readings of self-categorization theory (e.g., Turner, 1985) it is suggested that similarities and differences are used as a basis for categorizing oneself and others into groups, with ensuing categorizations distinguishing between one's own in-group and one or more out-groups. In line with findings from the minimal group studies that gave rise to the notion of social identity (e.g., Tajfel, Billig, Bundy, & Flament, 1971), it is also argued that, other things being equal, people tend to like and trust in-group members more than out-group members and so tend generally to favor in-groups over comparison out-groups (though for a discussion of the conditional nature of such effects see Haslam, 2001; Reynolds, Turner, & Haslam, 2000; Turner, 1999). In the context of work group or organizational membership, this can lead individuals to be more positively inclined toward the members of their work group or organization if they are similar to self (i.e., categorized as in-group) rather than dissimilar (outgroup). It can also affect individuals' relationships with the group (e.g., as evident on measures of group identification or group cohesiveness; e.g., Doosje, Ellemers, & Spears, 1995; Hogg, 1992), their interaction with fellow group members (e.g., as evident on measures of communication and social influence; e.g., Bhappu, Griffith, & Northcraft, 1997; McGarty, Haslam, Hutchinson, & Turner, 1994; van Knippenberg, 1999) and overall group functioning and performance (e.g., as evident on measures of social laboring and cooperation; Tyler & Blader, 2000; van Knippenberg, 2000a; Worchel, Rothgerber, Day, Hart, & Butemeyer, 1998).

Whereas the social categorization perspective concentrates on the relational element of group composition, the information/decision-making perspective focuses more on the task-related aspects of diversity. This perspective predicts that heterogeneous groups should outperform more homogeneous groups for a number of reasons. In particular, it is argued that, compared to employees in homogeneous groups, members of heterogeneous groups are more likely (1) to possess a broad range of task-relevant skills, abilities, expertise, and information that are distinct and nonredundant; and (2) to have different opinions and perspectives on the task at hand. Task performance may be enhanced as a result because (1) diverse groups may bring more task-relevant information and expertise to bear on the job in hand and (2) the need to reconcile different viewpoints may force the group to process task-relevant information more elaborately (De Dreu, Harinck, & van Vianen, 1999; Janis,

1972) thereby preventing the group from opting too easily for a course of action on which there seems to be consensus (cf. Turner et al.'s discussion of *groupthink* in chapter 7, this volume).

As should be evident from the brief discussion of diversity research presented above, research offers support for the social categorization as well as the decision-making perspective. Moreover, commentators have suggested that these perspectives do not necessarily contradict each other: it is possible, for example, that diversity simultaneously leads to more negative affective–evaluative reactions to the group but also to higher task performance. One could thus make a distinction between the relational and the task-related aspects of group functioning (a distinction maintained in approaches to other organizational topics, notably leadership; e.g., Fleishman & Peters, 1962), and argue that diversity has different effects in different domains.

But is it as simple as that? Analyses of the role of relational conflict (e.g., Jehn, 1995) and social identification (e.g., van Knippenberg, 2000a) suggest that negative relational responses to dissimilarity are detrimental to task performance. This is corroborated by a recent study by Jehn, Northcraft, and Neale (1999). In a survey of work groups, these researchers made a distinction between different types of diversity: informational diversity, social category diversity, and value diversity. They predicted and found that informational diversity was positively related to work group performance, whereas social category diversity and value diversity were negatively related to performance. The effects of the different forms of diversity were mediated by the *type* of conflict they seemed to induce (Jehn, 1995). Informational diversity was associated with task conflict (disagreement about task content), which was expected to benefit task performance by engendering more elaborate processing of task-relevant information. On the other hand, social category diversity and value diversity were associated with relationship conflict (disagreements about personal preferences and interpersonal interaction), which was expected to be detrimental to task performance. Moreover, informational diversity interacted with social category diversity and with value diversity so that informational diversity was positively related to performance mainly when social category and value diversity were low (i.e., social category and value diversity "spoiled" the positive effects of informational diversity).

The Jehn et al. (1999) study seems to summarize nicely the state of the art in diversity research with the distinction between different forms of diversity helping to make sense of apparent contradictions in the social categorization and information/decision-making perspectives. In combination, these perspectives predict that diversity will have negative effects to the extent that it engenders subgroup division in the workplace (i.e., *separatism* leading employees to see their colleagues in purely in-group/out-group terms; Berry, 1984) but positive effects to the extent that diversity is associated with divergent perspectives on the task that promote more elaborate and critical processing of task-relevant information. Extending these points, it can also be argued that diversity in demographic characteristics that appear to be relatively stable and nonnegotiable such as gender, ethnicity, and age (i.e., social category diversity) will more commonly be associated with separatism (partly because such categories are more likely to be politicized) and therefore have more potential to lead to negative outcomes than diversity on more fluid and negotiable dimensions such as information, opinions, and expertise. Conversely, diversity on task-relevant dimensions (i.e., informational diversity), such as functional background or expertise should be more likely to improve task performance.

In this respect, it is important to note that the distinction between social category diversity on the one hand and informational diversity on the other is not a hard one. Informational differences may be a basis for social categorization processes too (i.e., different areas of expertise may be seen as social categories; differences of opinion associated with informational differences may be a basis for subcategorization) and social category differences may be associated with informational differences. In addition, differences that may be a basis for social categorization in one situation need not be so in the other (cf. Jackson, 1992; Turner, 1985). What may seem meaningful differences between people in one situation (e.g., between different functional expertises in a production unit) may seem irrelevant differences in another situation (e.g., when the production unit has a conflict with the sales department). Indeed, social categorization processes may not only work to accentuate differences between categories, but also to trivialize differences within what is seen as a single category (Turner, 1985). In this sense the perception of difference is not only input for categorization processes, but also the *outcome* of social categorization processes.[1]

The above points clearly relate to the relative merits of diversity defined at different levels. However, in line with the findings of Jehn et al., the most important point here relates to the *interaction* between these different levels—specifically, the fact that homogeneity on category-defining dimensions (whatever their basis) seems to be a precondition for informational diversity to have beneficial effects. This suggests that groups need common ground, or shared identity, to help turn divergent perspectives into constructive debate rather than detrimental conflict (cf. Eggins, Haslam, & Reynolds, in press; Jehn et al., 1999; see also chapter 14, this volume; Reynolds, Turner, & Haslam, in press).

BALANCING SIMILARITY AND DIVERSITY

The social categorization perspective and the information/decision-making perspective discussed by Williams and O'Reilly (1998) have so far led largely separate research lives. To integrate these perspectives, van Knippenberg, De Dreu, and Homan (2001) propose the Categorization–Elaboration Model (CEM) presented in Figure 4.1. Building on studies like the study by Jehn et al. (1999), the CEM makes the distinction between social category diversity and informational diversity. The CEM posits that social category diversity may have a positive effect on task performance because it stimulates the processing (and the availability) of task-relevant information. This positive effect is, however, only expected to emerge when group members believe they share a common group membership at a higher level (i.e., social category homogeneity). In the case of social category diversity, subcategorization processes are more likely to result in intergroup biases, lowered superordinate-level identification and group cohesiveness, and relational conflict that will be detrimental to task performance. The CEM thus integrates the social categorization and information/decision-making perspectives in suggesting that the social categorization perspective describes the preconditions (i.e., categorization as a single unit rather than subcategorization as different subgroups within the work unit) for the positive effects of diversity described by the information/decision-making perspective to emerge.

It is important to note that even though social category diversity will often occur on demographic dimensions and informational diversity on task-relevant dimensions (cf. Jackson, 1992; Jehn et al., 1999; Pelled, Eisenhardt, & Xin, 1999) there is nothing that inherently links any dimension of difference to either level. Gender, for example, can represent a basis for social category or informational difference. In the same vein, dimensions that are typically associated with informational diversity, such as differences in functional background, may also be a basis for social categorization (e.g., between rival professions). When applied to the effects of demographic diversity, the model should thus be understood to propose that (1) demographic differences

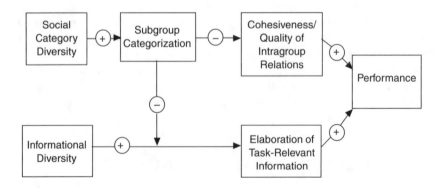

FIGURE 4.1. The Categorization-Elaboration Model (CEM) of group composition and task performance. Adapted from van Knippenberg, De Dreu, & Homan, 2001.

are more likely to result in subcategorization only to the extent that they are perceived to define social category diversity, and (2) that demographic diversity can have a positive effect on performance when it contributes to informational diversity in the context of perceived social category homogeneity.

In addition, it should be noted that, although this has been discussed to a far lesser extent in the organizational diversity literature, predictions from the information/decision-making perspective are compatible with the social identity perspective on social influence and group decision making (e.g., Turner, 1991; see also Haslam, 2001). The social identity approach also predicts the dysfunctionality of similarity when it emerges at *both* social category and informational levels. Indeed, group decision-making processes that have typically been seen to be dysfunctional, such as conformity to majority positions, self-censorship, and groupthink, can be seen to flow from social identity processes that emerge in the context of dual-level homogeneity (Turner, 1991). Conversely, research in minority influence (examining a group's openness to dissenting views) has shown that minorities will only impact upon majority opinions when the minority is perceived to be a part of the ingroup (Clark & Maass, 1988; David & Turner, 1996, 1999). Research in both these areas thus points to the fact that a shared social identity *prefigures* the positive impact of divergent perspectives. From an information/decision-making perspective too, it seems obvious that common ground (i.e., "speaking each other's language") is necessary for employees to be able to benefit from the diversity of perspectives associated with group heterogeneity (cf. Dunbar, 1995). Indeed, in order for an organization to benefit from diversity it seems to be important for its members to have a shared mental model of "who knows what," which allows them to locate the extra information that members with different perspectives may bring to a particular task (cf. Stasser, Vaughan, & Stewart, 2000; Wegner, 1986; Weick & Roberts, 1993).

Thus, both the social identity and information/decision-making perspectives argue against the utility of homogeneous workgroups, but at the same time they also point to the need for such groups to have, and to acknowledge, common ground. A key question for research and practice thus relates to the question of how to manage organizations so that social categorization processes do not undermine the potentially superior performance of diverse work groups. How can the demands for similarity and diversity be balanced? Our integrative review of the literature, as summarized in the CEM displayed in Figure 4.1, suggests that to avoid the potentially detrimental effects of diversity and to enjoy the potential fruits of diversity, organizations need to minimize the reality (and employees' awareness) of social categorical differences that might promote subgroup separatism.[2] Indeed, in this vein, studies addressing the management of intergroup relations have identified the potential benefits of *de*categorization strategies (interventions focused on making group members' unique characteristics as individuals salient, leading group members to see each other as individuals rather than as subgroup members) or *re*categorization strategies (interventions focused on making shared group membership salient, leading group members to see each other as members of the same superordinate group rather than as subgroup members) as a remedy against subgroup separatism and conflict (e.g., Gaertner, Mann, Murrell, & Dovidio, 1989; Sherif, 1966). But because decategorization tends to undermine group identification and cohesiveness, recategorization is typically presented as a preferred strategy (e.g., Gaertner, Rust, Dovidio, Bachman, & Anastasio, 1994, 1996). Nonetheless, stressing sameness to prevent subgroup categorization ignores the important possibility (that has, indeed, been virtually ignored in diversity research) that *diversity itself may be an aspect of social identity*, and that, where this is the case, downplaying within-group differences can also reduce group identification and cohesiveness. This is a point that we elaborate on in the next section.

DIVERSITY AS AN ASPECT OF IDENTITY

The discussion so far, and indeed research into organizational diversity in general, seems to suggest that diversity may have beneficial effects, but only if individuals do not see people as fundamentally different from themselves. Amongst other things, this means that group members can express different opinions and have different perspectives, but should at some higher level see themselves as similar to each other. But are people really as intolerant of differences as this conclusion suggests? Are group cohesiveness and a shared group identity always stronger the more similar group members are to each other? In what follows, we argue against this view and instead propose that rather than necessarily being an obstacle to a shared social identity, diversity may itself be an important aspect of such an identity's *content*.

A first important observation in this argument is that members of work groups necessarily differ on an almost infinite number of dimensions (from eye color and sexual preference to car color and toothpaste preference). Nonetheless, in the normal course of events most of these differences appear to have a negligible impact on group processes and performance. Moreover, even "obviously important" differences, such as differences in sex, age, or ethnicity have often been found to have minimal impact on group members' responses to the group (Williams & O'Reilly, 1998). This is all the more noteworthy in view of the fact that even the most trivial of categorizations may, in principle, be associated with intergroup discrimination and bias (Brewer, 1979; Tajfel, 1970). This is not to say that we should doubt the existence of intergroup bias in organizations, but it does suggest that any such bias is not a routine or automatic response to diversity (cf. Haslam, 2001; Turner, 1999). One reason for this, we argue, is that *identity-based beliefs about the nature and value of diversity mediate between the social world and employees' reactions to it*.

Elaborating on this point, we can surmise that group members not only hold beliefs about who is in their group and about its place within an organization or society, but also about the desirable composition of the group itself (i.e., *composition beliefs*). A simple example illustrates the way in which these beliefs can be relatively independent of the extent to which a social self-category is believed to be superior to other social categories (i.e., intergroup bias). Consider how you would feel about your work group being composed of individuals from different countries who all speak different languages and are not fluent in each other's language. Most likely, you expect the group to function less smoothly and less effectively than when all members would have the same mother tongue. This may seem a rather trivial example, but its significance lies in the fact that you probably believe in the functional superiority of language-homogeneous groups without necessarily believing that individuals who speak one language are better at their job than individuals who speak another. Conversely, you may believe that your group will function better if it is composed of individuals with varying levels of experience and expertise, because relative laypersons and novices may force more expert and experienced group members to articulate, and therefore to more consciously consider, why they approach tasks and problems in a certain way—even though you may also believe that the more expert and experienced members of the group are better at their job. In a similar vein, regardless of your beliefs about the differences between men and women, or between people with different ethnic backgrounds, you may believe that the composition of organizations should reflect the composition of society, and that organizations that are biased in their composition toward certain demographic groups are flawed in a societal sense, or you may prefer diverse groups over homogeneous groups because diverse groups allow individuals to be both a group member and a distinct individual at the same time (cf. Brewer, 1991).

Such beliefs about the value of diversity or homogeneity can affect group members' reactions to the composition of their group, because they can determine the extent to which diversity is seen as something that is, or should be, a part of the group's identity (cf. Jetten, Postmes & McAuliffe, 2002). Put differently, composition beliefs may be seen as beliefs about what makes the group a group, or what makes the group a good group. Individuals may believe that the things they have in common are what make them a group. But, especially in work contexts, they may also believe that it is the unique characteristics of each group member that make them a team in which the whole is more than the sum of its parts. The important implication of this argument is that if—for whatever reasons, be they ideological, instrumental, or other—group members believe that diversity rather than homogeneity contributes to the "groupyness" of their group (i.e., the normative fit of that social self-category; Oakes, 1987) and makes that group better, then they are likely to identify more with the group, be more committed to it, and be more satisfied with their group membership, when the group is heterogeneous rather than homogeneous. On the other hand, if group members believe that their group's identity is defined by homogeneity, they should react more favorably to perceived homogeneity among its members than to perceived diversity.

In a first test of these ideas, we conducted an experiment in which we suggested to participants that they would work in a four-person group on a computer-mediated task (van Knippenberg, Haslam, & Platow, 2000). Group composition was manipulated by giving bogus feedback about a nonexistent personality dimension labeled "cognitive style"(i.e., the choice of a fake personality characteristic allowed us to study group composition effects unconfounded by prior beliefs about these dimensions). Allegedly, a distinction could be made between individuals with a Type H style and individuals with a Type P style. Participants were given bogus feedback about their own cognitive style (always H) and were allegedly placed in a group that was either homogeneous on the HP-dimension (HHHH) or heterogenous on that dimension (HHPP).

Before the group composition manipulation took place, the task was introduced. Groups were to work on an idea generation task. Importantly, there were two task conditions. In the *unique ideas* condition, group members were instructed to come up with as many unique solutions to the problem of reducing the number of bike thefts in the city of Amsterdam. Each group member would enter ideas individually, but ideas would be checked for overlap: each idea could contribute only once to the group total. In the *shared ideas* condition, group members were instructed to come up with solutions to the same problem, but in this condition ideas could only contribute to the group product if they were proposed by at least three out of four group members. A measure of participants' composition beliefs (i.e., beliefs about the extent to which homogeneous all H or all P groups and heterogeneous HP-groups would perform well on the task) indicated that participants believed that homogeneity would lead to superior performance in the shared task condition and heterogeneity to superior performance in the unique task condition.

In line with our hypotheses, group identification was affected by the interaction of group composition and task. The means for this interaction are presented in Figure 4.2. From this it can be seen that individuals assigned to a homogeneous group identified more with their group in the shared ideas condition than in the unique ideas condition. Conversely, in the unique ideas condition, identification was higher when the group was heterogeneous than when it was homogeneous. Moreover, composition beliefs were found to mediate the effect of task in the interaction with composition. That is, group members identified more with a particular type of group (homogeneous or heterogeneous) when faced with a particular type of task because they believed that a particular composition was more appropriate and would help them perform the task better.

The findings of this study thus suggest that whether or not individuals identify with a homogeneous group or with a diverse group depends partly on

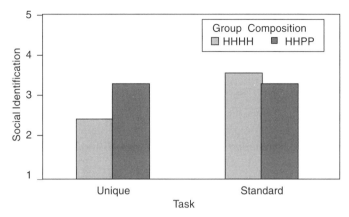

FIGURE 4.2. Work group identification as a function of task and group composition. From van Knippenberg et al., 2000.

their composition beliefs. In the van Knippenberg et al. (2000) study, we also assessed intergroup bias in perceptions of the ability of groups composed of Type H versus Type P individuals to perform the task at hand. There was no overall bias (nor was this expected), but individual differences in bias moderated the effect of group composition on identification: group members responded more negatively toward a heterogeneous group the more biased they were against Type P individuals. Importantly, however, the interaction between task and group composition was independent of this effect. That is, intergroup bias affected identification with the heterogeneous group, but this effect was independent of the effect of composition beliefs. This finding is significant because it indicates that beliefs favoring homogeneity should not be equated with biases against other social groups, nor should beliefs favoring heterogeneity be equated with lack of bias against individuals from other social categories. Another reason why these findings are important is that they show that the potentially positive effects of diversity are not limited to performance measures, but can also impact on other variables such as group identification—a variable on which prior analyses had suggested diversity would have negative consequences (cf. Williams & O'Reilly, 1998).

    In a second study, we sought to examine the role that composition beliefs play in actual organizational settings (Haslam & van Knippenberg, 2000). In a survey, 151 employees from a range of workplaces were asked to respond to a number of items relating to their perceptions of, and attitudes toward, a salient workunit of which they were a member (e.g., a team or department). The study assessed (1) work group composition in terms of sex, age, and social class; (2) composition beliefs about sex, age, and social class; (3) whether respondents perceived their beliefs about diversity to be shared by other members of their workunit; (4) identification with the work unit, interpersonal attraction to members of the work unit, turnover intentions, and self-reported efforts on the job (cf. *generalized compliance*; Organ, 1988). The main hypothesis of the study was that work group composition and composition beliefs would interact to affect identification, interpersonal attraction, and so on (cf. van Knippenberg et al., 2000), but that this effect would mainly be observed when composition beliefs were socially shared. This prediction was based on the notion that individual beliefs would be held more strongly to the extent that there was perceived to be group consensus (i.e., social sharedness) regarding the appropriateness of the group's composition (cf. Turner, 1991). Accordingly, social sharedness should contribute to a group climate that favors either diversity or homogeneity (i.e., contingent on composition beliefs) and thus enhance the effects of individual composition beliefs.

Although the three-way interactions implied by this hypothesis were not obtained for sex composition and not for all dependent measures, results generally confirmed predictions. As an illustrative example, we present the age composition by composition beliefs by social sharedness of composition beliefs interaction for identification. This interaction is displayed in Figures 4.3a and 4.3b. Decomposition of this interaction indicated that, as expected, the simple composition by composition beliefs interaction was not significant when the social sharedness of composition beliefs was low. When composition beliefs were more socially shared, in contrast, the simple interaction was significant. When composition beliefs favored age diversity, more age diversity was associated with higher identification. Conversely, when composition beliefs favored age homogeneity, more age diversity was associated with lower identification.

These findings are important for a number of reasons. First, in conjunction with the van Knippenberg et al. (2000) laboratory findings, they establish

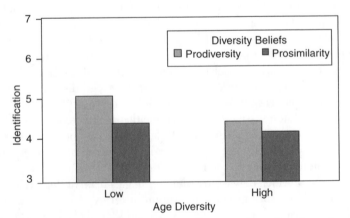

FIGURE 4.3a. Work group identification as a function of age diversity and composition beliefs when social sharedness of composition beliefs is low. From Haslam and van Knippenberg, 2000.

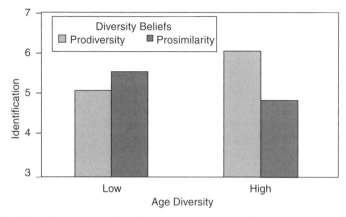

FIGURE 4.3b. Work group identification as a function of age diversity and composition beliefs when social sharedness of composition beliefs is high. From Haslam and van Knippenberg et al., 2000.

the moderating effect of composition beliefs on the effects of group composition with a high level of both internal and external validity. With some confidence, we may thus conclude that diversity itself is not inherently "good" or "bad," but to a certain extent diversity really is "what you make of it." Again, it is important to point out that composition beliefs should not be equated with (lack of) intergroup bias. As our earlier discussion and the findings from the van Knippenberg et al. (2000) study illustrate, such beliefs may be relatively independent of intergroup bias, because they are bound to the particular group in question and the particular social and task context in which the group operates. Second, by demonstrating that this moderating influence of composition beliefs is primarily observed when composition beliefs are socially shared, these findings corroborate the proposition that diversity (or homogeneity) may be an aspect of identity. That is, it is not individual composition beliefs per se, but rather consensually shared beliefs that determine individuals' reactions to their group's composition. This suggests that composition beliefs are not something that group members "bring to the scene"(i.e., a group composition variable), but may instead be the product of group processes tied to the particular group in its particular context. In this sense, diversity is very much "what the group makes of it." It is also important to note that the Haslam and van Knippenberg findings corroborate our earlier observation that research findings for a given group composition dimension may appear inconsistent in the sense that diversity on that dimension may have either positive, negative, or no effects. In the interaction we discussed here, all three outcomes were observed for the same dependent variable. When the social sharedness of beliefs was low, age composition was unrelated to identification, but when beliefs were more socially shared, age diversity was either positively or negatively related to identification contingent on the content of beliefs. In this sense too, these findings underscore the importance of attending to composition beliefs in diversity research.

MANAGING DIVERSITY

As our review of diversity research indicates, the general gist of diversity studies would seem to point to the value of downplaying differences to prevent subcategorization processes that can promote subgroup separatism. Our research into composition beliefs suggests, however, that awareness of differences between categories need not be problematic and indeed may bolster identification with the group when composition beliefs favor diversity and beliefs in the value of diversity are widely shared in the organization. Indeed, recategorization that encourages a sense of similarity within a common ingroup (Gaertner et al., 1996; Mayo, 1933) would be expected to have detrimental effects if it erodes the differences that are the basis of identification fueled by prodiversity composition beliefs. Contingent on the content of composition beliefs, group identification and cohesiveness might thus actually be promoted by an awareness of within-group differences.

Interestingly and importantly, recent developments in research in intergroup relations also point to the benefits of acknowledging differences between groups in a context in which the identities of the (sub)groups are secure, albeit for different reasons (e.g., Eggins et al., in press; Gaertner & Dovidio, 2000; Hewstone & Brown, 1986; Hornsey & Hogg, 2000; van Leeuwen, van Knippenberg, & Ellemers, 2001a, 2001b; for discussions of these perspectives see chapters 12, 14 this volume). This research suggests that an emphasis on homogeneity can actually backfire, because it can create motivational pressures to assert subgroup distinctiveness and encourage discriminatory behavior against the other subgroup (Brown & Wade, 1987; Jetten, Spears, & Manstead, 1997). Where important differences are perceived to exist in the workplace, effective management of diversity would therefore seem to require an acknowledgement rather than denial of differences between members of different societal or organizational groups (Reynolds, Eggins, & Haslam, 2001; see chapter 14, this volume).

However, our research into composition beliefs adds an important qualification to this conclusion, suggesting that recognition of differences will only have a beneficial effect in the context of shared composition beliefs that favor diversity. To integrate the "subgroup distinctiveness perspective" with our earlier review of the literature, we may therefore propose that whether the predictions of the CEM (subgroup distinctiveness as a threat to group functioning) or the subgroup distinctiveness perspective (subgroup distinctiveness as a precondition for good intergroup relations) hold is contingent on composition beliefs. When composition beliefs favor homogeneity, subgroup distinctiveness is likely to have detrimental effects (cf. the CEM), whereas when composition beliefs favor diversity, subgroup distinctiveness is likely to have beneficial effects (cf. the subgroup distinctiveness perspective). To a considerable extent, then, the management of diversity can be seen as an ideological exercise, because much of it is necessarily focused on the management of composition beliefs.

What, then, will lead people to share a belief in the value of diversity? Although a range of factors can be assumed to play a role here, two that we consider to be particularly important are *instrumentality* and *ideology*. As in our experimental research (van Knippenberg et al., 2000), employees may favor diversity for instrumental reasons: that is, they may believe that diverse groups will outperform homogeneous ones. To the extent that there are grounds for believing this (e.g., on creative and group decision-making tasks; cf. the information/decision-making perspective), organizations can communicate these grounds to team members and work with them to explore the benefits that flow from diversity. However, a second experiment using the same paradigm as the van Knippenberg, Haslam, and Platow (2000) study suggests that such instrumental concerns will only come into play when members are actually concerned about task performance (cf. task orientation; West, 1990): only when group members considered the task to be important did task requirements and group composition interact to affect identification (van Knippenberg, Platow, & Haslam, 2001). At some higher level, then, the instrumental values of diversity will only be apparent, and attempts to communicate them will only be heeded, when employees share a social identity with management that leads all parties to have compatible organizational perspectives (cf. Haslam, 2001; van Knippenberg, 2000a). Like beliefs about diversity, beliefs about what is instrumental are therefore grounded in identity rather than in any sense "given."

Leading on from this observation, we come back to the point that beliefs about the nature and value of diversity may be an expression of *ideology*. Accordingly, and just as in society at large, individuals in organizations would be expected to embrace a *composition ideology* that favors either diversity (cf. multiculturalism) or homogeneity (cf. monoculturalism; Chen & Eastman, 1997; Nahavandi & Malekzadeh, 1988). Indeed, the beliefs that lie at the heart of these ideologies are a natural consequence of large-scale political processes that surround the necessary debate about which differences in society are important and which are trivial, which differences are worth accentuating and which need to be suppressed, which are higher-order and which are lower-order. Clearly too, looking over the last 100 years of organizational practice in Western countries, we can see that the content of these beliefs has changed. Where once it was seen as acceptable and desirable for workunits to be largely homogeneous with respect to dimensions such as class, sex, ethnicity, and age, now these views are much more likely to be contested. Indeed, the massive upsurge of research interest in organizational diversity that has occurred over the last 10 years is a highly visible symptom of this fact.

This change has been the product of a number of factors (e.g., cultural, historical, economic, legal). Importantly, though, as we noted at the very start of this chapter, it has been associated with significant changes in the composition of the workplace, which, we believe, make multicultural composition ideologies more relevant, more prevalent, and more necessary than they once were. As Chen and Eastman (1997) argue, this means that while organizations were once keen to pursue the ideal of a "strong" organizational culture (Peters & Waterman, 1982), which promotes a high degree of sameness, such cultures are unlikely to be suited to contemporary organizations because they require a level of homogeneity which rarely exists (or which could only be achieved through a policy of separatism). Instead, these authors propose that contemporary organizations need a civic culture that focuses on relational values such as equity and respect for differences (cf. Tyler, 1999; see chapter 9, this volume) and in which differentiation of organizational groups as well as integration of organizational groups should be core cultural values. Although working from a slightly different perspective, Chen and Eastman's conclusion sits comfortably with much of the analysis and data that we have discussed in this chapter. Here we have argued that in order to harness their potential, organizations need to promote a sense of shared social identity, but we have also shown that the content of that identity needs to recognize and incorporate psychologically and socially *real* differences (e.g., in background, perspective, values, and goals). Indeed, it is the salience of a superordinate identity that makes the reality of difference a basis for organizational strength rather than weakness—translating the potential for separatism into a source of vitality and creativity.

As other chapters in this volume testify (e.g., chapters 3, 12, 14), creating and nurturing an organizational identity of this form requires that organizations give voice to, and respect, intragroup differences. Importantly though, it is also an ideological endeavor in which all employees, practitioners, and researchers have a role to play. For this reason, sound diversity management involves (1) the development and promotion of organic social identities that help organizations deliver greater justice and service; but also (2) negotiation, debate, and argument in which the ideology of diversity management is left open to interrogation and challenge. It is through the marriage of these activities that much of the recent progress in diversity management has been achieved. A similar recipe seems likely to maximize the likelihood of progress in the future.

NOTES

1. We would suggest that, in principle, all dimensions of difference may result in social category diversity. Nonetheless, stable features of social and political reality serve to make certain dimensions appear a more "natural" basis for demographic differentiation between people and hence make them a more likely basis for intergroup division. Importantly though, as that reality changes, so will the categories used to describe and experience it (cf. Haslam, Turner, Oakes, McGarty, & Reynolds, 1998). This is most apparent in the changing views about the nature of "racial" categories over the last 30 or so years, with the result that most researchers no longer believe "race" to be a valid demographic category at all (for a relevant discussion see Hopkins, Reicher, & Levine, 1997).
2. This suggestion presupposes that higher-level organizational conflict is not desirable. However, in some cases (e.g., where an organization's superordinate goals are corrupt) this is not the case, and indeed we would argue that conflict over higher-level goals can be important in order to promote pluralism and vitality at a societal level (e.g., chapters 12 and 14 this volume; Haslam, 2001, chapter 11).

PART III

COMMUNICATION AND DECISION MAKING

5

A Social Identity Approach to Communication in Organizations

TOM POSTMES
University of Exeter

*U*ncontroversially, this chapter argues that communication plays a central role in organizations. The argument that practitioners and academic students fail to do justice to its importance is perhaps somewhat more controversial. In the first section of this chapter I provide an overview of the field of organizational communication, with the aim of identifying some of its shortcomings. Although this field is much too diverse to do justice to within the confines of a few paragraphs, I shall do my best to indicate the breadth of the field, extract some common theoretical assumptions, and identify scope for improvement. The remainder of this chapter is concerned with exploring how the social identity approach could inform research into, and practice of, organizational communication, and tackle some of these problems.

Two sets of questions are addressed here. The first concerns matters of theory and process with regard to communication in general, not restricted to organizations per se. In particular, one purpose is to examine its relationship with social identity. This theoretical section is quite extensive, in part because there is a lot of ground to cover, but also because a careful consideration of theoretical issues is essential: it not only informs practice, but it seeks to address what some see as the central problem of the field of organizational communication to date—that it is atheoretical (Gardner, Paulsen, Gallois, Callan, & Monaghan, 2001; Tompkins & Redding, 1988).

The second set of questions concerns matters of application. The central issues addressed here pertain to the ways in which social identities play a role in organizational communications across interpersonal and corporate levels.

This section also addresses the issue of whether practitioners and scholars would benefit from taking the implications of the social identity approach for organizational communication into account.

THE FIELD OF ORGANIZATIONAL COMMUNICATION

There is no textbook of organizational communication (or, for that matter, of related fields such as organizational theory and organizational psychology) that fails to observe that communication and organization are closely entwined if not synonymous. Communication has been called the "life blood of the organization," the "glue" that binds it all together, the "force that pervades the organization," or better yet "the organization embalming fluid" (Goldhaber, 1993; Katz & Kahn, 1972; Kreps, 1990). Moreover, it is often pointed out that an act of organization necessarily involves an act of communication, that communication is the essence of organization, or—to reverse matters—that communication is the process of organizing (Johnson, 1977; Weber, 1947; Weick, 1969). All this reflects the fact that any form of organization entails coordination of human activity, and that coordination is only possible with a fair amount of information exchange. Whilst in theory such information could be a one-way stream of directives from a leader, in practice information can only be exchanged by *communicating* (i.e., a recursive process of signaling meaning). Communication serves essential functions ranging from the maintenance of interpersonal relations among coworkers to the dissemination of strategic organizational objectives. That managers often spend over half their time communicating, illustrates the pivotal role of communication in enabling organizations to function and achieve their objectives (Henderson, 1987; Mintzberg, 1983b).

It would be hard to imagine a better starting point for any discipline than that provided in the previous paragraph: this topic is of crucial importance for organizations. Yet beyond this point the studies of mainstream organizational communication tend to be a bit of a disappointment. If the source of this discipline is as powerfully persuasive and as irresistible as a sweeping current, then what follows is a near-endless description of the meandering branches and trickling streams that, when taken together, form a delta of heterogeneous topics and perspectives. Paying homage to the ubiquity of communication simultaneously signals its complexity and the main problem that impedes the field of organizational communication. Precisely because communication is omnipresent, the study of it is so diverse that cumulative research is rare. In this way, the field as a whole is theoretically fragmented, often trailing theoretical developments in its sister fields (Allen, Gotcher, & Seibert, 1993; Tompkins & Redding, 1988).

The complexities of the topic are illustrated by the many typologies that have guided the segmentation of the field of organizational communication into different subdisciplines (e.g., Goldhaber, 1993; Greenbaum, 1974; Katz & Kahn, 1972; Thayer, 1968). These are summarized in Table 5.1. Although this list is by no means complete, and is restricted to internal communication (i.e., communication within the boundaries of the organization), it illustrates that treating organizational communication as if it were a unitary phenomenon is a gross simplification. I will now briefly elaborate on each of these typologies, in order to give the reader a flavor of the theoretical underpinnings of this field.

Locus

As a logical starting point, communication may be subdivided according to the locus of sender and receiver in the organizational hierarchy. For example, it may originate from or be directed toward different levels such as the executive, managerial, and blue-collar employees. Although different social groupings could be involved (e.g., based on gender, religion, cultural background, race), these are not yet mainstream, despite an increasing interest in diversity issues (e.g., see chapter 4, this volume). As a rule, analyses of the locus of senders and receivers tend to be individualistic, focusing, for example, on information requirements, managerial objectives, or organizational roles.

TABLE 5.1. Typologies of organizational communication.

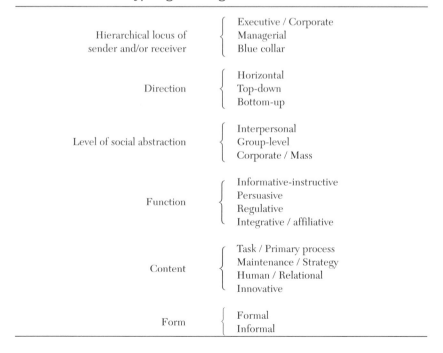

Hierarchical locus of sender and/or receiver	Executive / Corporate Managerial Blue collar
Direction	Horizontal Top-down Bottom-up
Level of social abstraction	Interpersonal Group-level Corporate / Mass
Function	Informative-instructive Persuasive Regulative Integrative / affiliative
Content	Task / Primary process Maintenance / Strategy Human / Relational Innovative
Form	Formal Informal

Direction

Communication may also be characterized by its *direction* in the organizational hierarchy: top-down or bottom-up, or horizontal. Again, this is about the place of communication in the social system, and reflects the centrality of the structural approach in the field. Traditionally, students of organizational communication are concerned with the formal structure of organizations, and identifying who needs to know what (cf. Mintzberg, 1983b). Following the example set by organizational sciences more generally, the focus is often on "how to get things done" from a managerial perspective. In communication audits, this ideal type is then compared with the reality of information provision (Downs & Adrian, 1997; Greenbaum, 1974).

Level of Social Abstraction

Another relevant division from a psychosocial point of view is whether information is exchanged between individuals, within or between groups, or at the level of the organization or a large division. This distinction is widespread, and guides the structure of major textbooks. At the individual and interpersonal level, communication research has primarily focused on interpersonal relationships in work settings. This, arguably, is the most developed field within communication science, with a tradition of examining the processes by which relationships are established and maintained, and the communicative aspects of motivation and control. The theoretical bases have partly evolved from humanistic and scientific management ideologies as expressed in the managerial, organizational, and social–psychological literatures. These include the human relations approach (Leavitt, 1972; Likert, 1961), motivational theories (Herzberg, 1987; Maslow, 1943), and theories of interpersonal relationships. Alternative approaches that are quite prominent are more *network based.* The analysis of (inter)personal communication networks is a major topic in organizational communication (Monge & Contractor, 2001). There is no underlying theoretical dimension to this work, however: it is mostly method-driven research.

The analysis of communications in groups is largely an extension of interpersonal research, partly derived from the group dynamics literature in social psychology, and incorporating insights from the interpersonal communications literature. At the level of corporate communications, the field is characterized by a structural approach, often influenced by humanistic ideals. Many studies fall in the mass communication tradition (McQuail, 1994). Also, the field devotes considerable attention to issues of corporate culture and communication climate (Deal & Kennedy, 1982; Hofstede, 1980) as guides for the organization of corporate communication (Redding, 1973). Finally, there recently has been a significant increase in studies of the implications of the organizational context for organizational communication (Sutcliffe, 2001). To some extent, these analyses are sociologically or politically inspired, often blended in with core assumptions of traditional management theories.

Function

The purpose of communication for sender or receiver has guided a range of distinctions (e.g., Greenbaum, 1974). Most common is the distinction between (1) informative–instructive functions (the exchange of information for the purpose of transferring meaning); (2) persuasive functions; (3) regulative functions (communication to coordinate activity); and (4) integrative or affiliative functions (the establishment of social relationships and social roles). Given that these distinctions are theoretically grounded in an understanding of individual motivations, the analyses tend to be individualistic—leaning on the attitude and attitude change literature, and social–psychological analyses of leadership and interpersonal attraction.

Content

Typologies that focus on *content* (Goldhaber, 1993) often distinguish communication about the primary process and the task at hand. Maintenance information pertains to policy and regulation of the organization, and its longer-term strategy. Human and relational communication deals with feelings, affection, or dislike for people or groups, morale, motivation, encouragement, and a range of other socioemotional content. Finally, some theorists consider innovative content as a separate category. This is communication dealing with new plans, projects, and directions.

Form

The final distinction contrasts formal and informal communications. Formal communication uses designated channels of communication and fits within the organization's formal structure, whereas informal communication does neither.

Although this is a short and somewhat crude introduction, it highlights two features of the field, the first of which is its diversity and fragmentation (Tompkins & Redding, 1988). This diversity is partly due to the nature of the object of study: Most actions occurring in an organization involve some form of communication, and in fact many actions are no more than communication. Inevitably, then, the range of phenomena that this field covers is too broad for most theoretical approaches to cope with successfully.

The second feature that emerges from this review is that despite the diversity, there is a metatheoretical unity to the field that reflects the dualisms of agency/structure and individual/society (Giddens, 1984; Turner, Hogg, Oakes,

Reicher, & Wetherell, 1987). On the one hand there are analyses at the corporate level that tend to be unconcerned with individual factors and which focus almost exclusively on the structural determinants such as culture, communication climate, and hierarchical structure. On the other hand, the field is dominated by individualistic analyses, reflected in studies of interpersonal communications, leadership, persuasion, negotiation, motivation, and informational approaches, all of which tend to ignore structural influences (Nykodym, 1988).

That this dualism resurfaces in the field of organizational communication is especially ironic, because scholars from both camps acknowledge that communication is the process which bridges the gap between individual and structure, and thereby holds the key to understanding their reciprocal influence. The social identity approach has some useful implications for the field of organizational communication in this regard, primarily because it presents a framework within which the interaction between the two levels can be understood. As such, the approach could point the field in a new direction, providing a framework within which all "types" of organizational communication can be analyzed and understood, enhancing our theoretical understanding of the elementary bases of coordination while informing practice at the same time.

THE SOCIAL IDENTITY APPROACH

A social identity approach to communications in organizations begins where our analysis of the shortcomings of the field stops: with the observation that both individual and structural factors are essential to understanding coordinated human activity. The key problems in the analysis of the interaction between the two are twofold. On the one hand, the question is how structural factors influence individual thought and action despite the undeniable autonomy of the individual. On the other hand, it is a challenge to understand the processes by which individual thought and action (co)determine social structures.[1] In answering both questions, communication plays a vital role. However, before we turn to the role of communication per se, let us first examine how the social identity approach deals with these two questions in the abstract.

In order to explain the influence of social and structural determinants on individuals, the social identity approach postulates that the social is not external to the self, but that it is internalized through a *social identity* (Haslam, 2001; Tajfel, 1981a; Turner, Hogg et al., 1987). These social identities are not merely individual conceptions of a group, social category, or organization. They are—to some extent at least—*socially shared* conceptions of what the defining features and boundaries of these structures are.[2] Social identities therefore provide a common interpretive framework encompassing a view about how the group is defined in relation to other groups, and is embedded in a common perspective on group history or a shared sense of future direction. They often include syntactic and symbolic conventions, and may have ideological ramifications. They reflect group *norms*, that is, a group-specific set of conventions, rules, and possible sanctions. "We-ness" carries with it at a minimum the anticipation of a common understanding that simultaneously delineates, implicitly or explicitly, what is normative and antinormative. In other words, if a common identity is salient and recognized among group members, they would expect to speak a common language.

A social identity may determine individual thought and action through the twin processes of social (or self-) categorization and social identification. The categorization of oneself as a member of a social group is in part dependent on the salience of categories (believed to be a matter of category accessibility, and fit; Oakes, 1987; see McGarty, 1999, for a recent and extensive discussion). Moreover, categorization may also be imposed on a person, even if this person challenges the category membership or meanings attributed to it, as is the case in stigmatized groups. Social identification goes beyond the (cognitive) knowledge of being a group member: it describes the affective consequences of (aspirant) group membership. Thus strong identification with a certain social group increases the likelihood that the group's social identity is self-defining. Both processes of categorization and identification—the first tending to be more situationally and contextually determined, the latter more enduring and long-term—enhance the likelihood that individuals will come to define themselves in terms of a certain social identity (see chapter 1, this volume). If this is the case, then the norms and properties that are commonly ascribed to the social group become internalized; they become subjectively interchangeable with personal norms, influencing thought and guiding action.

This rough sketch of the social identity approach provides the ingredients that may answer our first question, showing how structural factors can influence individual thought and action. To the extent that social structures can be transformed into social identities (groups, categories, or organizations that may be seen by the individuals in them as "we" structures), they will affect individuals once they define themselves as group members. The way these structures then influence individuals depends on the content of the identity; for example, on the specific norms, conventions, ideology, stereotypes, and culture of the group in question. This view may be applied readily to organizations. Hewlett Packard, for example, invests heavily in promoting its identity (the "HP way"). The social identity approach provides an insight in how this identity may elicit a certain HP-style behavior in employees, and under what conditions this is likely to happen, namely when employees categorize themselves as group members, and when they identify with HP.

The second question—concerning the processes through which individual thought and action (co)determine social structures—is more of a challenge, and unfortunately a rather limited amount of research in the social identity tradition has addressed it. One way in which the social identity content of a certain category or group is established is by means of comparison, implicit or explicit, with other social groups or categories. The principle of metacontrast specifies how this comparison will affect the ideas about the in- and out-group (Turner, Hogg et al., 1987). The general idea is that the differences between groups are accentuated, and differences within groups are minimized, both of which create group distinctiveness. It should be added that groups have some leeway when making such comparisons. Although certain aspects of social reality are relatively undeniable in the sense of having real (material or social) consequences, with regard to the *interpretation* of a comparison outcome there is a flexibility of meaning of the comparison dimension and an opportunity to choose among different available comparison dimensions (also termed social creativity). For example, this would mean that employees of an R&D department could define their group as innovative and resourceful (but not wasteful or irresponsible) in comparison to accountancy, but when comparing themselves to the sales department they could define themselves as thorough and scrupulous (but not stuffy or nerdy, cf. Doosje, Haslam, Spears, Oakes, & Koomen, 1998; Dutton, Dukerich, & Harquail, 1994). This general principle could, especially over longer periods of time, shape social identities. The Macintosh corporation, and the Jobs/Sculley mythology surrounding it, is exemplary in this regard. This company appears to have thrived on distinctiveness, and this contributes to its appeal for consumers.

Another possible way in which social identity may be formed is through induction (e.g., Turner, 1982). Group members may observe other group members' behaviors and induce from these more general properties of the social category or group. This is especially likely when group members are in a position to share their observations with each other (such as social norms, Sherif, 1936). Examples of how such norms emerge to regulate productivity in work groups can be found in the classic Hawthorne studies (Mayo, 1949). In these studies, groups of workers developed norms of production over the course of longer periods of time. These norms were enforced by correcting transgressions verbally or even physically. Induction may also partly explain the strong influence that history and prior experience have on the content of norms and social identities (Postmes & Spears, 2001). It should be pointed out that since social identities provide common interpretive frameworks, group members will expect to have similar interpretations of history and experiences: indeed, groups tend to further this by devoting considerable time to the collective interpretation and valuation of past events (i.e., mythologizing).

COMMUNICATION AND SOCIAL IDENTITY

In the above discussion of the social identity approach, direct reference to communication has been remarkably absent. Nonetheless, communication plays a pivotal (but often covert and underexposed) role in social identity processes. Its importance becomes evident when asking *how* the processes described above actually work. When one reflects on this, communication appears a key factor in determining the salience of social identities. Also, communication is essential for the interaction between the social and the individual which enables identity formation.

The salience of social identity is easily and powerfully influenced by a variety of communicative processes, some of which are subtle and occur unconsciously. There is a host of experimental evidence for this, even if it is not always framed as being about communication. For example, if experimenters address group members collectively (your group) rather than individually (you), this has powerful implications for the way in which people make decisions, evaluate their group and other groups, develop a sense of cohesion and unity, and so on (e.g., Spears, Lea, & Lee, 1990). Another experimental manipulation of identity salience that speaks to the power of communication is asking people to simply don some public sign expressing group membership: communicating group membership in such a public fashion elicits strong identification and strengthens group influence (e.g., Gaertner, Mann, Murrell, & Dovidio, 1989; Worchel, Rothgerber, Day, Hart, & Butemeyer, 1998). However, more private expressions of group membership can also powerfully affect the salience of group membership. Examples can be found in research asking people to list things their group does well, or to describe other aspects of their group (e.g., Haslam, Oakes, Reynolds, & Turner, 1999). Almost without exception, the literature has reported that such communication about the group or its membership exerts a strong influence over its members.

A further way in which communication influences the salience of social identity (and vice versa) is highlighted in research on communication accommodation theory (Giles & Coupland, 1991). This theory explores the convergence and divergence between speakers' language as part of the process by which language use reflects and creates social structure. Convergence refers to an assimilation of vocabularies, accents, and rates of speech, and is generally believed to signify social identification. Divergence is the reverse process of accentuating linguistic differences, and signifies social distancing, or the recognition and accentuation of an intergroup difference. Such processes can be quite powerful, and have direct implications for organizations. For example, it has been found that job applicants are recruited for jobs that are seen as "fitting" the social stratum conveyed by their accents, illustrating that language serves as a cue for social categorization (e.g., Giles, Wilson, & Conway, 1981).

Similar findings are contained in research on the linguistic intergroup bias, although to date, these have not been tested in organizational contexts. This research shows that there is a tendency to communicate negative information about the out-group and positive information about the in-group in more abstract terms, thereby reinforcing a favorable stereotype of one's own group over others (Maass, Salvi, Arcuri, & Semin, 1989). Consistent with communication accommodation theory, the social context of intergroup relations prompts a certain use of language. Follow-up studies have shown that such subtle language differences may also have considerable impact on others' impressions of these people (Wigboldus, Semin, & Spears, 2000). It is not hard to see how, in such a fashion, even a few turns in a friendly chat may invoke a huge, invisible social system of personal and intergroup relations. As communication accommodation theory outlines, such conversations are at the same time both the cause and consequence of such systems—utterances invoke social identities as much as they are activated by them.

One final way in which communication may enhance identity salience and identification is through the definition of what an organization actually is (Postmes, Tanis, & DeWit, 2001). Thus, corporate communications may define what the organization stands for, and thereby elicit organizational identification and commitment (Deal & Kennedy, 1982; chapter 11, this volume). This process was illustrated in recent studies which showed that vertical communication in organizations (i.e., strategic corporate information from CEOs and direct communication with management) was strongly predictive of affective organizational commitment, whereas horizontal communication (informal communications with colleagues) was much less predictive (Postmes et al., 2001). Of course this does not mean that informal and friendly interaction is unimportant, but it does reflect the theoretical principle that interpersonal processes are not as informative about the group as are factors which determine the position of the group as a whole (Tajfel, 1978). Interpersonal interaction is often not the best way of defining who *we* are.

This implies that, in Western cultures at least, task-related and strategic organizational communication are better placed than interpersonal communications to create distinctiveness of the organization, to set the organization apart in the eyes of its employees, and make it a salient entity. This phenomenon was observed in a recent study we conducted in 12 major information technology (IT) industries in the Netherlands ($N = 214$). We asked samples of about 20 employees in each organization to characterize the communication within their organization as a whole and among employees, using a Katz and Braly-type checklist (Katz & Braly, 1933). Two latent factors of organizational communication were distinguished in a structural equation model: an interpersonal factor (composed of adjectives such as personal, friendly, pleasant, open, and their opposites), and a task-oriented factor (composed of terms such as task-oriented, businesslike, professional, and their opposites). As displayed in Figure 5.1, the model showed that of these two factors only the task-related dimension influenced organizational commitment. Moreover, as predicted by the social identity approach this was mediated by the distinctiveness of the organization (captured by several questions; e.g., "this organization has a clear and distinctive identity in comparison with other organizations in its branch"). This result suggests that task-related (but not interpersonal) aspects of communication influence organizational distinctiveness, which in turn predicts organizational commitment. The importance of this result is underlined by the extreme competitiveness of the job market for respondents: they were highly qualified IT experts whose median tenure (2.5 years) suggests that changing employers is easy for them. That organizational communication can increase the distinctiveness of the organization and thereby increase commitment reflects the fact that communication plays a powerful role in enhancing the salience of organizational identity.

Beyond salience, communication is also relevant to identity formation, as suggested by the findings displayed in Figure 5.1. It is here that distinguishing between language and identity can sometimes be hard. The importance of communication to the formation of social identity is implicit in the work of Festinger and Sherif. Festinger, for example, suggested that social validation is essential for people to develop a sense of social reality (Festinger, 1950). This sense-making process depends not merely on the informational value of inputs from others, but also on whether the other is seen as a valid source of information (Turner, 1991). Recognition of a shared identity is crucial in this regard, with in-groups being more influential than out-groups (Mackie & Cooper, 1984). It should also be noted here that the influence of opinion leaders (and to a certain extent of the media) can be ascribed to the fact that the information they provide us with is most acceptable to us when they are prototypical our in-group or social category (McGarty, Haslam, Hutchinson, & Turner, 1994).

Social validation is, of course, closely linked to the processes of norm formation and consensualization of stereotypes and other views (Sherif, 1936). Both these processes can be seen as indispensable to, and partly synonymous with, identity formation. In the area of norm formation, the critical role of communication is illustrated in classical studies (Festinger, Schachter, & Back, 1950; Lewin, 1947; Newcomb, 1943) as well as more recent research. Postmes

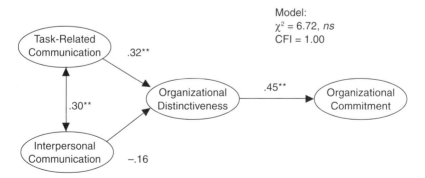

FIGURE 5.1. A structural equation model of communication as a predictor of affective organizational commitment, mediated by distinctiveness, in 12 IT firms (°° p < .01).

and colleagues (2001; Postmes, Spears, & Lea, 2000) showed that the individual preferences of members of online groups flourish into fully fledged social norms as communication within the group unfolds. Recent research of Haslam and colleagues also points to the power of conversation in small groups in shaping consensual views (Haslam et al., 1999; Haslam et al., 1998). All these studies illustrate the same underlying principle: groups are transformed as their members communicate, and communication is often geared to this transformation process. Members exchange information and views, not merely in order to learn what others think, or to obtain information that enables them to do their task. Rather, groups actively engage in collective sense making in order to reduce the uncertainties they face, and through this process they simultaneously define what is consensual and normative within the group (Weick & Roberts, 1993).

The upshot of this process is that individuals rely on social identities to make sense of their social world. Our social groups provide us with the tools to resolve uncertainty and coordinate our responses. Communication plays an essential role as a mediator between individual meanings, and as a constructor of social meanings. Yet, at the same time, communication is only possible because it draws upon a common understanding, a common language and interpretive framework, as contained within a common identity. Communication serves its function of collective sense making, then, because it is grounded in an already existing system of meaning. Social identity is crucial for communication to be effective in that it provides a common interpretive framework, enabling groups to make sense of the world. Simultaneously, any effort at sense making will define and transform social identity, altering the shared system of meaning which the social identity provides.

In sum, this section provides some indication of what the social identity approach has to offer students of organizational communication. Especially important here is the fact that it offers a coherent theoretical perspective that can inform communication practices. The power of this analysis is that it transcends the traditional levels and divisions in the field of organizational communication that were identified in this chapter's introduction. In particular, it identifies an opportunity to resolve the dualism of individual and structure, allowing communication to be valued in its proper and most important function: as enabling *coordinated* action. As a consequence, it forces us to reconsider what we consider to be the functions of communication in an organizational context. Classically these functions are identified along the lines of (1) information, (2) influence, (3) coordination, and (4) affiliation. The social identity approach broadens our focus to also consider the functions of communication that have both an individual utility and a distinct *social utility*. These functions are (1) the establishment of social reality through social validation; (2) the shaping, solidifying, and maintenance of social structure; (3) the communication of relationships, the affirmation of existing identities, and the creation of new ones. Through this shift in emphasis, the social identity approach has much to offer for the field of organizational communication. Its theoretical and practical utility are even greater because it offers an escape from the reductionistic individualism that plague this field, while avoiding the pitfalls of aspecific structuralism.

PRACTICAL CONSIDERATIONS

If the foregoing has been abstract and theoretical, this final section examines more practical consequences of the social identity approach. It provides some concrete examples of the ways in which social identities can be taken into account in organizational contexts, and of how this approach may inform strategies for communication between people, in groups, and at the corporate level.

Much of the research in the tradition of the communication accommodation theory addresses the influence of social identities in interpersonal communications. One obvious example is the interaction between manager and employee: without acknowledgement of the intergroup dynamics that may become salient in such interaction (e.g., based on status, race, or social class), powerful misunderstandings or conflicts may arise. Managers trying to break the ice in a Monday morning meeting with employees by recounting the exciting weekend on the golf course are not likely to capitalize on a social identity shared with employees (unless their employees play golf, of course). Identity-informed sensitivity in communication may go a long way. Accommodating the content and style of communication to an audience increases the likelihood of engaging a common in-group identity. If one succeeds in presenting oneself as *prototypical* for this in-group, the consequences are powerful (see chapter 8, this volume; Reid & Ng, 2000). This is by no means an easy thing to do, because research points to the fact that accommodation can be achieved (or not) by means such as topic choice, language intensity, interruptions, response latency and speech rate, turn duration, language choice, speaking time, and accent mobility (Shepard, Giles, & LePoire, 2001). Moreover, in order to get it just right, one needs to be sensitive to the many norms and conventions that govern our interactions and appreciate the others' perspective on the situation (Giles & Coupland, 1991).

Once a common in-group identity has been established, this has a positive outcome for the classic goals in communication discussed above: in providing information, in influencing, coordinating, and affiliating. The last is the most obvious: Identification breeds interpersonal attraction (Hogg, 1992). If members of academic staff accommodate their communication properly when talking to a student, they are liked more, and vice versa (Jones, Gallois, Barker, & Callan, 1994; also Street, 1984). Mackie and Cooper (1984) illustrated that in-groups exert stronger influence than out-groups, and a series of impressive studies by Wilder provide evidence that information given by in-group members is also better recalled (Wilder, 1990). Aune and Basil (1994) showed that when students were approached to make a charity donation their contributions more than doubled when the phrase "I'm a student too" was added to the request. In all these instances, the proper use of language in interpersonal encounters can give off strong cues to shared identity, adding to the power of the interaction.

In groups, communication has even more powerful identity effects. Communication has a strong influence on alignment among group members, on whether existing identities become salient, and on how new identities are formed. Concrete instances of how this may happen were already discussed briefly before. In two recent studies, we used a variety of communicative prompts to activate a common ingroup identity (Haslam et al., 2000). For example, group members were asked to write down what their group stood for, and they wore badges publicly expressing the group goal. Much like the battle cries of a warring tribe ("Once more unto the breach dear friends. . . . Cry 'God for Harry! England and Saint George!'"), such utterances have the effect of whetting the appetite of the group for the action that follows. Such public statements of group adhesion—even if not spontaneous—have powerful impacts on group performance, in the case of the above study leading the group to persevere in the face of adverse conditions.

Identity may also be conveyed and strengthened by nonverbal means. Uniforms and dress may cue status, prestige, or expertise, but may also serve to cement individuals into their role (Platow et al., 1999). In a very telling study, Johnson and Downing (1979) showed that clothing conveys normative cues that do not just influence the audience, but also affect the people that wear them. In this study, students who were made to wear Ku Klux Klanlike robes became more aggressive, while students dressed up in nurses' uniforms became less so. Similar effects were obtained by Reicher (1984), who showed that the norms of student groups influenced individual attitudes more strongly when these individuals were addressed as a group and when they were primarily identifiable as members of that group: how people are visually identified not only affects behavior, but also their beliefs.

Once a common identity is in place, it may affect a range of group outcomes, including communication. For example, Moreland and colleagues conducted a study in which group members were either instructed individually or in groups how to perform the complex task of building a transistor radio (Moreland, Argote, & Krishnan, 1996). When they subsequently had to assemble the radio in a group, those who had received collective instructions far outperformed those who had been individually instructed. Group instructions led to greater group salience, but also led to greater knowledge of who knew what, and who had what capabilities; in effect it resulted in enhanced collective (or "transitive") knowledge of the task at hand. Finally, the group training changed the communication within the teams with respect to pronoun use (less use of "I" and "you," more of "we") and with regard to the coordination of activities (the development of shared understanding of the task diminishing the communication required, and enabling symbolic references in interaction).

The program of research on the Social Identity Model of Depersonalization Effects (SIDE) (see also chapter 6, this volume) makes further points with regard to the interaction between identity processes and communication in groups. This research shows, on the one hand, that social norms may emerge when social identity is salient, and that these influence communication content and styles of expression. Thus, the outcomes of identity processes are codetermined by identity salience and the *content* of identity. On the other hand, this research also makes clear that "the group" is not just a cognitive concept, but that social interaction is required for identity to be expressed in groups, and for it to exert a social influence on group members. Thus, interaction and communication between individuals serves to establish and strengthen group norms (Haslam, 1997). This process may be initiated by identity salience, but it in turn forms and strengthens social identity. The implication is similar for practitioners and social psychologists, but in some sense it is more urgent for the latter: although teams are increasingly popular in organizations and organizational psychology, social–psychological research devotes less and less attention to people in interaction (Haslam & McGarty, 2001). That this is unfortunate is an understatement. For where communication gives voice to social identity, silence suffocates it.

In the final paragraphs of this chapter it is appropriate to discuss organizational communication in a wider sense. By this I refer to all communications within the organization, ranging from high to low, from corporate to interpersonal, and their impact on identification and commitment to the organization as a whole. For decades, there has been a strong tendency to argue that organizations should stop sending decrees from on high. Instead it is argued that the emphasis should be on networks of employees, or on corporate communications that are "individuated." These recommendations are informed by a belief that interpersonal and team communication by superiors (e.g., "management by walking around") are more effective than announcements made by CEOs. In management theory today, horizontal integration is in, vertical distance is out, networks are in, hierarchies are out: The personal touch works magic, whereas a CEO is just another face in a magazine or on the screen. Thus, management theory proposes that interpersonal communications and social processes in teams are vital to *modern* organizations (Foy, 1994; Lawler, Mohrman, & Ledford, 1995; V. Smith, 1997).

The social identity approach suggests otherwise. It proposes that interpersonal communication can be important and effective in particular conditions. However, it underlines the importance of communicating at a *social level*, and the value of rather more *impersonal* information. Information about organizational tasks and strategies is impersonal, as is the value of company shares. Yet, Figure 5.1 illustrates that impersonal "facts" and knowledge can perform important social functions. The social identity approach especially warns us against ignoring the *social* dimension. The social can be a certain intergroup dynamic such as the competition between R&D and sales for additional funds, or it can be the patterns of existing identities such as gender, class, and race. In all these examples, the social identity approach argues that impersonal and social factors may exert a strong influence on individuals (and on interpersonal relations). What is lacking in the traditional approach of focusing on the individual and on interpersonal relations is that it (1) underestimates the degree to which these supraindividual factors influence individual thought and behavior, and (2) has no clear theory that allows us to understand and predict their influence. In this regard, individualistic and interpersonal approaches to organizational communication can only ever offer partial understanding.

In sum, the social identity approach offers concrete insight into how communications may interact, subtly or blatantly, with the myriad identities and identifications that can be found in the organization. The social identity approach may inform the field of organizational communication, avoiding the pitfalls that characterize this field: the reduction of social events to individual phenomena, and the reverse fallacy of ignoring individual influences in a social system. Most importantly, however, the social identity approach allows us to *begin* grasping the immense importance of communications within organizations. Coordinated activity is only possible with communication, because we use communication to inform and persuade others, and to affiliate with them or instruct them. At the same time, though, communication is essential for the *establishment of social reality* through social validation, for the shaping and maintenance of social structure and social identities, and for transforming this into a social system that we cannot deny. Communication is at the same time the *product of social reality* and only successful and possible if it "speaks to" a social framework of the form provided by social identity. Communication and identity are thereby joined at the hip: each is distinguishable in its own right, but parting them will disfigure both.

ACKNOWLEDGMENT

This research was supported by a fellowship of the Royal Netherlands Academy of Arts and Sciences, KNAW. I would also like to thank Astrid Homan for her help with the literature search.

NOTES

1. This definition implies that, although social identities are represented in individual cognition, they are simultaneously properties of the social organization itself because they depend on some degree of consensus among those who share this identity, thus making its existence possible in the first place. Between the individual and the social there is reciprocal interaction; to ask which is cause and which effect is futile.

2. I am well aware that the distinction between these two levels is to some extent problematic, the two being in reciprocal interaction and therefore only distinguishable as "ideal types." The distinction is maintained here initially for analytic purposes, and because it suggests an opening for a key problem in the field. As the description of social identity theory progresses in this chapter, the solutions to the dualism become more apparent.

LIVERPOOL JOHN MOORES UNIVERSITY
LEARNING SERVICES

6

Social Processes in Electronic Teamwork
The Central Issue of Identity

MARTIN LEA
University of Manchester
RUSSELL SPEARS
University of Amsterdam
PAUL ROGERS
University of Manchester

*T*he use of computer-mediated communication (CMC) has become an accepted part of organizational life. A recent international benchmarking study showed that 83% of business organizations in the G7 major industrialized democracies now use electronic mail on a daily basis. Moreover, 43% of organizations provide remote access to e-mail and intranets while employees are away from the office (Department of Trade and Industry, 2000). At the macrolevel, CMC technologies have played a central role in reshaping organizational structures and redefining organizational boundaries in relation to the current economic landscape and the increasing globalization of markets (Monge & Fulk, 1999). For example, CMC has been a key factor in the cross-border integration of national organizations for the European Single Market that emerged in 1992 (Lea, O'Shea, & Fung, 1995). The emergence of e-commerce and the World Wide Web have meant that CMC technologies have become instrumental in publicly defining and presenting a coherent organizational identity, and electronic networking among professional communities is a mechanism by which organizations may change from traditional hierarchical to market-based relationships (Pickering & King, 1995). "Think globally, act locally" has become the mantra of the virtual or networked organization empowered by international teams of knowledge workers; and computer-based communication technology is at least the symbol, if not always the functional heart, of the new decentralized, "flat" organization of work (Castells, 1996; Lea et al., 1995; Winter & Taylor, 1999).

CMC presents organizations with a range of new opportunities and risks relevant to their ubiquitous concerns about cost, efficiency, effectiveness, and control. On the one hand, CMC offers unrivaled communication speed, overcoming space and time restrictions, even enabling a round-the-clock, around the world, pattern of knowledge working as important documents and reports are finalized for just-in-time delivery. Group discussions and decision making can occur in real time, unhampered by the need for workers to be colocated. Indeed, computer networks, conferencing systems, bulletin boards, and e-mail distribution lists make group communication in the medium as easy and cheap as one-to-one interactions, and arguably some of the most profound effects have been on the way individuals work together in groups or teams. Since the 1980s, terms such as *teleworking* and *computer-supported collaborative work* (CSCW) have entered the vocabulary of organizations to describe these new ways of remote working.

In remote-team working, concerns have often focused on what Sproull and Kiesler (1991) described as "second-level effects": social changes brought about by CMC that go beyond the foreseen efficiency or productivity gains. For example, some accounts of the medium suggest that better group decision making should obtain in CMC, because the medium strips away the social inefficiencies of face-to-face communication, creating a more rational communication medium (Johansen, Vallee, & Collins 1978; Pinsonneault & Heppel, 1998; Rice, 1984). CMC should encourage expression of a wider range of opinions by more people to a larger audience, uninhibited by constraints of status and power, the symbols of which are not as readily communicated in the medium (Sproull & Kiesler, 1991; Weisband, 1992). In this respect, CMC has been hailed as a democratizing, empowering medium, capable of diminishing the power of organizational hierarchies and facilitating lateral as well as bottom-up communications (Perry, 1992; Sproull & Kiesler, 1991). Equally, however, it has been argued that CMC disempowers workers, who are more easily and comprehensively monitored and controlled through CMC than in face-to-face arrangements (Botan, 1996; Sewell, 1998; Zuboff, 1988). Additionally, some approaches have argued that social norms are poorly communicated in CMC; that the capacity for social influence is diminished; that acquaintance-ship takes longer and relationships are more difficult to establish; and that CMC reduces trust and accountability, and encourages the spread of anti-social attitudes and activities that subvert organizational aims (Kiesler & Sproull, 1986; Sproull & Kiesler, 1991; Walther, 1992, 1995; Zmud, 1990; see Spears & Lea, 1994 for a review of power relations in CMC).

However, although many accounts describe the kinds of effects CMC may have on organizational communication, they seldom provide a detailed explanation of the mechanisms by which postulated changes actually occur. As

Pickering and King (1995) point out, until such mechanisms are specified and studied in detail, much of the rhetoric surrounding the transformational power of organizational CMC remains superficial. In this chapter we argue that issues of identity are central to understanding how communication technologies affect organizational practice. We develop this argument by first reviewing some of the dominant approaches to understanding the social–psychological processes implied or held responsible for CMC effects. We highlight the common themes underpinning these approaches, and trace their origins. As we hope to make clear, despite the variety of approaches, they rely nevertheless on a small set of common assumptions about the nature of CMC. Chief among these is the assumption that the reduced bandwidth of telecommunications determines the social character of communication in CMC—or rather its lack of sociality. This technical feature has been used in various ways to predict a range of social outcomes of CMC use in organizations. However, we argue that the predictions do not correspond with the actuality of CMC use. In the second half of the chapter, we discuss a theoretical blind-spot common to these approaches that can be overcome by adopting a social identity approach to organizational CMC. We argue that this approach can account for many of the varied and context-dependent effects that have been observed in group CMC within a single unifying conceptual framework.

THEORETICAL APPROACHES AND THEIR COMMON FOUNDATIONS

Comparative social–psychological analyses of media focus primarily on the relative availability of various social–informational cues in different media in comparison with face-to-face interaction. The origins of this approach have been traced back to the engineering concept of *communication bandwidth* (Lea, 1991; Lea & Giordano, 1997). Bandwidth refers to the quantity of information that can be transmitted along a given channel, such as a cable, in a given transmission time. The problem of how to increase bandwidth and thus maximize the efficiency and decrease the costs of telecommunications has been a longstanding engineering concern that has driven technical developments ever since the first experiments with telegraphy in the 1840s (Martin, 1971). Anxieties about the social consequences of reduced communication bandwidth also appeared in popular science and engineering journals following widespread diffusion of the telegraph and telephone (Marvin, 1988, pp. 86-96), and continue to be voiced today with respect to CMC (for examples, see Lea, O'Shea, Fung & Spears, 1992; Lea & Spears, 1995). The engineering emphasis on reduced bandwidth and concerns about its social effects paved the way for social-psychological models of media effects that employ various theoretical constructs to quantify the amount of *social* information carried by different media.

The earliest of these was *social presence*, which first gained ground in social science research in the 1970s following experiments funded by the British Royal Mail comparing communication by telephone, audio, and video (Short, Williams, & Christie, 1976), and subsequently has been applied extensively to research on CMC (e.g., Johansen, 1977; Rice 1984, 1993; Rice & Love, 1987). Social presence comprises a number of dimensions including "intimacy" (Argyle & Dean, 1965), "immediacy" (Wiener & Mehrabian, 1968) and the personal-impersonal dimension (Champness, 1973). A series of user-rating studies found that communications media could be ranked according to social presence (namely from business letters at the bottom, through telephone or single-speaker audio, multiple-speaker audio, and television, up to face-to-face communication at the top). CMC, in its text-based form, devoid of audio and visual channels, has assumed a relatively low position in this hierarchy (Rice, 1993; Short et al., 1976).

The concept of *media richness*, developed by Daft and Lengel (1984, 1986), applies information theory ideas more specifically to the organizational context, and identifies resolving ambiguity and reducing uncertainty as the main goals of organizational communication. The central proposition is that richer media are more suited to communicating equivocal information. Communication failures can be explained therefore by a mismatch between the equivocality of a communication task and the richness of the chosen medium. Four factors have been proposed to determine media richness: (1) the ability of the medium to transmit multiple cues; (2) the immediacy of feedback; (3) the use of natural language; and (4) the personal focus of the medium. Once again, CMC is judged to be a relatively poor medium according to these criteria and therefore best suited to fairly routine, unequivocal communication tasks.

A clear implication of approaches that rely upon the bandwidth or information-processing capacity of a medium to explain its effects is that differences between media should reduce or be eliminated once temporal factors in communication have been taken into account. This is the central theme of the social information processing approach, which attempts to clarify the effects of bandwidth restriction in CMC as retarding rather than removing social information exchange from interaction. The limited bandwidth of CMC forces social information into a single linguistic channel, which retards impression formation relative to face-to-face interaction (Walther, 1992, 1995). CMC is consequently argued to be less personal and evaluations of others less positive, than face-to-face interaction of equal duration, but that the differential should diminish over time. However, tests of such propositions revealed that the temporal factor does not have a consistent effect on limited bandwidth CMC. Some studies found more personal focus and greater attraction in short-term CMC than face-to-face, directly contrary to predictions (Walther, 1995, Walther & Burgoon, 1992).

To summarize, these three approaches, which have their roots in the engineering concept of communication bandwidth, argue that limited information exchange has deleterious effects on various social aspects of communication that underpin organizational use of CMC. However, evidence that the "social capacity" of CMC can be determined in such a direct manner from its informational capacity is weak. Although social presence and media richness approaches explicitly collapse multidimensional scales onto single factors, many studies suggest that additional dimensions are needed to account for variations in media perceptions or choice that are unexplained by the original concepts (D'Ambra, Rice, & O'Connor, 1998; Dennis & Kinney, 1998; Rice, 1993; Trevino, Daft, & Lengel, 1990; Valacich, Paranka, George, & Nunamaker, 1993). The need for these additions undermines the notion that a single informational concept is sufficient to explain media perceptions and choice.

More crucially, the assumed media hierarchy is further undermined by studies of actual media use. Large variances relative to very small mean differences between media suggest that other factors influence CMC use in organizations, and a growing number of studies have identified some of these additional influences (Burke & Chidambaram, 1996; Fulk & Boyd, 1991; Hiemstra, 1982; Dennis & Kinney, 1998; Lea, 1991; Rice, 1987, 1992, 1993; Steinfield, 1986; Sumner, 1988; Trevino et al., 1990; Walther, 1994).

One pattern that can be discerned is that the assumed media hierarchy holds better when communications are primarily focused on interpersonal concerns, but can be overturned for communication tasks (such as decision making, bargaining, and collaborative work) in which group and intergroup concerns are arguably uppermost (Morley & Stephenson, 1969; Short, Williams, & Christie, 1976; Walther, 1997). Furthermore, equating the information-processing efficiency of media with their social and organizational efficiency ignores not only the fact that the communication of meaning does not have a simple correspondence with the amount of information exchanged, but also the political reality of communication in organizations. This is that media can be strategically employed in equivocal situations precisely in order to distance communication or increase uncertainty (e.g., communicating on a need-to-know basis, managing disputes, "whistle-blowing," cataclysmic announcements, and e-mail dismissals). Media choice in these circumstances may not be so much a matter of increasing communication efficiency as applying new communication norms, and reducing their contestability. Ultimately it is a matter of using media to maintain and reinforce (or sometimes undermine) existing power relations.

Indeed, a number of other prominent approaches have argued that, particularly in organizational contexts, CMC brings *advantages* to communication precisely because of the reduction in social cues in the medium. These approaches suggest that there is a downside to interpersonal contact, and that CMC is advantageous in that it allows communicators to resist the power and influence of others, precisely because it creates conditions that undermine interpersonal bonds (e.g., Sproull & Kiesler, 1991). While there are several aspects to this argument (Spears & Lea, 1994; Spears, Lea, & Postmes, 2001), we focus here on two aspects of particular relevance to the organizational context: (1) the role of "electronic weak ties," and (2) the functions of reduced cues in group process, and group decision support theory in particular.

The concept of electronic weak ties distinguishes "weak" connections in CMC from the "strong" ties based on proximity, frequent contact, interaction history, personal acquaintanceship, and ongoing relationships that characterize face-to-face contacts. In the organizational context, the presence of weak ties connecting people are seen as advantageous for information gathering and problem solving, because they expose one to a greater diversity of information and knowledge than if one relied solely on face-to-face contacts for advice and information. This argument is predicated on the observation that physical proximity increases the chances of interacting with people who are similar to us, whereas the relaxation of constraints on the size and proximity of one's audience in CMC allows one to communicate with a greater number of diverse individuals. These relaxations, together with the lack of social cues in CMC, also mean that motivations for providing information and advice are likely to be different from the motivations of people in close proximity, as information and advice-givers in CMC are more likely to be merely casual acquaintances or strangers with respect to the information seeker. If advice and information provided in CMC is freed from the constraints of personal relationships, it is more likely to provide candid, independent, and novel solutions to problems (Constant, Sproull, & Kiesler, 1997).

Rather than acquaintanceship and interpersonal concerns motivating information providers in CMC, weak-tie theory suggests that a self-identity that is characterized by strong organizational identity and commitment encourages norms of information giving, general reciprocity, sensitivity, and concern to solve others' problems. Pickering and King (1995) similarly suggest that a strong professional identity that transcends organizational identity binds individuals connected by weak ties into occupational communities and motivates analogous behavior in interorganizational CMC.

However, while weak-tie theory recognizes self-identity as a source of behavior in CMC, in addition to interpersonally motivated behavior, the approach does not detail the mechanisms that account for prosocial behavior, and particularly how prosocial, identity-based behavior might initiate and persist in CMC even after personal acquaintanceship develops. Also missing is a framework to predict the circumstances and mechanisms by which interorganizational CMC moves beyond local interests, and becomes motivated by superordinate identities deriving from membership of professional groups. Interpersonal commitment that might account for prosocial behavior seems to be fundamentally contradictory to the weak-tie concept, but it is not clear that this approach, focusing primarily on the lack of interpersonal ties among communicators, provides enough of a theoretical framework to explain commitment without interpersonal connections. However, if the leverage provided by weak ties is to extend beyond casual e-mail exchange to encompass dispersed work teams, which are characterized by an interaction history, developing acquaintanceship, and regular intensive interactions on- and offline, such an explanation must be found.

While the weak ties approach offers the tantalizing suggestion that self-identity may be relevant to understanding how prosocial behavior can occur in a supposedly impersonal medium, our own social identity approach (presented in the second section of this chapter) goes much further to elaborate an explanatory framework for a wide range of behavior in the medium—including impersonal, antisocial behavior and prosocial behavior—in which social identity is central. In line with this, the conclusion that may be drawn from the observation of weak-tie behavior is not that CMC connections are weak in their entirety, but that their weakness is confined to the interpersonal basis for connections and motivating behavior. However, while CMC may be *interpersonally* weak because of the reduced cues in the medium, nevertheless CMC may be *socially* strong in that it facilitates contacts among dispersed individuals who share a common group identity. Furthermore, the reduction of personal cues and interpersonal communication behavior in CMC may further contribute to the importance of the social identities that group individuals together in the medium because it raises the relative salience of the group over the individual in the specific communication situation (Lea & Spears, 1991; Spears & Lea, 1992, 1994). In order to further develop this social identity argument we examine two approaches that specifically address group behavior in CMC: group decision support theory, and the reduced social cues approach.

Group decision support theory (GDS) identifies additional organizational advantages that accrue from a reduction of cues in group CMC. According to this approach, reduced social cues and anonymity can help overcome process losses and social dysfunctions generally associated with group work (Jessup, Connolly, & Tanisk, 1990; Nunamaker, Applegate, & Konsynski, 1987; Valacich, Dennis, & Nunamaker, 1991). These dysfunctions, rooted in the ways in which group members adapt their individual behavior to the group, can result in production blocking due to unequal participation, free-riding, social loafing, evaluation apprehension, conformity pressures, and groupthink (Steiner, 1972; Stroebe & Diehl, 1994). Anonymity, it is argued, can reduce the undesirable social influences of the group over the individual by reducing the power of the group, thereby liberating the individual from conformity pressures (Nunamaker, Briggs, Mittleman, Vogel, & Balthazard, 1997; Pinsonneault & Heppel, 1998). At the same time, the reduction in cues reduces the interpersonal immediacy or sense of presence of other group members and the capacity of other group members to exert interpersonal influence over the individual, undermining attachment to the group and evaluation apprehension (Nunamaker, Dennis, Valacich, Vogel, & George, 1993; Vallacich, Dennis et al., 1991, Vallacich, Jessup, Dennis, & Nunamaker, 1992).

The software designs of various computerized group decision support systems (GDSS) are based on GDS theory, and evaluations of such systems have generally attributed their effects (such as improved decision quality, increased quantity of decision proposals, and longer times to reach consensus) to the anonymity that such systems provide. However, the validity of this conclusion is undermined by a number of contextual factors (such as task complexity, group size, and member proximity) that moderate anonymity's effects (Postmes & Lea, 2000). In general, GDS theory invokes reduced accountability and reduced personalization as processes that reduce social influence in anonymous GDSS groups, but because GDS theory is imprecise about the mechanisms that underpin anonymity's effects it cannot easily explain how moderating factors can undermine its power. The crucial premise is that anonymity frees rational individuals from the deleterious effects of the group, allowing individuals to express themselves in accordance with their true (personal) identities, and reach "group" decisions by acting as an aggregate of rational individuals rather than as members of a dysfunctional grouping (for a review, see Postmes & Lea, 2000).

In contrast to GDS theory, the *reduced social cues* approach (RSC) takes the opposing premise namely, that reduced cues and anonymity in CMC release the irrational individual from the positive effects of group constraint. These conditions encourage psychological states that undermine the social and normative influences on individuals or groups, leading to more deregulated and extreme ("antinormative") behavior (Kiesler, 1986; Kiesler, Siegel, & McGuire, 1984; Siegel, Dubrovsky, Kiesler, & McGuire, 1986). Deindividuation, or the reduced self-awareness and deregulation of behavior accompanying immersion and anonymity in a group, attenuates normative influence, and reduces evaluation concern (e.g., Diener, 1980; Postmes & Spears, 1998; Zimbardo, 1969) by reduced feedback consequent upon the slowness and inefficiency of message exchange in CMC. The reduction in social cues engenders disinhibition, and undermines status and power differentials evident in face-to-face groups, leading to more equalized and egalitarian participation (e.g., Dubrovsky, Kiesler, & Sethna, 1991; Kiesler & Sproull, 1992). In group discussions and decision making, these factors expose communicators to a greater number of extreme arguments, leading to group polarization and extreme decision making (Kiesler et al., 1984).

However, independent studies have shown that the specific group context for the communications crucially influences anonymity's effects in CMC. Thus, and contra deindividuation theory, research has shown that self-awareness and evaluation concerns are often increased in anonymous CMC (Lea,

Spears, & de Groot, 2001; Matheson & Zanna, 1988, 1989). Greater group polarization in CMC is not associated with reduced social influence (Lea & Spears, 1991; Postmes, Spears, Sakhel, & de Groot, 2001), nor does it necessarily produce uninhibited behavior or risky decisions (Hiltz, Turoff, & Johnson, 1989). Status and power are not always equalized in CMC discussions, and CMC can even enhance status-related groupings (Postmes, Spears, & Lea, 1998; Postmes & Spears, 1999; Weisband, Schneider, & Connolly, 1995). In many of these studies, the crucial factors that emerge to influence CMC behavior are the degree to which a specific group or social category is salient for the communicators, and second, the specific group norms associated with the salient group.

RSC and GDS theories differ fundamentally in their presumptions about the nature of an individual's true or fixed self-identity—rational or irrational—on which the anonymizing effects of CMC are played. Indeed, the general conclusion to be drawn from this brief review is that identity emerges repeatedly, either implicitly or explicitly, as a central issue to be addressed in order to explain the range of behavior in CMC. However, the theoretical approaches reviewed here either neglect to place identity center stage, or fail to clarify specific identity-based processes that they implicitly invoke. Indeed, the concept of identity to which they default is rather individualistic—and consequently, social relations are interpersonal—when what often seems to be required is an expanded theory of identity and social relations operating at the group level. Instead, the concept of the group in this theoretical tradition remains paradoxically negative and individualistic, being grounded in interdependence theories that define the group as outside and subsuming of self, rather than a form of self-definition per se. As a result, the analysis of how identity interacts with the technical features of CMC has remained ad hoc, if not post hoc.

This individualistic and interpersonal perspective on social relations in theories of group CMC seems to be a legacy of earlier bandwidth-based analyses and the assumption there that face-to-face contact is the ideal form of social interaction between individuals qua individuals. This bias may in turn explain why approaches that focus specifically on group CMC, such as weak ties, GDS, and RSC, have failed to develop an analysis of identity. However, once the group dimension to identity and relating is acknowledged, the focus on the degree of approximation to face-to-face interaction in CMC arguably becomes less critical. More specifically, to the extent that people define themselves in terms of meaningful social identities (as a team member, as a professional, etc.), these social self-categories can form the basis not only for a social self-worth, but also a distinctively social relationship with others. The approach presented in the next section develops the social basis for interaction and places identity issues center stage in an analysis of communication contexts in order to better predict and explain the full range of behaviors observed in CMC.

A SOCIAL IDENTITY APPROACH
TO ORGANIZATIONAL CMC

Our approach is a broad social identity-based analysis of CMC effects that is sensitive to both the social and technical features of different communication contexts. It developed out of a social identity analysis of deindividuation and influence processes (Reicher, 1984, 1987; Spears, Lea, & Lee, 1990) that in turn is based on social identity and self-categorization theories (Tajfel & Turner, 1986; Turner, 1987). This focus is in many ways tailor-made for the organizational context. Social identity theory has provided theoretical tools for understanding social effects in organizations, as in organizational identity approaches for example (Albert & Whetten, 1985; Ashforth & Mael, 1989). However, simple translations of the general theory to the organizational context would not be sufficient to account for the effects of organizational communication technologies, and specifically how technological features interact with the social forms of implementation and use. If we can accuse some of the earlier approaches to CMC of degrees of technological determinism, there is a danger that simply applying social identity theory without providing an analysis of technological features would produce an equally problematic social determinism.

The Social Identity Model of Depersonalization Effects (SIDE; Reicher, Spears, & Postmes, 1995; Lea & Spears, 1991; Postmes & Spears, 1998; Spears & Lea, 1992, 1994) is therefore grounded in the social identity tradition (with its analysis of self and group processes) and integrated with an analysis of CMC features and contexts of use. These include different types of anonymity and identifiability found in various forms of CMC (e.g., electronic mail, computer-conferencing, and video conferencing) as well as conditions such as physical distribution or copresence (e.g., web-based group support systems, and electronic meeting rooms). A fundamental claim is that the apparent paradox surrounding CMC's effects is resolved by recognizing that different aspects of one's identity can be salient in different communication contexts, and that the same features in CMC will produce differential outcomes depending on which aspects of identity are salient. In accordance with its social identity foundations, the model proposes that the self is not a fixed entity, but is socially defined in context. Although our identity as unique individuals may be salient in many interpersonal situations, in intergroup contexts, where group identity is salient, we are likely to see ourselves and others in terms of this identity, and act in accord with its norms.

In order to develop a systematic framework, the SIDE model draws an important distinction between different sorts of social cues that may be present or absent in CMC: the interpersonal cues, which identify and individuate the communicators vis-à-vis one another, and conversely cues to the communicators' social features, such as group identity and category membership, which we refer to as *social* cues. We argue that cues about social groups and categories are often made salient independently of the actual content of mediated communication or else can be communicated within CMC relatively independently of bandwidth considerations (e.g., cues to organizational affiliation, status, gender, etc.). Compared to interpersonal cues, which are filtered out, social cues have more opportunity to influence interaction, and the definition of the self and situation. Although these social cues may be trivial in information theory terms, they can exert powerful effects. The consequence of reduced interpersonal cues in CMC then, is not loss of self-awareness and release from social influences (as proposed by deindividuation- and bandwidth-based approaches), but rather a shift of self-focus from personal to specific group-based aspects of identity.

Much of the SIDE analysis has focused on the relative anonymity provided by text-based CMC. Anonymity can have two classes of effects, termed *cognitive* and *strategic* (Reicher et al., 1995; Spears & Lea, 1994). The cognitive effects relate to the salience of a particular identity (personal identity or a group identity) and more precisely refer to issues of contextual self-definition. Anonymity can function to enhance group salience by reducing attention to individual differences within the group—a process of depersonalization of self and others. The strategic dimension refers to whether the individual or group member feels able to express behavior in line with a particular identity, given that this is salient. This is particularly relevant in intergroup contexts in which a power relation is present between groups. In this case anonymity from a powerful outgroup may enable members of the other group to express group normative behavior that might otherwise be punished or sanctioned by this group. We outline the operation of these cognitive and strategic dimensions in turn, together with their implications for the organizational context.

THE COGNITIVE SIDE: SELF-DEFINITION AND SOCIAL NORMS

A central SIDE prediction is that under conditions where a group identity is salient, communication and behavior will be more in line with the salient group norms than under conditions where personal identity is salient. The effects of anonymity and reduced interpersonal cues in CMC further enhance this group-based identity and behavior. It should be apparent that this prediction contrasts sharply with the GDSS and RSC approaches, which argue that anonymity releases individuals from social influences and norms. However, numerous studies have now shown that anonymous CMC in group-salient conditions leads to increased social influence in line with group norms, compared to face-to-face interaction or conditions of identifiability (Lea & Spears, 1991, 1992; Lea, Spears, Watt, & Rogers, 2000; Postmes et al., 1998, 2001). For example,

Lea and Spears (1991) showed that the attitudes of CMC discussion groups polarized more in a normative direction when they were anonymous and group identity was salient than when identifiable, or when personal identity was salient. Similarly, Lea et al. (2000) found greater individual shifts to consensus following anonymous salient group discussions in CMC. Lea and Spears (1992) also showed that idiosyncratic communication styles were interpreted as group normative under conditions of anonymity and high group salience. Thus, rather than anonymity inducing extreme behavior in CMC by reducing social influence, in fact, it enhances both group normative behavior and interpretations of expressed behavior in line with group norms.

Other studies have shown that conflicting observations of CMC behavior, rather than necessitating multiple, opposing explanations, can be accounted for within a single framework as behavior that is dependent upon specific identity-related norms enhanced by anonymity. "Flaming" behavior (usually interpreted as an example of uninhibited, deregulated, antinormative behavior inherent in organizational CMC; Sproull & Kiesler, 1986) has been accounted for in this way as reflecting context-dependent normative social influence (Kayany, 1998; Lea, O'Shea et al., 1992). A study by Postmes et al. (2001) illustrates the importance of the direction of group norms in anonymous CMC. Groups surreptitiously primed with either an efficiency-based, businesslike norm, or a prosocial norm, adhered to their primed norm in their subsequent CMC and communicated these norms to unprimed members of their group. However, this was only true of anonymous group members, and not those who were identifiable and individuated. Another analysis of real-life CMC groups showed that group norms defined communication patterns within groups, that conformity to group norms increased over time, and that communication outside the group was governed by different social norms (Postmes, Spears, & Lea, 2000). These studies explain one aspect of the apparent paradox that CMC can sometimes appear to be more efficient, impersonal, and task-focused, and at other times more socioemotional and relationship directed.

Recent research using path analysis has started to unravel the complex pattern of effects of anonymity and, in so doing, has provided direct support for the identity processes that mediate the effects of anonymity on behavior in group contexts. These anonymity effects include: enhanced identification with the group and self-categorization as a group member; self-stereotyping and stereotyping of others; as well as increased feelings of accountability and duty within the group (Lea, Spears, Watt, & Rogers, 2000; Lea, Spears, Watt, Berg, & Te Haar, 2001; Postmes, Spears, & Lea, 1998; Postmes, Tanis, & DeWit, 2001). For example, Lea, Spears, Natt, Berg et al. (2001) found that anonymity increased communicators' tendencies to categorize themselves as members of the group and that this, in turn, depersonalized their perceptions of others in favor of group-stereotypical perceptions, and group-based attraction.

More specifically relevant to the organizational context, field studies have now begun to show how these same identity processes operate over the longer term in real-life computer-mediated work teams to affect group productivity (Lea & Rogers, 2001a; Lea, Rogers, & Postmes, 2002). These studies examined the communication and behavior of small collaborative workgroups that used computer conferencing over a six-week period to research a specific topic and prepare a written report. The composition of each group meant that international, interorganizational, and interdisciplinary boundaries were present that could potentially undermine team members' identification with their work group (cf. chapter 4, this volume). Results showed that anonymity at the start of CMC collaborations increased feelings of belonging to the group, just as in laboratory experimental studies. The development of a superordinate group identity over competing identities encouraged the subsequent emergence of "team players"—prototypical communicators who were perceived by the group as embodying the essence of the group and laboring for the collective benefit of the group rather than for themselves. The presence of these high group-identifying team players in turn significantly increased group productivity (cf. chapter 2, this volume). Further study also showed how these group players channeled intragroup conflicts to produce superior quality group products (Lea & Rogers, 2001a).

One general conclusion of studies conducted within the SIDE framework then is that, although anonymity can accentuate normative tendencies, there are no generic effects or outcomes of CMC. Group norms can even be individualistic, adding an extra level of complexity to the analysis. This deference to the importance of content and context forms a key divergence with the other social–psychological approaches reviewed earlier that explicitly predict an impersonal task focus in anonymous CMC. For related reasons, we should also be cautious about assuming that anonymity always leads to more group-level effects. This may depend on the nature of the group or category and whether its group essence is designated by visible features or not. For example, a special feature of gender categorization is that it is readily cued by visible features, so that identifiability may render gender salient at the same time as it individuates people. In recent research, we have tried to separate the generally individuating effects of visibility from particular cases of category cuing. We have shown that visibility can render gender more salient, whilst undermining the salience of categories that are not visibly designated, such as nationality (Lea, Spears, Watt, & Rogers, 2000; Lea, Spears, Watt, Berg, & Te Haar, 2001).

The cognitive dimension of SIDE perhaps provides a less straightforward analysis of CMC than that offered by some of the earlier approaches; however, its greater complexity affords much richer implications. Clearly from this analysis, no understanding of technological effects can be understood independently from the particular contexts of implementation and use. To understand and anticipate social effects requires an analysis of not only task and technology, but also of the relevant identities made salient (personal, group), the relations between the communicators (interpersonal, intragroup, intergroup), and the content of (local) group norms activated in the communication context.

Although complex, we think the flexibility of SIDE and its sensitivity to context mean that it is well placed to capitalize on a range of organizational concerns. The cognitive SIDE analysis suggests that it may be possible to give local norms greater effect in anonymous CMC (emphasizing cooperation, task focus, group effort, etc.). The availability of anonymous CMC to accentuate identity-based differences may be a double-edged sword, but one that can be used to cut the suit according to the cloth. The organizational structuring of work can be tailored to capitalize on social differences where these are seen as desired, as in the case of creative tasks, brainstorming, and intergroup competition (e.g., by creating small work teams or subgroups, or even emphasizing personal identity). Where social differences are seen as destructive or deleterious, as in the case of interorganizational teamwork, or larger scale organizational mergers, for example, the institution of a superordinate identity coupled with isolation and anonymity of CMC may function to undermine intergroup boundaries and divisions during interactions.

One practical development from the SIDE model, then, has been to explore how the design of a CMC system to support interorganizational group working can be developed from social identity principles. The aim has been to create a CMC environment that is more congruent with the psychological meaning of the group task for participants than the default organizational CMC systems in use, such as e-mail and computer-conferencing systems, and current computer-supported collaborative work systems. A significant determinant of task productivity is the congruity between a person's self-definition and the features of the task environment (Haslam, 2001, p. 322), and designs of collaborative work environments that encourage clear and strong definitions of (1) the group itself and (2) the self-identity of members in relation to the group, have potential to raise group productivity (Lea, Postmes, & Rogers, 1999; Lea, Spears, Watt, Berg, & Te Haar, 2001; Lea, Spears, Watt, & Rogers, 2000). Of course, social engineering of this kind will be limited by the commitments to the identities evoked: The effect of anonymity, for example, remains a moderating one that only has meaning in the context of existing social relations. But equally, the current forms of CMC systems should not be taken as incontestable technical determinations of the social form of organizational CMC.

The Strategic SIDE

While much of our research has focused on the cognitive dimensions of the SIDE model, anonymity versus identifiability can affect how people strategically present different identities depending on the groups or audiences to whom they feel accountable. Individuals are generally more willing to adopt positions perceived to be against the interests or wishes of powerful out-groups and authorities when they are anonymous or physically isolated from them, or when they perceive themselves to have the collective support of fellow in-group members (Reicher & Levine, 1994; Reicher, Levine, & Gordijn, 1998). While CMC can isolate people, removing them from the copresence of fellow in-group members, and thereby cutting them off from visible social support, it also provides an effective alternative channel through which support can be communicated and collective action initiated and coordinated (Spears, Lea, Postmes, 2000).

The strategic dimensions of the SIDE model can have additional implications in contexts where we feel identifiable to the in-group as well as to the out-group. For example, an Internet study by Douglas and McGarty (in press) showed that people tended to stereotype a negative out-group (in this case, right-wing racists) more clearly when identifiable to other like-minded people, than when anonymous. This is contrary to the effect that might be expected from the cognitive component of SIDE, whereby group effects are usually exacerbated by anonymity. In this case, when identifiable to the in-group, participants presumably wanted to emphasize their opposition to a repugnant out-group in line with the in-group expectations. Greater compliance when accountable to an in-group may be motivated by the loss of face or credibility in failing to meet its standards, or more positively by the duty to live up to them (Lea, Spears, Watt, & Rogers, 2000; Lea & Rogers, 2001b).

However, identifiability can cut both ways, and may also paradoxically undermine the sense of group belonging (the cognitive effect) that can enhance commitment to its ideals. In one study using structural equation modeling, Lea and Rogers (2001b) found evidence for these two "opponent processes." Whereas anonymity reduced communicators' feelings of accountability, because they were less individually identifiable to others (a strategic effect), it simultaneously increased their feelings of accountability because it increased communicators' self-perceptions of belonging to a meaningful group rather than being one of a number of disparate individuals (a cognitive/self-definition effect). Such findings have helped to enrich the SIDE model, suggesting that there are complex interactions between the strategic and cognitive dimensions; accountability is a question of strategic self-presentation, but also reflects the priorities of self-definition.

Consideration of strategic effects shows the relevance of the SIDE model for understanding the effects of status and power differentials central to the organizational context. Again these will depend on the social structures and identities in which personnel are embedded, and how these are managed or manipulated. Thus, workers in the company or organization who have access to e-mail may be subject to strategic influences relating to power and status differentials at a number of different levels. E-mail networks can form systems of "panoptic" surveillance where communication, work rate, or recreational activity is recorded by the company at some level, in ways that make employees strategically constrain their behavior (Botan, 1996; Sewell, 1998; Spears & Lea, 1994; Spears, Postmes, Lea, & Wolbert, in press). Distributed forms of working may make the employee feel relatively disempowered compared to the colocated work team or collective copresence characteristic of the open-plan office. However, e-mail also forms a channel of contact with others in the organization (and outside it) who might not otherwise be reached, and who might provide the support networks to encourage resistance to powerful others.

However, it would be misleading to locate an analysis of power and status differentials in CMC purely in the strategic dimension of SIDE. Isolation in CMC can actually individuate, making collective forms of identification less salient and thereby disempowering workers (Spears & Lea, 1994). Anonymity can also have effects on the salience of the intergroup context, and thus enhance the impact of associated power differentials; it can strengthen group boundaries and reinforce power relations associated with them. For example, a study by Postmes and Spears (1999) showed that when gender identity was salient, anonymous CMC tended to reinforce gender inequalities in participation, compared to identifiable CMC. Other research also supports the accentuation of status differences within CMC in relation to gender and other attributes (e.g., Herring, 1996; Weisband, et al., 1995). This has implications not just at the micro level of team-work, but for employment practice and for the macrolevel structuring of organizations.

CONCLUSION

Computer-mediated communication affords a number of risks and opportunities for organizations. However, it should be clear from our review that defining them and how they operate is by no means straightforward. Simple comparative approaches, focusing on bandwidth features for example, are insufficiently flexible to account for the varieties of behavior observable in CMC, while the ad hoc addition of a limited range of contextual factors creates confusion rather than clarity about the processes responsible for the practical impacts of CMC.

Although a lot of work remains to be done, the social identity approach to organizational CMC is a promising one in many respects. The issue of social relations lies at the heart of understanding organizational communication, and the SIDE approach is unique in recognizing that many CMC contexts have intergroup features, rather than a strictly interpersonal focus, and that these in turn have significant implications for group behavior and teamwork. However, an analysis of the specific social relations pertaining in different CMC contexts is insufficient on its own, and the SIDE approach combines this with analyses of the technical features associated with CMC use, the kinds of social information provided by different forms of CMC, and the different contexts of its use, and considers the social perceptions and forms of action that these CMC features in turn engender.

Of course the situation is yet more complex: the theories that we mobilize to account for CMC in turn shape our subsequent social, and technical, constructions of CMC systems, with contingent effects on CMC behavior, and therefore upon subsequent theorizing. Nevertheless, this sensitivity to the social meanings of computer-mediated communication contexts within a coherent theoretical framework of identity and social relations can provide organizations with significant leverage to understand and improve their emergent electronic teamwork.

ACKNOWLEDGMENTS

Financial support for this work was provided under project grant GR/M25933 (SIDE-VIEW) from the UK Engineering and Physical Sciences Research Council (Multimedia and Network Applications Programme), and RTD grant IST-2000-26075 (COMMORG) from the European Commission Framework 5 (Information Society Technology Programme).

7

Identity Metamorphosis and Groupthink Prevention
Examining Intel's Departure from the DRAM Industry

MARLENE E. TURNER
San Jose State University
ANTHONY R. PRATKANIS
University of California, Santa Cruz
TARA SAMUELS
San Jose State University

*I*n 1969, a nascent Intel Corporation announced its first product: static random access memory components for computers (Grove, 1996). In 1970, it introduced another major innovation: dynamic random access memory (DRAM; Burgelman, 1994). As the first to develop a viable manufacturing process, Intel largely captured the market for this product (Botticelli, Collis, & Pisano, 1997). In contrast to many start-up businesses, the company experienced 14 consecutive years of profits. However, just 15 years later, Intel withdrew completely from the DRAM market and announced its first quarterly loss in nearly 15 years (Pollack, 1985). In short, the company that had pioneered this innovation had ceded a billion dollar market to its competitors (Burgelman, 1994). Reactions to the announcement were mixed. *Electronic News* interpreted the move as further indication of competitive pressure from Japanese manufacturers (Wirbel & Ristelheuber, 1984). The *New York Times* suggested, "Intel's decision to drop out of the dynamic RAM market will have little impact on the company, because sales of those chips amounted to less than 5 percent of revenues" (Pollack, 1985). A memory market analyst for Dataquest, Inc. noted that Intel's departure from the market was expected and that Intel, technologically, was very good but simply could not compete at current prices (Wilder, 1985).

Inside Intel, the story was told a bit differently. Andrew Grove, then president of Intel (1996), recalls that the company had been losing money on memory components for some time. When business slowed during the recession of the early eighties, other products could not compensate and losses mounted. He notes: "The need for a different memory strategy, one that would stop the hemorrhage, was growing urgent. We had meetings and more meetings, bickering and arguments, resulting in nothing but conflicting proposals. . . . It was a grim and frustrating year" (Grove, 1996, pp. 88–89). Albert Yu, then Director of Strategic Staff and later Senior Vice President, writes,

> As Intel had invented semiconductor memory, we had strong emotional ties to it and were spending most of our R & D dollars on it. . . . In an interesting twist, almost 40 percent of Intel's revenues and 100 percent of our corporate profits in 1984 came from microprocessors but we were investing more than 80 percent of our corporate R&D in memories! (Yu, 1998, p. 124)

Eventually, after much emotional turmoil, the decision was made to withdraw from the DRAM market.

Intel today is routinely on *Fortune* magazine's list of most admired companies. It is a world leader in microprocessors and is widely hailed as an innovation machine and one of the best-managed companies in the world. At the time, the decision to abandon the DRAM market was anything but clear-cut (Donlon, 1997; Gillmor, 2000). The computer industry was still relatively nebulous; uncertainty about market and industry trends was enormously high. In retrospect, the decision was clearly the right one. Interestingly, although Intel's decision to abandon the DRAM market has been exhaustively and admirably analyzed both in the scholarly literature (Burgelman, 1994) and in a series of business cases (Botticelli et al., 1997; Burgelman, Carter, & Bamford, 1999; Cogan & Burgelman, 1989), it has not yet been analyzed from a group process perspective.

In many ways, the situation facing Intel resembles, rather strikingly, other circumstances in which groups made disastrously poor decisions—those in which groupthink as social identity maintenance (SIM) played a role. The SIM model proposes that groupthink (or extreme concurrence seeking) occurs as members attempt to maintain a shared positive image of the group when experiencing a collective threat. We argue that the antecedent conditions most prominently associated with this form of groupthink were indeed characteristic of Intel's circumstances. Further, we suggest that certain symptoms of groupthink as social identity maintenance were evident in the decision-making processes. Most intriguingly, unlike many other groups such as the NASA Challenger launch team (Moorhead, Ference, & Neck, 1991), the

Nixon White House Watergate group (Raven, 1974), and a California city council grappling with earthquake retrofit ordinances (Pratkanis & M. E. Turner, 1999) that appeared to face similar pressures, Intel ultimately did *not* succumb to these pressures. In this chapter, we suggest that this accomplishment is due in large part to identity destruction and recreation activities established by Intel's management. To make our case, we will examine the context and the processes associated with the decision to exit the DRAM market and examine evidence supporting our view that the circumstances were indeed conducive to groupthink as social identity maintenance. We then consider the steps Intel management took to circumvent the occurrence of these processes. This analysis extends work on the SIM model in two ways. First, it demonstrates quite compellingly how identity maintenance processes are conducive to groupthink, even in quite adverse situations. Second, it highlights the crucial yet delicate process of identity metamorphosis as a method for overcoming groupthink tendencies. To provide a framework for our analysis, we first discuss the SIM perspective on groupthink.

GROUPTHINK AS SOCIAL IDENTITY MAINTENANCE

Groupthink enjoys an uneasy fame in the organizational and management literatures. It is indeed one of the more recognizable concepts ever proposed. Groupthink is often unquestioningly reported in popular books, periodicals, textbooks, and even scholarly outlets. It is not surprising, then, that groupthink has assumed a central role in popular and organizational culture. What is extraordinary, however, is the limited empirical research on the concept and the overwhelmingly equivocal support for the groupthink model (M. E. Turner & Pratkanis, 1998a, 1998b).

Janis's classic formulation (Janis, 1972, 1982), as well as his more recent reformulation (e.g., Janis, 1989), hypothesizes that decision-making groups are most likely to experience groupthink when they are highly cohesive, insulated from experts, perform limited search and appraisal of information, operate under directed leadership, and experience conditions of high stress with low self-esteem and little hope of finding a better solution to a pressing problem than that favored by the leader or influential members.

When present, these antecedent conditions are hypothesized to foster the extreme consensus-seeking characteristic of groupthink. This in turn is predicted to lead to two categories of undesirable decision-making processes. The first, traditionally labeled *symptoms of groupthink*, includes illusion of invulnerability, collective rationalization, stereotypes of out-groups, self-censorship, mindguards, and belief in the inherent morality of the group. The second, typically identified as symptoms of defective decision making, involves the incomplete survey of alternatives and objectives, poor information search, failure to appraise the risks of the preferred solution, and selective information processing. Not surprisingly, these combined forces are predicted to result in extremely defective decision making performance by the group.

Recent reviews of groupthink research draw three major conclusions regarding the state of the groupthink theory (M. E. Turner & Pratkanis, 1998b). First, case and laboratory research rarely document the full constellation of groupthink effects (e.g., Callaway & Esser, 1984; Callaway, Marriott, & Esser, 1985; Flowers, 1977, Fodor & Smith, 1982; Kroon, 't Hart, & van Kreveld, 1991; Leana, 1985; Longley & Pruitt, 1980; Raven, 1974; 't Hart, 1990; for further reviews see Aldag & Fuller, 1993; Esser, 1998, Park, 1990). Second, both laboratory studies and case research provide conflicting findings regarding the adequacy of operationalizations and conceptualizations of key antecedents of cohesion and threat. Only rarely have threat or cohesion had consequences for groupthink symptoms or decision quality (see M. E. Turner & Pratkanis, 1998a for a more detailed review). A third conclusion drawn from groupthink research is that questionable support has been provided for the causal sequences associated with the original model. No research has supported the hypothesized links among the five antecedents, the seven groupthink symptoms, and the eight defective decision-making symptoms.

Clearly, then, some reformulation of the groupthink concept is warranted. We suggest that groupthink can be a useful concept *if* the specific conceptualization accounts for the unique situational components inherent in it. To meet these goals, we proposed a SIM model of groupthink (M. E. Turner, Pratkanis, Probasco, & Leve, 1992; Turner & Pratkanis, 1998a). This perspective underscores the prominence of the group's social construction of its internal processes and external circumstances. Groupthink then becomes a process of concurrence seeking that is directed at maintaining a shared positive view of the functioning of the group. In the next section, we examine the particular

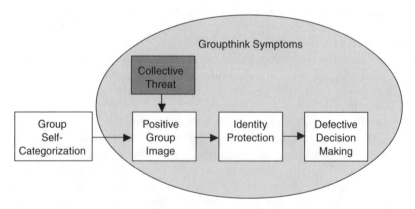

FIGURE 7.1. A Social Identity Maintenance Model of Groupthink.

nature of identifiable, antecedent conditions and then discuss the process by which these conditions lead to the consequences of groupthink.

GROUPTHINK AS SOCIAL IDENTITY MAINTENANCE: COHESION AND COLLECTIVE THREAT AS PRIME ANTECEDENTS

The SIM model proposes that groupthink occurs when members attempt to maintain a shared positive image of the group. Two assumptions underlie this notion. First and most simplistically, group members must develop a positive image of the group. Second, that image must be questioned by a collective threat. These two conditions, then, are essential for the development of groupthink as social identity maintenance. Yet, how do these conditions arise and what specific components of each antecedent condition are essential?

DEVELOPING A SHARED POSITIVE GROUP IMAGE: THE ROLE OF SELF-CATEGORIZATION AND SOCIAL IDENTITY

Developing a Positive Image

How do groups develop a positive image? One route involves the interplay of self-categorization processes and social identity maintenance. According to this perspective (J. C. Turner, 1981; J. C. Turner & Haslam, 2001), group members must categorize themselves as a group (e.g., Kennedy men, Nixon White House, Intel developers) rather than, say, as a set of unique individuals (see Hogg, 1992 for a complete discussion of this). In other words, members must perceive the group as indeed having a social identity. The SIM model suggests that groups who do not meet this precondition will be unlikely to develop groupthink as social identity maintenance. In short, simply drawing together a group of individuals (despite their level of mutual attraction) will be insufficient to produce this form of groupthink. Note that the SIM perspective diverges from some traditional approaches that define cohesion in terms of mutual attraction (e.g., Lott & Lott, 1968) but is consistent with the notion of cohesion as pressure to maintain the group (Cartwright & Zander, 1953). Nevertheless, this categorization, in turn, has crucial implications for the development of groupthink.

The Consequences of Categorization

Categorization has three consequences for groupthink. First, when categorization occurs, the group tends to develop positive views of itself (J. C. Turner,

1981). Categorization leads groups to seek positive distinctiveness for the in-group and to exhibit a motivational bias for positive collective self-esteem (J. C. Turner, 1981; J. C. Turner, Hogg et al., 1987). Thus, we see that members tend to develop a positive image of the group and, importantly, are motivated to protect that image. Categorization may also operate by reinforcing the similarities between the individual and other group members and making the group identity (as opposed to the group members themselves as unique individuals) attractive, thus serving as the basis for cohesion (Tajfel, 1981a; J. C. Turner, Hogg et al., 1987). Finally, categorization provides the basis upon which the collective threat operates.

COLLECTIVE THREAT: QUESTIONING THE GROUP'S IMAGE

A Shared Threat

A second condition highlighted by a SIM perspective is that the group should experience a collective threat that attacks its positive image. We define threat as a potential loss to the group (cf. Argote, M. E. Turner, & Fichman, 1989). It is critical that the threat be collective in nature and that it question or attack the group's identity. A threat to an individual member of the group is not likely to engender the groupthink-like consequences that a collective threat will. For example, a threat to a single member may result in the dismissal of that member in order to maintain the group's image. With respect to the development of groupthink-like consequences, this shared threat has some critical consequences for group processes.

The Consequences of Collective Threat

When threatened, individuals and groups tend to narrow their focus of attention to threat-related cues (Kahneman, 1973; M. E. Turner, 1992, M. E. Turner & Horvitz, 2000). In instances where the collective identity is threatened, the group tends to focus on those cues that can help maintain the shared positive image of the group that is invoked by social categorization. Thus, the overriding task of the group becomes image protection or even enhancement. Under certain circumstances, this can have detrimental consequences for group functioning. This is especially the case when high cohesion coupled with a social identity exacerbates identity protection motivations.

WHEN THE COLLECTIVE IDENTITY IS THREATENED: THE INDEPENDENT AND INTERACTIVE EFFECTS OF COHESION AND THREAT ON DECISION EFFECTIVENESS AND GROUPTHINK SYMPTOMS

Consequences for Decision Effectiveness

The SIM model holds that threat and cohesion should interactively affect group decision effectiveness. Under nonthreatening circumstances, cohesion, as we have defined it, can in fact have facilitatory effects on group decision performance. When group goals favor effectiveness and productivity, cohesion enhances the accomplishment of those goals. In short, cohesive groups tend to be better at achieving their goals (see M. E. Turner, Pratkanis et al. 1992 for a brief review of this literature, see Shaw 1981 for an extensive treatment).

A collective threat that strongly questions the group identity, however, can fundamentally change those goals because the cohesive group is motivated to protect that identity. Unchecked, this type of threat is likely to induce the group to focus on threat-relevant activities and goals. In this case, the goal of the group is transformed from the pursuit of effective functioning to the maintenance, protection, and even enhancement of the threatened image. Not surprisingly, when the task is complex and uncertain (as in most groupthink decisions), this focusing of attention detracts from the decision-making process to such an extent that performance is impaired. Indeed, experimental evidence provides strong support for this perspective. Highly cohesive groups operating under threatening conditions performed significantly more poorly than did highly cohesive groups operating under nonthreatening conditions (M. E. Turner, Pratkanis et al., 1992; M. E. Turner & Pratkanis, 1994b). Moreover, cohesion by itself and threat by itself each had facilitatory effects on group performance.

Consequences for Groupthink Symptoms

The SIM model suggests that groups that have a social identity and that experience a collective threat will have an overriding need to engage in identity protection. Thus, group members' reports of their decision-making processes are likely to reflect that motivation. We would expect then that group members are likely to use defensive strategies designed to protect or even enhance the image of the group. The manifestation of these motivations can vary considerably, with many routes to identity protection possible. Prior research has suggested that cohesion may be associated with more risky decisions (Thompson & Carsrud, 1976), greater social influence, agreement, and conformity (e.g., Festinger, Schachter, & Back, 1950), and more discussion of ideas (e.g., Leana, 1985). A collective threat can likewise have a variety of consequences for group processes. Prior research has demonstrated that threat can increase rationalization about the group decision (Janis & Mann, 1977), produce denial (Lazarus & Folkman, 1984), exacerbate premature closure (Janis, 1982; Janis & Mann, 1977), and limit participation in group processes (Hall & Mansfield, 1971; for a review of this literature see M. E. Turner & Horvitz, 2000). Thus, again, the specific components of the group situation are paramount in predicting the effects of the antecedent conditions. Once again, empirical evidence bears this out: groupthink symptoms tend to be quite pliable and vary depending on particular circumstances (see M. E. Turner, Pratkanis et al., 1992, M. E. Turner & Pratkanis, 1998a, 1998b).

THE ROLE OF ADDITIONAL ANTECEDENTS AND SYMPTOMS

The classic formulation of the groupthink model incorporates three other antecedent conditions: directive leadership, limited search and appraisal of information, and insulation from experts. The SIM model holds that these antecedents will have limited utility under conditions of groupthink as social identity maintenance (although they may be important in other forms of groupthink; see further Kramer, 1998; Whyte, 1989). In fact, a review of the existing empirical literature upholds this view. Studies investigating the effects of leadership style and discussion procedures (e.g., restricted vs. participatory discussion) show no adverse effects on performance and few effects on most groupthink symptoms (Callaway & Esser, 1984; Callaway et al., 1985; Courtwright, 1978; Flowers, 1977; Fodor & Smith, 1982; Leana, 1985). Similarly, procedures designed to limit group discussion (e.g., directive leadership, instructions emphasizing avoiding disagreement) tend to produce fewer solutions, less sharing of information, and fewer statements of disagreement, but do not affect other outcomes (nor do they adversely affect solution quality measures; e.g., Flowers, 1977; Leana, 1985). Thus, poor information processing procedures and insulation tend *not* always to be important for the production of groupthink.

DESIGNING INTERVENTIONS TO PREVENT GROUPTHINK AS SOCIAL IDENTITY MAINTENANCE

According to the SIM model, the prevention of groupthink is predicated on two overall goals: the reduction of social identity maintenance and the stimulation of constructive, intellectual conflict (see M. E. Turner & Pratkanis, 1994b; 1997). However, the SIM model suggests that the risks of inappropriately implementing interventions can be quite high.

Interventions designed to reduce pressures for identity protection include the provision of an excuse or face-saving mechanism, the risk technique, and multiple role-playing procedures. Providing an excuse for potential poor performance appears to reduce the group's need to engage in identity-protection tactics and increases the group's focus on problem solving, in turn enhancing performance (M. E. Turner, Pratkanis et al., 1992). The risk technique is a structured discussion situation designed to facilitate the expression and reduction of fear and threat (see Maier, 1952, for a complete discussion). Finally, multiple role-playing procedures can be accomplished by having group members assume the perspectives of other constituencies with a stake in the decision (see Fisher, Kopelman, & Schneider, 1996 for a good application of this technique) or of another group member.

Procedures for stimulating constructive conflict include structured discussion principles and procedures for protecting minority opinions, as well as linking the role of critical evaluation to the group identity. These recommendations can be given to the group in a variety of ways. One method is to provide training in discussion principles for the group leader either only or, more preferably, for all members. This approach may work well when there is sufficient time, resources, and motivation to complete such a program. A second method is simply to expose group members to these recommendations. Research has demonstrated that decision quality may be enhanced with this minimal exposure (M. E. Turner & Pratkanis, 1994a; see M. E. Turner & Pratkanis, 1998a for a more detailed discussion of interventions for overcoming groupthink). Finally, constructive evaluation can be made a part of the normative content of the social identity, as in jury instructions (Neck & Moorhead, 1992).

These approaches do not guarantee success. Much prior research shows that people evaluate conflict extremely negatively (e.g., O'Connor, Gruenfeld, & McGrath, 1993) and are motivated to avoid it. We can predict that groups operating under groupthink conditions would be especially susceptible to these pressures and might interpret any interventions as threatening the group identity. If so, they will heighten rather than reduce pressures toward groupthink. In such cases, we offer three pieces of advice: (1) make the intervention early in the groupthink-type situation before collective rationalization becomes the norm; (2) introduce strategies that can reduce, obviate, or redirect identity protection motivations; and (3) link the intervention strategy to the identity in a supportive rather than threatening way.

INTEL ABANDONS THE DRAM MARKET:
THE DECISION CONTEXT

Intel was founded in 1969 by Robert Noyce and Gordon Moore, former Fairchild Semiconductor executives, to exploit Noyce's innovation of the integrated circuit and the promise of silicon technology. They also recruited Andrew Grove, then Assistant Director of Research at Fairchild. In 1970, after the typically intense, pressure-filled effort associated with most start-up businesses, they, as Andy Grove terms it, "hit the jackpot," designing a computer memory chip they named, in a manner dear to engineers' hearts, the 1103 (Grove, 1996, p. 83).

Indeed, this chip became the world's largest selling semiconductor and accounted for over 90% of Intel's revenue in 1972. Gordon Moore noted, "We made just the right choice in the early days. . . . It took real work to get by. We had seven years using this technology without competition and this really helped us financially. We did a variety of memories, and we were first to market with each major memory technology" (quoted in Burgelman et al., 1999, p. 5). This trend continued until the late 1970s when a few American competitors began to enter the market. Although Intel occasionally became a second or third mover, it generally led the market trend (Grove, 1996). A secondary product for Intel was the microprocessor, which Intel originally developed for use by a Japanese calculator company. In 1974, the 8080 8-bit microprocessor was introduced and was used by MITS to produce the Altair, arguably the first "personal" computer. This industry became crowded with a number of competitors, including Motorola, Zilog, National Semiconductor, Texas Instruments, and many others (Yu, 1998). While its competitors introduced 16-bit microprocessors in the mid-1970s, Intel did not do so until 1978, with the development of the 8086 chip. After that, Intel began a major development effort, with intensive work on the next generation chip and development tools.

In the early eighties, the world of memories changed for Intel: enter the Japanese producers. Eventually, Japanese companies began to beat the American companies to market with the next generation chips. Moreover, their quality was higher and their manufacturing yields better. Downward price competition was cutthroat. Jackson (1997) reports the price of DRAM dropped 75% in one year. As a result, Japanese companies began to take more and more market share. The popular press was filled with dire warnings about Japanese competitiveness and American lack thereof (e.g., Bylinsky, 1981).

The world of microprocessors also was turbulent but in quite a different way. In 1980, IBM adopted the Intel microprocessor for its PC. As Grove puts it, "demand for it exploded far ahead of IBM's expectation. IBM, in turn, looked to us to help them ramp up production of the IBM PC. So did all of IBM's PC competitors. In 1983 and the early part of 1984, we had a heated-up market. . . . We were booking orders further and further out to guarantee a supply. We were scrambling to build more capacity, starting factory construction at different locations, and hiring people to ramp up our production volumes" (Grove, 1996, p. 88). Press reports were equally optimistic, with reports of profits quadrupling being common (Day, 1984; Leeke, 1984). In January 1984, in response to a securities analyst question about when Intel would meet demand for its microcomputer products, Grove joked, "We're going to catch up in the next recession." He went on to comment, "The next 5 years will be as exciting, as turbulent, as unpredictable, and hopefully as rewarding as the last have been" (quoted in Day, 1984; p. 49).

He was right about three of his four predictions. In late 1984, the recession hit and orders imploded. Intel could not ramp down fast enough to keep from building inventories while orders still dropped. They continued to lose money in memories. Now that microprocessors were no longer profitable, those losses "really hurt" (Grove, 1996, p. 88). By November, reports of losses and layoffs began (Moad, 1984). These continued through 1985. This episode almost resulted in the death of Intel. The company lost money for two years and flirted with bankruptcy (Morgenson, 1997). It was under these conditions that Intel decided to abandon the product that had skyrocketed the company to success—the memory chip—and focus its efforts on the microprocessor.

EVIDENCE FOR GROUPTHINK AS SOCIAL IDENTITY MAINTENANCE AT INTEL

Was this a case of groupthink as social identity maintenance? Recall that this form of groupthink is predicated upon two core antecedents, a group identity and a collective threat to that identity. Let us examine the evidence regarding each of these.

The Group Identity: Intel, the Memory Company

Gordon Moore described Intel as follows: "You have to recognize that Intel was formed by a group of technologists" (quoted in Hayashi, 1987; p. 55). That background was to have profound effects on the development of the Intel culture and the Intel identity. In creating Intel, Noyce and Moore intentionally set about demolishing the rigid, hierarchical structures typical of organizations of the day. At Fairchild Semiconductor, Noyce had intentionally established an organization that blurred authoritarian relationships between workers and managers. He instituted a modest dress code, induced sense of equality by using cubicles instead of offices, and ensured workers at every level were empowered to make decisions (Kwan, 2001). These ideas also permeated the organization Noyce and Moore created at Intel. Gordon Moore, commenting on the open office plan, noted, "It's convenient. You can stand up and see who's around and holler over the partitions" (Morkes, 1993, p. 32).

A second core aspect of the culture was a practice that came to be known as constructive confrontation (Grove, 1984, 1996; Yu, 1998). In constructive confrontation, employees deal with conflict instead of avoiding it, attack problems head on (and do not attack the person), provide constructive criticism, and concentrate on solving the problem and providing rationale for any objections and criticisms. Moore himself embodied the approach, saying, "We thrive on problems and like to find them so we can solve them. That's an old R&D view—there's nothing to do unless you've got a problem" (Morkes, 1993, p. 32). In theory, this process will allow information to be culled from all sources and will produce higher quality decisions and more acceptance of any decisions made. A former Intel product manager said of the process, "Grove was always the toughest, in terms of asking pointed questions that would basically put you on the spot in front of your peers. A strategy you had spent months on would fall apart in five minutes if you weren't prepared" (Schmitt, 1986, p. 1F). Dennis Carter, Grove's technical assistant, said, "He asks incredibly insightful questions. If there is a weak two-by-four, he will find it. When you walk into that meeting room, you walk in as prepared as you can be" (Sheridan, 1997, p. 69).

Third, Noyce and Moore wanted to create a place that was safe for bold ideas, recognizing that competing in a fast-paced industry necessitated innovation (Kwan, 2001; Yu, 1998). From the outset, sensible risk taking was central to the Intel culture. However, this was not to say that a freewheeling uncontrolled organization developed. Procedures such as Grove's infamous "Late List" attest to the structured aspects of Intel. Employees who arrived at work after 8:05 a.m. were required to sign a late list at the security station—despite the fact that they might have been at work the previous day until midnight or later (Jackson, 1997). Interestingly, this seemed to be a more psychological tactic than anything else. No punitive action would be taken against the late employee. However, it was a public embarrassment to have one's name appear on the list. Thus, control was clearly a central tenet of the Intel culture (Yu, 1998).

To a large extent, Intel was an embodiment of its three core executives, Noyce, Moore, and Grove. Moore commented that they each had different strengths and took the lead in different domains (Clancy, 1997). Noyce was the incredibly bright free thinker who had innumerable ideas—both extraordinary and impractical. Grove, like Noyce, was very bright but was entirely different in that he was highly focused and a superb manager. Grove noted that Moore was the technically brilliant big thinker, the strategist, and the company problem solver—the person who could solve the seemingly intractable problems. Like its founders, the company was also supremely confident. Customers reported that they were told to simply accept Intel's products. This attitude was also characteristic of employee groups; the memory design team was likewise described as a self-assured team with a can-do attitude (Graham & Burgelman, 1991).

But, most of all, Intel *was* its innovative products. More than that, Intel was *memories* (Grove, 1996). Computer memories were the technology drivers of the company. Technology drivers were the products on which new technologies were developed and refined. These products tended to be the easiest to test. After problems had been rectified with memories, the technology would be applied to other products (Grove, 1996; Yu, 1998). Moreover, the best developer team in the company was assigned to the memory division. As Grove notes, "Our priorities were formed by our identity; after all, memories were us" (Grove, 1996, p. 88).

Summary.   We suggest that Intel did, indeed, meet the criteria of our first antecedent condition of groupthink as social identity maintenance. Intel clearly categorized itself as the memory company. Moreover, this identity was undoubtedly a positive one. Intel viewed itself as an innovative, can-do, technology leader. And it was this identity that was directly and perilously challenged by a collective threat.

The Experience of a Collective Threat

Unquestionably, the situation that Intel faced was perceived as critically threatening, in particular to Intel's identity as the memory company. Grove termed it a "crisis of mammoth proportions" (Grove, 1996, p. 82). Japanese competition and economic recession together had enormous impacts on Intel. Dramatic losses in market share, decreases in unit prices, and dwindling sales had drastic effects on financial performance (see Burgelman, 1994; Cogan & Burgelman, 1989; Graham & Burgelman, 1991 for a complete analysis). Moore observed, "We went from almost 100% market share to zero" (Hayashi, 1987, p. 55). Intel in fact was losing badly on all fronts (Yu, 1998). Grove noted, "Intel equaled memories in all of our minds. How could we give up our identity? How could we exist as a company that was not in the memory business? It was close to inconceivable" (Grove, 1996, p. 90).

Media coverage exacerbated the problem. In as little as three months, stories about Intel changed from trumpeting the company's capturing of a strategic market niche and touting its management practices (Grove, 1984) to excoriating its first operating loss in 15 years (Greer, 1985). The emotional turmoil associated with the situation is immediately apparent in recollections of the participants. Yu (1998) termed it wrenching and painful, while Grove (1996) called it grim, frustrating, and discouraging. Burgelman and colleagues aptly describe the anguish and uncertainty that characterized the corporation (Burgelman, 1994; Burgelman et al., 1999; Cogan & Burgelman, 1989).

Summary.   Clearly, Intel experienced its situation as threatening. For our purposes, it is key that the threat be perceived as a challenge to the positive image of the group. In this instance, we see a company that has defined itself as the premier firm in a particular industry lose all external indications of that status. In turn, this undoubtedly questioned the positive image Intel had developed and fiercely motivated it to protect that image.

Wherefore Other Traditional Groupthink Antecedents?

One question that can be raised about our characterization of this decision as a social identity maintenance form of groupthink centers on the role of other traditional groupthink antecedents and concurrence-seeking. Should not other groupthink antecedents likewise be present?

In our discussion of the SIM model, we argued that these are neither necessary nor sufficient conditions for groupthink as social identity maintenance. Consistent with prior research, our examination of Intel provides support for this perspective. Let us first consider the issue of directive leadership. It is clear that Intel had three very strong leaders in Noyce, Moore, and Grove. Yet, their leadership established an intriguing form of both discipline and freewheeling discussion, confrontation, and creativity. Thus, this type of leadership seems at odds with traditional groupthink formulations. However, recall that prior research evidence demonstrates very little support for the hypothesized effects of directive leadership (see M. E. Turner et al., 1992; M. E. Turner & Pratkanis, 1998).

What about the role of inadequate search and evaluation procedures as well as insulation from experts? Once again, Intel seems directly at odds with the requirements of the traditional model. The use of the constructive controversy technique and the practice of holding one-on-one meetings with subordinates (Lenzner, 1995) most certainly conflict with the model. Again, however, prior research has convincingly demonstrated that, although procedures designed to limit discussion may in fact reduce solution alternative generation and so forth, they have very little effect on decision quality or other outcomes in groupthink situations. Thus, once again, we find evidence that is both consistent with prior research and supportive of the SIM model.

It was also clear that Intel had information regarding the nature of the threat facing it and was not insulated. As early as 1980, in an interview published in the *Harvard Business Review*, Noyce warned of the threat of Japanese competition (Salerno, 1980). Grove (1986) details how employees who had visited Japan told of Japanese manufacturing capabilities. Jackson (1997) discusses how company customers clearly and publicly communicated information about Intel's product quality problems. Once again, prior research has demonstrated that groups succumbing to groupthink can have adequate information search procedures and access to experts. The question is: what do they *do* with that information? Previous research also has shown that groups exhibiting SIM groupthink tendencies may identify high quality solutions but reject those alternatives as unacceptable (M. E. Turner & Pratkanis, 1994). Again, it appears that the intragroup decision-making process becomes of paramount importance.

Summary. Consistent with much prior research (see M. E. Turner & Pratkanis, 1998 for a review), little evidence for the role of information processing, directive leadership, and isolation from experts was obtained. It seems apparent that these are neither necessary nor sufficient conditions for groupthink as social identity maintenance.

Evidence for Groupthink Symptoms

This in turn leads us to yet another question: Were symptoms of groupthink manifested? Let us first examine the issue of mindguards and conformity. On the one hand, we see that Intel did indeed encourage discussion and conflict. Employees describe contentious meetings and numerous debates on the issue of just what to do about the memory market. Yet, we suggest that this disagreement was more apparent than real. The central belief, that Intel was *the* memory company, was not in contention until very far down the road. Rather, the discussions centered about how to more effectively run the business of memories—a practice that did little to question Intel's identity or the suitability of their course of action. In fact, even after the decision to abandon the market was made, Grove (1996) reports that a rational, objective discussion of the idea was almost impossible. Other research likewise has obtained evidence that groups may engage in superficial conflict in order to reinforce their image. For example, in analyzing the decision of the Johnson White House to escalate the Vietnam War, Janis (1982) notes that groups can limit objections to issues that do not threaten to shake the confidence of the group members in the rightness of their collective judgments. Interestingly, such a strategy allows the group to report that it actually tolerated dissent and encouraged full evaluation—both positive and negative—of the group decision even though it actually did not (see Pratkanis & M. E. Turner, 1999 for other examples). And, this in turn enhances the image of the group as a competent, objective evaluator. This was particularly important for Intel, as this constructive controversy was a significant part of its identity.

We can also see evidence for collective rationalization. Despite contradictory information from a variety of sources, managers at Intel continued to believe that they could recapture the memory market. Denigration of outgroups was also apparent. Managers discounted the Japanese as credible threat, frequently pointing to the previously shoddy products produced by Japan in the 1950s (Jackson, 1997). Along the same lines, it was quite clear that any attempt to recapture the market would require an investment of upwards of $100 million at a time when Intel was losing money (Yu, 1998). That this option was seriously discussed is further evidence for rationalization and a belief in their own illusion of invulnerability—that despite the odds, Intel could do it.

And what about the defective decision making associated with groupthink? As a culture of engineers, Intel employees were use to making a careful appraisal and evaluation of options to reach the best decision. In contrast, the DRAM decision was characterized by Grove as a "year of aimless wandering" (1996, p. 89). The need to protect their image as "memory makers" led to a denial or selective reinterpretation of the obvious facts of the situation. Although many of these facts were known, they were difficult for Intel employees to accept. Thus, a decision-making process was beginning to emerge that showed selectivity in information processing. Much of their effort went into how to recapture the memory market and not a reappraisal of the risks of this strategy.

Summary. Consistent with prior research, the preceding discussion once again provides evidence for the pliability of groupthink symptoms. Again, we see that groups can be quite creative and adept at finding ways to protect a threatened identity.

CIRCUMVENTING GROUPTHINK—SUBSTITUTING SOCIAL ROLES AND SHATTERING THE SOCIAL IDENTITY

The manner in which the decision was made to abandon the DRAM market has become the stuff of business legend. Grove (1996) reports it best:

> I remember a time in the middle of 1985, after all this aimless wandering has been going on for almost a year. I was in my office with Intel's chairman and CEO, Gordon Moore, and we were discussing our quandary. Our mood was downbeat. I looked out the window at the Ferris wheel of the Great America amusement park revolving in the distance, then I turned back to Gordon and I asked, "If we got kicked out and the board brought in a new CEO, what do you think he would do?" Gordon answered without hesitation, "He would get us out of memories." I stared at him, numb, then said, "Why shouldn't you and I walk out the door, come back and do it ourselves?" (p. 89)

From the perspective of groupthink as social identity maintenance, this exchange had two key points. First, taking the perspective of a new CEO was clearly an instance of role substitution. Recall that role playing procedures can provide additional sources of information that can impact the decision itself, provide alternative perspectives on information already at hand, and provide needed perspective on the attack on the group identity. Second, the process of getting out of memories would involve the destruction of Intel's corporate identity and the construction of another.

A New Intervention for Circumventing Groupthink: Identity Metamorphosis

The destruction and reconstruction of the new identity consisted of several initiatives: the destruction of the old identity, the construction of the new identity, the redeployment of resources to be consistent with the new identity, and reinforcement of the new identity. It was a long and arduous process. Several obstacles contributed to this. First, the Intel culture was quite strong. Breaking that down was a difficult and emotional process. As Grove said, "Denial can blind people. We found it very, very hard to face up to the DRAM decision. Financially, it should have been easy. In retrospect, it should have been easy strategically too. Yet we, Intel management, were at each others' throats over this" (Sherman, 1993, p. 58). Second, Intel had been a winner in many areas. The possibility of admitting defeat was daunting: "This was a very difficult option for us to swallow: admitting defeat on something that the corporation was created and founded on" (Yu, 1998; p. 124). Third, the resource redeployment issues were inescapable. Layoffs and plant closings were inevitable.

However, Intel had several advantages that helped make the process possible. First, and perhaps foremost, was the supportive relationship between Grove and Moore. Grove certainly had the competencies to carry out the task. However, he also had the political power necessary to accomplish the changes. Grove notes: "I could do pretty aggressive things because I had the security of the relationship behind me. . . . We both took so much for granted that we didn't even bring it up. But it's a very important deal when you are running a business where you take risks and things go up and things go down. But we've come through a bunch of hard times and the support that we give each other was never questioned" (Clancy, 1997, p. 18). This freedom to act without recriminations and the political support was probably crucial to the success of the transformation.

Second, Intel's history of innovation, participatory decision-making, and open discussion certainly made the process easier. Employees had been encouraged to air their opinions, and to disagree. While this made the exit process very difficult in some ways, it also facilitated the process. Employees were skilled in acquiring new information and evaluating that information. Management had access to a great variety of useful information as a result (Burgelman & Grove, 1996). It also meant that employees could assimilate—at least cognitively, if not emotionally—information about the transition more easily. The culture of innovation likewise provided a basis upon which the new identity could be fabricated. It provided new markets and technologies but also represented a core value that could be reinterpreted and redeployed in service of the new identity. More importantly, just a short time after Intel announced its decision to abandon the DRAM industry, it announced the development of a new microprocessor, the 386 (Yu, 1998). This ability to continue to innovate and to produce new products likely was key in reassuring employees that the new identity was viable.

Implementation of this process was a key challenge. Even after Moore and he made the decision to exit the memories market, Grove (1996) reports that he approached discussions about the idea tentatively. Not surprisingly, he met with enormous resistance. He recounts the tale of attempting to trap one waffling manager into writing a memo which laid out the position—to no avail. Grove also found that he had to replace the manager of the memories division. The manager was so tied to the division that he could not execute the decision. A new manager, even though directly charged with getting Intel out of memories, later convinced Grove only to cease R&D expenditures on new memories but to continue R&D on current products (which at the time were generating enormous losses and constituted 5% of sales).

In reorienting its identity, Intel was in the enviable position of having developed a strong microprocessor business. Thus, the question of "if not memories, then what?" was readily (if not easily) answered. The communication of this new identity was easier than Intel anticipated. Customer reaction was nonchalant. Many customers simply wondered why it took Intel so long (Grove, 1996). Grove reports that his communication to the memory development team went surprisingly well. He forcefully told them, "Welcome to the mainstream" and underscored Intel's new focus on microprocessors (Grove, 1996, p. 93). Numerous communication sessions were held to inform employees about the transition and to demonstrate why the change was crucial (Yu, 1998). In a fascinating footnote, Grove (1996) delineates the transition process as evinced in Intel's annual reports. As he says:

> Note the evolution: "Intel is a manufacturing of electronic 'building blocks' used by Original Equipment Manufacturers (OEMs) to construct their systems." *1985 Intel Annual Report*, p. 4. "Intel designs and manufactures semiconductor components and related single-board computers, microcomputer systems and software for original equipment manufacturers." *1986 Intel Annual Report*, p. 4. "The company originally flourished as a supplier of semiconductor memory for mainframe computers and minicomputers. Over time, though, the face of computing, and Intel, have changed. Microcomputers are now the largest, fastest-growing segment of computing, and Intel is a leading supplier of microcomputers" *1987 Intel Annual Report*, p. 4. (quoted in Grove, 1996, p. 210)

The resource deployment process necessary for reorientation took almost two years, as a result of the incremental change process used. Fortunately, at Intel, empowerment was taken seriously. Consequently, middle managers had been allocating successively more and more resources such as plant capacity toward the more profitable microprocessor line (Grove, 1996). Grove termed this divergence between middle management resource allocation and top management strategy "strategic dissonance" (Burgelman & Grove, 1996; Grove, 1996). This dissonant allocation eased the eventual redeployment process. But, changes were necessary. The memory development team, arguably the best in the company, had to be reoriented toward microprocessors. Despite some strategic dissonance in allocation, microprocessors had not enjoyed full corporate support: the development team worked in older facilities; R & D dollars had been relatively sparse. Capacity had to be redirected. Intel eventually laid off a third of its workforce and closed a number of plants (Grove, 1996; Yu, 1998).

Later, Grove was careful to reinterpret Intel's early participation in the DRAM market as a positive event in the company's history, noting the early innovativeness of Intel and its subsequent accomplishments. In this way, Intel's old identity was called into the service of its new identity.

In 1987, Intel again announced a profit (Feibus, 1987). The identity metamorphosis and reorientation had paid off.

Other Potential Interventions for Ameliorating Groupthink

Would any of our two categories of interventions for preventing groupthink been successful for Intel? It is possible that early implementation of procedures designed to reduce identity protection pressures might have been successful. It would have been imperative that any intervention be undertaken in a way that did not increase the experienced threat. But, in this case, the magnitude of the threat and the strong entrenchment of the identity likely would have limited the success of these interventions unless they were forcefully and consistently applied. Our recommendations regarding the stimulation of intellectual conflict had been in place at Intel almost since its inception. However, the threat to the company's identity focused attention on finding ways to protect that identity and the conflict stimulation procedures became a mechanism for achieving that goal. Thus, in order to be effective in these types of situations, these types of procedures need to be coupled with the compelling mechanisms for reducing identity protection pressures. Moreover, interventions, particularly in the types of situations that Intel faced, need to be presented in such a way that they are in service of the group identity.

CONCLUDING REMARKS

In this chapter, we have argued that Intel's decision to abandon the memory market was a case of groupthink circumvented. The company clearly faced a situation in which the key components of groupthink as social identity maintenance were characteristic. The company faced a collective threat to a positive social identity or image. And indeed, groupthink-type processes were apparent as the company grappled with this dilemma. However, unlike many other groups, Intel did not succumb to groupthink. By a process of role substitution and identity metamorphosis, the company was able to refocus its efforts and regain its economic vigor.

This chapter suggests that groupthink as social identity maintenance is indeed a viable perspective on the groupthink phenomenon. It also highlights another strategy that may be necessary to avoid the deleterious consequences of groupthink: identity metamorphosis. It is not likely that more modest interventions would have been effective in Intel's situation. Intel's identity was firmly entrenched and the environmental conditions were extremely harsh.

The chapter also highlights some important points about the implementation of these extensive types of interventions. The extensive nature of procedures such as identity metamorphosis poses some particular requirements. First, they require that implementers have sufficient power and influence to be able to persuade others and execute the necessary dismantling. Second, when such a drastic identity reorientation is necessary, it is likely that incremental steps will be difficult. For example, the desegregation of baseball was accomplished because it was presented as inevitable and was implemented largely as a *fait accompli* in the host team (cf. Pratkanis & M. E. Turner, 1994). Intel's unsuccessful experience with incremental implementation lends support to this view. Finally, the process of identity metamorphosis can be a delicate one. Emotional ties to the identity are often strong and groups are highly motivated to protect that identity. Thus, managing those ties becomes crucial. Acknowledging the prior contributions of the old and celebrating the future contributions of the new identity is vital.

In sum, groupthink as social identity maintenance is not an inevitable consequence associated with the key antecedent conditions, nor is a progression toward failure predetermined once this form of groupthink has manifested itself. As Intel has shown, interventions that reduce pressures toward identity protection, stimulate intellectual conflict, and when necessary, shatter and rebuild identity can be invaluable.

ACKNOWLEDGMENT

The first author is grateful to the College of Business Summer Grant program for providing partial support for this research.

PART IV

LEADERSHIP AND AUTHORITY

8

Social Identity Analysis of Leader–Member Relations
Reconciling Self-Categorization and Leader–Member Exchange Theories of Leadership

MICHAEL A. HOGG
ROBIN MARTIN
University of Queensland

*L*eadership is a critical concern for organizations. Businesses can thrive or perish largely due to the quality of organizational leadership. Not surprisingly, organizational psychology places the study of leadership very high on its agenda (e.g., Bass, 1990a; Yukl, 1998)—it is a booming research field that generates an enormous amount of literature spanning the complete range from weighty research tomes to fast-moving self-help books.

In recent years, organizational psychologists have paid particular attention to transformational leadership and the role of charisma. Charismatic leaders are able to motivate followers to work for collective goals that transcend self-interest and transform organizations (Bass, 1990b; Bass & Avolio, 1993; see Mowday & Sutton, 1993, for critical comment). This focus on "charisma" is particularly evident in "new leadership" research (e.g., Bass, 1985, 1990b, 1998; Bryman, 1992; Burns, 1978; Conger & Kanungo, 1987, 1988a) which proposes that effective leaders should be proactive, change-oriented, innovative, motivating, and inspiring, and have a vision or mission with which they infuse the group. They should also be interested in others, and be able to create commitment to the group, and extract extra effort from and empower members of the group.

In contrast to organizational psychology, social psychology has experienced a decline in interest in leadership over the past 20 to 25 years. In very recent years there has, however, been a revival (e.g., Messick & Kramer, in press; van Knippenberg & Hogg, in press; also see Hogg & Terry, 2001). This chapter is a part of this revival. After brief introductory comments, we critically discuss leader–member exchange (LMX) theory (e.g., Graen & Uhl-Bien, 1995), a major organizational psychology approach to leadership, and the social identity theory of leadership (e.g., Hogg, 2001a, 2001b, 2001c; Hogg & Reid, 2001), a major vehicle for social psychology's new interest in leadership. We then explore the relationship between these theories. Our thesis is that social identity theory provides an overarching model of leadership in groups that generates parameters for the operation of LMX in contrast to other more group-oriented processes, and thus can encompass LMX processes.

SOCIAL PSYCHOLOGICAL RESEARCH ON LEADERSHIP

Leadership is about dealing with people, usually within a group, and about changing people's behaviors and attitudes to conform to the leader's vision for the group. For this reason, one would think that the study of leadership ought to be a paradigmatic topic for social psychology. Indeed, leadership was an important focus for many years, particularly during the boom years of small group dynamics (e.g., Cartwright & Zander, 1968; Shaw, 1981), and it was a component of some of social psychology's classic research programs (e.g., Bales, 1950; Hollander, 1958; Lippitt & White, 1943; Sherif, 1966; Stogdill, 1974). This tradition of leadership research culminated in Fiedler's (1965, 1971) contingency theory, which suggested that the leadership effectiveness of a particular behavioral style is contingent on the favorability of the situation to that behavioral style.

During the 1970s and 1980s, however, there was a new emphasis in social psychology on attribution processes, and then social cognition (e.g., Devine, Hamilton, & Ostrom, 1994; Fiske & Taylor, 1991). These developments were associated with a well-documented decline in interest in groups (e.g., Steiner, 1974, 1986), that carried across to the study of leadership. The previous edition of the *Handbook of Social Psychology* had a chapter dedicated to leadership (Hollander, 1985), whereas the current edition (Gilbert, Fiske, & Lindzey, 1998) does not. The study of small group processes and of leadership shifted to neighboring disciplines, most notably organizational psychology (Levine & Moreland, 1990, 1995; McGrath, 1997; Sanna & Parks, 1997; Tindale & Anderson, 1998).

In the meantime, social psychology has, with the help of social cognition, become more sophisticated in its methods and theories (Devine et al., 1994), and, with the help of social identity theory, has begun once again to focus on group processes, intergroup phenomena and the collective self (Abrams &

Hogg, 1998; Moreland, Hogg, & Hains, 1994; Sedikides & Brewer, 2001). There has been a revived focus on leadership (e.g., Chemers, 2001; Lord, Brown, & Harvey, 2001; Messick & Kramer, in press; van Knippenberg & Hogg, in press), an integration of social cognition and social identity approaches within social psychology (Abrams & Hogg, 1998), a closer relationship between social identity theory and organizational psychology (e.g., Haslam, 2001; Hogg & Terry, 2000, 2001; van Knippenberg & Hogg, in press; and this current volume), and the development and exploration of social identity analyses of and perspectives on leadership (e.g., de Cremer, in press; Duck & Fielding, 1999; Fielding & Hogg, 1997; Foddy & Hogg, 1999; Hains, Hogg, & Duck, 1997; Haslam, McGarty, Brown, Eggins, Morrison, & Reynolds, 1998; Haslam & Platow, 2001b; Hogg, 1996, 2001a, 2001b, 2001c; Hogg, Hains, & Mason, 1998; Hogg & Reid, 2001; Platow, Hoar, Reid, Harley, & Morrison, 1997; Platow, Reid, & Andrews, 1998; Reicher, Drury, Hopkins, & Stott, in press; Reicher & Hopkins, 1998; van Vugt & de Cremer, 1999).

This recent social–psychological focus on leadership has raised some concerns about contemporary organizational psychology leadership research. Although most research now acknowledges that leadership is a relational property within groups (i.e., leaders exist because of followers, and followers exist because of leaders), the idea that leadership may emerge through the operation of ordinary social–cognitive processes associated with psychologically belonging to a group, has not really been elaborated.

Instead, recent organizational psychology has two emphases. (1) There is an emphasis on individual cognitive processes that lead people to categorize individuals as leaders. The social orientation between individuals is not considered, and thus group processes are not incorporated. (2) There is an emphasis on whether individuals have the charismatic properties necessary to meet the transformational objectives of leadership. It may be noted that leadership is a matter of situationally attractive individual characteristics rather than group processes.

Both these perspectives have attracted criticism for neglecting the effects of larger social systems within which the individual is embedded (e.g., Hall & Lord, 1995; Lord, Brown, & Harvey, 2001; Pawar & Eastman, 1997; also see Chemers, 2001; Haslam & Platow, 2001a). Lord et al. (2001) explain that leadership cannot be properly understood in terms of a leader's actions or in terms of abstract perceptual categories of types of leader. They advocate a paradigm shift in how we understand leadership. Haslam and Platow (2001b) independently express this concern, and warn against any explanation of leadership that rests too heavily, or at all, on invariant properties of individuals and their personalities.

One well-established organizational approach to leadership that may circumvent some of these concerns is leader–member exchange (LMX) theory.

LEADER–MEMBER EXCHANGE (LMX) THEORY

LMX is an analysis of leadership processes in work contexts that differs from most other leadership theories because it focuses on the dyadic relationship between a leader and specific subordinates (Gerstner & Day, 1997; Graen & Uhl-Bien, 1995; Liden, Sparrowe, & Wayne, 1997; Schriesheim, Castro, & Cogliser, 1999). The central premise is that within work units, the quality of leader–subordinate exchange relations can vary widely along a continuum ranging from low to high quality LMX. Low-quality LMX relationships, sometimes termed "out-group exchanges" (Dansereau, Cashman, & Graen, 1973), are ones in which subordinates are disfavored by the leader and thus receive fewer valued resources. Leader–subordinate exchanges simply adhere to the terms of the employment contract, with little attempt by the leader to develop or motivate the subordinate. In contrast, high-quality LMX relationships, referred to as in-group exchanges (Dansereau et al., 1973), are ones in which subordinates are favored by the leader and thus receive many valued resources. Leader–subordinate exchanges go beyond the formal employment contract, with managers showing influence and support, and giving the subordinate greater autonomy and responsibility. LMX theory predicts that effective leaders should develop high LMX relationships with their subordinates, which should enhance subordinates' well-being and work performance.

Research Findings

In reviewing the LMX area, Graen and Uhl-Bien (1995) have proposed that research and theory should progress through four distinct stages: (1) Vertical Dyad Linkage (VDL), with a focus on differentiated dyads (namely, in-groups and out-groups); (2) leader–member exchanges (LMX), examining the quality of the LMX relationship and its outcomes; (3) a prescriptive approach to dyadic relationship building; and (4) the aggregation of differentiated dyadic relationships into groups. Research at the first stage, examining the Vertical Dyad Linkage (VDL), showed that, contrary to prevailing beliefs, managers do differentiate amongst their subordinates in terms of the quality of their relationships (Dansereau, Graen, & Haga, 1975; Johnson & Graen, 1973; Vecchio, 1982). Indeed, research shows that over 90% of managers vary greatly in the quality of their relationship with their subordinates (Liden & Graen, 1980). Part of the reason for this is that managers have limited resources and therefore direct these to a smaller number of their subordinates who take primary responsibility for helping with work-related issues. Differentiation in quality of relationships may be a functional strategy adopted by managers to achieve optimal performance when resources are limited or when there are many demands placed upon them (e.g., work complexity, managing many individuals).

Research in the second stage described by Graen and Uhl-Bien (1995) examines the antecedents and outcomes of different LMX relationships. In a review of the antecedents of LMX, Liden et al. (1997) identified four main factors that affect the quality of LMX: member characteristics (e.g., performance, personality, and upward influence behavior), leader characteristics (e.g., leader ability), interactional variables (e.g., demographic compatibility and similarity), and contextual variables (e.g., leader workload, high time pressure). In terms of the outcomes of LMX, subordinate ratings of LMX with their leader has been found to be positively related to job satisfaction (e.g., Major, Kozlowski, Chao, & Gardner, 1995), well-being (e.g., Epitropaki & Martin, 1999), organizational commitment (e.g., Kinicki & Vecchio, 1994), and organizational citizenship behavior (Townsend, Phillips, & Elkins, 2000).

The third stage of research described by Graen and Uhl-Bien (1995) has examined the development of an effective leadership relationship or partnership (see the leadership making model; Graen & Uhl-Bien, 1991; Uhl-Bien & Graen, 1993). This research shifts attention away from a simple dichotomy between superiors and subordinates to examine leadership as a *partnership* between individuals. A number of longitudinal studies has examined how leadership partnerships develop over time, and has found performance improvements where a leader improves the quality of the leader–subordinate relationship (e.g., Graen, Scandura, & Graen, 1986; Scandura & Graen, 1984).

The final stage of research expanded the level of analysis from dyadic relationships to the group level. The majority of research into LMX focuses on the leader-subordinate relationship without acknowledging that each dyadic relationship occurs within a system of other relationships (Cogliser & Schriesheim 2000; Graen & Scandura, 1987; Schriesheim, Castro, & Yammarino, 2000). To date, there has been very little research directed at this issue. One exception has been Sparrowe and Liden's (1997) examination of LMX development from a social network perspective (see also Wayne, Shore, & Liden, 1997).

Critical Summary

Research on LMX demonstrates the importance of examining leader–subordinate relationships as a dynamic system of exchanges. However, the area has not been without criticism (e.g., Dienesch & Liden, 1986). The measurement of LMX is problematic (e.g., Keller & Dansereau, 2000), and some researchers have found that LMX fails to predict important outcomes, such as performance (e.g., Vecchio, 1998). Nevertheless, the broad consensus is that leaders can, and do, have a very different quality relationship with their subordinates—some subordinates are treated as in-group members and afforded certain "privileges" while others are treated as out-group members and are excluded and marginalized in the workplace (Schriesheim et al., 1999).

From our own perspective we feel that there are two key criticisms that we would like to highlight. First, as noted above, the vast majority of research in LMX is, quite explicitly, located at the dyadic level, with very little theorizing or empirical work examining LMX at the group level. This is rather surprising given that leadership essentially involves individuals managing and leading groups of subordinates, each of which involves different LMX relationships. From social–psychological research on group processes, especially on social comparison processes, we know that people do not act alone, but continually compare themselves with others in order to evaluate themselves and their behavior (e.g., Suls & Wheeler, 2000). Presumably, then, group members will make comparisons with each other, and these comparisons will be influenced by whether their LMX relationship is of the "in-group" or the "out-group" variety. Effectively the group is textured into a variety of subgroups that are defined by their LMX relationships, and the interaction between these subgroups may very well acquire all the familiar characteristics of intergroup behavior—in-group favoritism, ethnocentrism, out-group denigration, and so forth. This will have far-reaching consequences for subordinates' reaction to their work—a possibility that has not been explored by LMX research.

The second issue we wish to highlight concerns the process whereby subordinates evaluate their LMX relationship. Current theorizing suggests that people simply evaluate their own LMX relationship in an absolute sense. We feel, however, that this is an oversimplified account. It is more likely, following Kelley and Thibaut's (1978) social exchange theory, that subordinates evaluate the quality of their LMX relationship not only in the absolute sense (low vs. high) but also with reference to their "perception" of other subordinates' LMX relationship. More broadly, evaluation of LMX relationships will be influenced by concerns of what is considered to be "fair" within the context of the organization (Scandura, 1999). Notions of equity, prior LMX history, comparison with other LMX relationships, and procedural justice, amongst other factors, are likely to play an important role in determining LMX quality.

These two critical points or limitations go, we feel, to the same overarching issue, leadership, and the nature of leader–subordinate relationships need to be understood in the context of a deeper and more textured analysis of group processes, intergroup behavior, and the nature of group membership. Leaders lead groups that, among other things, furnish people with a sense of identity, and that exist in a wider intergroup comparative context. Furthermore, differentiated leader–subordinate cliques within the group may establish powerful intergroup relations within the group.

SOCIAL IDENTITY THEORY OF LEADERSHIP

Some of these limitations may be addressed by the recently formulated social identity theory of leadership (e.g., Hogg, 2001a, 2001b, 2001c) that has been developed within the social identity perspective in social psychology. Because the social identity perspective (e.g., Hogg & Abrams, 1988; Tajfel & Turner, 1986; Turner, Hogg, Oakes, Reicher, & Wetherell, 1987) has been fully overviewed elsewhere (e.g., Abrams & Hogg, 2001; Hogg, 2001d, in press), we will only describe the recent leadership theory here.

The social identity approach to leadership integrates two notions: (1) leadership is a relational property—leaders and followers are interdependent roles embedded within a social system bounded by common group–category membership; and (2) leadership is a process of influence that enlists and mobilizes others in the attainment of collective goals—it imbues people with the group's attitudes and goals, and inspires them to work toward achieving them (e.g., Chemers, 2001; Lord et al., 2001). In addition, from the social identity perspective, we consider a group to exist psychologically when people share a collective self-definition.

A key insight of the social identity approach is that the basis of perception, attitudes, feelings, behavior, and self-conception is contextually fluid. Self-conception can vary from being entirely based on idiosyncratic personal attributes and the unique properties of a specific interpersonal relationship, to being entirely based on a shared representation of "us" defined in terms of an in-group prototype—a fuzzy set of attributes that optimizes the ratio of in-group similarities to in-group–out-group differences. In the latter case, the situation represents a group situation and perceptions attitudes, feelings, and behavior acquire the familiar characteristics of inter- and intragroup behaviors—conformity, normative behavior, solidarity, stereotyping, ethnocentrism, intergroup discrimination, in-group favoritism, and so forth.

Another way to put this is that the more that an aggregate of people is a salient basis for self-definition as a group member, then the more strongly is self-definition, perception, cognition, affect, and behavior based upon prototypicality. When group membership is the salient basis of self-conception people, including self, are represented and treated in terms of the relevant in- or out-group defining prototype. Self-categorization depersonalizes self in terms of the in-group prototype (producing self-stereotyping, conformity, normative behavior, social attraction, social identification, and so forth), and it depersonalizes perception of others so that they are seen as more or less exact matches to the relevant prototype. Prototypicality is the yardstick of life in salient groups.

The implication of this idea for leadership is quite straightforward. As group membership becomes increasingly salient, leadership perceptions, evaluations, and effectiveness become increasingly based on how group prototypical the leader is perceived to be. Where group membership is contextually or enduringly salient, people self-categorize in terms of the in-group prototype and become depersonalized—they conform to the in-group prototype and exhibit normative behavior. In a highly salient group, the prototype, or at least its key elements, is likely to be relatively consensual, and thus the group as a whole appears to be influenced by a single prototype that prescribes a single norm or goal. Social identity research on conformity and social influence shows that self-categorization produces conformity to an in-group prototype. The prototype may capture the central tendency of the group, or may be displaced from the central tendency such that it is polarized away from a relevant outgroup (for reviews see, Abrams & Hogg, 1990; Turner, 1991; Turner & Oakes, 1989).

Relative Prototypicality and Influence

Within any salient group there is a prototypicality gradient, with some members being more prototypical than others. Because depersonalization is focused on prototypicality, group members are very sensitive to prototypicality, which is the basis of perception and evaluation of self and other members, and thus people notice and respond to subtle differences in how prototypical fellow members are—they are very aware not only of the prototype, but also of who is most prototypical (e.g., Haslam, Oakes, McGarty, Turner, & Onorato, 1995; Hogg, 1993).

Within a salient group, then, people who are perceived to occupy the most prototypical position are perceived to best embody the behaviors to which other, less prototypical, members are conforming. There is a perception of differential influence within the group, with the most prototypical member appearing to exercise influence over less prototypical members. This "appearance" arises in part due to the human tendency to personify and give human agency to abstract forces—perhaps a manifestation of the fundamental attribution error (Ross, 1977) or correspondence bias (e.g., Gilbert & Malone, 1995). In new groups, this is only an "appearance" because the most prototypical person does not actively exercise influence; it is the prototype, which he or she happens to embody, that influences behavior. In established groups the appearance is reinforced by actual influence.

Where the social context is in flux, the prototype will likewise be in flux. As the prototype changes so will the person who appears to be most prototypical and thus most influential. Under conditions of enduring contextual stability the same individual may occupy the most prototypical position over a long period, and so appear to have enduring influence over the group. In new groups this person will be perceived to occupy an embryonic leadership role; although leadership has not been exercised. There is nascent role differentiation into "leader" and "followers."

Thus far, social identity processes ensure that as group membership becomes more salient, and members identify more strongly with the group, prototypicality becomes an increasingly influential basis for leadership perceptions. However, it is important to keep this in perspective—prototypicality is not the only basis of leadership. People also rely on general and more task-specific schemas of leadership behaviors (what Lord and his colleagues call leader categories or leader schemas; e.g., Lord, Foti, & DeVader, 1984). However, the importance of these schemas is either unaffected by self-categorization, or it diminishes as group prototypicality becomes more important. In either case, leadership schemas should become less influential *relative* to group prototypicality as group membership becomes psychologically more salient.

Social Attraction

Social categorization and depersonalization not only affect perceptions, but also feelings (e.g., Hogg, 1993; Hogg & Hains, 1996). They transform liking based on personal preferences or interpersonal relationships (personal attraction), to liking based upon prototypicality (social attraction). In-group members are liked more than out-group members and more prototypical in-groupers are liked more than less prototypical in-groupers. Where there is a relatively consensual in-group prototype, social categorization renders more prototypical members socially popular—there is consensual and unilateral liking for more prototypical members.

From the point of view of leadership, prototype-based consensual social attraction furnishes the person occupying the most prototypical position with the ability to actively influence, because he or she is able to secure compliance with suggestions and recommendations he or she makes. If you like someone you are more likely to agree with them, and to comply with their requests and suggestions (e.g., Berscheid & Reis, 1998). In this way, the most prototypical person can actively exercise leadership by having his or her ideas accepted more readily and more widely than ideas suggested by others. This empowers the leader, and publicly confirms his or her ability to influence. Consensual depersonalized liking, particularly over time, confirms differential popularity and public endorsement of the leader. It imbues the leader with prestige and status, and begins to reify the nascent intragroup status differential between leader(s) and followers. It allows someone who is "merely" prototypical, a passive focus for influence, to take the initiative and become an active and innovative agent of influence.

Social attraction may also be enhanced by the behavior of highly prototypical members. More prototypical members tend to identify more strongly, and thus display more pronounced group behaviors; they will be more normative, show greater in-group loyalty and ethnocentrism, and generally behave in a more group-serving manner. These behaviors further confirm prototypicality and thus enhance social attraction. A leader who acts as "one of us," by showing in-group favoritism and intragroup fairness, is not only more socially attractive, but is also furnished with legitimacy (e.g., Platow, O'Connell, Shave, & Hanning, 1995).

Attribution and Information Processing

Prototypicality and social attraction work alongside attribution and information processing to translate perceived influence into active leadership. Attribution processes operate within groups to make sense of others' behavior. As elsewhere, attributions for others' behavior are prone to the fundamental attribution error (Ross, 1977) or correspondence bias (Gilbert & Malone, 1995); a tendency to attribute behavior to underlying dispositions that reflect invariant properties, or essences, of the individual's personality. This effect is more pronounced for individuals who are perceptually distinctive (e.g., figural against a background) or cognitively salient (e.g., Taylor & Fiske, 1978).

We have seen that when group membership is salient, people are sensitive to prototypicality and attend to subtle differences in prototypicality of fellow members. Highly prototypical members are most informative about what is prototypical of group membership (Turner, 1991), and so in a group context they attract most attention. They are subjectively important and are distinctive or figural against the background of other less informative members. Research in social cognition shows that people who are subjectively important and distinctive are seen to be disproportionately influential and have their behavior dispositionally attributed (e.g., Erber & Fiske, 1984; Taylor & Fiske, 1975). We have also seen how highly prototypical members may appear to have influence due to their relative prototypicality, and may actively exercise influence and gain compliance as a consequence of consensual social attraction. Together, the leadership nature of this behavior and the relative prominence of prototypical members are likely to encourage an internal attribution to intrinsic leadership ability, or charisma.

In groups, then, the behavior of highly prototypical members is likely to be attributed, particularly in stable groups over time, to the person's personality rather than the prototypicality of the position occupied. The consequence is a tendency to construct a charismatic leadership personality for that person that, to some extent, separates that person from the rest of the group and reinforces the perception of status-based structural differentiation within the group into leader(s) and followers. This may make the leader stand out more starkly against the background of less prototypical followers, as well as draw attention to a potential power imbalance; thus further fueling the attributional effect.

It should be noted that this analysis views charisma as a product of social–cognitive processes operating under conditions of self-categorization, and not as an invariant personality attribute that determines leadership effectiveness. In this respect our analysis is consistent with Haslam and Platow's (2001) critical appraisal of the role of charisma in contemporary transformational leadership theories.

Maintaining Leadership

Thus far we have seen how prototype-based depersonalization fairly automatically imbues the most prototypical member of a group with many attributes of leadership—for example, status, charisma, popular support, and the ability to influence. These attributes also allow the leader to actively maintain his or her leadership position. The longer an individual remains in a leadership position the more he or she will be socially "liked," the more consensual social attraction will be, and the more entrenched the fundamental attribution effect will become.

Social contextual changes impact upon prototypicality. Thus, over time and across contexts, the leader may decline in prototypicality while other members become more prototypical. This opens the door, particularly under high salience conditions, to a redistribution of influence within the group. An established leader is well placed in terms of resources to combat this by redefining the prototype in a self-serving manner that marginalizes contenders, making them appear highly aprototypical, and centralizes self, making self appear highly prototypical. This can be done by accentuating the existing in-group prototype, by pillorying in-group deviants, or by demonizing an appropriate out-group. Generally all three tactics are used, and the very act of engaging in these tactics is often viewed as further evidence of effective leadership (e.g., Reicher, Drury, Hopkins, & Stott, in press; Reicher & Hopkins, 1996).

Leadership endurance also benefits from consensual prototypicality, because of the latter's effect on social attraction. In groups with less consensual prototypes, there is less consensus of perceptions of and feelings for the leader and thus the leader may have less power and may occupy a less stable position. It is in the leader's interest to maintain a clearly defined and consensual prototype. One way to do this is to construct and then foment rejection of in-group deviates—a process that clarifies the prototype that the leader best represents (see Marques, Abrams, Páez, & Hogg, 2001). Another strategy is to polarize or extremitize the in-group relative to a specific "wicked" out-group. These processes are most likely to operate in extremist groups with all-powerful leaders (e.g., Hogg, 2001b; Hogg & Reid, 2001).

RELATING SOCIAL IDENTITY AND LEADER-MEMBER EXCHANGE (LMX) PROCESSES OF LEADERSHIP

We have taken some time describing the social identity theory of leadership. The theory has attracted solid empirical support, mainly regarding the central role of prototypicality in salient groups (de Cremer, in press; Duck & Fielding, 1999; Fielding & Hogg, 1997; Foddy & Hogg, 1999; Hains, Hogg, & Duck,

1997; Haslam, McGarty, Brown et al., 1998; Haslam & Platow, 2001b; Hogg, 1996, 2001a, 2001b, 2001c; Hogg, Hains, & Mason, 1998; Hogg & Reid, 2001; Platow, Hoar, Reid, Harley, & Morrison, 1997; Platow, Reid, & Andrews, 1998; Platow & van Knippenberg, 2001; Reicher, Drury, Hopkins, & Stott, in press; Reicher & Hopkins, 1998; van Knippenberg, van Knippenberg, & van Dijk, 2000; van Vugt & de Cremer, 1999).

Of most relevance to a comparison with LMX theory, is the key idea that as group membership becomes more salient, the basis of effective leadership changes from leadership schemas, personal relations, idiosyncratic preferences and so forth, to group prototypicality. The sorts of groups that mediate high salience include those that are high in entitativity (e.g., Hamilton & Sherman, 1996), high in cohesiveness (e.g., Hogg, 1993), under external threat (e.g., Ellemers, Spears, & Doosje, 1999), critically important to self-conception, and occupy minority status. An example would be an established organization confronting a hostile takeover, or a start-up company struggling to establish a niche in a competitive market.

In these high-salience groups, there is the paradox that leaders are simultaneously "one of us" and "separate from us." The processes described in the previous section construct a relationship within the group in which the leader stands alone in "opposition" to a consensual and relatively homogenous majority of followers. Under these circumstances the leader's relationship to the followers is one in which the latter are treated and related to as an undifferentiated corpus of group members. Followers are not differentiated and treated on an interpersonal basis—the leadership style does not personalize individual followers.

Things are very different in low salience groups. Such groups are ones in which there is a degree of membership diversity, and there is some disagreement on what the group stands for and what the prototype looks like. The group may not be highly cohesive, may not have high cohesion as an entity, may not feel under threat, and so forth. The group is more heterogenous and the followers are more highly individuated. Leadership endorsement is less based on prototypicality and more strongly grounded in people's leadership schemas, personal preferences, and so forth. Under these circumstances, the leader clearly cannot relate to the followers as an undifferentiated whole. Instead the leader needs to develop individual relationships with followers—relationships that cater to idiosyncrasies of the particular follower's preferences, personality, and so forth. A separate LMX relationship needs to be established with specific individuals or groups of individuals, if the leader is to be effective.

Thus, the clear prediction is that as group membership becomes more salient, leader-member relations will become less interpersonal and more depersonalized. LMX theory may account for leader–member relations in low- or moderately salient groups, but social identity theory accounts for leader–

member relations in high salience groups and also accounts for the process that shifts between the different leader–member relations.

We can describe one study that provides some indicative support for this idea—though further systematic research is required and is currently underway. Hogg, Martin, Weeden, and Epitropaki (2001, study 2) administered a questionnaire to 439 respondents performing a range of jobs in seven UK service and manufacturing companies. The principal dependent variable was a 3-item scale measuring perceived leader effectiveness ($\alpha = .85$). There were two predictor variables: (1) a 5-item scale measuring the extent to which respondents felt that the company encouraged people to work in teams or not ($\alpha = .85$)—high scores approximate a high salience group and low scores a low salience group, and (2) a 2-item scale measuring the extent to which the leader's style treated subordinates as unique individuals or as one of the team ($r = .43$, $p < .001$). Stepwise regression revealed that after demographic variables had been removed at Step 1, perceived leadership effectiveness was predicted by salience ($\beta = .326$, $p < .0001$), by leadership style (beta = .372, $p < .0001$), and by the interaction of salience and style ($\beta = .080$, $p < .04$). The interaction generally supports predictions derived from the social identity model described in this chapter. For ease of presentation, Figure 8.1 displays cell means for the 2×2 interaction, based on median splits. It shows that in low salience groups leaders who adopt an interpersonal leadership style are perceived to be significantly more effective than leaders who adopt a depersonalized leadership style, and that this difference disappears in high salience groups. Put differ-

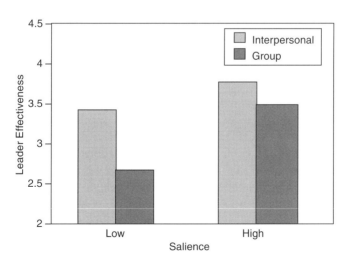

FIGURE 8.1. Perceived leader of effectiveness as a function of group salience and leader–subordinate leadership style. (From Hogg, Martin, Weeden, & Epitropaki, 2001, Study 2.)

ently, the leadership effectiveness of a depersonalized leadership style is significantly increased in high salience groups—the effectiveness of an interpersonal style is not significantly changed.

Some Implications for Organizational Leadership

On the basis of the leadership analysis presented in this chapter, we can make concrete prescriptions for organizational leadership (e.g., Hogg & Terry, 2000). By default, leaders should strike a balance between, on the one hand, relating to followers as distinct individuals and establishing personal relationships with them, and, on the other hand, relating to them as undifferentiated representatives of the organization. As the organization becomes more diverse, less cohesive, lower in entitativity, and prototypically less consensual, leaders would do well to shift towards a more interpersonal leader–member relationship pattern. A depersonalized relationship pattern, one that treats followers as undifferentiated and interchangeable members of the organization, would probably offend and alienate followers, and thus reduce leadership effectiveness.

There are clear leadership effectiveness costs to a mismatch between organizational entitativity and the leader–member relationship pattern. However, appropriate strategies may minimize these costs. Where this is the case, one intriguing possibility is that leaders may be able to increase organizational entitativity and thus organizational identification in fragmented groups by developing a more depersonalized leader–member relationship pattern, and decrease organizational entitativity and thus organizational identification in overly cohesive groups by developing a more interpersonal leader–member relationship pattern.

Some Links and Caveats

One implication of the social identity analysis of leader–member relations is that some group contexts are better suited to personalized relationships and others to depersonalized relationships. Although people may vary in their preferred leader–member relationship pattern, we believe that the group context will have a stronger effect on leader–member relations—in fact the preference itself will be grounded in specifics of the group context. This contrasts with earlier social–psychological models of leadership that identified leadership styles that were relatively enduring properties of individuals (e.g., Bales, 1950; Fiedler, 1965, 1971; Lippitt & White, 1943; Stogdill, 1974).

If group contexts influence leader–member relationship patterns, the possibility exists that cultural differences in self-conception and relationship patterns may have a higher order influence. Research on cultural differences has identified a general difference between individualistic and collectivist cultures, that is reflected at the individual level in idiocentric and allocentric individuals (e.g., Triandis, 1989) who have independent or interdependent self-concepts (Markus & Kityama, 1991). Brewer and Gardner (1996) go further to identify three types of self-conception—collective, individual, and relational. Taken together, these distinctions would seem to identify people (and cultures) who might prefer personalized leader–member relations, and those who might prefer depersonalized leader–member relations. However, it is not clear exactly how the cultural variables might map onto the leader–member relationship variable. For example, someone with an interdependent self might prefer a personalized leader–member relationship as it pivots on close relationships, but might also prefer a depersonalized relationship as it may set up the possibility of greater interdependence among followers.

One thing that we do know is that social identity processes themselves are influenced by collectivism-individualism. Social identity processes are more likely to occur in groups that are collectivist and have an ideology that promotes comparisons, than those that are individualistic or have an ideology that does not promote comparisons (Hinkle & Brown, 1990). Thus depersonalized leader–member relationships will be more effective in the former groups.

CONCLUSIONS

The aim of this chapter has been to explore the relationship between the LMX theory of leadership and the social identity theory of leadership. We critically reviewed LMX theory and concluded that identity dynamics and intergroup processes associated with leadership had been underexplored, and that the social identity perspective provided a way forward. We then described the social identity model of leadership and its articulation with LMX processes.

The core message of this chapter is that when people do not identify very strongly with a group (the group has low entitativity, is not very cohesive, has low self-conceptual importance, and so forth), leadership effectiveness is based on the leader's match to situation-specific and more global leadership schemas, and on the leader nourishing interpersonal leader–subordinate relationships that treat each subordinate as a unique individual. When people do identify very strongly with a group (the group has high entitativity, is very cohesive, has high self-conceptual importance, and so forth), leadership effectiveness is based on the leader's match to the group prototype, and on the leader nourishing a more depersonalized leader–subordinate relationship that treats all subordinates in much the same way, simply as undifferentiated members of the group. The implication for organizations, and other group leadership settings, is that incumbent or potential leaders need to pay close attention to the entitativity, cohesiveness, and self-conceptual importance of the group in order to know what processes and properties will maximize his or her leadership effectiveness.

Although there is reasonably solid empirical support for the LMX theory of leadership and for the social identity theory of leadership, there are few direct tests of the interactive ideas we have presented here. We reported one indicative, but promising, study conducted in an organizational setting. A larger program of empirical research is currently underway. A distinct strength of the social identity perspective is that it specifies social–cognitive generative processes that underpin leadership and tie leadership to group processes and group membership. Such processes allow one to predict the conditions under which more interpersonal or more group oriented leader-member relations and leadership styles will be most effective.

9

Interpersonal Treatment, Social Identity, and Organizational Behavior

HEATHER J. SMITH
Sonoma State University
TOM R. TYLER
New York University
YUEN J. HUO
University of California, Los Angeles

I magine that you are about to meet with your immediate work supervisor about a recent conflict with a colleague; that you are about to discuss a grade you have received from a professor; or that you are about to discuss your taxes with an IRS auditor. What will you care about in such situations? Will it be most important that the authority gives you the outcome that you want? Or will it be more important that he or she listens to you and treats you with respect? When people are asked to imagine these types of situations, they typically report that they think that their personal outcomes are the most important issue to them and it is their outcomes that will determine how they react to their experiences with authorities (Tyler, Huo, & Lind, 1999; also see Miller & Ratner, 1998). However, research shows that people in the actual situation often are more concerned with how authorities treat them (i.e., with procedural or process issues) than they are with the favorability or the fairness of the outcomes they receive when dealing with those authorities (see chapter 15, this volume; Messick, Bloom, Boldizar, & Samuelson, 1985; Mikula, Petri, & Tanzer, 1990). When people feel they have been fairly treated, they are more likely to cooperate in social dilemmas, show greater organizational commitment, more support for authorities, more voluntary compliance with rules and regulations, and greater acceptance of (unfavorable) decisions (see Tyler

& Lind, 1992; Tyler, Boeckmann, Smith, & Huo, 1997 for an overview). In contrast, people who feel unfairly treated by authorities are more likely to act aggressively or retaliate in the workplace (e.g., Miller, 2001), are more likely to steal from or sabotage their workplace (e.g., J. Greenberg, 1993), and are more supportive of sit-ins and strikes (e.g., Leung, Chiu, & Au, 1993),

Justice researchers distinguish between distributive justice (how fair are decision outcomes) and procedural justice (how fair are the methods for making outcome decisions; Brockner & Wiesenfeld, 1991; J. Greenberg, 1987; G. Greenberg & Baron, 2000). Procedural justice includes both structural aspects of decision making and treatment quality by decision-makers (sometimes defined as interactional justice; Bies & Moag, 1986; G. Greenberg & Baron, 2000, Tyler & Blader, 2000). In this chapter, we outline a relational model of authority in which we link findings about the importance of the quality of the treatment that people experience from group authorities to their emotional attachment to groups and to their self-categorization as group members.

The relational model of authority seeks to explain why and when people care about issues of process, and in particular, why and when they will care about the quality of authority treatment. We argue that group authorities don't just distribute resources; they also communicate information about the person's value to the group. Our research shows that people draw such identity relevant information from the quality of their treatment by authorities during their interactions with key group authorities (Tyler & Smith, 1999). Further, this information influences both people's voluntary actions on behalf of the group and their self-images (Tyler & Blader, 2000). The relational model of authority builds upon the insight articulated by social identity and self-categorization researchers that people incorporate important group memberships (or social identities) into their self-concept (Ellemers, Spears, & Doosje, 1999; Tajfel & Turner, 1986; Turner, Hogg, Oakes, Reicher, & Wetherell, 1987). People strive for positive social identities and they will be particularly sensitive to information about both their group's value and their value to the group (Ellemers, Spears, & Doosje, 1999; Schmitt & Branscombe, 2001a).

TWO VIEWS OF WHAT PEOPLE WANT FROM AUTHORITIES: THE INSTRUMENTAL AND RELATIONAL MODELS

The traditional view of authority relations is found within both social exchange and interdependence theories (Thibaut & Kelley, 1959) and realistic group conflict theories (Campbell, 1965; Sherif, 1966; Taylor, Moghaddam, Gamble, & Zellerer, 1987). These theories suggest that people's interactions with authorities are shaped by their desire to gain benefits and avoid costs when dealing with others in groups, organizations, or societies. According to this view, people should be most concerned about the amount and quality of the resources that they receive from group authorities. If group authorities are successful in securing resources and can dispense those to group members, or if they can wield credible threats of potential sanctions for undesirable behavior, people will cooperate with those authorities. This focus on the costs and benefits of particular authority–subordinate relationships shapes analyses of organizational power in which power is defined as the capacity that one person has to influence the behavior of another person. According to the dependency hypothesis, power is linked to the extent that the person controls important, scarce, or nonsubstitutable resources (Fiske & Dépret, 1996; G. Greenberg & Baron, 2000; Robbins, 1998). Similarly, leader-member exchange theory (Graen, Novak, & Sommerkamp, 1962; Robbins, 1998) proposes that leaders' relationships to selected in-group members are qualitatively different from leaders' relationships with other out-group members. In-group members give and get more attention and more rewards from leaders than do out-group members.

In contrast, the relational model of authority argues that the way that authorities behave is important because the behavior of group authorities tells people about the nature of their relationship to the group (Tyler & Lind, 1992). When people are treated fairly, this fair treatment communicates the message that they are important and included within the group, organization, or society. On the other hand, when people are treated unfairly, this unfair treatment communicates the message that they are marginal or excluded from the group, organization, or society. It is the self-relevant implications of procedural treatment that make the behavior of authorities such a powerful influence on people's attitudes and behaviors.

In the relational model, fair treatment is defined in terms of three elements: (1) evaluations of whether authorities' motives can be trusted (benevolence); (2) judgments about whether authorities' actions are based upon the nonbiased examination of facts (neutrality); and (3) evaluations of the degree to which authorities are treating people with the dignity and respect appropriate for full group members (status recognition, Tyler, 1989; Tyler & Blader, 2000). In addition to our own work, research on interactional justice also strongly suggests that when reacting to authorities, individuals are attuned to these relational issues (Bies & Moag, 1986; Bies & Shapiro, 1987).

As a first test of the relational model, we can compare the predictive power of relational judgments and instrumental judgments when people are making judgments about authorities. Instrumental judgments include evaluations of the favorability and the fairness of the outcomes received from the decisions made and policies enacted by the authority. These judgments reflect people's assessments of the quality and quantity of the resources being received from the group and from the group's authorities. If treatment by group authorities communicates identity-relevant information to group members, relational judgments about treatment by those authorities should predict people's group-related behaviors and their feelings about themselves independent of the influence of instrumental judgments.

Table 9.1 presents the results of a recent survey of 404 employees varying from low-income and part-time employees to long-time and highly compensated executive and technical staff (see Tyler & Blader, 2000, for details). This analysis focuses directly on the influence of the quality of the authority treatment that people experience from the authorities with whom they are dealing. This influence can be compared to the influence of instrumental judgments including outcome favorability, outcome fairness, and the structural aspects of the decision-making processes.

As Table 9.1 shows, the quality of the treatment that the employees studied receive from organizational authorities predicts a great deal of the variance in a wide variety of dependent measures, ranging from job satisfaction to employees' willingness to go above and beyond their job requirements (extrarole behavior, Folger & Konovsky, 1989; Organ & Moorman, 1993). For example, 36% of the variance in job satisfaction was explained by four judgments: outcome favorability, outcome fairness, structural aspects of decision making, and quality of treatment received. Of those four factors, treatment quality is most strongly related to job satisfaction. The same four factors explain 19% of the variance in extrarole behavior. Again, treatment quality is most strongly related to extrarole behavior.

This pattern of results supports our argument that people place considerable weight on the quality of their interpersonal treatment by groups and group authorities (and much less weight on instrumental judgments). Perhaps most strikingly, people place more weight on the quality of their interpersonal treatment than they do on the quality of the decision making that they believe is

TABLE 9.1. The relationship among outcome favorability, treatment quality, and key organizational measures.

Predictors	Outcome Measures				
	Job satisfaction	Organizational commitment	Compliance with authorities	In-role behavior	Extrarole behavior
Outcome favorability	.10	.21°°°	−.04	.12	.02
Distributive justice	.12°	.03	−.01	−.03	−.11°
Structure of decision-making	−.04	−.07	.12	−.12	−.18°
Treatment quality	.50°°°	.52°°°	.20°	.35°°°	.62°°°
Adjusted R^2	37%	40%	7%	10%	19%

Note. N = 404. After Tyler and Blader, 2000, p. 121.
°$p < .05$
°°$p < .01$
°°°$p < .001$

occurring. These findings support the argument that how authorities treat people is the key to people's connection to the group and to group authorities.

We find the same pattern of results in interviews with community residents who describe their encounters with police and the legal system (Tyler & Huo, 2000), interviews with community residents about water regulation authorities (Tyler & Degoey, 1995), interviews with employees in a public sector work organization in Northern California (Huo & Tyler, 2001a) and other survey studies of employees in for-profit organizations (Tyler, 1999). What is striking about all of these studies is that the quality of people's interpersonal treatment not only predicts people's feelings toward supervisors and other authorities, and their commitment to organizations, institutions, and communities, but it also influences their actual behavior.

As the relational model of authority predicts, the quality of people's treatment is more important than are the outcomes they receive for predicting group-oriented behavior. This pattern of results leads us to view treatment by authorities as the key factor that mediates the relationship between group members and the groups to which they belong. Such an image contrasts sharply with the suggestions of the traditional social exchange and interdependence models, which link the relationship between people and groups to issues of resource exchange.

SOCIAL CATEGORIZATION MODERATES THE IMPORTANCE THAT PEOPLE PLACE ON THE QUALITY OF THEIR TREATMENT

An even stronger demonstration of the importance of the relational model would be to show that people care more strongly about the treatment quality by group authorities when the group the authority represents is important to their sense of identity and self. Information that you are a marginal or excluded group member should be less important if you don't care about the group, but the same information should be very important if the group is central to your self-definition, and hence to the basis of your feelings of self-esteem and self-worth. As suggested by social identity theory (Doosje, Ellemers, & Spears, 1999), group members' reactions to particular group memberships and their willingness to act in terms of group norms depends upon the salience of the group membership and the relative importance members attach to the membership. For example, group members who identify closely with the group will support collective improvements even at the expense of their own personal interests (Ellemers, Wilke, & van Knippenberg, 1993; Ellemers, Spears, & Doosje, 1997). In the same situation, group members who do not identify with the group will focus on personal risks and benefits.

To explore whether the salience of particular group memberships shapes reactions to treatment by group authorities, 335 public sector employees were asked to describe a recent conflict they had in their work setting and to talk about how their supervisor resolved it (see Huo & Tyler, 2001a; Tyler, Lind, Ohbuchi, Sugwara, & Huo, 1995). The results showed that when the supervisor shared the same ethnicity as the employee (i.e., the supervisor was an in-group authority), relational judgments shaped their views about the supervisor's legitimacy (i.e., their right to make binding decisions that workers should obey, Tyler, Lind et al., 1998), as well as their willingness to cooperate with the supervisor's suggestions for how to handle the problem (Huo & Tyler, 2001a). When the supervisor was a member of a different ethnicity (i.e., the supervisor was an outgroup authority), instrumental judgments shaped employees' judgments about the legitimacy of their supervisor and their willingness to cooperate. Further, when employees were dealing with an in-group supervisor, they accepted the decisions of an authority if they were fairly treated by that authority, whereas if the supervisor represented an out-group, employees accepted their decisions if those decisions were favorable to them.

We tested the same argument using an experimental design in which outcome favorability, quality of treatment, and the group affiliation of the authority were independently manipulated (Tyler & Smith, 1999). In this experiment, a graduate student responsible for grading a social skills test was presented to students as either an in-group member (from the student's university) or an out-group member (from a rival university). Later, the graduate student entered the room and treated the student fairly or unfairly by either carefully grading their work performance, or doing a superficial job. Independently, the study manipulated whether the student received a favorable outcome (97% correct) or an unfavorable outcome (43% correct).

Students in the experiment were also asked whether they would be willing to help the graduate student's supervisor in further studies (voluntary extrarole behavior; Tyler & Smith, 1999). The results showed that if the test grader and advisor represented an in-group (i.e., were from the student's own school), the willingness to help further was significantly related to how fairly the test grader treated the student, and not to the outcome the student received. In contrast, if the test grader and advisor represented an outgroup (i.e., were from another university), the willingness to help those authorities further was significantly related to favorable outcomes, but not to how fairly the test grader treated the student.

In this research, we find that how in-group authorities treat people influences their behavior, as we would predict from the relational model's assumption that treatment by an authority communicates information about a person's value to the group. Further, outcome favorability does not influence people's behavior when the authority represents an in-group. So, for in-group authorities the key issue is quality of interpersonal treatment, not resources. This finding contradicts the key prediction of traditional social exchange and interdependence models, which suggest that people should be concerned with the possible costs and benefits associated with their interaction with a particular authority. This should be true regardless of the authority's group affiliation. Whether the authority represents an in-group or an out-group does not change the material rewards and costs that an authority can deliver to group members.

GROUP IDENTIFICATION MODERATES
THE IMPORTANCE OF RELATIONAL TREATMENT

Our explanation for this pattern of results assumes that the categorization differences illustrated in the research described above occur because the differences in group membership served as a proxy for higher or lower degrees of "identification" with the group whom the authority represented. In fact, the in-group/out-group effects we have outlined are consistent with the relational perspective only if we assume that people identify more strongly with in-group authorities than with out-group authorities.

It is important to recognize that identification with particular groups or social categories is a subjective psychological experience that is not necessarily defined by objective membership characteristics. Although it is natural to assume that people identify with their in-group more than with an out-group, people are potential members of a variety of different groups and social categories, some of which will be more important to their sense of self (Brewer, 1991; Crocker & Luhtanen, 1990; Turner et al., 1987). A more direct test of the argument is to measure how much people identify with the group the authority represents, and to explore whether quality of treatment is more important when people identify more strongly with a group.

To test this idea, we divided a sample of Chicago employees into two groups based upon the degree to which they indicated that their work organization was central to their sense of self (Tyler & Smith, 1999). We then examined the degree to which employees were willing to accept their supervisor's decisions because: (1) the outcome of the decision favored them or (2) they were fairly treated by their supervisor during the process in which the decision was made. For employees who identified more strongly with their work organization, their acceptance of their supervisor's decision was more closely related to the quality of their supervisors' treatment of them than by the favorability of their outcomes. In contrast, outcome favorability and not quality of treatment, shaped the opinions of those who identified less strongly with the organization.

As a second test of this idea, we focused on 205 employees of a public university who worked with supervisors from a different ethnic background (Huo, Smith, Tyler, & Lind, 1996). Our earlier research suggests that in this cross-ethnicity management context, there is considerable likelihood that employees will focus on the instrumental implications of their supervisor's behavior. This occurs because from an ethnic group perspective the supervisor is an out-group member (Fiske & Dépret, 1996). Our concern was with whether identification with the larger organization could encourage employees to focus on how a supervisor from a different ethnic background treats them rather than on the outcomes they receive. As predicted by the relational model, employees who identified more strongly with the overall work organization focused on the quality of their treatment by their supervisor when evaluating the fairness of their experience and when determining whether or not to accept their supervisor's decision. In contrast, instrumental judgments were much more important to acceptance decisions among employees who did not identify as strongly with the organization.

These results suggest that, even in cross-ethnic interactions, employees cared about how fairly supervisors treated them, and that concern was greater when they identified more strongly with the organization that the supervisor represented. Hence, if we consider subjective identification with a group, rather than simple group membership, we continue to find results consistent with the predictions of the relational model.

THE QUALITY OF THE TREATMENT RECEIVED FROM AUTHORITIES SHAPES WHETHER A PERSON FEELS RESPECTED IN THEIR GROUP

Why do people place greater emphasis on the quality of their treatment by authorities when those authorities represent a group with whom they identify? We believe that people care about relational issues because these aspects of their experience communicate information about their self-worth. Initial evidence for a link between procedural fairness and the self-concept occurs in a set of experiments conducted by Koper and her colleagues (Koper, Van Knippenberg, Bouhuijs, Vermunt, & Wilke, 1993). In two different experiments, treatment quality (defined as how an experimenter graded a test) influenced participant's self-esteem. However, the relational model of authority predicts that if the source of this information does not represent an important reference group, the treatment quality by authorities will be less important as a source of information about identity. In other words, the argument that people learn identity relevant information from authorities can predict *when* people will care how authorities treat them. However, the next step of our argument requires us to specify more completely the information that we believe in-group authorities communicate to group members by their treatment.

We propose that the enactment of procedures, particularly by group authorities, tells people whether they are valued by the group represented by the procedures or authorities, (i.e., treatment communicates respect; Tyler,

Degoey, & Smith, 1996). Respect is a psychological construct that captures people's views of their value to the group. Feelings of respect represent an entire group's opinions rather than the sum of idiosyncratic interpersonal relationships with a variety of people (Ellemers, Doosje, & Spears, 2001; Emler & Reicher, 1995). Because authorities represent the group, people typically see their behavior as representing the views of the group (Haslam & Platow, 2001a).

We view feeling respected by an important reference group as being a central part of people's social identity. According to social identity and self-categorization theories (Tajfel & Turner, 1986; Turner, Hogg et al., 1987), both personal or idiosyncratic attributes and the groups and categories to which we belong shape our self-concepts. However, most social identity and self-categorization research focuses on people's knowledge, attachment, and evaluations of the entire group to which they belong. Whether people view the group as valuable is clearly important. However, we also believe that people's beliefs about whether the group values them can be equally, if not more, important (Smith & Tyler, 1997; Tyler & Lind, 1992). As suggested by Branscombe, Ellemers, Spears, and Doosje (1999), the possibility that one might be demoted or excluded from an important group can be as threatening to one's social identity as stigmatizing or challenging the entire group's status.

In Table 9.2, we summarize the results from a number of different studies in which people's feelings of respect from a reference group and personal self-esteem were measured. Both social identity theory (Noel, Branscombe, & Wann, 1995; Schmidt & Branscombe, 2001a) and other recent models of self-esteem (Leary & Baumeister, 2000) suggest that feeling included or excluded from an important group should influence personal self-esteem. For example, Leary and Baumeister (2000) propose that personal self-esteem is best defined as an internal monitor of the possible social exclusion by other people.

As shown in Table 9.2, from groups as large as the United States, in which people could not know every member of the group, to small housing cooperatives and sororities, in which members know each other intimately, feeling respected by other group members is significantly related to personal self-esteem. Interesting, in the studies in which a collective measure of self-esteem (Luhtanen & Crocker, 1992) was included, respect also is significantly related to collective self-esteem, supporting the hypothesized group-based nature of respect. Table 9.2 also presents the correlations between feeling respected by one's group and discretionary group-oriented behavior—actions that promote the group's goals but are not necessarily prescribed by the group (e.g., extrarole behaviors or voluntary deference to decisions, Folger & Konovsky, 1989; Organ & Moorman, 1993). We have also referred to these behaviors as assertive behaviors (Tyler & Smith, 1999), because they reflect proactive behaviors on the part of group members. In fact, discretionary be-

TABLE 9.2. The relationship among respect from group members, self-evaluations, and group-oriented cooperative behavior.

Study	N	Personal self-esteem	Collective self-esteem	Discretionary/ assertive behaviors
Smith & Tyler (1997), university as student	200	.43	.42	.20
Smith & Tyler (1997), sororities	83	.32	.63	.45
Tyler, Degoey, & Smith (1996), families	335	.47	—	.45
Tyler, Degoey, & Smith (1996), university as employee	335	—	—	.22
Tyler, Degoey, & Smith (1996), nation as citizen	502	.34	—	—
Smith et al. (1998), experiment 1	115	.34	—	.16°°
Smith et al. (1998), experiment 2	119	.33	—	—
Smith, Tyler, & Daubenmeir (2002), cooperatives	193	.22	.24°	.19
Smith, Tyler, & Daubenmeir (2002), construction workers	49	.46°°°	—	—
Tyler & Blader (2000), employees (average effect size)	404	.33	.39	.22
Average Effect Size		.36	.39	.27

°Correlation is with the identification subscale of the collective self-esteem scale.
°°Sample size is 108.
°°°Correlation is with a measure of self-efficacy.

haviors represent an important group asset. When environment requirements can change quickly, flexible, creative employee behavior is particularly valuable.

Table 9.2 also includes the data obtained from the set of experiments (Smith et al., 1998) described earlier. There is also recent experimental evidence that shows a direct influence of feeling respected by *other group members* on self-evaluations and behavior (in contrast to a single group authority). For example, in three different experiments, Simon and Sturmer (2001) directly manipulate respectful treatment from other group members independently of how negative or positive the actual feedback is. Across three experiments, respectful treatment by other group members increased collective self-esteem and participants' willingness to engage in group serving behavior. In a different set of experiments, Ellemers, Doosje, and Spears (2001) also directly manipulate respect from other group members (operationalized as other group members' evaluations of the participants' descriptions of their personal behavior). They find that high respect from the in-group leads to more self-esteem than low respect, particularly if respondents identify more closely with the in-group. Moreover, the respect manipulation also influenced participants' willingness to help the group and discriminate against an out-group (Branscombe et al., 2001).[1] Further, Ellemers and her colleagues (2001) show that the influence of respect depends upon the source of the information. The same positive information from an out-group made participants feel worse rather than better. More importantly, this information was communicated by an entire team of individuals rather than single identifiable individuals, supporting that respect represents a group level variable (Ellemers, Doosje, & Spears, 2001).

Having shown that feeling respected by other group members is related to self-evaluations and group-oriented behavior, the next question is whether the quality of the treatment that people receive influences their judgments of how respected they are by the group. Earlier we showed that treatment by in-group authorities, or by authorities representing a group with whom a person identifies, is more closely related to the willingness to help and the acceptance of supervisors' decisions than are measures of outcome favorability. Now the question is whether feeling respected is more closely related to the quality of the treatment that people receive or to the favorability of their outcomes.

In two different laboratory experiments (H. J. Smith, Tyler, Huo, Ortiz, & Lind, 1998), we manipulated the group affiliation of an authority responsible for people's treatment and outcomes. In the first experiment (described earlier), participants who were treated unfairly by the test grader from the participant's own university reported feeling significantly less respected by other people than participants who were treated fairly, regardless of the outcome. In a second experiment, students completed three timed tasks for which they could earn points toward participation in a subject payment lottery. However, as sometimes is the case in the "real world," the computer that students were using would unexpectedly freeze and the students would lose time for their task of earning points. Afterwards, students could e-mail an unseen supervisor (presented as either from their university or from a rival university) about the computer problems. This supervisor responded to the participants' e-mail messages with either three very polite and considerate messages or an initially polite message followed by two rude and insensitive messages (a manipulation of treatment quality). As predicted, unfair treatment by an in-group authority led to feeling less respected by other people, particularly when outcomes were negative.

Having shown that when the authority represents an in-group, the quality of treatment by an authority shapes feelings respected by other, we can test the complete pattern of relational model predictions (see Figure 9.1). According to the relational model of authority, identification with the group or organization the authority represents determines whether people will pay more attention to relational or instrumental justice concerns. When people identify with the organization, how key organizational authorities treat them influences their feelings of respect from the organization as a whole, and consequently their personal self-evaluations and their willingness to help the organization.

To test the full model, we asked university students to describe a recent

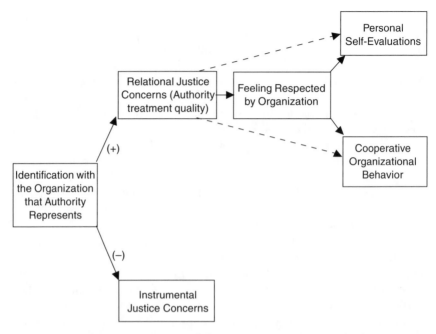

FIGURE 9.1. A relational model of authority.

conflict with a faculty or staff member of the university (Smith et al., 1998). As the relational model predicts, how fairly students felt the staff treated them was related to lower feelings of respect from the university community, but only if they identified with the university. If they did *not* identify with the university, unfair treatment by the faculty member was actually associated with feeling more respected.

In this survey, we also asked students how they felt about themselves (personal self-esteem) and whether they put in a great deal of effort beyond what is expected to make university successful, make innovative suggestions, and volunteered to do things for university that are not required (extrarole or discretionary behaviors). For students who identified closely with the university, the quality of the treatment received from an authority was related to both personal self-esteem and to discretionary behavior helping the group. Given the relationship among treatment quality, respect, and personal self-esteem, we could explore whether feeling respected by other members of the university community mediated the relationship between authority treatment quality and personal self-esteem or discretionary behavior. However, this pattern should only occur for students who identified closely with the university. For students who do not identify with the university, authority treatment quality should not predict self-evaluations or group-oriented behavior. When we included feeling respected in the regression equation for personal self-esteem and extrarole behavior for high identifiers, the original relationship between quality of treatment and personal self-esteem/extrarole is reduced significantly. In contrast, there is no relationship between the quality of the treatment received, feeling respected and the two outcome variables for low identifiers.

Thus far, we have focused on studies that examine the quality of people's treatment by authorities within hierarchical conflicts, but in a recent study of housing cooperative members (Smith, Tyler, & Daubenmeir, 2002), we find the same pattern among general evaluations of procedural fairness, feeling respected by group members and personal self-esteem. These results suggest that the relationships we are describing apply more generally to procedures (not just a single enactment of procedures by an authority) and even to cooperative groups with clearly nonhierarchical group structures. We also find the same pattern of relationships in a questionnaire study of concrete construction workers' experiences with their immediate work supervisors (Smith, Tyler, & Daubenmeir, 2002).

WHAT ABOUT MULTIPLE GROUP MEMBERSHIPS?

The evidence we have described supports our argument that people can be relationally oriented when responding to group authorities, but only if these authorities represent a group with whom people identify. Further, we show that fair treatment shapes whether people feel respected by group members, and it is feeling respected that shapes personal self-esteem and group-oriented behavior. However, one could argue that this research is based on an overly simplified conception of group and organizational life in which individuals and authorities are either members of the same group or are organized into separate groups through the process of social categorization.

In fact, most people belong to a variety of different groups and social categories (i.e., a member of the work organization may also perceive herself as being a woman, an ethnic minority, and a member of the management team). Given the complexity of group identities, it is worth considering how multiple group memberships might shape the relationship between treatment quality and people's self-evaluations and group-oriented cooperative behavior (van Knippenberg & van Schie, 2000). Moreover, a multiple-group framework provides an opportunity for us to consider whether and to what extent social and cultural diversity will disrupt social relations within an organization or other structured groups.

We have studied this question by evaluating the influence of social identification on relational justice concerns in contexts where people may experience tension between loyalty to two different groups (e.g., the larger society and one's ethnic group). A typology of acculturation orientations developed by

Berry (1984) offers a framework from which to consider the influence of multiple group identities. In Berry's typology, attachment or identification with a superordinate group (e.g., society or work organization) is crossed with identification with a subgroup (e.g., ethnic group membership) to produce four categories of people, each with a different acculturation orientation: (1) assimilators (strong superordinate identification, weak subgroup identification); (2) separatists (weak superordinate identification, strong subgroup identification); (3) biculturalists (strong identification with both the superordinate and the subgroup); and (4) alienated (weak identification with both the superordinate and the subgroup).

A relational model of authority suggests how individuals within each of these categories will respond to interactions with authorities who share his or her group membership at the superordinate level but not at the subgroup level (e.g., a white employee responding to interactions with a Latino supervisor). We predict that assimilators will emphasize quality of treatment in this situation because his or her primary form of identification is with an overarching category that includes the authority. In contrast, we predict that separatists will emphasize instrumental issues in a similar situation because his or her primary form of identification is with the subgroup that excludes the authority.

Biculturalists identify strongly with both the superordinate group and the subgroup. This group provides an interesting test of the effects of multiple group memberships. The relational model does not make an a priori prediction of how biculturalists would respond to an authority in the situation we described. However, the response of this group is likely to generate potentially important insight into the dynamics of culturally and ethnically diverse organizations. If a person with dual identities evaluates authorities primarily in terms of their instrumental interest, then one of the likely costs of valuing and acknowledging diversity is the inevitability of subgroup conflicts that may threaten organizational cohesion. On the other hand, if a person with dual identities evaluates authorities and policies primarily in terms of how he or she is treated, then it may be possible for authorities to smooth over internal conflicts and maintain organizational cohesion. It is important to recognize that while the relational approach may benefit the organization by maintaining positive relations between subgroups, it may be costly for individuals who relinquish their pursuit of self or subgroup interest for the good of the collective.[2]

In the Huo et al. study (1996) described earlier, workplace employees were asked to recount a recent encounter with their supervisor. Individuals were organized into one of the three categories based on their self-reports of how much they identified with the university and their ethnic group. Analyses were conducted separately for each group to determine whether outcome favorability or treatment quality best predicted willingness to cooperate with the decisions of the supervisors. The findings show that decision acceptance was closely related to the belief that the outcome was favorable (e.g., receiving a promotion or a raise) for separatists. In contrast, decision acceptance was closely related to perceptions of fair treatment among *both* assimilators and biculturalists. This pattern of results offers an interesting insight into the dynamics of diverse groups. It suggests that diversity will not necessarily hinder authorities' ability to gain cooperation. Diversity disrupts the relational processes we described only when individual's attachment to their subgroup outweighs their attachment to a more inclusive category that they share with the authority (for a related discussion, see chapters 12 and 14, this volume).

In this project, we assumed subordinate and superordinate identification are independent constructs. In other words, greater identification with a superordinate category does not mean less identification with a subordinate category. Although this assumption seems reasonable in light of theories of acculturation (Azzi, 1992; LaFromboise, Coleman, & Gerton, 1993; Phinney, 1990), we recently acknowledged that this view may be inconsistent with other theoretical perspectives (Huo & Tyler, 2000b). The strongest challenge comes from self-categorization theory (Turner, Hogg et al., 1987). According to the principle of functional antagonism derived from self-categorization theory, simultaneous superordinate and subgroup identifications are inherently incompatible. When a superordinate category is made salient, subgroup boundaries become blurred and perceptions of differences among subgroup members dissipate and are replaced by perceptions of similarity. A second challenge is suggested by social dominance theorists (Sidanius & Pratto, 1999) who propose that superordinate and subgroup identities should be negatively related for subordinate (i.e., minority) groups in diverse societies. According to the instrumental perspective of social dominance theory, members of subordinate groups should either place their loyalty in their subgroup or to the dominant group, but not both.

We put these challenges to the test using data collected from a recent telephone study of California residents (see Huo & Tyler, 2001a for study details). White, Latino, and African-American respondents in this study described and evaluated recent encounters with either the police or court officials. They also indicated how much they identified with the United States as a superordinate category and their particular ethnic group. Factor analyses revealed that the two types of identification were empirically distinct, and further, the two types of identification were positively (as opposed to negatively) related for each of the three ethnic groups. Together, these findings support our prior assumption that superordinate and subgroup identification are distinct constructs rather than two ends of a single dimension. We sought to replicate the earlier findings by entering interaction terms comprised of the appropriate group identification measures and fair treatment into a regression analysis. In support of the relational prediction, greater identification with the United States was associated with a greater emphasis on treatment quality than instrumental judgments when people decide whether to accept an authority's decisions. Further, subgroup identification did *not* influence the way individuals respond to superordinate authorities. These results bolster our original conclusion that the operation of relational processes is dependent upon the individual and the authority experiencing a common group membership but that this process is not disrupted by subgroup identification.

Although the evidence that subgroup and superordinate identification are independent constructs appears to contradict the social categorization theory principle of functional antagonism, this may be a context in which the superordinate category represents what Haslam (2001) has termed an "organic social identity." In a group characterized by organic solidarity, each member or subgroup contributes toward building a sense of shared identification through their uniqueness. We argue that the premise underlying an organic social identity is consistent with the multicultural celebration of difference which asserts that distinct ethnic loyalties cannot only coexist but they, in fact, function to promote a common national identity through their ethnic identity (Berry, 1991; de la Garza, Flacon, & Garcia, 1996). This line of reasoning leads to the conclusion that to the extent that the shared superordinate identity is defined in terms of all relevant subgroup identities, dual identification is not only possible but is easily sustainable.

CONCLUSIONS

Our research shows that people care about receiving fair treatment by group authorities because it communicates how much the group or organization respects them. People who feel respected by groups that are important to them enjoy higher personal self-esteem and will pursue creative ways to help the group. However, if people do not identify with the group authority the group represents, they appear to care more about the favorability of their outcomes than about the respectfulness of their treatment. When people don't care about the organization the authority represents, relational justice does not communicate any self-relevant information, and consequently, does not shape people's behavior. In fact, there is recent experimental evidence that people define procedural fairness differently in intergroup contexts than they do in intragroup contexts (Platow, Reid, & Andrew, 1998). Participants in intergroup and intragroup contexts viewed the same leadership behavior as equally neutral, trustworthy, and respectful, but rated the intergroup leader as significantly less procedurally fair than the intragroup leader.

On the one hand, fair treatment by organizational authorities can encourage employees to accept less than favorable outcomes or decisions when resources are scarce. On the other hand, fair treatment can draw attention away from structural inequities and problems. Group members might tolerate great inequities in resources because they feel "valued" by their organization

(Martin & Harder, 1994; Haney, 1991). Further, unfair treatment by an important group representative can diminish or threaten people's self-esteem and lead to passivity, or in some cases, increased interpersonal violence. Baumeister, Smart, and Boden (1996) argue that feeling disrespected provokes aggressive reactions among people with high (but perhaps unstable) personal self-esteem. Procedures and how they are enacted are often an afterthought in many organizations. Our research illustrates the potential costs of ignoring what procedures and authorities who enact them communicate to people about their value to the organization.

NOTES

1. In a related research tradition, researchers have examined how participants react to the suggestion that they are not as prototypical a group member as they assumed or as are other group members (Schmidt & Branscombe, 2001a; Hogg, Hains, & Mason, 1998). Although prototypicality, being liked as a group member, and being respected as a group member are most likely positively related, we do not think they are the same thing. In fact, when members of a sorority pledge class were asked to nominate the most representative, the most liked, and the most respected members of their class, nominations for most liked and most representative were more closely related ($r(80) = .77$, $p < .05$) than were nominations for most representative and most respected ($r(80) = .56$, $p < .05$) and most liked and most respected ($r(80) = .56$, $p < .05$. The distinction between respect and liking may be similar to the distinction made in the organizational power literature between position and personal power (Robbins, 1998).
2. The fourth group of the alienated is excluded from our analysis because they expressed very little interest in either of the relevant groups. Inclusion within the relational model is premised upon individuals valuing at least some form of group membership.

10

On the Social Psychology of Power and Powerlessness
Social Power as a Symptom of Organizational Division

KATHERINE J. REYNOLDS
Australian National University
MICHAEL J. PLATOW
LaTrobe University

*P*feffer (1992) has described the challenges and difficulties faced by people who have power in organizations. He acknowledges that obtaining power and using it can be a dirty business. Often the powerful and powerless disagree, those who attempt to develop a power base can make enemies, and those exercising power do upset others and can make mistakes. The mistakes, of course, are not inevitable, and perceptions of good and bad, of success and failure, depend often on whether one agrees with the strategy taken and outcome sought. In Pfeffer's view, what is inevitable is that those who are powerless are less likely to strive for specific outcomes for the organization as a whole. They will remain passive recipients of others' desires to achieve these outcomes and to shape the organization. For this reason, for this lack of striving, Pfeffer agues that powerlessness can lead to organizational failure. It is powerlessness, thus, not power, that is an organization's last dirty secret.

Many believe that powerlessness is self-inflicted, and that some people in organizations simply choose to opt out of decision making and responsibility taking. In some cases this may occur. However, powerlessness is tied to something more functional; it is tied to people's actual ability to achieve their goals and control resources in the way they desire. In this manner, powerlessness can be a direct outcome of specific organizational processes and practices. These practices—the values, goals, and norms that define the organization

173

and the way people work—may influence, inter alia, both in-role and extrarole productivity and performance, employee turnover, and social conflict. If this is true, then organizations can more easily move to minimize powerlessness and benefit from the untapped resources that may emanate from the active engagement of its members.

In this chapter, we argue that power use and, hence, powerlessness are symptoms of intergroup categorization within an organization, and a sign of the organization's failure to work as a unified collective. To be sure, neither the unified collective nor intergroup categorizations guarantee organizational success; both unity and division create fiascos as well as advancements (e.g., Janis, 1982; Moscovici, 1976). But our fundamental thesis remains thus: To understand fully social power in organizations, we must understand the nature of social categorizations and employees' social identities within them.

RESOURCE POWER: CONTROL, LEGITIMACY, AND VALUE

Our analysis starts with a simple truism: Individuals and groups can, and do, have resources (e.g., money, goods, information; Foa & Foa, 1980), and can, and do, *control* them. People garner control over resources; with force or with legitimacy, they can keep these resources; and the holders of these resources can distribute them to others as they see fit (cf. chapter 15, this volume). When these events transpire, people have both reflexive control over their own outcomes (i.e., people's own behavior reflects the resources back to themselves) and fate control over the outcomes to others (i.e., people's behavior affects others' outcomes regardless of what these others do; Thibaut & Kelley, 1959; Kelley & Thibaut, 1978). We refer to these forms of control as *resource power*.

In most organizations in Western industrialized nations, resource power is largely associated with management, who, by their position within the organization, are seen as the legitimate purveyors of such power. Management—and other authorities, such as teachers and political representatives—have either been granted the right over access and control of resources by some (nominally) consensual agreement within the broader community (French & Raven, 1968; cf. Locke, 1764/1952; Platow, 2000; Rousseau, 1762/1967), or have simply acquired access by hook or by crook. While the former instance of acquisition is considered legitimate from the outset, the latter can come to be seen that way if, by commanding the lion's share of the resource, those with resource power develop rules and ideologies that, in time, legitimate the existing differential distribution of resources (Cohen, 1986; Platow & Hunter, 2001; Walster & Walster, 1975).

We ought not to forget, of course, that nonmanagement, general employees of organizations also have resource power. Their resource is largely their labor (Marx, 1867/1906). They can give it to or withhold it from others as they, the general employees, see fit. Unfortunately, economic realities in most Western industrialized nations prohibit withholding, if only because the provision of labor in exchange for needed resources (i.e., money for food) has been legitimated into the dominant ideology, as well as the real social and political structure. Creative ways of withholding labor, such as sabotage (Rocker, 1938/1981), are often seen as illegitimate and legislated against. And "go slow" and "work clumsily" tactics to maintain employment fairness (i.e., "for bad wages, bad work"; Rocker, p. 20), when instituted on an individual basis, will often only result in job loss. Of course, one not so extreme employee use of power that is more likely to lead to continued employment is simply not to engage in extrarole behavior, not to "go the extra mile."

In the end, resource power, as we are using it, is simply the ability to control how and to whom resources are distributed. If the resources are of no value to others, then resource power remains just that (i.e., power over resources), and is it impotent to change people's behavior in any way. However, if the resources *are* of value, then those with fate control can affect the behavior of others. It is in this case that simple resource power is translated into *social power*.

SOCIAL POWER AND SOCIAL INFLUENCE

It is important for our discussion to clarify precisely what we mean by social power, and to differentiate it from the related, but distinct, concept of social influence. Social power and social influence appear similar, and are often used interchangeably because they both relate to the effects that individuals and groups have upon one another (Blau, 1964; French & Raven, 1968). Sometimes these effects come about through the control of rewards and punishments, sometimes through the control of information, and sometimes through people's status as authorities, experts, or friends. But in our current analysis, when we speak of social influence, we mean actual persuasion (Turner, 1991); we mean contemplated evaluation of information leading to internalized changes in attitudes, values, and behaviors. This is the outcome of systematic (Chaiken, 1987) or central-route (Petty & Cacioppo, 1986) information processing resulting in some internal conversion (Moscovici, 1985). It relies heavily upon the social validity and perceived strength of arguments. Social power, in contrast, we reserve specifically for changes in attitudes, values, and behaviors that are primarily compliant (Festinger, 1953; Kelman, 1961). These changes are the outcome of one's functional dependence in the social relationship for either material outcomes (French & Raven, 1968) or information (Cialdini, 1993; cf. Chaiken, 1987; Petty & Cacioppo, 1986). Thus, when employees internalize the views of managers because they believe the managers are right, this is social influence; when employees comply with the views of managers because managers control valued resources, this is social power.

To date, social influence more so than social power has received the bulk of theoretical and empirical attention within the social identity approach (Turner, 1987, 1991; Turner & Oakes, 1989). Out of this work has emerged the simple but critical fact that we are influenced by in-group members not by out-group members. It is others who share important, context-dependent similarities to us—people with whom we self-categorize—who can provide us with meaningful, *socially valid* information about the world, who can lead us to change our opinions and internalize new values (Abrams, Wetherell, Cochrane, Hogg, & Turner, 1990; Mackie, 1986).

But how does information, that may appear to be socially neutral, become "socially valid"? To answer this, consider Cialdini's (1993) concept of social proof. People are moved by social proof when there is social consensus about the correctness or appropriateness of a particular attitude or behavior. Cialdini's simple example is the oft used television industry technique of recording canned laughter over dubiously humorous material. The clear goal is to inform and persuade viewers that the material is actually funny. However, recent research by Platow, Haslem et al. (2002) questions whether all social proof is equally socially valid. The answer they provide is a resounding "no." When people listen to recorded jokes in which audience laughter (i.e., social proof) is said to come from in-group members, they laugh more, laugh longer, and *privately* rate the material as more humorous than when the audience laughter is said to come from out-group members. It is thus in-group members who socially validate information and, hence, provide us with social proof.

The research demonstrating social influence from in-group members is very robust, and more complex analyses clearly show that social influence derives from deeper cognitive processing of information to in-group than out-group communications (Mackie, Worth, & Asuncion, 1990; McGarty, Haslam, Hutchinson, & Turner, 1994; Platow, Mills, & Morrison, 2000). Shared group membership does not simply act as a persuasion cue to which we thoughtlessly conform. Instead, shared group membership informs us of the level of social validity of the information, of its relative veridicality; we can place our trust in the information provided to us by in-group members (cf., Foddy, Platow, & Yamagishi, 2001) and, hence, will be more persuaded by them when they forward strong arguments, than we will be by outgroup members.

So what is social power and from whence does it come? As we said, social power is the ability to get people to comply, to go along with, to do one's bidding in the absence of actual cognitive conversion and internalization. And it is out-group members who must resort to social power precisely because of their status as out-group members (i.e., people who we do not trust and who do not provide us with socially valid information; Turner, 1991). This analysis, however, appears less than satisfying, if only because we are left asking why anyone would comply with out-group members. Surely, we would leave behind people with whom we do not identify, we would simply disengage from those whom we do not trust and who do not provide us with socially valid information. It is, however, this ability (or inability) to "leave behind," to "disengage," to exit that forms the actual basis of social power (or social powerlessness; Kelley & Thibaut, 1978; Thibaut & Kelley, 1959). Thibaut and Kelley make it very clear that in social relationships in which people can mutually affect each other's outcomes, social power comes to those who *can* leave the relationship. Those who cannot leave are powerless. These people have no viable substitutes and are at the mercy of those with power (see Mintzberg, 1983a).

When people have nowhere to go, when people cannot leave (or believe they cannot leave) the current relationship, they have no choice but to accept the will of others in the relationship. When people can move easily from one relationship to another, however, they can demand and receive more from those with fewer alternative relationship options. Those with power can make a personal decision to exit out of the relationship or threaten to exit out. Simply put, the more functionally dependent people are on a particular relationship, the less social power they have within that relationship, and vice versa (Emerson, 1962). In an unskilled labor market, for example, workers have very few real options to move from one job to another, and they must resign themselves to their current jobs and the wills of their more highly skilled employers. This is why the creative use of resource power by "go slow"and "work clumsily" tactics are often not an option for individual employees; job loss is simply not an alternative. The well-trained CEOs, however, can sell their wares more easily, and can threaten to leave the organization if their wills are not followed; these are the socially powerful (the so-called gold collarworkers).

The critical variable in this analysis is the real or perceived availability of alternatives to the current relationship. Even dissatisfied employees will remain in their current jobs if they have no other alternative options (Rusbult, Farrell, Rogers, & Mainous, 1988); those with no alternatives are precisely the people most at risk for social powerlessness. They are the people that Pheffer warns may be an organization's "last dirty secret." These are the people most likely to try to exercise their resource power in such a way that they can maintain employment by failing to "go the extra mile" for the organization. In our terms, not striving for the organization, not taking responsibility, not rectifying errors, and being passive recipients of others' actions are not signs of powerlessness but of the restricted social power available to those individuals who are dependent on the current relationship.

SOCIAL INFLUENCE, SOCIAL POWER AND FOUR FORMS OF EXIT

Thus far, we have made the apparently incommensurable claim that social power is used by *out-group members*, but that it comes from their ability to leave a *social relationship*. How can we reconcile the apparent contradiction within an organizational context? First, we recognize that organizations represent valued and shared relationships, as people enter them to satisfy, inter alia, functional (e.g., money), value-expressive (e.g., helping), and identification needs and desires (Cartwright & Zander, 1968). Second, organizations exist with formal or informal subgroups, such as management staff and general staff. In organizations, it is the management subgroup that most often exerts (or tries to exert) social influence and social power over general staff (Kirkbride, 1992). As we suggested above, managers are often seen as legitimate purveyors of directives, of having the "right to manage."

Managers' abilities to manage other employees through social influence and internalization, or social power and compliance, is tied directly to the degree to which these other employees see themselves and managers as sharing a common group membership. There are two ways in which general employees can self-categorize with managers. First, they can see themselves and managers as members of the entire organization, pursuing a common mission (Gaertner, Dovidio, Anastasio, Bachman, & Rust, 1993). Highlighting common fates and providing mission statements, or referring to the organization as a "team," are ways in which managers work to create a shared sense of "us." Second, general employees can recognize their current nonmembership in the management subgroup, but can hold a social mobility ideology (Tajfel, 1975; Tajfel & Turner, 1979). With this, general employees accept the legitimacy of the social power differential, but believe that, through hard work, they can *exit up* from their relatively low status group to the higher status management group (Ellemers, 1993; Ellemers, van Knippenberg, & Wilke, 1990). In this manner, the management group is a group to which they aspire, effectively a future in-group (Moreland & Levine, 1982). In either of these two situations, managers need only offer sufficiently persuasive communications, and employees are likely both to follow and want to follow. Here we have true social influence.

In contrast, however, when general employees fail to self-categorize with management—either concurrently or in the future—then managers must rely on social power to elicit mere compliance. Organizational structure and management practice can easily lead general employees to view management as an out-group. One way this could come about is through the application of unfair management procedures and outcome distributions (see chapters 9 and 15, this volume). Unfair promotion practices, for example, can lead general employees to see only their reflections on the glass ceiling and recognize that they will never be promoted, that they will never move into the management group (see chapter 16, this volume). But if such a state of affairs is unsatisfying for general employees, again we ask, why don't they just leave? The answer is simple: They would if they could. And it is here, through leaving the organization, that the social power imbalance can move into equilibrium.

Three forms of leaving, or exit (Hirschman, 1970), can begin to balance the social power. The first is *psychological exit out*. In this instance, individual employees psychologically disengage from their work, putting in their required effort but failing to commit to extrarole behavior. This is precisely what Pfeffer (1992) was talking about in his analysis of powerlessness. The second form of exit is *full exit out*. Like exit up and psychological exit out described above, this is an individual solution to the social power imbalance. In full exit out, general employees (and management for that matter) simply leave the organization for another so that the relationship ends, as does the social-power imbalance. This, of course, assumes available alternatives to the individual. The third form of exit to balance social power is necessarily a collective endeavor (given the realities of organizational life and social power imbalances that the exit behavior is trying to rectify); this we refer to as *threatened exit out*. In simple terms, this is a strike.

In strikes, workers threaten en masse to exit and, in doing so, threaten not only to end the relationship but the very existence of the organization. It is through this collective threatened exit out that the once socially powerless can gain social power (Kirkbride, 1992; Platow & Hunter, 2001). Of course, threatened exit out, as we are discussing it, requires a shared social identity (e.g., as workers, Kelly & Kelly, 1992), and the concomitant shared ideology of instrumental social change (Hartley, 1992; Tajfel, 1975). In this manner, and quite paradoxically, the socially powerless *need* an "us" and "them" orientation; they need to form impressions and attributions of themselves and the socially powerful, not as unique individuals but as group members (cf. Ellemers, van Rijswijk, Bruins, & de Gilder, 1998). Efforts to individuate employees through organizational structure and policy (via resource power; see Keenoy, 1992), of course, can undermine the development of this shared social identity. If it has developed, however, and threatened exit out is initiated, then the calling in of strikebreakers and scabs represents management's recognition of the renegotiated social-power equilibrium, and a not so subtle attempt to disempower. But, inasmuch as managers have the legitimate right to manage, so too do general employees have the legitimate right to strike. Of course, by using threats instead of full exit out, workers actually signal inter alia continued commitment to the organization.

CLARIFYING THE STEREOTYPING EVIL OF SOCIAL POWER

Our analysis thus far allows us to clarify one of the supposed evils of social power: intergroup stereotyping. Consider Fiske, Bersoff, Borgida, Deaux, and Heilman's (1991) analysis of the discrimination case in which a female employee of Price Waterhouse was refused promotion. As part of a larger team, Fiske et al. successfully argued to the United States Supreme Court that social power relations between the senior management and the female employee caused stereotyping—in this case, gender stereotyping—which led to discriminatory behavior (in the form of nonpromotion). Arguing from a cognitive miser perspective (Fiske & Taylor, 1984), Fiske et al. claimed that the social powerholders in organizations (specifically, senior managers), because of demands on their time and mental resources, cannot individuate and learn the personal characteristics of each employee. These managers must, instead, form broad impressions of others based on social categories. In the case at hand, the category was gender, and the employee, whose personal qualities should have led her to promotion, was denied that promotion. To Fiske et al., being in a socially powerful position *causes* powerholders to stereotype (and, hence, discriminate). Stereotyping is, thus, one of social power's evils.

The social identity analysis, however, suggests an alternative explanation, informing us that stereotyping is *not* the outcome of limited information processing (e.g., Oakes, Haslam, & Turner, 1994; Spears & Haslam, 1997). Stereotyping, like other group processes such as cooperation (Brewer & Schneider, 1990), social attraction (Hogg, 1992), and collective action (Reicher, 1987), is the outcome of social categorization (Haslam, Turner, Oakes, McGarty, & Hayes, 1992; Tajfel, 1981). Stereotyping is the process of forming impressions of "us" and "them" *as group members* and not as unique individuals because it makes sense to do so in the context in which we find ourselves. So how does this bear on Fiske et al.'s argument? Undoubtedly, social power and stereotyping co-occur. However, rather than one causing the other, we argue that they are both outcomes of the same process of social categorization (Reynolds, Oakes, Haslam, Nolan, & Dolnik, 2000; Reynolds, Oakes, Haslam, Turner, & Ryan, in press). If management stereotypes general employees as out-group members (or general employees stereotype management as out-group members, for that matter), then the organization is, by definition, failing in its pursuit of a single mission. It is, by definition, characterized by intergroup categorizations not framed by higher order similarities (chapter 14, this volume). Stereotyping is not one of social power's evils; stereotyping, like social power, is an outcome of intergroup categorization.

Of course, there is one other implication of our analysis. As we said above, for threatened exit out (e.g., industrial strikes) to be successful, the socially powerless *need* "us" and "them" impressions. For collective efforts to coalesce and act in concert, the socially powerless must develop and use social stereotypes (Haslam, Turner, Oakes, Reynolds, & Doosje, in press). These stereotypes provide the normative substrate of people's collective identities (cf. Haslam, 1997; Oakes, 1987; Reicher, Hopkins, & Condor, 1997). They allow people to define "us" and to know who "they" are. Do not be misled by our key theoretical point, however; we are not advocating discrimination or injustice. Rather, our claim is that, in order to harness social power to redress the imbalances in it, the socially powerless must recognize and capitalize on the inter-group nature of power use. When management uses social power against general employees, the employees should never be so naïve as to think they can further their own cause simply through social influence; it is necessary to fight fire with fire.

SOCIAL POWER AND THE CREATION OF LEGITIMATING BELIEFS

With functional dependence on information, socially powerful groups can do more than create impressions, descriptions (e.g., stereotypes), and missions of their own and other groups. They can create, as well, a set of beliefs legitimating their resource and social power through the select provision or framing of communications to both in-group and out-group members. This can come about through actual deceptive messages or a more subtle linguistic masking. For example, with deception, Ng and Bradac (1993; emphasis added) argue that: "Speakers may mislead their hearers by failing to reveal their true position and by failing to admit that they even have a position. Or, more subtly still, speakers may mislead their hearers by *presenting one model of reality while suppressing alternative models*" (pp. 118–119).

So, when workers and management are negotiating new contracts, management may frame holidays as a "privilege" to be granted, rather than an entitlement they may be trying to abolish (Kirkbride, 1992, p. 78). Here, management neither admits to having a position nor presents the alternative view that holidays are rights. Instead, they speak as if there is only one reality.

With the more subtle linguistic masking, by contrast, there is a "rendering of reality so to make it appear different from the 'actual' way of the world. Masking does not withhold true information or present false information as if true, rather it presents true information in an incomplete or partial way under the cover of one or more literary masks" (Ng & Bradac, 1993, p. 145). Thus, for example, even the slightest changes in communication voice (e.g., from active to passive) can alter general impressions, such as responsibility and liking of social actors (Trew, 1979). Platow and Brodie (1999) conclude from their empirical work on linguistic masking that:

> By using such masking techniques, skilled communicators have the ability to create and control the impressions held by readers and listeners . . . this may be particularly powerful in intergroup relations; in these contexts, leaders, for example, can create a reality that justifies potentially discriminatory behavior towards outgroup members, while maintaining support from ingroup members for their own positions. (p. 200)

SUMMARY OF THE THEORETICAL POINTS THUS FAR

So what is the theoretical message, thus far, for organizational psychologists, management, and union representatives? When we examine an organization, our instruments should be calibrated to measure at least three things: (1) reliance on the use of social power tactics, such as contingent control over valued resources (Ng, 1980; Pfeffer, 1981) or tricking people via the control of information (Cialdini, 1993; Ng & Bradac, 1993); (2) actual or threatened exit out by management and general employees (Tajfel, 1975; Thibaut & Kelley, 1959); and (3) the presence of mere compliance rather than internalization (Kelman, 1961; Turner, 1991). These are all *symptoms of power-based intergroup categorizations* within the organization. Sometimes these are symptoms of health, as they represent the nascent forms of social change and social creativity (Haslam, 2001; Haslam, Eggins, & Reynolds, 2001; Oakes & Haslam, 2001). However, it remains the case that true social influence and internalization will never obtain until there is a shared self-categorization between all parties within the organization. It is not until all members of an organization see themselves truly as partners, allied in a collective effort, will the perils of social powerlessness (and the oppressions of social power) dissipate.

SOME RECENT RESEARCH ON THE PERILS OF POWERLESSNESS

To assess empirically some of the perils of powerlessness, Reynolds and Uzubalis (2000; see also Uzubalis, 1999) conducted a study in a large retail company. They measured the degree to which the social categorical relationship between a supervisor and general employees affected the likelihood of employees engaging in organizationally beneficial behaviors (i.e., organizational citizenship behavior). The study respondents were led either to focus on their common group membership with the organization as a whole (i.e., the conditions for social influence), or to focus on the subgroup differences within the organization (i.e., the conditions for social power). They then read two scenarios. In one scenario, a supervisor asked employees to volunteer for a sales techniques course, perceived by employees as benefiting themselves more than the organization. In the other, the supervisor asked employees to work nine unpaid overtime hours, perceived by employees as benefiting the organization more than themselves. In both requests, the supervisor had relatively high resource power (i.e., ability to administer rewards and punishments).

The research design allowed Reynolds and Uzubalis (2000) to determine whether—despite the relatively high levels of resource power—shifts in the social-context framing would affect the relative social influence of the supervisor. To examine this, the critical response measure was employees' reported "happiness" with following the request. This measure was used because it better reflects employees' underlying attitudes to the request; it is possible to be willing to do something through compliance (because of an anticipated reward or punishment) without being happy about it.

It was anticipated that in the subgroup identity condition, employees would be primarily motivated by their own individual concerns, and that requests for collective contributions at the organizational level would fall on deaf ears (i.e., there would be no social influence). This is exactly what happened. The employees were much happier to attend the sales course for their own personal advancement ($M = 4.62$) than volunteer for the unpaid overtime for the collective welfare ($M = 1.84$) *despite the relatively high levels of resource power possessed by the supervisor*. However, when a sense of shared social identity with the supervisor was made salient, social influence was expected to be enhanced. This, again, is exactly what happened. While employees' reported happiness to attend the sales course remained relatively high ($M = 4.00$), their happiness to volunteer for unpaid overtime was substantially enhanced ($M = 3.09$).

In a related unpublished laboratory study by Reynolds, Ryan, and Turner (2002), the effects on individual productivity were measured as a function of the group membership and the relative resource power of a task leader. The leader was selected through either a formal leadership inventory (i.e., the person who scored the highest became leader) or informally on the basis of the group members' names (i.e., the person with the last initial closest in the alphabet to "Z" would be leader). Following previous work, this manipulation of leader selection was used to vary the extent to which the leader would be identified as a member of a salient in-group or as an out-group member. Specifically, the formal selection of leaders was expected to *reduce* shared social identity salience, as well as the associated group commitment and cohesiveness, by highlighting individual *differences* between group members (Haslam, McGarty et al., 1998).

Once chosen, the leader was provided with either high or low resource power by experimental manipulation. High power leaders, for example, had the ability to make decisions and these decisions had to be followed. This manipulation, of course, represents more than resource power; it was, by experimental design, social power (primarily because group members were provided with no alternative groups in which to exit). In this manner, the manipulation of power should *also* have served as a manipulation of social categorization (Reynolds et al., in press).

The task set before the group was to produce as many paper airplanes as possible within a series of quality controls. The main prediction was that productivity would be highest when the leader selection procedure and resource power coincided to maximize a shared social identity with group members (i.e., informally selected leaders with low resource power). In contrast, however, productivity was expected to be lowest when the leader selection procedure and resource power coincided to maximize the *intergroup* relationship between the leader and group members (i.e., formally selected leaders with high resource power). As shown in Figure 10.1, this is exactly what happened. Indeed, in this instance—in which alternative relationships were unavailable and there was no opportunity for firing—group members *did* adopt a "go slow" strategy (Rocker, 1938/1981) in response to the high resource-power out-group leader. Figure 10.1 also shows intermediate levels of productivity in contexts in which leader selection and resource power resulted in ambiguous group membership.

The results of these two studies support our argument that the nature of social categorical relationships between those who hold resource power affects: (1) the overall level of social influence, and (2) the amount of in-role and extrarole behavior that group members perform. Under conditions in which the resource-power holder was more likely to be categorized as an in-group member, people engaged in behaviors that benefited the organization (i.e., unpaid overtime, increased output). When the resource-power holder was perceived as an out-group member, however, people behaved in ways more consistent with Pfeffer's (1992) analysis of the negative implications of powerlessness. Note again, however, that group members *did* have the resource power of their labor, and they chose to withhold it in response to resource-powerful outgroup leaders.

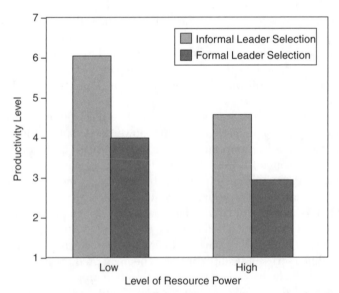

FIGURE 10.1. Mean level of individual productivity as a function of leader resource power and selection method.

IMPLICATIONS FOR ORGANIZATIONAL PRACTICE

The social identity analysis of power has some important implications for organizational practice. As we said above, it suggests that true influence and internalization of managerial directives, for example, will emerge only when there is a shared sense of "us." However, a shared sense of "us" will come about only when employees psychologically perceive themselves and other organizational members—management included—as the same, identical, or interchangeable with each other (Turner, Hogg, Oakes, Reicher, & Wetherell, 1987). Organizational structure and practice (e.g., fair procedures and outcome distributions) will go a long way to create this shared social identity. But intergroup categorizations, such as "management" and "general employees" (and, hence, social power use), mitigate against this shared social identity. The very process of management providing "directives" reinforces the salience (indeed, highlights the reality) of the intergroup categorization.

There is one organizational practice, however, that creates not just psychological interchangeability, but functional interchangeability *while simultaneously recognizing the real resource and social power of all employees.* This is, of course, participative decision making. With participative decision making, there is a mutual recognition of the special skills, knowledge, and basic labor resources that general employees bring to an organization. There is also the admission that the organization *depends* on these resources for its very survival. And it is this dependence that allows the resource power to be converted into social power, signaling the beginning of promotive interdependence (Deutsch, 1968), cooperation toward a mutually desired goal (Sherif & Sherif, 1953), functional interchangeability, and ultimately, a shared sense of "us" (Platow & Hunter, 2001; Walker & Crogan, 1998).

Although some authors report mixed success with some programs (Harley, 1999; Kelly & Kelly, 1991; Parker, 1993; Wagner, 1994), certain forms of participation have had a significant impact on job satisfaction, productivity, and turnover (i.e., full exit out; Cohen & Ledford, 1990 cited in Ledford, 1993; Kelly & Kelly, 1991; Lawler, 1993; Ledford, Cummings, & Wright, 1992 cited in Ledford, 1993). In the limited space available, we discuss the possible implications of participative decision making for the theoretical and empirical points we have discussed thus far.

Ledford (1993) describes three types of participative decision making. These differ from each other in the extent to which resource power is shared within an organization (see also Lawler, 1986) and, hence, the degree to which: (1) organizational members are functionally interchangeable, and (2) the mutual dependence is recognized and embraced. The first of these is *suggestion involvement.* This requires the least recognition of general employee resource and social power by management, and instantiates the lowest degree of functional interchangeability. With suggestion involvement, employees can make suggestions for change (they have "process control" or "voice"), but are not involved in actual decision making (they do *not* have "decision control"; see chapter 15, this volume). Because general employees' abilities actually to shape organizational policy is highly constrained, if not truly absent, Keenoy (1992, p. 99) considers this more as a "unilateral pretension" on the part of management. To be sure, voice can go a long way to create a shared sense of social identity (chapter 9, this volume). But voice that falls on deaf (or even merely censored) ears, is neither social power nor social influence; it is simply impotent.

The second type of participative decision making Ledford (1993) describes is *job involvement.* In this case, management grants general employees the ability to make decisions about their specific work, and often includes the introduction of self-managed work teams. In these teams, employees take over a series of managerial functions, such as work design and problem solving. Here we have the ability for social power *and* social influence to emerge. As long as management's paternalistic granting of decision-making abilities is seen for what it is (i.e., paternalistic granting and, hence, tokenistic), then an intergroup relationship is likely to be maintained between general employees and management; and this relationship will be characterized by social power and mere compliance (with management remaining more socially powerful). The work teams themselves, however, can provide the basis for a shared social identity and, hence, true social influence and internalization, not to mention strong work motivation, creativity, and productivity (Haslam, Powell, & Turner, 2000; Reynolds, Eggins, & Haslam, 2001; van Knippenberg, 2000a).

One particularly insidious outcome of job involvement, and the team concept in particular, is "management-by-stress" wherein "a kind of worker empowerment takes place, but only insofar as it conforms to an even more carefully regimented shop-floor regime" (Parker, 1993, p. 250). Management-by-stress is characterized by structural changes in organizations such as just-in-time resource systems and the use of teams and interteam antagonism. Parker highlights both the positive and negative consequences of such schemes, including work intensification and increased productivity, as well as unpaid overtime, forced redundancy, stress, and burnout. Parker (1993) cites a paper by Rosenfeld (1989) in which Canadian Auto Workers claim that the "truth is that management's agenda is not about surrendering its power but of finding more sophisticated ways to extend it." Indeed, rather than overcoming the problems of social power use, job involvement may simply serve to increase them (see also chapter 3, this volume).

To some extent, the negative outcomes of job involvement emerge because employees identify more with their work, take more collective responsibility, and increase their output. In this way, the organization benefits from the social motivations that stem from psychological identification with a work team or group. However, if employees feel there is a fundamental problem with the organizational system, they have very little social influence (or social power) to change it. They are unable to inform decisions and challenge organizational activities that perpetuate negative outcomes (e.g., feelings of exploitation, work practices that promote burnout). Over time, any negative feelings could diminish employees' self-categorization as a team or organizational member and impact negatively on organizational outcomes. Consequently, any gains from such participation schemes are likely to be difficult to maintain over time.

To overcome these problems, the third type of participative decision making Ledford (1993) describes is *high involvement* (or "cooperative alternatives," Keenoy, 1992, p. 106). In this instance, general employees help manage the organization and are involved in decision-making in a range of areas related to organizational activity. Here, finally, is functional organizational interchangeability. Here, finally, general-employee resource power is recognized and treated with respect (cf. chapter 9, this volume). And here, finally, social power and mere compliance are most likely to wither away as employees self-categorize as equal organizational members, engaging in mutual social influence and internalizing the goals and values of the collective enterprise.

Unfortunately, given the structure of most organizations in Western industrialized nations, managers often view high involvement participation as difficult to implement because it often requires significant change to the organizational structure. But this difficulty obtains only because the current ideologies, legitimated through social power differentials (as described above), blind people to considering other possibilities. Ledford (1993) argues explicitly that high involvement strategies are rare because "they are inconsistent with the dominant management ideology and the fundamental design principles of most contemporary organizations" (p. 150; see also Conger & Kanungo, 1988b; Lawler, 1992). Simply put, those with social power in organizations prefer suggestion and job involvement over high involvement participation. But recognizing the psychological process that led to the legitimization of these ideologies equips general employees with at least some of the tools (if not weapons) they need to create an equilibrium in the social power imbalance and work toward a common and shared social identity.

Overall, the organizational benefits that stem from employee participation are most sustainable when the participation results in real resource power for general employees, leading to admission of mutual dependence, functional interchangeability, and, ultimately, the creation of psychological interchangeability, shared social identity, and mutual social influence. This does not mean that high involvement will always be a success story for organizations. There are always going to be points of conflict between subgroups with different organizational interests (chapter 14, this volume). But, because high involvement strategies involve genuine functional interchangeability between organizational members, they have the most potential to address these differences, create a shared self-category, and deliver social identity-related organizational dividends.

CONCLUSION

In this chapter, we have outlined a social–psychological analysis of power and powerlessness. Based on theory and research within the social identity approach, we were able to distinguish between social influence and internalization, on the one hand, and social power and compliance on the other. Social influence is a product of shared self-categorizations (Turner, 1991). Social power, however, is the outcome of resource power, intergroup categorizations, and dependence (i.e., inability to exit). By recognizing social power's intergroup nature, we were able to clarify the co-occurrence of power and stereotyping, and highlight why stereotyping on the part of the socially powerless may allow for collective action (i.e., threatened exit out) to redress the power imbalance. With our theoretical analysis as background, we presented new empirical evidence showing that directives from socially powerful out-group leaders will lead people to employ their own resource power to "go slow," while in-group leaders can influence people to "go the extra mile."

Our fundamental lesson, then, is that the blurring (actually, the removal) of the boundaries between management and employees—created through, for example, high involvement participative decision making—can create the shared self-categorization and social identification with the organization conducive to social influence and internalization, as well as productivity and commitment. Our advice for participative decision making is offered with caution, however, as partial empowerment of employees to make suggestions or decisions about their job but not to negotiate and shape the ideology of the organization in general may have negative consequences.

We, like others, believe that the most sustainable organizational dividends ensue when general employees have a genuine power sharing arrangement within the organization (e.g., Lawler, 1992; see also chapter 14, this volume). Under conditions where social categorical differentiation continues to exist between the power holders and more powerless others, "powerlessness" will remain an organization's last dirty secret.

PART V

CHANGE AND CHANGE MANAGEMENT

Identity, Culture, and Change in Organizations
A Social Identity Analysis and Three Illustrative Cases

NAOMI ELLEMERS
University of Leiden

O rganizations are often described as dynamic systems that continually have to adapt to societal, economical, and competitive market considerations in order to become or remain successful (see also chapter 7, this volume). As a result, in most if not all organizations at least some resources are devoted to developing new products, strategies, skills, or managerial policies (e.g., Huber & Glick, 1993). Consequently, in scientific Industrial/ Organizational psychology as well as in more popular handbooks on management, substantial effort is devoted to analyzing such change processes in order to understand how to achieve organizational change (also referred to as organizational learning, development, or redesign) most effectively.

Whereas a range of relevant factors and processes has been addressed in this literature, the aim of this chapter is to examine the specific role of culture and identification in organizational change. This is in line with contemporary insights that, for the functioning of modern-day organizations, identity processes have become equally if not more important than characteristics of the organizational structure (Albert, Ashforth, & Dutton, 2000). The term *culture* is commonly used to denote important goals and values in the organization that determine how people perform their jobs, and guide the way they interact with each other; identity indicates the extent to which individual workers are committed to the culture, in the sense that they subscribe to these goals and values or have internalized them into their self-image as workers (Albert & Whetten, 1985; Dutton, Dukerich, & Harquail, 1994). Thus, to the extent that change involves a redefinition of the goals and values that are important

LIVERPOOL
JOHN MOORES UNIVERSITY
AVRIL ROBARTS LRC
TEL. 0151 231 4022

to the organization, or requires people to interact with each other in a different way, it is obvious that both the nature of the culture and the degree of commitment to it is likely to impact upon the change process in important ways.

The first part of this chapter aims to summarize how organizational culture and identity are usually conceived in mainstream organizational psychology, and how they are seen to affect processes of organizational change. The second part will examine how an analysis in terms of social identity processes may further contribute to our understanding of these processes. Finally, three cases will be presented in order to investigate the validity of an analysis in social identity terms, and to illustrate further the consequences of culture and identity for organizational change.

ORGANIZATIONAL CULTURE AND IDENTITY: ENDURINGNESS VS. ADAPTABILITY

An influential analysis by Albert and Whetten (1985) considers organizational culture and organizational identity as closely related concepts, with the term *culture* mainly referring to the content of important organizational values (defining the system), and *identity* to the strength of commitment of individual workers to that culture (defining the self; see also Fiol, Hatch, & Golden-Biddle, 1998). Albert and Whetten's (1985) definition of organizational identity is commonly cited in the literature. It refers to three necessary criteria, according to which an organizational identity (1) encompasses what is *central* to the organization; (2) indicates how the organization is *distinct*; and (3) provides an *enduring* sense of continuity. While this general definition has been widely adopted, the third criterion (*enduringness*) has been subject to considerable discussion, particularly in the context of organizational change.

Some theorists subscribe to the view of enduringness. They maintain that—even when faced with a crisis due to environmental change—organizations try to retain their current values (Starbuck, Greve, & Hedberg, 1978), and propose that identity maintenance can constitute an important (if not always explicit) function of the business strategy (Gagliardi, 1986; chapter 12, this volume). Indeed, resistance to change is sometimes explained by arguing that the desired change does not fit the identity of the organization (Fox-Wolfgramm, Boal, & Hunt, 1998). This leads to the conclusion that in order for organizational change to be successful, it has to be preceded by a corresponding change in identity (Barr, Stimert, & Huff, 1992).

However, others have emphasized that for organizations to deal adequately with environmental change, it is crucial that they show some degree of "adaptive instability" (e.g., Gioia, 1998). In other words, the requirement that organizational identity adaptively responds to changing circumstances implies that the criterion of enduringness cannot always apply (Gioia & Thomas, 1996). Indeed, in more recent publications it is even argued that, from a postmodern perspective, identity itself is nothing more than a social construction. According to this reasoning, the "existence" of an identity is an illusion, and this in turn would render the issue of enduringness simply irrelevant (Gioia, Schultz, & Corley, 2000). A similar argument has been proposed from a psychodynamic point of view, where it is assumed that organizational learning is hampered by so-called collective ego defenses (Brown & Starkey, 2000). In this view, efforts to maintain continuity of identity are considered maladaptive, while a "wise" organization is characterized by an adaptive self-concept.

CHANGE MODELS

A review of recent developments in the area of organizational change has classified research as dealing with four different topics (Armenakis & Bedeian, 1999). Specifically, researchers in this area have addressed issues of (1) *content* (the nature of the change); (2) *context* (the role of the environment); (3) *process* (how change evolves); and (4) *outcome* (which criteria indicate the achievement of change). In view of our current discussion, any insights into the *process* of change would seem particularly relevant. To date, work in this area has mainly focused on the question of the number and nature of the different phases that should be distinguished in this process, resulting in models containing anything from four (Isabella, 1990) or five (Judson, 1991) to eight (Kotter, 1995) or nine (Galpin, 1996) phases, describing how change is effected.

These phases are usually described as stages of a continuing process that progressively develops over time. This is not only evident from the terms that are used to describe the change process (e.g., Albert & Whetten, 1985, characterize the organization as "drifting towards" the next phase), but also from the fact that some theorists even specify the amount of time that is necessary for each phase (e.g., Judson, 1991). In this perspective, resistance has been conceptualized as just another stage in the change process, implying a certain inevitability both in its occurrence, as well as in its dissolution (Jaffe, Scott, & Tobe, 1994).

At first sight, this would seem to suggest that these change models mainly address so-called first-order change that involves incremental adaptation of the organization; for example, to enhance its efficiency. However, similar statements are made with reference to second-order change that is more fundamental and obtrusive, because it also impacts upon the current goals and norms of the organization (see also Pettigrew, Woodman, & Cameron, 2001; Sashkin & Burke, 1987). Theorists have suggested that second-order change may be difficult to achieve when it affects the existing culture (Vollman, 1996), or implies a loss of identity (Albert & Whetten, 1985). However, this has not resulted in a further analysis of this issue, because it is generally assumed that those who manage change are not in the position to address this particular source of resistance (Fitzgerald, 1988; Judson, 1991).

Accordingly, the change process has mainly been analyzed in terms of the effects of infrastructural provisions and reinforcement mechanisms, or has examined different techniques of communication and diffusion of information (Armenakis, Harris, & Feild, 2001; Galpin, 1996; Pasmore & Fagans, 1992), usually aiming at alleviating *instrumental* concerns that are viewed as the primary source of resistance to change (Judson, 1991), or at least as the main source of resistance that is affected by acts of management. Indeed, a recent issue of the *Academy of Management Journal* that was devoted to organizational change, takes a similar approach. When setting the agenda for future research, methodological difficulties (instead of theoretical questions) are proposed as the main challenge in gaining further insight into the change process (Pettigrew et al., 2001). This is reflected in the 10 papers published in this issue, that mainly describe examples of *business* processes and how these are transformed, rather than focusing on understanding the *psychological* processes involved in organizational change.

Thus, although researchers who examine organizational culture and identity seem to agree that a central question for theory and research is how identity facilitates or hinders organizational change (Whetten & Godfrey, 1998), previous efforts to examine the change process, or to develop change models, have paid little systematic attention to culture change and the identity processes involved in such change (Woodman, 1989). Accordingly, it has been suggested that insights from related fields of science might be necessary to gain further insight into important sources of resistance to change (Armenakis & Bedeian, 1999).

SOCIAL IDENTITY AND CHANGE

In the context of social identity theory, it has been extensively argued and empirically demonstrated that people prefer membership in a group that can be distinguished positively from other groups, while they tend to resist association with groups that provide them with a negative identity (see Mullen, Brown, & Smith, 1992, for an overview). However, social identity theory was originally formulated to understand identity processes in *dynamic* situations (Tajfel, 1974). Indeed, considerable work has been conducted in order to show that the relative standing of the group may be subject to change (see Ellemers & Barreto, 2000, for an overview). Accordingly, it seems that people may strategically adapt their patterns of identification with different possible groups in order to accommodate the effects of prospective change. For instance, one way to cope with inclusion in a negatively valued group is to dissociate the self from that group, at least when there is scope to gain access to another, more attractive one. Alternatively, people may opt to work together for the improvement of their collective plight (as an alternative to individual distancing), providing that such group-level change seems feasible (e.g., Ellemers, van Knippenberg, & Wilke, 1990; Ellemers, Wilke, & van Knippenberg, 1993).

Most of the empirical work and further theoretical refinements in this tradition have focused on the effects of change prospects for those who are *dissatisfied* with the status quo, and hence tend to perceive change primarily in terms of the opportunities it offers for position *improvement* of individuals or collectives (Ellemers, 1993). However, in his theory, Tajfel also explicitly considers the consequences of change for those who are happy with the status quo. He argues that when external circumstances render the maintenance of subjectively valued group characteristics insecure, this is likely to result in feelings of threat, which in turn should elicit attempts to preserve the current systems of social relations (Tajfel, 1975). Indeed, with reference to similar arguments proposed within relative deprivation theory, Tajfel (1978) posits that insecurity about the future of a subjectively attractive group causes feelings of threat and elicits resistance to change (Ellemers, Doosje, Van Knippenberg, & Wilke, 1992).

More recently, it has been argued from a social identity perspective that the implications of prospects for change are likely to be different, depending on the extent to which the individual identifies with the group and what it stands for (Doosje, Ellemers, & Spears, in press; Ouwerkerk & Ellemers, in press). That is, while change is unlikely to impact upon the identity of those who are loosely connected to the group, people who identify strongly with the group may feel the self is implicated if the outcomes or fate of their group are subject to change (Branscombe, Ellemers, Spears, & Doosje, 1999; Ellemers, Spears, & Doosje, in press). Thus, according to a social identity perspective, people who perceive their identity as group members as positive and distinct from other groups, should feel jeopardized by any change that may challenge the current standing or distinctiveness of their group, but only to the extent that they identify as members of that group. This implies that when change is viewed as implicating a loss of distinctive group features or important group values, this is likely to elicit resistance, especially from those who identify strongly with the group in its current form (see chapter 12, this volume, for a similar argument in relation to organizational mergers).

One important implication of approaching change from this specific point of view—that is, with a focus on subjectively attractive groups instead of groups that are disaffected by their current standing—is that it places the value of identification (or commitment to the group) in a different perspective. Indeed, social identity theorists as well as researchers in the area of organizational commitment generally tend to accentuate the positive outcomes of identification or group commitment (e.g., Ellemers, 2001b). That is, those who take pride in their membership in the organization and feel strongly committed to it are generally seen as reliable workers, who internalize group norms, and are willing to invest effort to help achieve collective goals (e.g., Armenakis & Bedeian, 1999; Dutton, Dukerich, & Harquail, 1994; Woodman, 1989; see chapter 6, this volume). However, whether or not such adherence to characteristic features and values of the organization is desirable not only depends on the point of view that is taken (i.e., is it desirable for the workers, for management, or for both?) but is also determined to an important extent by the *content* of these features and values and how these relate to some preferred end state (see also chapters 2 and 3, this volume). In view of our present discussion, this implies that, from the perspective of those who desire and approve of change, strong identification with or commitment to a particular work or organizational culture can result in undesirable outcomes, in particular when the underlying view of how things should be done is in flux—as it is likely to be during organizational change. As a result, commitment to the (previous) culture is not only likely to elicit resistance to change, but can even result in *dis*identification with the organization as provisioned by the agents of change (see also Dukerich, Kramer, & Parks, 1998).

As has been argued in the literature on organizational culture and identity (and is evident from the summary above), changing circumstances may seem to require adaptive change from the group. Our analysis in terms of social identity processes highlights the possibility that the adherence to (previously normative) attitudes and behaviors—shown by group members who strongly identify with the current culture—may seem maladaptive to those in the organization who no longer endorse the values underlying these attitudes and behaviors.

On the basis of a social identity analysis, more specific predictions can therefore be made about the psychological processes elicited by change prospects as well as their likely consequences. Specifically, we hypothesize that:

1. Those members of the organization who identify more strongly with the present culture are more likely to feel threatened by impending organizational change;
2. Such identity threat is an important source of resistance to change, or at least as important as other more instrumental considerations; and
3. To the extent that the change process explicitly addresses identity concerns, this may alleviate feelings of threat and hence reduce—or even eliminate—resistance tendencies.

While this argument may seem relatively straightforward, it is important to realize that, although the mechanisms involved may not be inherently complex, in order to derive a meaningful analysis of actual change episodes on the basis of these insights, one first has to examine the nature of the existing organizational culture, and assess the extent to which aspects of this culture are likely to be challenged by the impending change.

Having developed this argument, it is important to examine whether an analysis in social identity terms indeed provides further understanding of concrete cases of organizational change. The next section therefore discusses three cases of organizational change in which we assessed whether identity processes were relevant to the occurrence of resistance.

CASE 1: TEACHING INNOVATION IN SECONDARY EDUCATION

The first case presented here, consists of a large-scale teaching innovation in the context of secondary education in the Netherlands. In accordance with guidelines initiated by the Dutch Ministry of Education, starting in August 1999, all public secondary schools in the Netherlands were required to introduce new ways of teaching in their final years (which was indicated as "The Second Phase"). The main aim of this change was to provide a more adequate preparation for further education at the college or university level, as well as to get students acquainted with the work requirements of a dynamic and information-oriented society. One important way to achieve these goals was to turn the traditional schools into so-called houses of study. That is, instead of classroom teaching in particular subjects (e.g., English, physics) according to a fixed schedule, students would independently work on the acquisition and application of knowledge in a number of broad areas (e.g., culture and society, nature and technology).

For the teachers, this implied an important role change. While they were primarily working on the transfer of specialist knowledge to the students in the traditional system, after the teaching innovation they were required to provide guidance at a more general level, in order to facilitate the students' independent learning process (Veugelers, 1998). Thus, instead of teaching the students about the subjects they had been trained in, teachers were now supposed to "teach students how to learn." In public opinion media, there was considerable discussion about the rationale underlying this innovation, and there were several indications that teachers were generally not in favor of the proposed changes. Nevertheless, the schools were required to adopt the innovations by the date specified, and many school organizations requested their teachers to take additional training that was supposed to help them implement the new structure, for instance by showing them how to "teach students to learn." (Two years after the policy was introduced it became clear that the innovation had been unsuccessful, and steps were taken to adapt the Ministry of Education's formal guidelines accordingly.)

In the context of this change, we aimed to assess whether a social identity analysis might help elucidate the causes of resistance to the proposed innovation (van Maanen & Ellemers, 1999). We argued that the required role change was likely to impinge in important ways on the professional identity of the teachers involved. Thus, to the extent that teachers experienced identity threat as a result, this might in turn lead them to resist the impending change. In order to test the validity of this argument, we examined teachers from different schools, in the context of their participation in teacher training courses. At the time of our investigation, research participants had an average of 20 years of experience as school teachers in the traditional system.

In line with our theoretical analysis, we asked the participating teachers to indicate the extent to which they perceived the innovation as a *threat* to their professional identity (e.g., "I am afraid that my contribution as a teacher will become less important for what the students are going to learn"), and assessed their willingness to *change* (e.g., "I am prepared to exert myself to help implement the teaching innovations"). Principal components' analysis confirmed that the scales we used to assess these two constructs indeed represented two orthogonal dimensions. Nevertheless, the results of this study showed that there was a strong relation between perceived threat to professional identity on the one hand, and resistance to change on the other. That is, the more that teachers perceived the impending innovation as a threat to their professional identity, the less willing they were to implement the requested changes. Consistent with our second prediction above, this case thus provides some initial support for the argument that perceived identity threat can be a powerful source of resistance to change.

CASE 2: THE NATIONAL COUNCIL FOR CHILD PROTECTION

A second case of change that we examined, concerned the National Council for Child Protection in the Netherlands. This organization is a government institution, employing welfare workers and lawyers who are strongly motivated to help protect the rights of children. However, recent government policy resulting in budget cuts, had required the organization to increase its cost-effectiveness. In order to facilitate this transition from a normative to a more utilitarian organization (cf., Albert & Whetten, 1985), a firm of organizational consultants was hired. The consultancy firm redefined the work that was done in terms of certain "products" that were delivered, and developed norms as to the acceptable cost of each product, which was partly operationalized as the amount of time employees were allowed to spend on a particular case. Thus, instead of the ideological concerns and values that originally guided the work of employees at the National Council for Child Protection, they now were supposed to orient themselves to economic considerations, and minimize the costs of their efforts to help children at risk (see also Albert & Whetten, 1985). This caused a great deal of turmoil in the organization, and there were various overt indications of resistance to the proposed changes.

In terms of a social identity analysis, again this was a case of change in which the professional identity of the workers involved as well as the organizational culture that had developed were both heavily implicated. Hence, we predicted that the more workers identified with the organization and its culture, the more they would perceive the impending change as a threat to their identity, and the more they would resist the requested change as a result. In order to assess whether there was evidence for the occurrence of the hypothesized process, we asked employees who were about to participate in sessions designed to inform them about the impending changes to complete a number of questionnaires (Van der Weijden & Ellemers, 2000).

Employees from different regions of the country, and representing the full range of jobs within the organization participated in our investigation. On average they had been working for the Council for 13 years. In the questionnaire, we asked them about their identification with the Council and what it stands for (e.g., "The National Council for Child Protection is very important to me"), about the threat they experienced due to the impending change (e.g., "I think that the quality of my professional work will deteriorate when I have to work according to these norms"), and about their feelings of resistance to the intended changes (e.g., "I am against the introduction of cost-effective work norms").

The results of this study again were consistent with our social identity analysis, in line with both predictions 1 and 2 above. That is, regression analyses revealed that the more employees identified with the Council the more they experienced threat as a result of the request to start working in a more cost-effective way. Furthermore, the more they experienced such threat, the stronger their resistance to the impending change.

CASE 3: THE HUNGARIAN POLICE FORCE

The third case of change we examined was that of the Hungarian Police Force. After the revolt in 1989, there were a number of far-reaching political and societal changes in Hungary, which also had important consequences for the Hungarian police. Under the communist regime, the police had been an ideologically based political force, which was used by those in power as an instrument to oppress and control the public. After 1989, it was obvious that the police force had to transform into a public service institution, which required a fundamentally different kind of organization, as well as different norms of professional conduct. In order to help achieve these changes (and to foster control of criminal behavior and other illegal activities in central Europe), the

Hungarian Police Force received substantial help from police forces in other European countries. However, while most of this help was provided in the way of material support and equipment (computers, squad cars), the contribution of the Dutch police force took a different form. They developed a collaborative project (the "Police Partnership Program"), that established direct international exchanges between groups of individual police officers in order to introduce those working in Hungary to Western European standards of professional policing, and to help them adapt to their new identity in the police force.

For our study (Ellemers, Németh, & Mlicki, 2000), we approached all participants in the exchange program (from across 20 regions in Hungary) as well as a matched control group of colleagues who had not participated in the Dutch collaboration, to fill out a questionnaire. This yielded a 74% response rate and resulted in a sample that represented workers at different levels of the organization. The vast majority (83%) of research participants was male. On average participants had 14 years of organizational tenure. The questionnaire assessed identification with the communist ideology about policework (current organizational culture, e.g., "As a policeman, I should represent the state"), the experience of identity threat (e.g., "I feel questioned in my professional competence"), and resistance to change (e.g., "I am not willing to invest energy in any changes"). Again, a principal components analysis confirmed that these different constructs were represented in our data as independent measures. Additionally, we assessed a number of alternative considerations, representing more instrumental sources of resistance to organizational change (e.g., perceived capabilities and career prospects).

In the analysis of these results, we compared participants in the exchange program with those who had not participated, after correcting for the effects of any demographical differences (age, gender) or imbalance in other background variables (e.g., tenure, rank, and level of education). From a social identity perspective, the core hypothesis was that identification with the current organizational culture would cause feelings of threat and resistance to change. However, we expected that those who had been subjected to the exchange program, and hence had been given the opportunity to start developing a new professional identity, would experience less identity threat and accordingly report less resistance to change.

When comparing participants in the exchange program with the matched control group, it was clear that participants in the exchange identified less with the old organizational culture, and more with new professional standards for police work, experienced less threat, and displayed less resistance to change than those who had not had the opportunity to learn about the new professional identity they were supposed to adopt. Regression analyses examining the interrelations between these different variables were consistent with the hypothesized psychological processes. That is, we established that identification with the current organizational culture was a predictor of identity threat, which in turn predicted resistance to change. Conversely, adoption of the new professional identity resulted in less identity threat, and hence predicted more willingness to work at the achievement of change. Finally, results revealed that while instrumental considerations (such as perceived individual capabilities and career prospects) also affected the level of resistance, these effects were less strong and occurred relatively independently of the effects of identity concerns.

In sum, our observations with respect to this third case of change are again in line with a social identity analysis, as they corroborate all three hypotheses specified above. That is (a) we established that those who identified most strongly with the present culture were most likely to feel threatened by impending organizational change; (b) that this identity threat was an important source of resistance to change even in the context of other more instrumental considerations; and (c) that feelings of threat and resistance to change were reduced for those who were helped to adopt a new professional identity.

CONCLUSIONS

This chapter has summarized ways in which identity, culture, and change are usually approached in organizational psychology. On the one hand this revealed that the adaptibility versus enduringness of organizational culture and identity is likely to impact upon the success of organizational change in important ways (see also Dutton & Dukerich, 1991). On the other hand, however, it turned out that current change models have not systematically specified (or empirically examined) the psychological processes which may be directed at maintaining the current organizational culture, and hence foster resistance to change. In light of this lacuna, the aim of this chapter has been to develop an analysis in social identity terms, based on what this perspective has to say about the effects of identity maintenance, the experience of threat due to change prospects, and the behavioral responses that this is likely to elicit. Three cases of organizational change were presented in order to examine the validity of some specific hypotheses resulting from our social identity analysis, as well as to gain some initial insights into possible interventions that may successfully address identity-based resitance to change.

In line with the proposition of Armenakis and Bedeian (1999), it would seem that related fields of science (in this case, social psychology) may indeed yield insights that complement and further specify what we know about organizational change from the I/O literature. In this particular case, the incorporation of social identity insights in the analysis of organizational change enables us to gain a better understanding of the psychological processes involved, and yields some concrete suggestions as to what to take into account when designing procedures to facilitate the change process.

Obviously, in this chapter we focused on culture and identity in the context of change, without pretending to provide an exhaustive analysis either of the change process or of the range of possbile factors that may elicit resistance to change (for some discussion of these points see Veenstra & Haslam, 2000). However, while identity considerations were crucial in the three cases of change examined here, this is not necessarily true for other instances of change. Some changes will have little impact on organizational culture or people's identities, and hence these are less likely to be met with this particular form of resistance. Nevertheless, it does generally seem to be relevant to attempt to understand issues of culture and identity in change. First, culture and identity often constitute an important determinant of whether change can be successfully achieved, and second, culture and identity have not been systematically addressed in research on organizational change—perhaps because they have been deemed inaccessible to intervention attempts. However, the cases presented here show that it is possible to derive novel insights about culture, identity, and change in organizations by locating this topic at the crossroads of different areas of research.

What, then, are the novel insights derived here? First, it has become clear that—in contrast to what is often assumed—there may be a downside to high levels of identification with the organization or commitment to the organizational culture, at least, from the perspective of the proponents of change. While highly committed workers generally are willing to exert themselves on behalf of the collective, the nature of the organizational culture and the content of organizational values determine the direction and focus of the efforts that workers display. When this particular culture or these work values are no longer considered desirable (for instance by those who fear that they prevent the organization from adapting to environmental changes), high levels of identification and commitment may work against instead of for the organization.

A second important conclusion from this analysis is that the discussion in I/O psychology of whether culture and identity should be seen as adaptable or enduring seems somewhat irrelevant (see also Hatch, 1993). Instead, a more constructive approach would seem to involve attempts:

1. to uncover the *conditions under which* the organizational culture and identity can be considered as enduring (or not);
2. to predict *for whom* in the organization this is most likely to be important; and
3. to specify the *circumstances* that require either enduringness or adaptability of culture and identity for optimal organizational success.

For instance, in some business sectors (e.g., information technology) it is essential that organizations quickly adapt to a changing environment. Thus, under these circumstances it may be disadvantageous if workers cling to a particular way of getting things done. However, other organizations (e.g., those providing legal support) quite possibly thrive on an image of dependability, which may be conveyed by changing as little as possible (at least in the way clients are approached and service is provided). Within organizations there are also likely to be differences, as some constitutents may be more commit-ted to a particular culture than others, for instance depending on the nature or level of their job (see also Becker, Billings, Eveleth, & Gilbert, 1996). In-deed, while some managers maintain that they don't care what the nature of the business is or how it is carried out, as long as it runs well, such concrete work aspects are expected to be much more meaningful to those who are involved in the day-to-day activities of the organization, if only because what they are doing and how they are doing it is closely related to their professional expertise and standing in the organization.

Thus, by considering the social identity aspects of organizational culture and change, existing insights are put into an alternative perspective, and new questions emerge. While it has become clear that changes affecting the way people define themselves are likely to be met with resistance, this analysis also offers scope to better understand such resistance as ensuing from identity threat, and specifies that in order for a transition to be made a redefinition of professional identity may be required for those who were most committed to the organization as it was.

12

Organizational Identification Following a Merger
The Importance of Agreeing to Differ

ESTHER VAN LEEUWEN
Free University of Amsterdam
DAAN VAN KNIPPENBERG
Erasmus University Rotterdam

*M*ergers are unmistakably popular in the corporate world. Hardly a day goes by without newspapers reporting on yet another merger, acquisition, or takeover. Whereas initial reports of a merger typically describe a blissful state resembling that of a couple announcing their engagement, the optimistic attitude toward a corporate marriage generally does not last very long. Scientific and popular literature seem to be in agreement that mergers are a powerful source of stress, hostility, and resistance. One of the frequently cited consequences of a merger is a loss of psychological attachment to the organization (Buono, Bowditch, & Lewis, 1985; Dutton, Dukerich, & Harquail, 1994; van Knippenberg & van Leeuwen, 2001). It is often thought that a prolonged and even strengthened attachment to the old, premerger organization inhibits the adoption of the new postmerger organizational identity. In this chapter, an alternative approach to post-merger identification is presented, proposing that it is not the continuation of one's organizational identity that prevents the postmerger organization from being internalized, but rather a threat to the continued existence of that identity. We will first discuss the theoretical framework that constitutes the basis of our analysis. Subsequently, data from three experimental studies will be presented to illustrate our point, and finally, our argument will be discussed in the light of literature pertaining to organizational fit and merger integration patterns.

A SOCIAL IDENTITY APPROACH TO MERGERS

The theoretical approach lying at the core of our analysis is the social identity approach. Social identity theory (Tajfel, 1978; Tajfel & Turner, 1986), and self-categorization theory (Turner, 1985; Turner, Hogg, Oakes, Reicher, & Wetherell, 1987) can both be considered theories of the social self. Although the theories differ somewhat in their emphasis on motivational and cognitive aspects, there is consensus among them in the assumption that membership in social groups forms an important basis for self-definition. Self-categorization contributes to an individual's *social identity*, which is defined as "that part of an individual's self-concept which derives from his knowledge of his membership of a social group (or groups) together with the value and emotional significance attached to that group membership" (Tajfel, 1978, p. 63). The strength of a social identity is reflected in the degree of identification with the category in question. More specifically, social identification refers to the extent to which people view themselves in collective terms, consider themselves part of a larger grouping, and form a psychological bond with others that can exist independently of any physical contact (Deaux, 1996). Social identification can reflect membership in a broad range of groups, social categories, and social aggregates, including organizations. Ashforth and Mael (1989) propose that, through organizational identification, organizational membership reflects on the self-concept in the same way that (other) social group memberships do (see also Pratt, 1998). Moreover, social identification is related to an individual's functioning in an organizational context, thereby affecting a broad range of organizational outcomes such as attitudes toward the organization, commitment to the organization and its goals, effort and productivity, and organizational citizenship behavior (Dutton et al., 1994; Ouwerkerk, Ellemers, & de Gilder, 1999; van Knippenberg, 2000a; see chapter 2, this volume).

Given the importance of organizational identification for both practical (i.e., the organization's productivity) and theoretical reasons (i.e., the internalization of an altered aggregate as part of one's self-definition), the question arises as to how identification with the organization is affected by a merger. Organizational identification is affected by a variety of factors, many of which can also play a role in the complex process of merging (for a discussion of factors affecting identification, see, for example, chapter 1, this volume; Ashforth & Mael, 1989; Pratt, 1998; Hogg & Abrams, 1988; Tajfel, 1978a; Turner et al., 1987). One of these factors, however, is more or less embedded in the very definition of a merger and is central to the research presented in this chapter: a change to the organization's *distinctiveness*. As argued above (see also chapter 1, this volume), through organizational identification, organizations provide their members with a sense of who they are. Accordingly, the desire for self-definition may be one of the driving forces behind social and organizational identification (Hogg, 2000; Pratt, 2000). Distinctiveness may be derived from the organization's values and practices, its mission, or any other factor that provides the organization with a niche or otherwise differentiates the organization from comparable other organizations (Albert & Whetten, 1985; Dutton et al., 1994; Mael & Ashforth, 1992). Because these distinctive aspects of organizational identity play a special role in helping to define individuals as members of the organization, organizational distinctiveness is directly related to organizational identification (Dutton et al., 1994; Mael & Ashforth, 1992; cf. Brewer, 1991; see also chapter 13, this volume). Yet, when two companies merge to form one new organization, this distinctiveness, and thus part of the basis for individuals' organizational identification and sense of self, is threatened—indeed, it is scheduled to be formally eliminated. Mergers thus pose a *distinctiveness threat* (Jetten, O'Brien, & Trindall, in press; Jetten, Spears, & Manstead, 1999), and according to the social identity approach, people are motivated to resist such threats and to preserve their group's distinctiveness.

Despite the fact that a threat to the premerger organizational identity appears inherent to every merger, research in which mergers are conceptualized as a source of identity threat is very rare (for exceptions, see Haunschild, Moreland, & Murrell, 1994; Terry & Callan, 1998; Terry, Carey, & Callan, 2001; van Knippenberg, van Knippenberg, Monden, & de Lima, in press). The prospect of combining forces with an organization which was previously considered as clearly distinct from, and potentially even a competitor to one's own organization, can turn the merger into an arena for intergroup conflict. The "us versus them" mentality which is so often cited in the merger literature certainly attests to the argument that a merger raises strong concerns for the premerger organizational identity (e.g., Blake & Mouton, 1985; Haunschild et al., 1994; Terry et al., 2001). As a consequence, employees may reject the common organizational identity and, instead, cling to their old organizational identity.

PRESERVING PREMERGER ORGANIZATIONAL BOUNDARIES

To the extent that the "us versus them" problem is acknowledged in merger research, the cure typically prescribed is to stress the superordinate identity (e.g., Graves, 1981; Gaertner, Rust, Dovidio, Buchman, & Anastasio, 1996). Organizational practice too seems anxious to eliminate the premerger identities as soon as possible, as is, for instance, evident in the common practice in acquisitions of firing the acquired party's higher management in the hope of more smoothly assimilating the acquired organization's culture in the acquirer's own (cf. Cartwright & Cooper, 1992). In direct contrast with this prevailing line of reasoning, the present argument suggests that one should not deny, but rather preserve the premerger organizational identities to prevent resistance against the merger. If, as we propose, a major source of resistance against mergers lies in their threat to the premerger identity, preserving the distinctiveness of the premerger groups would reduce this threat, and thus reduce the resistance associated with this distinctiveness threat.

At first sight, preserving the premerger identities may seem to argue against the very purpose of the merger (i.e., forming one new organization), but in reality there is far less tension between merging and preserving a degree of distinctiveness for the premerger organizational identities. Mergers do not necessarily require the dissolution of premerger group distinctions. In fact, mergers vary widely in the extent to which they aim for a full integration. Some mergers, for example, are primarily administrative. Here common ground may be created between two organizations that has few implications for the way in which the constituting businesses are perceived by the members of the workforce. Other types of mergers involve more drastic changes, like a total restructuring of the aggregate, often accompanied by changes in job content and social environment. It should be clear that this latter type of merger may be more threatening to the premerger group identity than the first type, in which the preservation of the premerger group boundaries enables people to preserve their original identities.

Albert and Whetten (1985) describe how in nonmerger contexts organizations may differ in the extent to which they consist of a single, or of multiple identities. In *ideographic* organizations, subunits (e.g., departments) maintain subunit-specific identities, whereas in *holographic* organizations, members share a common identity across units. The distinction between ideographic and holographic organizations corresponds to the difference between organizations that have organic social identities and those that have mechanical social identities (cf. Haslam, 2001; see also chapters 4, 14, this volume). Research on organizational culture has similarly acknowledged the possibility of within-organization subcultures in addition to, or instead of, one overarching organizational culture (e.g., Martin, 1993). Thus, even in the context of mergers where organizations are integrated to form one new organization, it should be possible to preserve premerger identities. Maintaining subgroup distinctiveness in a merger is not incompatible with the act or aim of merging. Even so, the notion that maintaining group distinctiveness may have a beneficial effect on employees' attitudes toward the merger and the merged organization, is novel to merger research, and the present chapter is essentially the first to assess its merits (but see chapter 13, this volume). An important question, therefore, is to what extent this notion is supported by empirical evidence.

First evidence that maintaining premerger distinctiveness may engender more positive responses to a merger comes from research on intergroup relations. Working from the premise that threats to group boundaries can have aversive effects, a growing number of researchers are arguing in favor of the positive effects on intergroup relations of asserting these group boundaries (Gaertner et al., 1999; Hewstone & Brown, 1986; Hornsey & Hogg, 2000a, 2000b, 2000c). Asserting group boundaries in the context of an overarching common group identity (cf. premerger groups within a merged group) has been conceptualized as the adoption of a "dual identity"—a concept first put forward by Gaertner, Dovidio, and colleagues as part of the common in-group identity model (CIIM; Gaertner, Dovidio, Anastasio, Bachman, & Rust, 1993). Central to the CIIM is the notion that the imposition of a common identity can transform group members' perception of out-group members into one in which they are represented as in-group members, which should generate more favorable attitudes accordingly. The benefits of a dual identity are proposed to lie in the fact that the positive consequences of the adoption of a common identity can be accomplished even in those situations where eliminating the premerger group identities is impossible or undesirable. Others have taken this idea one step further by stressing that the maintenance of subgroup boundaries may even be a *prerequisite* for the favorable effects of a common group membership to occur (e.g., Hewstone, 1996; Hewstone & Brown, 1986; Hornsey & Hogg, 2000a, 2000b). Evidence in support of the benefits of a dual identity comes from both laboratory experiments and field research, most of which focused on domains of ethnic and/or national identities (see Bizman & Yinon, 2000; Brewer, 2000).

Bachman (1993, in Gaertner et al., 1993) applied the concept of dual identity to the context of mergers. Their results seem to contest the suggested benefits of a dual identity: The perception of the postmerger aggregate as two subgroups within a larger group was *positively* associated with bias in work-related measures. The authors suggest that the preservation of the premerger group identities, although beneficial in many other situations, may not be desirable after all in the context of mergers because the ultimate goal of the merger is the elimination of premerger group distinctions. Consequently, the prolonged salience of these subgroup identities may be diagnostic of serious problems that could affect the merged organizations' success. However, the reported salience of the subgroup identities could also be a reaction to the implementation of a structure in which these identities are *not* formally acknowledged. The Bachman study therefore does not seem to provide a conclusive answer to the question of whether the preservation of subgroup identities is a helpful or harmful strategy in the context of a merger.

To summarize, then, social–psychological research on distinctiveness threat and dual identity generally corroborates our proposition that reactions to a merger may be more positive when the distinctiveness of the premerger groups (i.e., organizations) is preserved within the merged organization. However, the evidence discussed above relates to attitudes toward the other group (i.e., the merger partner) in nonmerger contexts (aside from the inconclusive findings from the Bachman study). The question, therefore, remains whether preserving premerger group distinctiveness alone is sufficient to engender identification with and commitment to the merged organization.

THE IMPORTANCE OF POSTMERGER ORGANIZATIONAL ENTITATIVITY

Although the notion that the adoption of a dual identity may help to reduce intergroup bias is still a relatively novel concept, research supporting this idea is accumulating (Gaertner et al., 1999; Gaertner, Dovidio, & Bachman, 1996; Hornsey & Hogg, 2000a, 2000b, 2000c; Roccas & Schwartz, 1993). What has remained uninvestigated, however, are the consequences of this strategy for the adoption and strength of the common post-merger identity. In general, it could be argued that the recognition of premerger organizational boundaries, to the extent that it reduces feelings of threat to this organizational identity, should also be beneficial for postmerger identification. However, identification with the organization should not only be affected by the degree to which the premerger organizational identity is preserved, but also by the extent to which the organization comprises a meaningful and homogeneous entity (i.e., its degree of *entitativity*; Campbell, 1958). Entitativity is related to the "oneness and realness" of a group, as demonstrated by the findings that membership in groups high in entitativity is valued more than membership in groups that are low in entitativity (Lickel et al., 2000; Sherman, Hamilton, & Lewis, 1999), and that physically entitative groups are viewed as both physically and psychologically homogeneous (Dasgupta, Banaji, & Abelson, 1999).

How does organizational entitativity related to organizational identification? The relationship between postmerger entitativity and organizational identification was investigated in three survey studies of corporate mergers reported in van Knippenberg and van Leeuwen (2001). Perceived differences between the merger partners were negatively related to entitativity. Moreover, entitativity was positively related to postmerger identification in all three studies. Organizational entitativity thus appears to be a powerful determinant of meaningfulness and strength of the organizational identity (cf. Ashforth and Mael's, 1989, suggestion that holographic organizations may elicit higher levels of organizational identification than ideographic organizations).

At a more fundamental level, there is a clear link between entitativity and the *fit* of a category (Turner, Hogg, Oakes, Reicher, & Wetherell, 1987). The fit of a category refers to the degree to which perceived similarities and differences between people correlate with a particular level of categorization. Fit therefore holds two elements: a structural element that refers to the availability of a formal categorization, and a perceptual element that refers to the perceived variability within the aggregate, or between the aggregate and other possible aggregates. This variability results in perceived fit of a categorization on the basis of the principle of the *metacontrast ratio*. The metacontrast ratio is defined as "the ratio of the average difference perceived between members of the category and the other stimuli (the mean inter-category difference) over the average difference perceived between members within the category (the mean intra-category difference)"(Turner et al., 1987, p. 47). A particular group membership thus "fits" to the extent that perceived variability across people is systematically related to the variability in underlying group memberships. It is this match between formal group structure and perceived similarities or differences that turns a particular identity into a salient, and thus a meaningful one (Blanz, 1999; Brewer, Weber, & Carini, 1995; Oakes, Haslam, & Turner, 1994; Simon, Hastedt, & Aufderheide, 1997).

The literature on entitativity and fit thus suggests that the preservation of premerger organizational distinctions may reduce postmerger organizational entitativity (because it creates a differentiation within the organization), and thus postmerger identification. It should be clear that this notion is at odds with the previously advanced position that the preservation of premerger organizational distinctiveness favors the adoption and strength of the postmerger organizational identity. To resolve the apparent inconsistency between these two arguments, we conducted three experimental studies that address the interplay of these two process in determining postmerger identification.

EXPERIMENTAL EVIDENCE: DISTINCTIVENESS VERSUS FIT

Because the test of our theoretical argument requires an experiment to establish causality, and the manipulation of group distinctiveness in actual organizational mergers is not feasible, we tested our propositions in a series of laboratory experiments. The available evidence (see van Knippenberg & van Leeuwen, 2001) suggests that conclusions regarding the social identity processes involved in mergers generalize from the laboratory to the field (see also the discussion later in this chapter). Despite the huge differences between organizational mergers and mergers of ad hoc laboratory groups, there is thus reason to believe that the conclusions from the experiments discussed in the following are highly relevant to actual organizational mergers.

Research on the dual identity concept has demonstrated a general need to preserve premerger or subordinate identities. The first experiment reported here (van Leeuwen, van Knippenberg, & Ellemers, 2001b) was designed to investigate how preservation of premerger distinctiveness as a precursor to postmerger identification relates to the effect of the fit of the superordinate category (i.e., which was argued to be negatively affected by subgroup distinctiveness). The expectation tested was that high intergroup similarity would improve the fit of the imposed one-group structure, but that improved fit would only result in higher identification with the merged group when it did not threaten the premerger group identities. That is, identification was proposed to be higher under conditions that were conducive to both the preservation of the premerger identities and the entitativity of the merged group. This hypothesis was tested in a minimal group experiment (Tajfel, 1970; Tajfel, Billig, Bundy, & Flament, 1971), in which we manipulated (1) whether the premerger groups were structurally distinct or not within the merged group, and (2) the relative similarity of the premerger groups. We suggested to our participants that they were a member of one of two four-person teams (team A or team B) that would work on a computer-mediated brainstorming task. In reality, all participants were assigned to team B. After participants had worked on the brainstorming assignment (whilst confined to their separate cubicles), identification with this premerger team was measured. Participants were then given bogus feedback stating that, on the basis of their answers to a brief questionnaire they had filled out at the beginning of the experiment, the members of team A were either similar or dissimilar to the members of team B with respect to their association styles (a group characteristic that was purported to be highly relevant to the task at hand). In the second stage of the experiment, the groups were allegedly merged for a second brainstorming task. In the two subgroups condition, it was explained that this assignment consisted of two parts or problems, to be focused on by the members of the respective premerger teams (that were from hereon referred to as subgroup A and subgroup B). In the no subgroups condition, no such information was given and all members brainstormed about the same problem. Following this second brainstorming assignment, postmerger identification with the merged group was assessed. In addition, we assessed the perceived fit of the categorization as one merged group.

Premerger identification (identification with the original premerger group) and postmerger identification (identification with the combined postmerger group) were analyzed in a repeated measures analysis, and results were in line with expectations (see Figure 12.1). A three-way interaction revealed that similarity or dissimilarity in terms of group association styles interacted with the presence or absence of the formal acknowledgement of subgroups in determining whether the shift from pre- to postmerger identification was a positive or a negative one. A positive shift, indicating the adoption of the postmerger common identity, was found when similar group styles were combined with a distinctive subgroups structure, and when different group styles were combined with a structure in which no subgroups were acknowledged. Thus, similarity on the group structure dimension or the group association style dimension led to a stronger adoption of the postmerger common identity when dissimilarity on the other dimension preserved the premerger groups' distinctive identities. In the other two conditions (similarity or dissimilarity on both dimensions), a negative shift in identification revealed a rejection of the

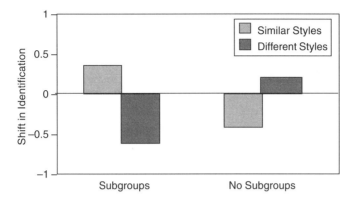

FIGURE 12.1. Mean shift in identification (post–premerger identification) as a function of group structure and group association styles

postmerger identity, compared to the strength of the premerger identity. Additional analyses showed that perceived fit of the postmerger common category was positively related to the adoption of this identity, but only in the subgroups condition. Mediational analyses further demonstrated that the effect of group styles on identification was mediated by perceived fit.

Results from this study support the notion that perceived homogeneity or fit of the superordinate category, and the need to preserve the distinctive premerger group identity, jointly affect the extent to which a common identity is adopted. As such, these findings make a clear case for the benefits of preserving subgroup distinctiveness when two groups merge—but in the context of a shared common group membership (cf. dual identity). Interestingly, it appears that one important way to prevent merger resistance as expressed by an "us versus them" mentality lies in the implementation of an "us and them" structure.

MORE EXPERIMENTAL EVIDENCE: DISTINCTIVENESS VERSUS SUPERORDINATE REPRESENTATION

In the van Leeuwen et al. (2001b) study, the merger was created as a "merger of equals"; that is, neither premerger group dominated the other in determining the nature of the postmerger group. Yet in organizational practice, such an asymmetry appears to be more the rule rather than the exception. Many mergers involve a dominant and a dominated partner and are thus psychologically, if not formally, more akin to acquisitions than to mergers of equals (Buono & Bowditch, 1989; Cartwright & Cooper, 1992; Hogan & Overmyer-Day, 1994). As we discuss in the following, there is good reason to expect that the degree to which the premerger group dominates the merger group is related to the preservation of that group's premerger identity within the merged group, and thus to postmerger identification. An obvious question would thus be how this preservation of identity through dominance within the merged group (or, conversely, lack of preservation of identity through being dominated) relates to the preservation of identity through subgroup distinctiveness.

Previous social identity analyses of mergers have typically focused on the idea that mergers force people to abandon their premerger group identities in exchange for a new one. Perhaps a better and more accurate description would be one in which a merger is construed as a process involving a partial change, but also a partial continuation of the premerger group identity. In this respect, dominance in mergers (i.e., acquiring vs. acquired partner) is probably a key factor in affecting the extent to which the merger is a continuation or a change of the premerger identity. Consider, for example, a merger between a relatively small, and a much larger organization. The larger party, in a sense, "takes over" the smaller one, resulting in a postmerger organization which is a clear reflection of the larger partner to the merger in terms of, for example, name, culture, and location. As a result, the members of the smaller organization may conceive of the merger as a highly intrusive event, changing their premerger organization to the point that it is completely dissolved within the postmerger structure. Yet the members of the larger organization may experience little change and indeed, perceive the merger more as a continuation or expansion of their premerger organization. In this respect, a parallel can be drawn to the phenomenon of "in-group projection" (Mummendey & Wenzel, 1999). In-group projection implies the projection of subgroup characteristics on a superordinate category, resulting in a perception of the superordinate group as more similar to one's own subgroup than to other subgroups that are also nested in it. Because group-defining attributes are usually positively valued attributes, subgroups that are (perceived as) more strongly represented in the superordinate group are more positively evaluated (Waldzus, Mummendey, Wenzel, & Weber, n.d.).

Elsewhere, we discussed a series of studies on the effects of in-group representation (i.e., the extent to which the postmerger group or organization is more similar to one premerger party than to the other) on postmerger identification (van Knippenberg & van Leeuwen, 2001). Two of these studies were conducted among employees recently involved in the merger of two town governments (Study 1) or two high schools (Study 2; D. van Knippenberg et al., in press). Although neither of these studies contained direct measures of in-group representation, there was strong anecdotal evidence that in both studies one party was more strongly represented in the postmerger structure than its partner (because it was larger or more economically sound than its partner). For members of the highly represented partner, premerger identification (with the original group) was positively related to postmerger identification (with the combined postmerger group) in both studies. For members of the partner which was only weakly represented, however, pre- and postmerger identification were unrelated. Moreover, both studies revealed postmerger identification to be lower than premerger identification, especially (or only) among members of the weakly represented group. Similar findings were obtained in two experimentally controlled studies in which in-group representation was measured or manipulated (van Leeuwen, van Knippenberg, & Ellemers, 2000a). In both studies, in-group representation strengthened the association between pre- and postmerger identification, thus providing clear evidence in support of the notion that through in-group representation the postmerger group is perceived as a continuation rather than a change of the premerger group identity.

Because in-group representation can lead group members to perceive the postmerger group as essentially a continuation of their own premerger group, the preservation of premerger group boundaries in a situation of unequals may have different consequences than it does in a merger of equals. Imagine, for example, a merger in which conditions of high in-group representation lead group members to perceive the postmerger group as essentially a continuation of their own premerger group. Locating the merger partner as a distinctive subgroup in the postmerger aggregate can then be construed as threatening to the continued group identity. In this respect, a parallel can be drawn to literature on acculturation and cultural diversity (e.g., Berry, 1980; Bradberry & Preston, 1992; Nahavandi & Malekzadeh, 1988; Roccas, Horenczyk, & Schwartz, 2000; Sears, Citrin, Cheleden, & van Laar, 1999). Research in these domains generally shows a fear among members of majority subgroups that members of minority subgroups will position themselves as distinct from the majority (i.e., a separation strategy). Conversely, fear exists among members of minority subgroups that the majority aims at assimilating them, thereby eliminating their distinctive subgroup identities. When one's own premerger group is strongly represented in the postmerger group, the combined postmerger group will be perceived as essentially a continuation of the premerger in-group. The preservation of pre-merger group distinctions (and with that, the continuation of the merger partner's distinctive group identity) violates the integrity of the postmerger group. For members who, through high in-group representation, perceive the postmerger group as a continuation of their premerger group, the preservation of subgroup distinctiveness should therefore have a negative effect on postmerger identification.

We conducted two experiments to investigate this proposition (van Leeuwen, van Knippenberg, & Ellemers, 2000b). In Study 1, in-group representation was manipulated in conjunction with out-group representation, such that the postmerger group was either a strong reflection of both premerger groups (high mutual representation), or a weak reflection of both groups, turning them into a "new" group (low mutual representation). In Study 2, in-group representation was manipulated relative to outgroup representation, such that high in-group representation was associated with low out-group representation (high relative representation), or low in-group representation was associated with high out-group representation (low relative representation). The experimental setup was highly comparable to that of our study presented earlier, as was the manipulation of subgroup distinctiveness (i.e., participants worked on the same task, or on different subtasks). High mutual in-group representation (Study 1) was manipulated by explaining to participants that, for the second phase of the experiment, both teams would be combined in a team whose name and logo either contained clear elements of both premerger teams (that is, the postmerger team was referred to as team AB and its logo was essentially a combination of both logos), or that a new team would be created out of the members of both premerger teams (resulting in a postmerger team with a different name [team C] and a different logo than those of either premerger teams; cf. Rousseau, 1998). Relative representation (Study 2) was manipulated by telling participants that their premerger team B would continue and be expanded by the members of team A in the second phase of the experiment (resulting in a postmerger team that was a clear reflection of the premerger in-group), or that their premerger team B would be dissolved and they would join team A (thus involving essentially a change in group membership for the members of team B).

Results from both studies supported the hypothesis that the effects of preserving distinctions between the premerger groups are contingent on in-group representation (see Figures 12.2 and 12.3). Irrespective of whether in-group representation was manipulated in conjunction with, or relative to

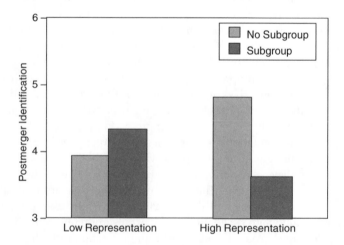

FIGURE 12.2. Mean level of postmerger identification as a function of subgroup distinctiveness and mutual representation

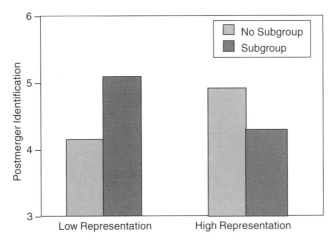

FIGURE 12.3. Mean level of postmerger identification as a function of subgroup distinctiveness and relative representation

out-group representation, the preservation of premerger group distinctions only favored postmerger identification under conditions of low in-group representation. Thus, postmerger identification was enhanced by the preservation of group distinctivenss under conditions of low mutual representation (Study 1) or low relative representation (Study 2). When mutual or relative representation was high, in contrast, the preservation of group distinctiveness reduced postmerger identification. Moreover, similar effects were obtained with respect to group members' willingness to exert themselves for the benefit of the postmerger group, as measured by the extent to which they felt responsible for working hard on the postmerger brainstorming assignment (Study 1), the amount of time they volunteered to do additional brainstorming to help their postmerger group compare favorably to other groups in this study (Study 1), and the number of ideas generated during the postmerger brainstorming assignment (Study 2).

Taken together, results from these experimental studies demonstrate the benefits and limitations of preserving group boundaries in a merger context. In those situations in which the representation of their own group in the postmerger group is low, the preservation of premerger group distinctiveness can secure the premerger identity and prevent resistance to the merger. However, when the postmerger group is essentially a reflection of one's premerger in-group, the existence of subordinate group boundaries may be threatening because it not only leaves the premerger *in-group* intact, but also the premerger *out-group*, thereby violating the integrity of a postmerger group, which is experienced as a continuation of the premerger in-group.

PRESERVING PREMERGER GROUP DISTINCTIONS: EVIDENCE FROM THE FIELD

Perhaps the most frequently noted fact about research in the psychology of mergers in reviews of the literature is that so little systematic research attention has been devoted to the psychological processes operating in mergers and acquisitions (e.g., Cartwright & Cooper, 1992; Hogan & Overmyer-Day, 1994). The experimental studies presented in this chapter are an important step in the direction of a more systematic approach to group-based reactions to mergers. An obvious question that remains to be answered, however, is how these experimental findings relate to mergers in the field.

A substantial part of the psychological–organizational science literature is devoted to the "fit" between the merger partners, but the conceptualization of fit is quite different from fit as defined in self-categorization theory (Turner et al., 1987). In merger literature, fit is described as the degree of compatibility between the merger partners. Compatibility means a "good match," which sometimes involves similarity, but at other times complementarity of the merger partners. *Cultural fit* thus refers to the degree of compatibility in organizational culture. *Organizational culture* refers to the "symbols, values, ideologies, and assumptions which operate, often in an unconscious way, to guide and fashion individual and business behavior" (Cartwright & Cooper, 1993a, p. 60). There seems to be general consensus in the merger literature that mergers are more likely to be successful when the cultures of the merger partners are similar (e.g., Buono, Bowditch, & Lewis, 1985; Cartwright & Cooper, 1993b; Hogan & Overmyer-Day, 1994; Marks & Mirvis, 1986; Walter, 1985; Weber, Shenkar, & Raveh, 1996). Cultural differences are assumed to lead to "culture clashes" that feed the "us versus them" mentality that is argued to be so detrimental to mergers. Only when the acquiring organization's culture (i.e., to which the acquired organization is assumed to assimilate) is consensually seen as more attractive than the acquired organization's culture, do cultural differences not amount in serious conflict (Cartwright & Cooper, 1992).

As opposed to good cultural fit, good *structural fit* appears to exist when the merger partners are different and complementary to each other, rather than similar. *Structural fit*, sometimes also referred to as *strategic fit*, can be described as the degree to which the merging firms augment or complement each other in terms of, for example, production or expertise (Jemison & Sitkin, 1986). As far as the consequences of structural fit for individual effort and performance are concerned, literature generally indicates a positive effect of complementarity. Based on a sample of 147 acquisitions, Krishnan, Miller, and Judge (1997) conclude that complementary backgrounds are positively associated with post-acquisition performance (see also Brush, 1996; Lubatkin, 1983; Van Oudenhoven & de Boer, 1995). Thus, functional distinctiveness seems to yield more positive results than functional similarity (for a discussion of functional diversity in nonmerger contexts see also chapter 4, this volume).

Organizations are more distinctive when cultures are dissimilar rather than similar, and when the merger partners are functionally complementary rather than supplementary. It would thus seem that our proposition regarding the effects of premerger group distinctiveness holds for structural distinctiveness, but not for cultural distinctiveness. Matters may be a little more complex, however. Distinctiveness and dissimilarity should not be equated. Dissimilarity can be a basis for distinctiveness, but if the aim of a merger is to integrate merger partners, dissimilarity in itself may not lead to preservation of distinctiveness; more formalized recognitions of premerger differences, or at least the absence of formalized denials, may be in order. Indeed, an important difference between the research on structural similarity and cultural similarity seems to be that in cases of structural diversity (i.e., complementary fit) the distinctiveness of the premerger groups is formally recognized, whereas in research on cultural similarity studies typically focus on situations where organizations are required to merge their cultures into one. As this merging of cultures will typically be associated with the suggestion that one is required to *adapt to the merger partner's culture* (Buono & Bowditch, 1989), it is not surprising that cultural differences are associated with more negative responses than cultural similarities—indeed, only when this suggestion is present are cultural differences between the merger partners associated with lower identification with the merged organization (van Knippenberg et al., in press). This suggests, in line with our earlier argument, that cultural differences need not be problematic if the merger partners are in a position to maintain their premerger cultures as subcultures within the merged organization (cf. ideographic organizations).

Perhaps even more directly related to the propositions advanced in the present chapter, is the research on merger integration patterns. Based on the degree to which a merger involved a change and loss of individuality of the group or person, Schoennauer (1967) identified three merger integration patterns. In the *absorb pattern*, the acquired organization's culture disappears as employees are completely absorbed by the acquirer. In the *combine pattern*, a new culture is created, which, despite the fact that it contains elements of both premerger organizations, is essentially different from either party. In the *blend pattern*, portions of both organizational cultures remain clearly identifiable. In Schoennauer's survey, most resistance was found in the absorb pattern, followed by the combine and the blend. Mottola, Bachman, Gaertner, and Dovidio (1997) investigated anticipated reactions to these integration patterns in a scenario approach, and found results consistent with Schoennauer's. Compared with the blend or combine scenarios, participants in the absorb scenario expected less organizational commitment, and had less positive perceptions of organizational support and of contact conditions. In addition, members of the acquired organization were expected to be more threatened by the merger than members of the acquiring organization. In a similar vein, Nahavandi and Malekzadeh (1988) applied the acculturation literature (Berry, 1980) to mergers, and proposed that mergers, and merger partners, may differ in the extent to which they strive for an integration of cultures (i.e., maintaining distinctive cultures; cf. Schoennauer's combine pattern) or an assimilation of the acquired culture into the acquirer's culture (cf. Schoennauer's absorb pattern). Both perspectives corroborate our line of reasoning in suggesting that postmerger organizational identification from members of the acquired organization (cf. low representation) will be higher if their organization maintains a degree of distinctiveness (e.g., integration, combine) than when their identity is lost in the merger partner's identity (assimilation, absorb), while the reverse holds for members of the acquiring organization (cf. high representation).

CONCLUSION

In some merger and acquisition literature, it is believed that the best approach to postmerger organizational unity is the creation of a new group, from which all elements reminiscent of the premerger organizations are eliminated (e.g., Graves, 1981). By effectively wiping out the structures and symbols that could serve to uphold the distinctive premerger organizational cultures, employees are considered most likely to abandon their premerger organizational identities. The abandonment of the premerger group identities is subsequently assumed to be a prerequisite for the adoption of a new, postmerger group identity. However, the present research suggests this last assumption to be wrong. The abandonment of the premerger group identity is not a precondition for the adoption of a postmerger common identity. Rather, it is the *preservation* of the original identity that helps to internalize the new structure and define oneself in terms of the altered group identity. Evidence supporting this notion can be found not only in experimentally controlled research, but also in the merger and acquisition literature pertaining to corporate fit and merger integration patterns.

The aim of a merger, short term or long term, is to combine two functionally distinct organizations into one. If much of the resistance to these forces of integration can be prevented by preserving group boundaries or symbols that serve to uphold the premerger group identity, then to what extent does this strategy clash with the integration policy of the merger? Surely, if employees' reactions to a merger were of no concern to those managing the merger, different structures and procedures might be implemented than if the employees' perspective was taken into account. But an organization is not a structure on paper alone, it does not exist without the people in it, and it cannot be restructured without considering their needs and desires. When implementing a merger, managers should abandon the idea that they are creating a new and homogenous entity on the spot. Although this goal may eventually be reached, the path that leads to it is long and rocky. Instead, managers as well as researchers should focus on finding ways by means of which the merged parties can harmoniously coexist in a postmerger structure characterized by a high degree of interdependency. The problems that face groups bound together by a common organizational goal are different from those facing groups that do not share this interdependency. For the merger to be considered a success, the parties not only need to be free of intergroup conflict and hostility, but they also need to cooperate with each other, share information, and provide help when needed. Given that the viability of a merger depends on employees' motivation to think and act on behalf of the combined postmerger organization, a focus on determinants of this kind of positive intergroup behavior certainly seems beneficial.

13

A Social Identity Perspective on Organizational Mergers
The Role of Group Status, Permeability, and Similarity

DEBORAH J. TERRY
University of Queensland

*I*n an effort to become more competitive in an increasingly complex corporate environment (Dunphy & Stace, 1990; Nahavandi & Malekzadeh, 1988), mergers and acquisitions are rapidly becoming one of the most common means by which organizations seek to achieve corporate growth through a diversification of their activity base. Cartwright and Cooper (1993a) referred to the sharp increases in mergers and acquisitions that have been observed in recent years as an "unprecedented wave" of such activity (see also Holson, 1999; Shrivastava, 1986). Contrary to the assumption that mergers are a potentially beneficial business practice, they typically engender negative reactions in employees (e.g., Ivancevich, Schweiger, & Power, 1987) and more than half of them fail to meet their financial expectations (Cartwright & Cooper, 1993; Marks & Mirvis, 1986; Shrivastava, 1986). Indeed, divestments have been found to be nearly as common as mergers and acquisitions (Cartwright & Cooper, 1993). Commentators have acknowledged that merger failures cannot readily be explained in terms of a lack of financial or strategic fit. Instead, it has been suggested that the extent of "cultural fit" or, more specifically, the extent to which the merger partners can be integrated into the new organization, is a critical factor in determining the success of a merger (Cartwright & Cooper, 1993).

Despite the recognition of the importance of the "human" side of an organizational merger (Schweiger & Ivancevich. 1985), the factors that influence the extent to which the merger partners can be integrated into the new

223

organization are not well understood. Given that an organizational merger involves the imposition of a new organizational identity on employees from previously distinct premerger organizations (Haunschild, Moreland, & Murrell, 1994), the notion of integration in such a context has a clear intergroup dimension. Employees of the two organizations are likely to be motivated to establish an optimal position for their own group in the new organization, thus a merger may well engender competitive and antagonistic intergroup relations. As noted by Haunschild, Moreland, and Murrell (1994), there are many examples of mergers failing because of the "us vs. them" dynamics that occur if employees do not relinquish their old identities (e.g., Blake & Mouton, 1985; Buono & Bowditch, 1989). However, until relatively recently, research on mergers has neglected the intergroup nature of this type of organizational change (cf. Haunschild et al., 1994; Mottola, Bachman, Gaertner, & Dovidio, 1997; Terry & Callan, 1998; van Knippenberg & van Leeuwen, 2001).

This chapter outlines an intergoup perspective, based on the social identity approach (Tajfel & Turner, 1979; see also Haslam, 2001; Hogg & Abrams, 1988; Hogg & Terry, 2001; Hogg, Terry, & White, 1995; Spears, Oakes, Ellemers, & Haslam, 1997; Turner, 1999), to an understanding of employee responses to an organizational merger. From this perspective, relative group status and beliefs concerning the sociostructural relations between groups are key factors that need to be considered in an effort to understand intergroup conflict in response to an organizational merger. An intergroup perspective has considerable potential to contribute to the current literature on organizational mergers, given that reducing such conflict and effectively managing organizational diversity in newly formed superordinate organizations is likely to have considerable benefits for employee well-being and morale, at the same time as enhancing the likelihood that the merger will be successful. The present chapter outlines the social identity perspective on employee responses to a merger, followed by a brief overview of the results of a longitudinal study designed to test aspects of the perspective in the context of a large-scale hospital merger.

THE SOCIAL IDENTITY APPROACH

The social identity approach (Tajfel & Turner, 1979; see also Haslam, 2001; Hogg & Abrams, 1988; Hogg & Terry, 2001; Hogg, Terry, & White, 1995; Spears, Oakes, Ellemers, & Haslam, 1997; Turner, 1999) is a general social–psychological perspective on group processes and intergroup relations, which is based on the original social identity theory (Tajfel & Turner, 1979) and its development, self-categorization theory (Turner, Hogg, Oakes, Reicher, & Wetherell, 1987). Central to the social identity approach is the social self; that is, the component of the self-concept, referred to as social identity, which derives from memberships in social groups and social categories, and contrasts with one's personal identity, which reflects one's characteristics as a unique individual. People have a repertoire of groups and social categories to which they belong—these vary in their overall importance to the self-concept, but are responsive to contextual cues in determining the extent to which they define self in a particular social context. Thus, social identity theory conceives of self as being defined in a dynamic manner by the group membership or categorization that is activated and hence salient in a specific context. When a particular social identity becomes the basis for self-definition in a particular context, people's attitudes and behavior accord with in-group norms, members of relevant out-groups are perceived in stereotypical ways, and intergroup attitudes and behavior have the capacity to become competitive, discriminatory, and conflictual.

According to social identity theory, two underlying sociocognitive processes account for group and intergroup phenomena. The first, social categorization, reflects the fact that when people define themselves as a member of a self-inclusive social category (e.g., a sex, class, team, organization), differences among individual in-group members are minimized, whereas distinctions between in-group and out-group members are accentuated. Self-categorization theory (Turner et al., 1987) identifies the process of social categorization as the cognitive basis for group phenomena. When a social identity is salient, people use available, and usually shared, social comparative information to construct a context-specific group norm—a group prototype. It describes and prescribes beliefs, attitudes, feelings, and behaviors that optimally minimize in-group differences and maximize intergroup differences (the principle of metacontrast). As well as underpinning the construction of a contextually salient in-group prototype, the process of self-categorization means that the self is depersonalized and assimilated to the group prototype. Thus, the self is transformed so that how one should behave, think, and feel is now defined in terms of the group prototype.

Self-enhancement, which is the second underlying process that is central to social identity theory, is predicated on the assumption that people have a basic need to achieve and maintain a positive sense of self, or self-esteem. Because the self is defined in terms of the group membership, people should be motivated to achieve a positive social identity by belonging to groups that compare favorably to relevant out-groups. Thus, people tend to make intergroup comparisons that favor the in-group, and they tend to perceive in-group norms and stereotypes that achieve this same goal. Building on the basic sociocognitive processes of categorization and self-enhancement, social identity theory explains the behavior of group members by taking into account people's subjective beliefs about the nature of the relationships between their own group and relevant out-groups. Central to group members' subjective belief structures and their efforts to attain a positive social identity, and hence a positive sense of self, are their beliefs about the permeability of intergroup boundaries.

IDENTITY MANAGEMENT STRATEGIES OF MEMBERS OF LOW AND HIGH STATUS GROUPS

Intergroup relations in the context of an organizational merger, as in other intergroup contexts, are complicated by the status and power differences between groups. However, as noted by Jost and Elsbach (2001), much of the extant work on intergroup relations in organizations assumes symmetrical relations between groups; however, relations between nested social groups in superordinate organizational structures (such as premerger organizations in a merged organization) and those that involve groups and social categories that extend outside the organization's boundaries, are likely to differ markedly in terms of status and power. Indeed, Van Oudenhoven and de Boer (1995) observed that merger partners are unlikely to be equal in status (see also Terry & Callan, 1998; Terry, Carey, & Callan, 2001; Terry & O'Brien, 2001).

From a social identity perspective, it is assumed that membership in low-status groups (i.e., groups that compare poorly to other groups) fails to provide members with a positive social identity. Thus, members of these groups should seek to gain membership in relevant high status groups, whereas members of high-status groups should seek to maintain both their membership in the group and the existence of the social category in an effort to maintain and enhance the positive contribution that the identity makes to their self-concept (Ellemers, Doosje, van Knippenberg, & Wilke, 1992; Zuckerman, 1979). In laboratory experiments, there is evidence that participants assigned to a high-status group show pride in their group, identify strongly with the group, and seek to maintain their group membership (Ellemers, van Knippenberg, de Vries, & Wilke, 1988; Ellemers, van Knippenberg, & Wilke, 1990; Sachdev & Bourhis, 1987). Similar findings have been reported in field research (Brown et al., 1986). In contrast, membership in a low-status group has been found to have a negative impact on strength of identification (e.g., Ellemers et al., 1990) and self-esteem (Brown & Lohr, 1987), and there is evidence that members seek to disassociate themselves from such groups (Ellemers et al., 1988).

According to social identity theory, there are three strategies that members of low-status groups can use to improve their social identity or, in other words, to achieve identity enhancement (Hogg & Abrams, 1988; Tajfel & Turner, 1979; van Knippenberg & Ellemers, 1993). Low-status group members may engage in individual mobility, which reflects efforts to seek membership in a relevant high-status comparison group. In contrast to this individualistic response, low-status group members may engage in group-oriented or collective strategies. Social competition is one such response, which involves direct strategies to change the negative standing of the group. A second collective response, referred to as social creativity, is a cognitive response that involves making intergroup comparisons that favor the in-group (also referred to as *in-group bias* and *in-group* favoritism) with the aim of positive reevaluating the in-group. To achieve this aim, intergroup comparisons may be made on new dimensions for comparison, a modification of values assigned to comparative dimensions, or the selection of a different comparison group (Hogg & Abrams, 1988; Lalonde, 1992).

In organizational contexts, it might be assumed that in-group bias or social creativity is likely to be an important way in which members of a low-status group seek to attain a positive social identity, given that the opportunities for social change may be limited. Moreover, in stable intergroup contexts, options for individual mobility may also be seen to be limited. Thus, in the pursuit of self-enhancement, members of low-status groups should engage in more in-group bias than members of high-status groups. This assumption is consistent with Tajfel's (1974) expectation that group differentiation is most marked when the classification is particularly salient or, in other words, personally relevant to group members. However, although there is some evidence that members of low-status groups do engage in more in-group bias than members of high-status groups (e.g., Brewer, 1979), other evidence suggests that in-group bias is most often exhibited among members of high-status groups (Doise & Sinclair, 1973; Hinkle & Brown, 1990; Sachdev & Bourhis, 1987, 1991), presumably as a consequence of status protection concerns. Moreover, low-status group members have been observed to acknowledge their position of inferiority, as reflected in a tendency to exhibit out-group favoritism (Hinkle & Brown, 1990; Spears & Manstead, 1989; Terry & Callan, 1998; see also Jost & Elsbach, 2001).

From a social identity perspective, it is relatively straightforward to reconcile these results by taking into account the status relevance of the dimensions or attributes on which in- and out-group members can be judged (see Bettencourt, Dorr, Charlton, & Hume, 2001; Mullen, Brown, & Smith, 1992; also Hinkle & Brown, 1990; Spears & Manstead, 1989; Terry & Callan, 1998). As noted previously, low-status group members may attain positively valued group distinctiveness through the use of social creativity in their intergroup comparisons. One way in which this may be achieved involves the pursuit of positive in-group differentiation on dimensions that do not form the basis for the status hierarchy, or that are only peripherally related to this hierarchy. Because the status-defining or status-relevant dimensions cannot be ignored (Lalonde, 1992), members of a low-status group may well acknowledge their relatively inferior status on the status-relevant dimensions (i.e., exhibit out-group favoritism on these dimensions). However, on the status-irrelevant dimensions, that is, on those dimensions not directly related to the basis for the status hierarchy, members of low-status groups should show positive differentiation.

In contrast to members of low-status groups, high-status group members should show in-group bias on the status-defining dimensions (Mullen, Brown, & Smith, 1992). This is because to do so serves to verify their dominant position in the intergroup context. Thus, among high-status group members, in-group bias should be more marked on status-relevant than status-irrelevant dimensions. In fact, on the latter type of dimension, a "magnanimous" out-group bias or "reverse discrimination" effect may be evident (Mullen et al., 1992). In other words, high-status group members may be willing to acknowledge that the out-group is better than the in-group on dimensions that are clearly irrelevant to the basis for the status differentiation (see also Sachdev & Bourhis, 1987; Turner & Brown, 1978), particularly in relatively stable intergroup contexts.

In a study of an airline merger, Terry, Hogg, and Blackwood (2001) found that in line with the expectation that an impending merger will heighten the salience of their relatively inferior status, members of the lower status organization engaged in more in-group bias than employees of the higher status organization (see also Haunschild et al., 1994, for a similar result in a laboratory study). Furthermore, as expected, in-group bias among the employees of the lower status organization was evident only on the status-irrelevant dimensions, whereas employees of the higher status organization showed evidence of in-group bias on the status-relevant dimensions, a pattern of results that has essentially been replicated during the aftermath of a merger between two scientific organizations (Terry & O'Brien, 2001). In the latter study, there was evidence linking the perceived threat of the merger to the amount of in-group bias exhibited by the low-status employees on the status-irrelevant dimensions, on the one hand, and the extent of in-group bias exhibited by the employees of the high-status organization, on the other. Thus, for both groups of employees, in-group bias on the expected dimensions was explicitly linked to the merger context, rather than reflecting a stable intergroup response. Indeed, the lack of evidence of outgroup favoritism by either group of employees presumably reflects the unstable and potentially conflictual nature of an organizational merger (cf. Terry & Callan, 1998, for contrary results in the anticipatory phase of a merger).

The motivational focus of the social identity approach means that it is well placed to explain how members of devalued or low-status groups maintain a favorable group image (Terry, 2000; see also Jost & Elsbach, 2001). As noted above, in the face of the identity threat associated with an organizational change, members of such groups have been found to exhibit in-group bias on status-irrelevant or socio-emotional dimensions, which are generic rather than likely to be status-defining in a particular business context (Terry et al., 2001; Terry & O'Brien, 2001; see also Hinkle & Brown, 1990; Spears & Manstead, 1989; Terry & Callan, 1998). As noted by Jost (2001), additional support for the social identity perspective on identity management strategies of low status group members includes Elsbach and Kramer's (1996) finding that in the face of negative national rankings, business school professors attained a positive social identity by positioning their school as being at the top of a subgroup (e.g., public university, metropolitan business school), and Ashforth and Kreiner's (1999) observations of the favorable self-evaluations that people involved in "dirty work" manage to attain through socially creative interpretations of their work, including the observation that: "exotic dancers and prostitutes claim that they are providing a therapeutic and educational service, rather then selling their bodies" (p. 421).

On the basis of his system justification theory of intergroup relations, Jost and Elsbach (2001) caution against an uncritical acceptance of the relatively optimistic message that the social identity approach—through the mechanism for social creativity—has for members of devalued groups. As noted, there is clear evidence that there are creativity mechanisms through which members of such groups can attain a positive social identity; however, Jost and Elsbach (2001; Elsbach, 2000; Elsbach & Bhattacharya, 2001) have argued that there are social and psychological costs of being a member of a chronically devalued group in an organizational context that may result in a disidentification with the organization. In research on intergroup relations in the context of a merger, this type of response has been observed. Terry, Carly, and Callan et al. (2001), for instance, found that employees of the low-status premerger organization were less strongly identified with the new organization than the high-status employees. There was also evidence that employees of the low-status premerger organization were less committed to the new organization and were less satisfied with their job than employees of the high-status premerger organization. From a social identity perspective, the extent to which employees will disidentify with the newly merged organization as a consequence of being in a devalued position will be dependent on their subjective beliefs about the nature of the intergroup relations in the organization, in particular those that relate to the permeability of the intergroup boundaries.

PERMEABILITY OF INTERGROUP BOUNDARIES

According to the social identity approach, subjective beliefs concerning the intergroup context are critical to an understanding of intergroup relations. The distinction between social structures in which the strategy of individual mobility is possible and structures in which the predominant belief is that the boundaries between groups are impermeable, thus precluding individual mobility (Tajfel, 1974; Tajfel & Turner, 1979), is central to social identity theory. Perceived permeability reflects the extent to which group members believe that the intergroup structure allows them to move from their own group to another group or, in other words, the extent to which intergroup boundaries are perceived to be open. If intergroup boundaries are perceived to be relatively open, then group members should perceive that they will have access to the opportunities and benefits afforded to the other group.

Impermeable boundaries, conversely, are those perceived to be in a fixed or closed state. They thus imply that changing group membership is not a feasible alternative, and that access to the opportunities and benefits afforded to members of the higher status group are precluded for members of the low status group.

According to social identity theory, the extent to which the boundaries that separate their own group from the high status group are perceived to be permeable is a critical determinant of the strategy that members of low status groups choose to adopt to improve their social identity (see also Taylor & McKirnan's, 1984, five-stage model of intergroup relations for a similar argument). When intergroup boundaries are perceived to be open or permeable, the dominant response of low-status group members is likely to be one of individual mobility. In other words, members of low-status groups—attuned to opportunities to enhance their identity—should respond favorably to the merger when they perceive that they have access to the opportunities that are afforded to members of the other group (Zuckerman, 1979). In contrast, when intergroup boundaries are perceived to be relatively impermeable, low-status group members should use collective strategies in order to satisfy their motivation to enhance their social identity. As noted above, one such strategy is social creativity or, in other words, in-group favoring intergroup differentiation on dimensions that are not related directly to the basis for the status differentiation (Tajfel, 1974; see Lalonde, 1992; Terry & Callan, 1998; Terry et al., 2001).

There is empirical support for the supposition that the extent to which intergroup boundaries are perceived to be permeable influences the way in which members of low-status groups deal with their inferior social identity. Wright, Taylor, and Moghaddam (1990) found that the perceived intergroup permeability was negatively related to participants' willingness to engage in a collective protest (see also Taylor, Moghaddam, Gamble, & Zellerer, 1987; Ellemers, 1993), a pattern of results that Lalonde and Silverman (1994) found was most marked when the social identity was made salient. There is also evidence for a link between perceived permeability and social creativity. Lalonde (1992) found that members of a team placed last in a competitive league (i.e., a low-status group in a low permeability situation) engaged in in-group bias on the attributes not related to performance.

Members of low-status groups—attuned to opportunities to enhance their identity—are likely to respond favorably to conditions of high permeability (see Zuckerman, 1979). In contrast, high-status group members are driven by identity protection motives (Tajfel, 1975; A. van Knippenberg & Ellemers, 1993). Thus, members of high-status groups are likely to respond negatively to the presence of permeable intergroup boundaries because of the threat that such boundaries pose to their high-status group membership. In support of this supposition, Ellemers, van Knippenberg, de Vries, and Wilke (1988) found that permeable group boundaries reduced in-group identification among low-status group members, but there was some evidence of an associated increase in identification among members of the high-status group. In a subsequent study, Ellemers, Doosje, van Knippenberg, and Wilke (1992) found evidence of status-protection strategies among high-status group members, but only if the group was a minority group.

In an initial effort to examine the role that perceptions of intergroup permeability may play in the context of an organizational merger, Terry et al. (2001) conducted a study of pilots involved in an airline merger. It was proposed that employees of the low-status premerger organization, who perceived the intergroup boundaries to be highly permeable, would be better adjusted to the merger (on both person- and job-related outcome measures), be less likely to engage in in-group bias (a collective response), and be more likely to identify with the new organization (reflecting the opportunity for individual mobility) than low-status employees who perceived the intergroup boundaries to be relatively impermeable. For the employees of the high-status premerger organization—presumably motivated by a need for social identity protection—an opposite pattern of results was predicted. Specifically, it was proposed that when intergroup boundaries were perceived to be relatively open, employees of the high-status premerger organization would exhibit poor adjustment to the merger, high levels of in-group bias, and weak identification with the new organization.

The merger involved two previously independent airline companies— one of relatively high status (an international carrier) and one of relatively low status (a domestic carrier). There was consistent evidence that perceptions of permeability influenced employees' responses to the merger. In relation to identification, organizational commitment, and job satisfaction, there was a positive relationship between perceived permeability and scores on each of these outcome variable for low-status group members but not for the high-status group members. Similar results were found on the person-related outcomes. For the employees of the low-status group, the perception that the intergroup boundaries in the new organization were relatively permeable was associated with higher self-esteem and better emotional well-being. There was also, as expected, some evidence that high levels of perceived permeability were associated with poorer emotional well-being and lower self-esteem for members of the high-status premerger organization. Perceptions of permeability did not influence in-group bias for the employees of the low-status premerger organization, which is contrary to the premise that when opportunities for individual mobility exist, collective responses such as in-group bias should decrease. It is possible that the unstable nature of relations in the merged organization meant that the extent of in-group bias was not influenced by perceptions of permeability—such a response may become evident later in the merger process.

These results are consistent with the basic premise of social identity theory that the dominant strategy of members of low-status group members faced with a clearly superior group is one of individual mobility if the group boundaries are perceived to be relatively open. That is, in the pursuit of identity enhancement, low-status employees, who perceived that the boundaries in the new organization were permeable, transferred their allegiance to the new organization—presumably reflecting a disidentification with their premerger organization. The fact that the negative relationship between perceived permeability and adjustment among the high-status employees was evident only on the person-related outcomes suggests that status protection motives are most likely to be reflected in self-relevant outcomes. It should, however, be acknowledged that the relatively weak permeability effects observed for the employees of the high-status group may be a consequence of the fact that the items used to assess permeability were more relevant to the low-status participants than the high-status participants, given that they focused on opportunities for status enhancement. More generally, the results of the research need to be replicated in a longitudinal design. The cross-sectional nature of the study of the airline merger meant that the temporal relationships between the predictors and the outcome measures could not be detected. Moreover, the contaminating effects of contemporaneous measurement may have inflated the relationships between the predictors and the outcomes.

PREMERGER ORGANIZATIONAL SIMILARITY

Although not typically considered as a sociostructural characteristic, the perceived similarity of groups in a specific intergroup context should also influence intergroup behavior. According to social identity theory, antagonistic intergroup responses are likely to be engendered when the distinctiveness of the in-group is threatened by similarity between the in- and the out-group—the similarity–differentiation hypothesis (Spears, Doosje, & Ellemers, 1997). However, this response may not be observed in a merger context, where the need for corporate diversification may mean that there are considerable differences, on multiple levels, between the merging organizations. To facilitate harmonious intergroup relations in this type of context, it may be preferable for the two groups of employees to perceive some intergroup similarity. This supposition is in line with similarity–attraction theory (Byrne, 1971), which would propose that intergroup relations should be more positive when the groups are perceived to be similar rather than dissimilar.

In contrast to laboratory research, field research has tended to support the intergroup similarity–attraction hypothesis (Brown, 1984), a pattern of results that may reflect the fact that similarity-differentiation is likely to occur only when groups are highly similar (such as in relation to the group memberships typically studied in the laboratory) and, hence, where the possibilities for positive distinctiveness are relatively limited (Diehl, 1988). On this basis, it was proposed that more positive responses to the merger should be exhibited among those employees who perceive that the premerger organizations are similar on a range of different dimensions, a situation that should facilitate acceptance of a shared, inclusive identity.

A LONGITUDINAL STUDY OF THE EFFECTS OF STATUS, PERMEABILITY, AND SIMILARITY ON EMPLOYEE RESPONSES TO AN ORGANIZATIONAL MERGER

The research focused on the merger of two previously independent metropolitan hospitals. Both of the hospitals were teaching hospitals—one was a 180-bed hospital specializing in obstetrics, gynecology, and neonatology, whereas the other was general adult hospital (870-bed medical and surgical hospital, with acute care and emergency services, and a full range of specialist services). In line with the underlying assumption of the social identity approach to organizational mergers, it was assumed that employees of the low status premerger organization would be most threatened by the merger and that this stress would emanate, most strongly, from identity-related concerns associated with the merger, in comparison to more general change-related or implementation stressors (H1). It was further proposed that, as a consequence of their relatively inferior status, employees of the low-status premerger organization would exhibit the most negative responses to the merger situation (H2). These effects were expected to be particularly marked for low-status group members who perceived that the intergroup boundaries were relatively impermeable for members of their group (H3a). In contrast, it was proposed that members of high-status groups would respond negatively to such a situation because of the threat that open boundaries poses to the existence of their high status group (H3b). In addition to examining the effects of premerger organizational status and the perceived permeability of the intergroup boundaries, the research was designed to examine the effects of the perceived similarity of the two premerger organizations. In line with similarity-attraction theory (Byrne, 1971, it was proposed that intergroup relations should be more positive when the groups were perceived to be similar rather than dissimilar (H4).

Among the hospital staff, pilot work indicated that the general hospital was widely regarded as being higher in status than the smaller specialist hospital. In line with the staged completion of the new shared hospital redevelopment, a gradual integration of the functional units and clinical support services occurred. The present analysis focuses on data collected from 206 employees working in the areas that were the first to merge. Time 1 data were collected prior to the merger, whereas the Time 2 data (collected one year later) were collected after the first group of units and services had moved into the new premises as merged units. The sample was representative of the overall organizational population. Around 70% of the sample was female, and the mean age was 43.32 years. They were employed across the full range of levels in the organization.

At Time 2, measures of perceived stress or threat associated with the merger were obtained. To assess perceived threat, employees indicated whether they had experienced a range of different stressors likely to be associated with a merger and, if they had, how difficult they had found the stressor. A preliminary principal components analysis revealed that the items assessed two dimensions of stress—one that pertained to identity-related concerns (10 items; e.g., "Loss of identity for your hospital" and "Fear that your hospital will be in a weak position in the integrated hospital") and one that pertained to change-related or implementation stress (6 items; e.g., "Insufficient information about the integration" and "Lack of opportunities to discuss the implications of the integration").

Perceptions of the permeability or openness of the intergroup boundaries in the new organization were assessed at Time 1 using two scales that comprised two items each. These scales each assessed perceived permeability for members of the employee's own premerger organization (e.g., "The opportunities that members of my premerger organization [specified in questionnaire] group have access to will" 1 decrease to 7 increase) and members of the other premerger organization (e.g., "The resources that members of the other premerger organization [specified in questionnaire] group have access to will" 1 decrease to 7 increase), respectively. To assess perceived similarity of the premerger organizations, participants compared the two hospitals, at Time 1, on variables such as culture, norms, values, work practices, etc.

A range of different outcome variables was assessed at both Times 1 and 2. These included common in-group identity (e.g., "At work, despite the different divisional backgrounds, it usually feels as though we are all just one group"; see Gaertner et al., 1996), strength of identification with the new organization (e.g., "How much do you identify with the new organization"), and strength of in-group identification. The latter variable was operationalized as the difference between strength of identification with the premerger organization and strength of identification with the merged organization (both assessed with four items)—high scores indicated high relative identification with the premerger organization. Anxiety in response to intergroup contact (see Stephan & Stephan, 1985) and self-esteem (Rosenberg, 1965) were also assessed.

As a check on the relative status of the two organizations and Times 1 and 2, participants indicated on a 7-point scale whether, compared to the other organization, their premerger organization was 1 low in status or 7 high in status. On the measure of the perceived relative status of the two premerger organizations, there was, as expected, evidence that, at both Times 1 and 2, participants from the high-status premerger organization rated their organization as being relatively higher in status than participants in the low-status premerger organization.

In line with predictions (H1), the employees of the low-status organization reported higher levels of stress associated with the merger than the employees of the high-status premerger organization. This finding was evident on the measures of both implementation and identity-related stress but it was most marked on the measure of identity-related stress (see Figure 13.1). Contrary to predictions, employees of the low-status premerger organization rated similar levels of stress in relation to implementation and identity-related stressors. However, in line with the social identity approach, employees of the high-status premerger organization rated identity-related concerns as being less difficult than the stressors associated with the implementation of the merger.

As predicted under H2, participants from the low-status premerger organization, at both Times 1 and 2, identified less strongly with the new organization than the employees of the high-status organization and, in relative terms, they were more likely to identify with their premerger organization than with the merged organization (see Figure 13.2). They were also less likely to perceive a common in-group identity than employees of the high-status premerger organization. On each of these measures, there was also a main effect for time, indicating that across the course of the merger—from the anticipatory phase to the immediate postmerger phase—responses to the newly merged organi-

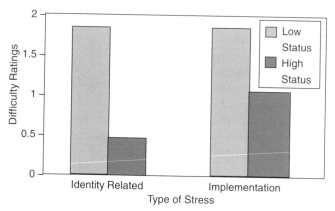

FIGURE 13.1. Difficulty ratings for identity-related and implementation stress for employees of the low- and high-status premerger organizations.

LIVERPOOL JOHN MOORES UNIVERSITY
LEARNING SERVICES

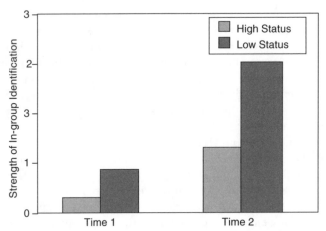

FIGURE 13.2. Strength of in-group identification at Times 1 and 2 for employees of the low- and high-status permerger organizations

zation worsened in terms of strength of identification with the new organization, strength of in-group identification, and common in-group identification. At Times 1 and 2, there was evidence that the employees of the low-status premerger organization perceived more intergroup anxiety than the employees of the high-status premerger organization.

These findings all accord with social identity theory, in that they show that an inferior group membership—a comparison that is likely to be heightened in a merger situation—has a negative impact on a person's social identity. In other words, affective responses to the newly merged organization were most negative among the employees of the low-status premerger organization (see also Brown, Condor, Mathews, Wade, & Williams, 1986; Ellemers, Wilke, & van Knippenberg, 1993; Sachdev & Bourhis, 1991). The present findings add to the consistent body of evidence linking premerger organizational status to employee responses to an organizational merger (Terry & Callan, 1998; Terry, Hogg, & Blackwood, 2001; Terry & O'Brien, 2001). Future research needs to disentangle the interplay among premerger organizational status, power, and size—although it can be assumed that these variables will typically co-occur, there may be circumstances in which dominance in terms of status, power, and size diverge.

In accord with H3a, there was evidence that Time 1 employees' perceptions of permeability for their own group predicted weaker in-group identification, stronger identification with new organization, and lower levels of intergroup anxiety for the employees of the low-status premerger organization but not for employees of the high-status premerger organization. These results replicate those reported by Terry et al. (2001) in a cross-sectional study of an airline merger. The fact that the effects of perceived permeability for the employees of the low-status premerger organization were observed longitudinally adds further support to a social identity perspective on organizational mergers. Specifically, the results are consistent with the basic premise of social identity theory that the dominant strategy of members of low-status group members faced with a clearly superior group is one of individual mobility if the group boundaries are perceived to be relatively open. That is, in the pursuit of identity enhancement, low-status employees, who perceived that the boundaries in the new organization were permeable, transferred their allegiance to the new organization.

There was also support for H3b—Time 1 perceptions of the permeability of the intergroup boundaries for the other organization predicted Time 2 levels of self-esteem and perceptions of a common in-group for the employees of the high status premerger organization, but not for the employees of the low-status organization. These results are in accord with the notion that members of high-status groups are influenced by their motives for identity protection and, as a consequence, are threatened by permeable boundaries. For the employees of the high-status premerger organization, the threat associated with a merger presumably emanates from the belief that they will lose the benefits and opportunities afforded to them as a consequence of being a member of a high-status organization. The evidence of status protection among the employees of the premerger high-status organization was considerably stronger than in the cross-sectional study of the airline merger. This is presumably because the present study obtained a focused measure of the extent to which the intergroup boundaries in the newly merged organization would be permeable for the employees of the low-status premerger organization.

The present research builds on Terry et al.'s (2001) study of an airline merger by demonstrating the proposed differential effects of intergroup permeability, as a function of premerger organizational status, in a longitudinal study. Future research on the interplay between perceived permeability and premerger status also needs to take into account the type of merger. In a merger situation where it is clear that the acquiring organization (likely to be the higher-status organization) is seeking to assimilate or absorb the acquired or lower-status organization (see Mottola et al., 1997), boundaries are likely to be perceived to be less permeable than in a merger that will yield a new fully integrated superordinate organization. Moreover, the effects of permeability—for members of both the low-status and high-status premerger organization—may be weaker in a merger with an absorb rather than an integration pattern. This is because the levels of threat are likely to be relatively low among the employees of the high-status premerger organization, whereas evidence of permeability may be perceived as tokenistic by members of the low-status organization.

There was considerable support for the similarity-attraction hypothesis (H4). The more employees perceived, at Time 1, that the organizations were similar, the better their scores on each of the Time 2 outcomes, with the exception of self-esteem. Thus, in line with the similarity–attraction hypothesis (Byrne, 1971), there was support for the view that intergroup relations are more positive when the groups are perceived to be similar rather than dissimilar. The finding that perceived similarity was associated with more rather than less—as would be predicted by a social identity perspective—harmonious integroup relations may be a function of the intergroup context under consideration. Given that a merger is often predicated on the basis of achieving organizational diversification (Cartwright & Cooper, 1992), perceived intergroup similarity may signal the presence of some common ground between the groups rather than being a threat to distinctiveness.

On the measure of the strength of in-group identification (and weakly on the strength of identification with the new organization), there was some evidence that the positive effect of Time 1 similarity was stronger for the employees of the low-status than the high-status premerger organization. Low-status employees who perceived that the two premerger organizations were highly similar were more likely to identify strongly with the new organization than those who did not. This result is not incompatible with the view that identity-related concerns are likely to be particularly salient for the employees of the low-status premerger organization. Specifically, the perception that the two hospitals were similar presumably engendered the belief that they would be compatible, and hence equally valued, partners in the merger.

SUMMARY AND CONCLUSIONS

The results of the research outlined above support the proposed interplay among premerger organizational status, beliefs about the sociostructural relations between the groups in the new organization, and employee responses to the merger. Overall, there was consistent evidence, across time, that the employees of the low-status premerger organization responded most negatively to the merger. Moreover, there was support for the view that stress engendered by identity-related concerns was more of an issue for these employees than for their counterparts in the high-status premerger organization. In line with the expectation that the identity management motives for the two groups of employees would differ, differential effects of perceptions of permeability for their own group, on the one hand, and permeability for the other group, on the other, were observed for the two groups of employees. The low-status employees were influenced by perceptions of permeability for their own group—presumably as a consequence of a motivation for status enhancement, whereas as a desire for status protection presumably underpinned the effects of perceived permeability for the other group on responses of the employees of the high-status organization to the merger.

In sum, the longitudinal study of the hospital merger provides strong support for the assertion that employee responses to an organizational merger can be usefully understood from an intergroup perspective and, more particularly, from a social identity perspective. As such, the study builds on recent cross-sectional field research (Terry & Callan, 1998; Terry et al., 2001; van Knippenberg, van Knippenberg, Monden, & de Lima, 2002) and laboratory studies (Haunschild et al., 1994; Mottola, Bachman, Gaertner, & Dovidio, 1997; van Knippenberg & van Leeuwen, 2001; see also chapter 12, this volume), in that it demonstrates the relevance of this perspective in the context of a longitudinal study of an actual organizational merger. More generally, the research underscores the importance of examining the effects of social identity and intergroup relations in organizational contexts. Although the importance of such research has been pointed out by a number of commentators (e.g., Ashforth & Mael, 1989; Haslam, 2001; Kramer, 1991; Hogg & Terry, 2000; Nkomo & Cox, 1996), there has been relatively little empirical research on group-based phenomena in organizational contexts. This is despite the fact that the centrality of the work role means that organizational membership is likely to be an important social identification, as are memberships in particular branches of the organization and memberships in different employee classifications.

At an applied level, the results of the present research have important implications for the implementation of organizational mergers. Clearly, they point to the fact that mergers are not only very stressful for employees but that the identity-related concerns—engendered differentially as a function of premerger organizational status—underpin a complexity that is unlikely to be addressed satisfactorily with generic organizational change management programs. Instead, organizations involved in mergers need to consider the extent to which cultural fit can be achieved or, in other words, the extent to which the premerger organizations can be effectively integrated into the new organization. This consideration will require a realistic assessment of the nature of intergroup relations between the two organizations and an acknowledgement of the likely status differential between them. For the employees of the low-status organization, efforts will need to be directed toward identifying the extent to which there is permeability between the intergroup boundaries and, hence, the likelihood that they main gain from the merger. In contrast, for employees of the high-status organization, the extent to which the status of the new organization will be enhanced as a consequence of the merger rather than compromised will need to be considered.

Assuming that there is justification for the merger not only on financial and strategic grounds, but also in terms of cultural fit, then explicit efforts will need to be adopted in an effort to engender harmonious relations in the newly merged organization. Ways in which this may be achieved include establishing favorable conditions for intergroup contact (see Hewstone, Martin,

Hammer-Hewstone, Crisp, & Voci, 2001 for a more detailed discussion of this issue), increasing the salience of a comparative outgroup or competitor and, therefore introducing a new basis for social categorization (Haunschild et al., 1994), encouraging perceptions of a common superordinate in-group (e.g., Gaertner, Rust, Dovidio, Bachman, & Anastasio, 1993; Gaertner & Dovidio, 2000), and changing the normative climate to ensure that it is supportive of the merger (see Terry, Hogg, & Blackwood, 2001). The usefulness of such strategies need to be examined in future research on organizational mergers, as does the identification of other group-level factors that may help to mitigate negative employee responses to an organization merger, particularly among employees of the lower status merger partner.

14

Working with Identities
The ASPIRe Model of Organizational Planning, Negotiation, and Development

RACHAEL A. EGGINS
KATHERINE J. REYNOLDS
Australian National University
S. ALEXANDER HASLAM
Exeter University

*C*ontemporary organizations and their employees are often told that they will not survive the new century (much less the new millennium) without a willingness to participate in ongoing change and innovation. Simultaneously, most organizations aim to run smoothly and effectively, with all parts working productively toward the achievement of core goals. This implies that the survivors of 2001 and beyond will be those organizations that manage to be both flexible and stable.

But partly because these demands are potentially quite difficult to reconcile, the capacity of any organization to function in such a way will clearly be greatly influenced by its systems of people management and decision making. Moreover, it would appear that a workable system will be one that not only functions efficiently but that also encourages and values creative input from its diverse constituents while maintaining a sense of shared purpose. We argue that this is the case for several reasons. First, an organization that values diverse opinions is more likely (1) to seek out, and benefit from, new and creative ideas; (2) to avoid chronic conflicts that result from a failure to tolerate difference; and (3) to be able to cope effectively with change. On the other hand, an organization that also fosters a sense of common purpose is more likely (1) to have a committed workforce; (2) to be characterized by fruitful cooperation over the long term; and (3) to move forward through leadership rather than coercion.

Following this line of reasoning, in this chapter we argue that an effective management model will be one that promotes collective diversity within a context of shared goals. The chapter applies principles from social identity and self-categorization theories (Tajfel & Turner, 1979; Turner, Hogg, Oakes, Reicher, & Wetherell, 1987) to show how organizational identities can first be brought to light and then used as a basis for planning and development. The model we have developed, the model for Actualizing Social and Personal Identity Resources (ASPIRe); Haslam, Eggins, & Reynolds, in press; Reynolds, Eggins, & Haslam, 2001), incorporates four phases of information gathering and group participatory goal setting. Amongst other things, these are designed to encourage the development of an *organic organizational identity*. This identity emphasizes shared values and goals but also accepts and encourages lower-level diversity and difference.

The first part of the chapter reviews some of the empirical research in areas of intergroup relations, conflict management, negotiation, stereotyping, and attitude change that provide a foundation for core features of the model. The remainder of the chapter then outlines how these ideas are integrated in the model. A key feature here is temporal sequencing that takes participants through discrete phases in which different levels of identity are rendered salient by means of intra- and intergroup activities. In general, these activities move from an emphasis on lower level (personal) identities, through to higher level (subgroup and then organizational) identities. At all times, however, the process is framed by superordinate-level issues, goals, and perspectives.

THEORETICAL BASIS FOR THE ASPIRE MODEL

Drawing on ideas put forward in social identity and self-categorization theories, we know that groups come to define themselves through a process of intergroup comparison, itself constrained by the historical, social, and psychological context within which they operate. This means that there is a clear link between the way groups related to each other and the way they define themselves. As self-categorization theory argues, we also know that patterns of shared attitudes and practices are associated with particular levels of social categorization (Turner, 1985). So, any description of an organization's goals, values, and purpose bears a relationship to the content of a social category defined at a superordinate level. However, we also know that at subordinate or subgroup levels, different goals and behaviors may be in operation. Norms associated with different levels do not operate in isolation from each other, because intergroup comparisons (at a subgroup level) are framed by people's shared membership of a superordinate category. Moreover, norms defined at different levels may develop and operate in concert or conflict with each other.

To give an example, the design and marketing divisions in an organization define their roles in the context of their common membership within the same organization. Despite this, they may or may not communicate and operate effectively. The two groups will work together more productively to the extent that they play *distinctive* but *mutually coordinated* roles in line with the same set of shared organizational goals. However, if each group views the other as playing an inferior or unimportant role, both may fail to communicate or consult appropriately about product development, with the result that organizational processes and products suffer. In the event of the latter scenario being played out, practices and relations could be improved through a process of reaching consensus about which goals and contributions are important. And we can see that our understanding of organizational functioning and change in this context might be enhanced by a capacity to describe and predict the processes underlying change in intergroup attitudes and relations.

Theories of intergroup relations are relevant to such issues because they are concerned with the question of how to encourage parties (often ones that are in conflict) to move harmoniously toward the achievement of mutually beneficial goals. While not all organizations are characterized by internal conflict, it is nonetheless the case that most are concerned with maximizing the potential for working together in pursuit of a common purpose. In light of this, it makes sense to consider models of intergroup conflict and cooperation that have essentially been developed with the same goal in mind.

Recent models in this field tend to focus on changing the social structure within which groups operate in order to develop productive social relations. These models are loosely extrapolated from ideas originally detailed in self-categorization theory (Turner et al., 1987) that suggests that (1) categorization is a natural process that underpins self-perception and our relations with others; (2) the self can be categorized at multiple levels (e.g., as an individual, as part of a group, as part of society); (3) relations between parties, be they individuals or groups, are framed by their shared membership of a superordinate category; and (4) parties define themselves on dimensions that contrast self-categories with other non-self-categories defined at the same level of categorization.

The first structural model of intervention, the *decategorization model*, argues that the process of categorizing people (into in- and out-groups) automatically leads to intergroup hostility (Rothbart, 1993; Rothbart & John, 1993). Accordingly, the model argues that conflict will be resolved to the degree that the people involved in it are encouraged to think of themselves as individuals instead of as members of opposing groups. This idea is based on an interpretation of social identity theory that has been countered by other theorists (Turner, 1999; see also Ellemers, Barreto, & Spears, 1999). As Turner argues, social identity theory-driven research suggests that in an intergroup context, participants do differentiate between people along group lines and do seek to perpetuate a positive view of the in-group, but this does not necessarily translate into negative perceptions of the out-group. According to the social identity perspective, conflict will arise only where (1) one group's self-definition is threatening to that of another group (e.g., where identities are mutually exclusive); (2) a superordinate categorization accepted by one group is unacceptable or threatening to the other; or (3) one group is unable to achieve a positive and distinct social identity (in line with social identity theory) due to the perceived action or position of the other group. Essentially, these three conditions amount to the same thing—suggesting that social conflict is associated with incompatible collective self-definitions within a given comparative context. According to this view, identification as a group member is necessary for people to behave as a group, but this behavior will only be negatively directed at other groups where they are seen as a significant impediment to achieving a valued social identity.

In view of these points, the decategorization perspective fails to take account of the social identity perspective's emphasis on the *interaction* between motivation, cognition, and social reality that means that categorization effects can be translated into more than one outcome. Similarly, another model of intervention—the *recategorization* or *common in-group identity model* (Gaertner, Mann, Murrell, & Dovidio, 1989; Anastasio, Bachman, Gaertner, & Dovidio, 1997)—recommends that group boundaries be downplayed in order to improve social relations and decision-making practices. However, in contrast to the decategorization perspective, the recategorization model promotes the development of a new, inclusive in-group, that places one boundary around conflicting groups and erases the boundaries between them—an approach that was also recommended by early advocates of the human relations school (e.g., Mayo, 1933, 1949). This model is in line with self-categorization theory's hypothesis that social cooperation is associated with the salience of a shared social identity (Turner, 1982; see also Haunschild, Moreland, & Murrell, 1994; Tyler & Blader, 2000). The primary recommendation of the recategorization model is, therefore, to encourage cooperation and productivity by engaging in activities that encourage the development of a shared identity.

Although these two categorization approaches have a common origin, their application has been shown to have different outcomes. For example, Gaertner et al. (1989) tested both approaches empirically. They began by categorizing participants into two groups, each of which took part in an in-group creating "survival task" exercise. Having established cohesive groups, the authors then looked at the impact of decategorization (promoting individuation) relative to recategorization (promoting membership of a superordinate group) on feelings of trust, friendliness, liking, and cooperative behavior expressed toward other former in- and out-group members. Each intervention was found to have a different impact on these measures, as predicted by self-categorization theory. In particular, the formation of a superordinate group (recategorization) seemed to elevate former out-group members to the levels of attractiveness also enjoyed by former in-group members. In contrast, individuation (decategorization) reduced former in-group members to the relatively lower levels of attractiveness of the former out-group. The authors concluded that recategorization was preferable to decategorization, in which intergroup division was fomented. This finding has since been supported by considerable further research (e.g., Gaertner, Dovidio, Mann, Murrell, & Pomare, 1990; Morrison, 1997).

However, despite the apparent success of recategorization in increasing cooperation, other research has demonstrated that it may not always be an effective strategy. Brown and Wade (1987) studied the effects of social categorization on group-based attitudes under certain conditions. In their study, two groups simultaneously performed a task that was classified as the same as or different to the task performed by the other group or was not classified at all ("undifferentiated" condition). The researchers also introduced the dimension of differential status after the task was performed and supposedly evaluated by the researchers, whereby each group was told that its competence was equally as high, equally as low, or was simply unequal to (without specifying a direction) that of the other group. Two contrasting hypotheses were proposed and tested. The first (based on the recategorization model), predicted that where group boundaries were meaningless (the unclassified, equal status condition) intergroup attitudes would be most favorable, as all participants experienced the benefits of in-group membership. The second was drawn from what the authors called the *differentiation model*. This predicted that intergroup attitudes would be most positive where each group was able to achieve a positive yet distinctive position (i.e., in the differentiated, equal status condition). According to the differentiation model, these conditions are important for favorable group relations as they allow group members access to a secure and valued identity. In contrast to the recategorization perspective, the model also predicts that intergroup attitudes would be more negative where the groups were not differentiated in terms of their tasks. This is because the opportunities for distinctiveness were reduced and the likelihood that group identities would be threatened was increased.

Supporting the differentiation model, Brown and Wade's research revealed that friendliness toward the out-group was greatest when the role of each group was clearly distinct. Relations between groups therefore changed as a function of intergroup distinctiveness. The availability of a superordinate categorization per se was therefore not associated with increased friendliness. Emphasizing equality of status between the groups did not increase friendliness either, leading the authors to suggest that, where distinctiveness is not available for each group, placing emphasis on common group membership (equality at a higher level of categorization) may, in fact, lead to a struggle for distinctiveness, contrary to the aim of the exercise. They concluded that emphasizing commonality or equality between groups may not be preferable to emphasizing the positive distinctiveness of groups. This is because efforts to emphasize commonality may actually increase hostility between groups or lead to their rejection of conflict resolution attempts where it encroaches upon the validity, legitimacy, and distinctiveness of their social identity.

Developing such findings, Hornsey and Hogg (1999, 2000) proposed a model of *subgroup relations* in which levels of identity threat posed by a superordinate category play a key role in determining the success or failure of category-based interventions in conflict situations. In line with the work of Brown and Wade, and others (i.e. Hewstone & Brown, 1986; Hewstone, Fincham, & Jaspars, 1981; see also chapter 12, this volume), they conclude that subgroups are keenly interested in the way in which they and other subgroups influence the definition of the superordinate group in which all subgroups share membership. Brown and Wade note that, when a superordinate identity is emphasized at the expense of the subgroup identity, subgroup members are threatened and may be expected to act to protect their distinctiveness by developing a hostile view of the out-group.

However, findings of this form do not mean that an emphasis on shared categories should be avoided. On the contrary, as work on the recategorization model demonstrates, a shared category can provide a framework for the development of a common outlook. Along these lines, several studies have investigated the effects on intergroup relations of *simultaneous* identification at superordinate *and* subgroup levels of social categorization. Huo, Smith, Tyler, and Lind (1996), for example, found that conflict between union members and work supervisors was open and defiant where union members did not also identify as part of an organization that included management. However, union members who identified at *both* sub- and superordinate group levels, expressed willingness to work to improve the conflictual relationship. Huo et al. concluded it was not necessary for people to relinquish allegiance to subgroup memberships in order to improve intergroup relations, merely that it was beneficial for them to also "care about their ties to the superordinate group" (p. 45).

As the above research shows, an awareness of identity issues is particularly important in a conflict situation where party lines are likely to be clearly drawn. In such a situation, the differentiation model cautions against a premature emphasis on superordinate identities. However, where groups also define themselves in terms of a shared categorization, subgroup relations may be at their most productive. We also have strong evidence to suggest that the imposition of non-fitting superordinate categories may be detrimental to social relations (Eggins, Haslam, & Reynolds, in press). In other words, positive and productive relations between parties seem to be associated with the presence of *mutual differentiation in the context of a shared perspective*. Haslam

(2001) describes this as a state of *organic pluralism* (see also Eggins et al., in press; Eggins, Haslam, & Ryan, 2000; Haslam, Powell, & Turner, 2000). Such a state appears to be a desirable destination when sustainable intra-organizational relations is a goal. The all-important question, though, is, How do we get there?

A PROCEDURALLY ORIENTED PERSPECTIVE

Increasingly, research indicates that an emphasis on perceptions of fairness and justice are important determinants of satisfaction with negotiation and other decision-making practices (Druckman & Harris, 1990; Pruitt, Peirce, Zubek, McGillicuddy, & Welton, 1993; Tyler & Blader, 2000). Along these lines, Susskind and Cruikshank (1987) argue that a process that is seen to be fair by the participants will, almost by definition, lead to an outcome that is also perceived to be fair. Generally, they feel that a fair solution is one that (1) involves all stakeholders (those who feel affected by the issue); (2) provides opportunities for review; (3) is perceived to be legitimate by stakeholders at the start, during, and at the end of negotiation; and (4) that also sets an acceptable precedent in the eyes of the community.

This approach is also consistent with the work of researchers drawing on social identity and self-categorization principles to study the relationship between social identity processes and perceptions of fairness in decision making (such as those carried out by public institutions like the court system (Lind & Tyler, 1988; chapters 9 and 15, this volume; Tyler, Boeckmann, Smith, & Huo, 1997; Tyler & Smith, 1998). In their group-value model of justice, Lind and Tyler (1988) argue that people are motivated to feel positively valued and, hence, are often more concerned with the *treatment* they receive in decision-making processes than with the *outcomes* of those processes. This argument is supported by a large body of research (chapter 9, this volume). It also fits with social identity theory, in which it was argued (e.g., Tajfel, 1978c) that groups are motivated to achieve valued identities and just social environments. So, where a perceived injustice exists and where group membership is salient, there will be pressure for collective action to redress that injustice (e.g., see Kelly & Breinlinger, 1996; Veenstra & Haslam, 2000). It follows that providing group members with fair procedures should reduce the need to achieve justice through conflict.

Drawing on this idea, Eggins, Haslam, and Ryan (2000) argued that representation in negotiation would provide such a procedure. Importantly, though, they suggested that such representation would need to occur at a level of identity that was normatively fitting (Oakes, 1987) in the light of participants' identity-based perceptions of the issues at hand. To examine this idea, Eggins et al. (in press) tested the relative impact of emphasizing subgroup and superordinate identities in a negotiation context where subgroup differences were salient. In their study, group members were presented with details of a negotiation process in which negotiators had discussed the issue at either a superordinate level or a subgroup level. They found that, regardless of the level at which an issue was framed, participants were more satisfied with a negotiation that had emphasized subgroup representation. They also perceived such a process to be more fair. So, while an emphasis on a superordinate self-category was not detrimental to participants' satisfaction, this was no better than a strategy of subgroup negotiation alone.

Eggins et al. (in press) went on to test the effect of subgroup representation during a three-phase negotiation process that required parties to reach agreement on an issue to do with health funding for men and women. In this study, participants made decisions about (fictional) interventions designed to improve the health of male and female students. They made these decisions first as individuals, then as members of a two-person subgroup, then finally as members of a four-person superordinate group. Half the participants completed the second phase with another person of the same sex. They therefore had their identity as males or females emphasized as a basis for agreement, and they also had the opportunity to develop a position that was representative of their sex in-group. The other half of participants completed this sub-group phase with a member of the opposite sex. They therefore did not have their social identity validated to the same degree and did not have the same opportunity to reach consensus with an in-group member prior to the final stage. Dependent measures focused on in-group identification, perceptions of the representativeness of agreed positions, perceptions of the out-group, and the nature of relations between negotiators in each phase.

As can be seen in Table 14.1, the results revealed that negotiators who were given the opportunity to represent consensual subgroup positions during negotiation (rather than being denied the opportunity to do so) identified more with their sex in-group. In addition, they were more positive about the negotiation process and the outcome, more favorably disposed toward the other party, and reported a more positive interaction in the formal phase of the negotiation. They were also more confident about the representativeness of their agreed outcomes at each phase. These findings are consistent with the argument that, where subgroup identities and issues form a basis for social relations, negotiation processes that are representative of subgroup differences may be beneficial. They also suggest that subgroups do care about procedural fairness, and can be positively influenced by a process that is representative at a relevant level of social categorization. In addition, they suggest that the validation of subgroup identities as an initial step in negotiation may actually contribute toward the development of a shared point of view, as such an approach validates group members and obviates the need for them to achieve distinctiveness through conflict. Further support for this argument was found in a

TABLE 14.1. Means for primary measures by phase of negotiation discussion and subgroup structure.

Phase	Condition	In-group identity	Expectation of sex in-group consensus	Perception of sex out-group as biased	Negotiators worked well together	Ease of agree-ment	Willingness to compromise in next phase
Phase 1	Same sex	5.19	4.68	3.02	—	—	4.25°
Individual	Mixed sex	5.09	4.35	3.34	—	—	4.82°
Phase 2	Same sex	5.60°	5.33°	2.71	6.35°	6.33°	4.31°
Subgroup	Mixed sex	5.13°	4.87°	2.64	5.96°	5.89°	4.89°
Phase 3	Same sex	5.54°	5.58°	2.19°	5.88°	5.27	—
Super-ordinate	Mixed sex	4.95°	4.86°	2.80°	5.20°	5.04	—

° = Means within the same phase that are significantly different at the .05 level.

second study (Eggins et al., in press) that revealed that the development of positive relations between negotiating subgroups was mediated by the presence of a salient superordinate identity.

Our argument in favor of subgroup representation in the organizational domain is given support by an analysis (Eggins & Ryan, 2000) performed on data obtained from the 1995 Australian Workplace Industrial Relations Survey (AWIRS) (Moorehead, Steele, Alexander, Stephen, & Duffin, 1997). This survey was given to employees from 200 organizations Australia-wide. In an analysis of the interaction between (1) identification with the union; (2) industrial relations decision-making practices; and (3) employee satisfaction, it was found that those who reported high allegiance to a subgroup within the organization (the union) as a whole reported less satisfaction with work and a poorer relationship with management compared to those who reported no allegiance to a union. However, it was also found that personal satisfaction of union-identifying employees was not uniform across the board but depended on whether or not those people had access to collective (union-based) versus individualized negotiation over industrial relations issues. In general, union-identifying employees were as satisfied with their jobs as people who did not identify with the union at all—provided they had access to union-based representation in dealing with management. In contrast, the *most* stressed and *least* satisfied employees were those who identified with the union but who had individual agreements. These findings suggest that where employees do identify with a subgroup like a union, it is important for management to recognize the need to allow these parties collective representation in negotiation.

This brief review suggests that an inclusively defined superordinate identity can encourage groups to work together productively. However, we have also seen that the recognition of subgroup identities may be just as important in seeking to achieve productive intergroup relationships. Even in conflict situations, the maintenance of subgroup identities can help to reduce the potential threat of change and increase the acceptability of solutions (Douglas, 1957; Stephenson, 1981, 1984). Encouragement of participation is also likely to extend the life of agreements that are consequentially seen as more representative and, hence, more generalizable to everyday functioning (Pruitt et al., 1993). The benefits of genuinely participatory processes in organizational contexts have been recognized for some time (Deery, Plowman, & Walsh, 1997). However, on the basis of the above research, we go one step further in arguing the case for how and why subgroup identities provide a particularly good basis for participatory planning and development.

The ASPIRe model has accordingly been designed to harness the potential associated with important subgroup social identities. It provides a process through which organizations can move in order to identify their identity resources and deploy these to resolve problems and formulate development strategies and interventions. Ultimately, it aims to contribute to the development of organizations that are more cohesive and at the same time capable of better recognizing relevant intraorganizational differences and of drawing upon these to help people work creatively for the benefit of the organization as a whole. In short, it aims to actualize social and personal identity resources in a manner that helps achieve multiple sets of collective goals.

TRANSLATING THEORY INTO PRACTICE: THE ASPIRE MODEL

The ASPIRe model represents an application of principles drawn from social identity and self-categorization theories. It draws on a large body of research findings to present a systematic approach to organizational development that aims to improve organizational functioning by promoting (1) the appropriate mapping of existing identities and social relations within organizations and (2) interventions designed to enhance the contribution of existing (but perhaps unrecognized) identities within the organization. Importantly, application of the model is, by necessity, participatory. Equally importantly, it brings people together to negotiate goals, issues, and differences within a framework defined by *organizational* goals, issues, and similarities. In any one organizational setting, application of the model will be driven by goals specific to that situation or organization. The model may, for example, be used to help clarify organizational values, resolve intergroup conflict, bring isolated groups in from the cold, improve communication between sections or groups, identify barriers to development, or coordinate subgroup goals and practices in line with goals defined at the organizational level.

Drawing on what we know about intergroup relations, the diagnostic phase of ASPIRe begins by involving organizational members as individuals to identify relevant social identities that may either form a useful basis for, or represent barriers to, organizational planning (see Figure 14.1 for a representation of the four phases of the model). At the end of this phase, managers make a choice about whether or not they wish to proceed with subsequent phases of the model. Should the process continue, members go on to meet in groups that are defined with respect to the categorical dimensions that were identified as important in the previous phase. In these groups, participants aim to establish a cohesive perspective on the issues that precipitated the process in the first place, from the unique viewpoint of their group. In the next phase, subgroups come together in a superordinate forum to present their views and to negotiate a coordinated response designed to achieve organizational-level outcomes. Finally, a forum is developed and given the task of translating identified issues and goals into organizational strategies and practices. The model can be used in an iterative fashion to deal with new issues as they arise, or to review the outcomes of a previous iteration. In this sense, the model pre-

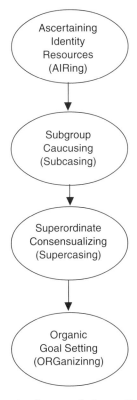

FIGURE 14.1. Actualizing Social and Personal Identity Resources: The ASPIRe model.

scribes a process for organizational functioning designed to be used in an on-going manner. It is not intended to be a one-shot intervention, and it is also important to recognize that the identities that form the basis for planning in relation to one issue may not be those most relevant to another issue.

However, we do claim that, regardless of the purpose for which it is used, ASPIRe can be a practical tool used not only to produce concrete planning outcomes but also to change the way people relate within and to the organization. ASPIRe is therefore differentiated from other approaches to participatory planning (such as the democratic dialogue approach developed by Gustavsen, 1985) by its use of meaningful identities as a basis for organizational development, rather than selection of participants based on their level in the hierarchy (the "deep slice" technique) or their position in the structure. ASPIRe is also distinctive in that it goes beyond attempts to educate participants about the democratic process (Gustavsen, 1986) or produce plans for action. ASPIRe does these things, but it is also a planning model that aims to develop a shared and functional organizational identity and alter intraorganizational relationships at a group level. Our research provides some evidence for the capacity of ASPIRe in this respect. Eggins et al. (in press; Experiment 2) tested the efficacy of subgroup participatory planning versus individualized participatory planning with regard to group functioning and identification. Participants took part in the study in groups of approximately 30 people and engaged in a three-phase planning process that required them to ultimately develop a plan for action that would allow banking institutions to improve their public image. The initial phase involved a brainstorming exercise in which a range of strategies were proposed and the top five strategies selected by the group. In the second phase, participants either worked in small groups of six or as individuals on a randomly assigned strategy, selected from the top five chosen previously. Their task was to develop a case in support of the adoption of their assigned strategy. Finally, all participants came together to present their cases and agree on the best strategy. Measures were taken at each phase and included assessment of participants' levels of identification at the subcategory level (people who worked on the same strategy in Phase 2) and the superordinate level (people working on the project) as well as their perceptions of social relations and the process itself. As can be seen in Table 14.2, results showed that the introduction of group-based procedures enhanced identification with the subcategory, as participants in the group structure condition identified more with the subcategory than those in the individual condition, once group interaction had taken place. This identification persisted into the final phase where parties came together into a superordinate group. While none of the negotiation were perceived as actively conflictual, we did find that subgroup negotiation procedures were associated with the perception that negotiation was relatively more conflictual. However, group negotiators also tended to perceive the negotiation process to be fairer and to place

TABLE 14.2. Ratings of the negotiation process as a function of negotiation structure and phase of the study.

Phase	Condition	Subgroup identity	Superordinate identity	Perception of conflict	Negotiators worked well together	Fairness of treatment	Input was valued
Phase 1	Group	2.99	3.38	2.21	3.53	3.94	3.25
	Individual	2.96	3.27	2.33	3.43	3.80	3.13
Phase 2	Group	3.50°	3.46°	—	—	3.96	3.42°
	Individual	2.76°	3.06°	—	—	3.78	3.07°
Phase 3	Group	3.47°	3.45	2.53	3.47	4.08	3.31°
	Individual	2.88°	3.30	2.33	3.43	3.69	3.02°

° = Means within the same phase that are significantly different at the .05 level.

greater value on their involvement. Interestingly, and in line with predictions drawn from the ASPIRe model, we also found that the relationship between subgroup identification and positive intergroup functioning was partially mediated by highly identifying participants' perceptions that their input had been valued. Also in line with ASPIRe-based predictions, we found that the relationship between subgroup identification and positive perceptions of negotiation were mediated by the development of identification at the superordinate level. This pattern suggests that the effects of subgroup involvement can be positive but are most so where they are associated with the feeling of being valued and, importantly, with the simultaneous emergence of a shared identity. We interpret these findings as support for our model, that argues that subgroup planning in the context of shared goals can pay dividends in terms of organizational identity and subgroup relations. We will now present a more detailed overview of the model.

The First Stage: Ascertaining Identity Resources (AIRing)

The ASPIRe model rests on an assumption that organizations must draw on and enhance meaningful and valued social identities if they intend to harness identity-based behavior to achieve organizational outcomes (Haslam, Powell, & Turner, 2000). Accordingly, rather than seeking to define these identities a priori (as most alternative models of diversity management do; e.g., Nicholas & Semmartino, 2000; see Reynolds et al., 2001, for a discussion), it begins with a process of establishing exactly which identities are seen by employees to be relevant to the workplace. Relevant social identities may be those which contribute positively to a person's sense of who he or she is and what he or she does at work (e.g., as a union member, as a creative employee, or as a teacher). Alternatively, members may pinpoint social categories that they feel actually constrain them or their capacity to work effectively, for example, as a junior, female staff member or as a casual worker. Participants may also identify categories that they feel should be valued and drawn upon but which are currently not. Examples of workers in this situation might include those with industry experience in an academic environment, or new employees in a workplace where novel approaches to work are perceived to be unwelcome.

In order to first establish which identities are important for organizational functioning, participants work through several steps in the AIRing phase. Initially, *all* members of the organization complete a standard questionnaire designed to tap into: (1) the groupings people see as relevant to the organization and (2) the perceived compatibility of subgroups, and of subgroup and superordinate identities. A sample of employees is then chosen to collectively reflect upon the dimensions of difference revealed to be relevant in the questionnaire. These participants are given the task of developing a range of alternative conceptual maps of the organization and its relevant subgroupings, taking into account the summarized feedback from the questionnaire. These maps illustrate relevant groupings within the superordinate framework provided by the organization. Finally, all members of the organization are asked to rank the resulting identity maps in order of their validity and acceptability as a basis for meaningful planning, thereby revealing which subgroupings are seen to be most important in the light of salient organizational issues. As a result of this process, the organization is able to gain valuable information about which subgroupings are seen to be relevant, desirable, or undesirable from the point of view of all employees. Unlike staff satisfaction surveys, this methodology also provides a clear picture of whether staff regard the organization as a whole, functioning system and of where they see themselves within this system.

On the basis of this information, managers decide whether or not they wish to proceed to the next phase of the model. This should be a decision that is based on input from all those subgroups identified as important in the AIRing phase. Should the organization choose to go ahead, the information produced in the AIRing phase informs the activities and clustering of participants in the next phase. However, it should be noted that even if a decision is taken not to proceed, the AIRing phase has already allowed employees to provide information in a way that legitimizes meaningful personal and social identities, and that gives them the opportunity to voice any discontent with self-defining identities that they see as illegitimate—all in the context of some shared purpose. In this sense, the information-gathering stage has in fact been something of an intervention in itself. On top of this, the participatory and social identity-based nature of the process means that, if it proceeds, employees are more likely to feel (and be) genuinely involved. Hence they should be more committed to any outcomes with which it is associated (Eggins et al., 2002). In line with this general rationale, the next phase of the model is explicitly designed to give participants the opportunity to meet in those groups that are associated with the social identities uncovered in this first phase.

The Second Stage: Subgroup Caucusing (Subcasing)

By the end of the AIRing phase, all employees in the organization have been given the opportunity to identify those subgroup dimensions that they see as most relevant to their work and organizational functioning. In the second phase of the model, members meet in groups formed on the basis of those dimensions (cf., Eggins, Haslam, & Reynolds, in press). Within each group, emloyees discuss target issues with several goals in mind. In particular, they engage in participative group goal setting (PGGS; Wegge, 1999; see also chapter 3, this volume) in which they identify organizational goals that, if achieved would allow them to: (1) work together better and (2) to do their job more effectively. As a part of this process they also (3) identify barriers to working effectively and (4) canvas ideas about how these might be overcome. As an exercise that incorporates both team building (Moreland, Argote, & Krishnan, 1996) and goal setting (Locke & Latham, 1990b) this activity also helps establish cohesive organizational units formed on the basis of relevant social identities (Hogg, 1987, 1992).

As well as moving the group and its members toward concrete goals (an activity that has reliably been shown to increase organizational output; Locke & Latham, 1990b), the establishment and validation of important subgroup identities within the context of a shared organizational identity should yield dividends in the form of improved intraorganizational communication and relations. Consistent with this view, justification for the activities in this phase is provided by the large body of work on social identity processes and intergroup relations reviewed above (e.g., Brown & Wade, 1987; Eggins et al., in press; Hornsey & Hogg, 2000). Importantly too, these activities should create a climate that encourages creative, diverse input, simply because the development and active recognition of distinct identities invites pluralistic production of distinctive ideas and approaches (Swann, Milton, & Polzer, 2000; also see chapter 3, this volume). However, because these identities have been actualized in the context of a superordinate framework of goals and values, group products and behaviors will not be so disparate as to be incompatible, but instead should have the potential to be organically aligned with the products of other subgroups. The next phase of the ASPIRe process is intended to help realize that organic potential.

The Third Stage: Superordinate Consensualizing (Supercasing)

The purpose of the third phase of the ASPIRe process is to engage in goal-setting activities that maximize the potential for integrated and coordinated organizational outcomes. In this phase, subgroups come together in a large forum where they: (1) present the products of the previous phase and in light of that information; (2) aim to reach consensus regarding shared goals that can improve organizational functioning. Accordingly, this phase places a strong emphasis on superordinate perspectives. However, such a perspective is explicitly built upon the lower level subgroup identities that formed the basis of participation in the subcasing phase. Indeed, consistent with notions of organic pluralism, the achievement of workable superordinate goals rests on the engagement of relevant subgroup entities. For this reason, supercasing begins by providing subgroups with an opportunity to voice their various positions. The representation of subgroup positions in this public forum not only serves to identify key points of difference and similarity between groups, it also provides the opportunity for groups to reflect upon the issues at hand from multiple social perspectives. As such, the supercasing phase acts as a forum for creative problem solving at an organizational level. In so doing, it also establishes a dynamic problem-solving approach as part of organizational culture.

Importantly, this phase also provides a forum in which valued subgroup identities are legitimized in the context of shared aims, thereby creating the conditions for successful and sustainable organizational relations (cf. Eggins et al., in press; Gonzalez & Brown, 1999; Haslam, 2001; Hornsey & Hogg, 2000; Huo et al., 1996, Jetten, O'Brien, & Trindall, 2002). Moreover, in seeking to (1) define goals commensurate with two levels of organizational identification and (2) reconcile differences and similarities at these levels, it instantiates a synergetic process of organizational development in which parties establish and renegotiate identities, goals, and practices.

The Fourth Stage: Organic Goal Setting (ORGanizing)

At the end of the supercasing phase, participants should have produced sets of goals that are relevant to identities defined at both subgroup and superordinate (organizational) levels. They should have a clear sense of themselves as members of both the one organization and its constituent parts and have a working sense of how these parts relate to each other as a whole system. In short, they should now view the organization and their own role within it from the perspective of an organic organizational identity. In this sense, the ASPIRe process can be seen to have both structural and psychological outcomes.

It clearly remains, though, to put the goals identified in the previous phases into practice. Participants will no doubt have already proposed a range of alternative mechanisms for doing so. However, we recommend that an ongoing representative forum be established to oversee and coordinate the implementation of these plans in a timely, effective, and orderly fashion. Again, it is important that this forum continues to be representative of the parties involved in the ASPIRe process. This will (1) mean that its resolutions continue to be seen as relevant to all employees (and therefore worthy of their commitment) and (2) ensure a continued payoff from the identity dividends created by ASPIRe. For this reason the ORGanizing phase is not intended to be a final point in the implementation of the model. In fact, given the fluidity of the self-categorization process and its sensitivity to social and other exigencies (e.g., see Turner, Oakes, Haslam, & McGarty, 1994), it is important to recognize that the relevance of the groupings that formed its basis will almost certainly change over time. For this reason, we see the ASPIRe model as outlining a process of *ongoing* organizational planning and development.

CONCLUSIONS

As outlined above, the ASPIRe model represents an attempt to uncover and work with multiple levels of employee identity and to use these as a basis for organizational developments at all levels. In this, the process is fully participatory and relates the identification of organizational issues and problems directly to their treatment and resolution. Indeed, at every stage it is employees who provide the content and the momentum to drive the process forward.

Implicit in the model, therefore, is the view that successful planning and development starts with a process of ascertaining those identity dimensions that are relevant to people's experience of work and that need to be harnessed in order for that experience to be enriched (Reynolds et al., 2000). This ensures that the identities with which an organization is attempting to work are meaningful for employees and that the process of identity-mobilization is self-relevant. And because participants should feel appropriately represented in the process, they are more likely to take emergent resolutions seriously.

In this way, the participatory nature of ASPIRe is something of an intervention in itself. However, unlike other participatory systems that often appear (and are) tokenistic (e.g., see Kelly & Kelly, 1994), ASPIRe is based on contributions from people acting in self-relevant and self-defined terms as group members as well as individuals. The process is, therefore, designed to legitimize employee involvement in organizational planning in ways that do not simply create pressure for conformity or preservation of the status quo. This involves the recognition of the multiple levels and diverse bases of identity that help create conditions that are conducive to the evolution of an organically functioning system that is characterized by both stability and vitality.

Although we believe this model accords fully with social identity and self-categorization principles, clearly much more large-scale empirical work remains to be done to establish its utility and viability—as well as its limitations. Points of detail also need to be clarified and these also need to demonstrate how the process can be tailored to specific organizational settings and demands. However, we believe that by helping to bridge the gap between theory and practice, and to translate some of the most important social identity research of recent years into a coherent framework for organizational development, the model has the capacity to take the field an important and much-needed step forward. Indeed, we believe that taking this step may prove to be one of the most positive in helping researchers and practitioners to realize fully the progressive potential of the social identity approach.

PART VI

PERCEIVING AND RESPONDING TO INEQUITY

15

The Importance of Social Identity and Self-Categorization Processes for Creating and Responding to Fairness

MICHAEL J. PLATOW
LaTrobe University
MICHAEL WENZEL
MARK NOLAN
Australian National University

*I*n this chapter, we discuss social–psychological and organizational contributions to understanding fairness within and between groups. This work on fairness has taken psychologists a long way from simple motivational models of personal self-interest; fairness rules do exist and people do follow them (Walster, Walster, & Berscheid, 1978). Unfortunately, however, despite the forward movement, theory and research on fairness has encountered several problems, but they are problems that a social identity analysis is particularly well suited to address. Two of these problems pertain to the scope of the fairness theories (Foschi, 1997). For example, the traditional analyses of fairness rest at an individual level (Doise, 1986), despite many fairness concerns—such as contract negotiations between labor and management—obtaining at an intergroup level (Tajfel, 1982, 1984; van Knippenberg & van Oers, 1984). Moreover, although most fairness theorists place a "moral community" (Deutsch, 1975, p. 142) or some other in-group (e.g., organization, work team) as the scope of application of their work, very little fairness research, if any, has allowed for the a priori identification of this scope condition.

Another problem with traditional fairness analyses is highlighted by debate over definitions of what ought to be considered work-task contributions. As we describe below, some justice theories emphasize the importance of group members' relative contributions to a task in determining what is and is not a fair resource distribution. However, in many situations, people attend to, and make decisions based upon, contributions other than those considered by researchers (or managers, for that matter; cf. Bruins, Platow, & Ng, 1995). This, again, is a problem of a priori prediction. A final problem with fairness analyses to date is that some of the hypothesized mechanisms for *why* people are fair rather than overtly self-interested have actually encountered empirical obstacles.

For these problems of scope, a priori prediction, and causal mechanisms, social identity theory (Tajfel & Turner, 1986), and self-categorization theory (Turner, Hogg, Oakes, Reicher, & Wetherell, 1987) have provided successful conceptual frameworks for advancement. Our discussion thus focuses primarily on how these theories have allowed the field to move forward, by helping solve old questions and by directing us to new ones. Before discussing these, however, we review, as background, two ways in which fairness is often discussed by social and organizational psychologists. The review is by no means exhaustive; instead, our intention is simply to present some basic concepts of the field before undertaking our main analysis.

INTRODUCTION TO TWO FORMS OF FAIRNESS

Social and organizational psychologists most often discuss two broad forms of fairness (Cropanzano, Byrne, Bobocel, & Rupp, 2001; Greenberg & Cropanzano, 2001). The first, known as "distributive fairness," forms the basis of the actual allocation of valued resources between people and groups in non-self-interested ways. A variety of forms of distributive fairness have been outlined theoretically and studied empirically (Deutsch, 1975, 1985; Marx & Engels, 1848/1986; Tornblom & Foa, 1983). These include a need-based rule, an equality rule, a rule that people should receive outcomes proportional to their contributions to the group effort (called "equity"), and a rule that people should receive outcomes proportional to their need so long as they contribute proportionally to their ability. Each distributive fairness rule places a different emphasis, or value, on what is important in the particular context. For example, the equality rule tends to place greater emphasis on interpersonal relationships by not differentiating between people, whereas the need rule emphasizes assisting the weakest individual or group in the community (Schwinger & Lamm, 1981).

The distributive fairness rule most often playing a formal role in organizations is equity. With this rule, potential recipients (e.g., employees) receive resources (e.g., money) proportional to some input or contribution to the organization. Sometimes the input is time spent at work each day, sometimes it is the number of products made, and sometimes it is status (Adams, 1965). Whatever the input is, people who have more of it will have claims to greater amounts of the resource; people who work longer, adjust more cogs, or have the title *leader* will earn more than those who do not. This rule has the positive feature of encouraging people to perform and produce, under the assumption that they will receive more if they produce more (Lawler, 1968). Importantly, however, fairness is maintained only when the ratio of the inputs to outcomes received for each person is equal to that of all other people in the same situation. So managers' high salaries may be justified by this rule, but only if the ratio of their salaries to their contributions to the organization is equal to that of each other employee; if it is greater, the managers are unfair, and simply conning the rest of the workforce (cf., Haslam & Platow, 2001b).

The second broad form of fairness studied by social and organizational psychologists is "procedural fairness." This focuses on the *manner* in which distributive decisions are made and people are treated. Like distributive fairness, procedural fairness takes a variety of forms. One form, known as "process control" (Thibaut & Walker, 1975, 1978), emphasizes the ability of all parties subject to a particular resource distribution to have their say about how the distribution ought to unfold. For example, in a dispute, a fair application of process control would be to allow all sides to have their say, rather than just one or a few sides. A second form of procedural fairness is "decision control." After each side has had its say, a decision must be made. Should all parties to a dispute make a joint decision, or should a third-party arbitrator (e.g., a judge) make the decision? In Anglo-American courts, for example, it is typically the latter, with a judge or jury making the final decision rather than the parties involved in the dispute. An interesting feature of process and decision control is that both must be distributed between group members in some manner, bringing us back to concerns of distributive fairness.

Procedural fairness is not limited, however, to process and decision control (see Greenberg, 1987). Consistency in applying rules across individuals, group members, or time, is an important procedural fairness rule, as is non-biased decision making (Leventhal, 1980; van den Bos, Vermunt, & Wilke, 1996). Recent empirical analyses also suggest that simple politeness and interpersonal respect serve important procedural fairness functions (Lind & Earley, 1992; Tyler, 1997; Tyler, Degoey, & Smith, 1996; see chapter 9, this volume).

THE SOCIAL IDENTITY ANALYSIS: RECONSIDERING THE PROBLEMS

The Relevance of Intergroup Processes

Early statements of social identity theory criticized social justice theories as examples of individualistic social psychology being used inappropriately in intergroup contexts (Tajfel, 1978, p. 47; Tajfel, 1979). Tajfel suggested that overly individualistic emphases misrepresent the full range of possible justice-motivated behaviors, including "exit" and "voice" (Tajfel, 1975; Tajfel, 1978c, p. 59). According to a social identity perspective, the psychology of the individual self is seen as disengagement or exit from groups, whereas an understanding of subgroup challenge or collective voice requires a nonindividualistic psychology allowing for a socially constructed sense of collective self (cf., Turner & Onorato, 1999). This distinction helped clarify notions of social change within social identity theory, and, in particular, what would become known formally as the *social beliefs continuum*.

The social beliefs continuum is anchored conceptually by *social mobility beliefs*, on the one hand, and *social change beliefs*, on the other. Social mobility beliefs lead to an understanding of society (or organizations within it) as a collection of individuals. The use of these beliefs to structure interpretations of social conflict, in turn, motivates the holder of these beliefs to seek group "exit" or to "bail out" when the group is threatened by injustice (Veenstra & Haslam, 2000, p. 168). At the other end of the continuum, *social change beliefs* lead to an understanding of society or organizations as a collection of subgroups that are motivated to find a group "voice" to "stand and fight" against perceived injustice (Ellemers, Spears, & Doosje, 1997; Veenstra & Haslam, 2000, p. 168). Social identity researchers build on these ideas by suggesting that social beliefs help determine which *identity-management strategies* (e.g., *social competition* or *social creativity*; see Tajfel & Turner, 1979) are used by aggrieved individuals or subgroup members within a particular moral community (e.g., the organization or a nation state).

The social beliefs continuum within social identity theory helps theorists to focus on people's thoughts relevant to intergroup relations and group-based perceptions of social structure implicated in many intergroup and organizational justice problems. Syroit (1991) has suggested that a person's positioning on the social beliefs continuum, in turn, helps to structure perceptions of injustice. Specifically, Syroit argues that people's use of social mobility beliefs to cognitively structure a conflict leads to perceptions of interpersonal injustice; in contrast, the use of social change beliefs to help understand a particular conflict leads to perceptions of intergroup injustice. In this way, using particular social beliefs to make sense of violations helps to define the very type of psychological harm and injustice that is perceived in organizational and other sociopolitical contexts.

Adopting an intergroup analysis also acknowledges the relativity of social perception deriving from subgroup positions within the broader moral community (Turner, Oakes, Haslam, & McGarty, 1994). People's understanding of intergroup injustice should be understood as being constructed from the perspective of subgroups whose members desire identity recognition as well as material outcomes, and who pursue their subgroup interests within the social reality of a larger moral community. An understanding of motivated relative perception in organizational, and other social and political contexts, aids an understanding of how each subgroup disputant within a moral community may develop differing, partisan and socially mediated construals of the same critical issues. These construals of critical issues may cover a variety of concerns for organizational management. For example, construals may relate to social understandings of the critical issues themselves, the effect of status-based treatment (van Knippenberg & van Oers, 1984), concepts of blame and responsibility, and the perceived purpose of antidiscrimination law, affirmative action policies, and human rights law as protections against injustice (Nolan, 2002; Nolan & Oakes, 2000). Construals that may differ between groups could also relate to the nature of distributions and procedures, and the appropriateness of subgroup recognition or diversity within organizations (chapter 14, this volume).

Inclusive Social Categories

In addition to arguing for an intergroup analysis (e.g., Adams 1965; Azzi, 1992, 1993; Cohen, 1991; Hegtvedt, 2001; Huxtable, 1998; Jasso, 1993, 1994; Lind & Tyler, 1988; Markovsky, 1985; 1991), social justice scholars have also reasoned that judgments of fairness and justice have group or categorical boundaries. Resource distributions, in particular, require the definition of a circle of recipients who are considered for the allocation (Eckhoff, 1974; Deutsch, 1975). For example, a corporation may have to decide whether to allocate surplus profits within the segment that produced the profits, between all staff of the organization, or to all people with a stake in the business, including shareholders and the community at large. Because distributive fairness presupposes such boundaries, Walzer (1983) has gone so far as to suggest that "the primary good that we distribute to one another is membership in some human community" (p. 31), which subsequently influences our distributive choices. The boundaries of our fairness behaviors can follow along either concurrent group distinctions or temporal dimensions (e.g., when our concerns for the environment include or exclude the likely shares of future generations in such resources; Cohen, 1991).

The concepts *scope of justice* and *moral exclusion* (Deutsch, 1975; Opotow, 1990, 1995, 1996), as well as Lerner's (1977) *just versus non-just worlds* are related to this discussion. These, however, refer to boundaries beyond which one's moral reasoning does not extend and which thus exclude some beings from morals and rights altogether. Following Eckhoff (1974), we regard boundaries as inherent in fairness itself, rather than determinants of the withholding of fairness, because fairness judgments necessitate the definition of a *category of potential recipients* (Wenzel, 2000, 2001). Consequently, for a better understanding of fairness itself, we need to explain and predict how people define the boundaries of distributive and procedural rules. We can achieve this by understanding the psychological process of social categorization, of differentiating people as potential recipients and nonrecipients (Wenzel, 1997, 2000, 2001).

Tyler and his colleagues (Lind & Tyler, 1988; chapter 9, this volume; Tyler, Boeckmann, Smith, & Huo, 1997) have specifically employed a concept of justice boundaries in their *group value model* of procedural justice. Challenging self-interest accounts of procedural fairness (Thibaut & Walker, 1975), Tyler and colleagues argue that people want to be treated fairly as members of a group they share with the decision maker because fair treatment acknowledges their membership and status in the group, and maintains the values of the group. Thus, similar to distributive justice, procedural justice has its boundaries because people want to be, and feel entitled to be, treated in accordance with principles of fairness when they feel or aspire to belong to a group that includes the authorities and other potential recipients of the authorities' treatment.

The group value model argues for a social identity basis of procedural justice, and research in this tradition has tended to equate distributive justice with personal self-interest (e.g., Smith & Tyler, 1996). Wenzel (2000, 2001, in press), however, contends that the distributive justice motive is likewise founded on a sense of inclusive social identity. Following the Aristotelian principle that equals should be treated equally, and those who differ should be treated differently, distributive justice necessarily involves the process of categorization (Perelman, 1963). Nondifferentiating justice notions (e.g., equality; Cohen, 1987) are derived from the perception that all potential recipients are the same in that they share membership in the inclusive category defining the boundaries of the justice problem. Differentiating justice notions (e.g., equity; Cohen, 1987) are derived from the perception that the potential recipients are differentially prototypical of the inclusive category and represent, to different degrees, important values of that category (Oakes, Haslam, & Turner, 1998). Thus, equal treatment confirms one's social identity in terms of the inclusive category (e.g., the organization), while differential treatment confirms the importance of identity-defining values of the inclusive category. In either situation, it is identification in terms of the inclusive category that motivates people toward justice.

To examine these ideas, Wenzel (in press, Study 2) conducted a laboratory study in which participants worked independently on a task but their joint achievements entitled them to a bonus that they were asked to allocate to the most deserving member. Feedback about individual achievements showed one member as being outstanding on the task dimension that constituted the group's strength (and thus value), while the participants themselves were outstanding on the alternative task dimension that was not a distinctive quality of the group. When participants were led to identify strongly with their group, they found the member representing the group's strength as more deserving, counter to their personal self-interest, compared to participants with relatively low in-group identification. In another study (Wenzel, in press, Study 3), group-value based justice was similarly pitted against the interests of participants' subgroup, while identification with a more inclusive group and with the sub-group were manipulated. Results indicated that entitlement judgments were based on perceived group values (the in-group's or out-group's strength, de-pending on the level of subgroup identification) when inclusive identification was high. However, entitlement judgments were based on group interest, and the in-group or out-group member was favored directly (depending on the level of subgroup identification) when inclusive identification was low.

The justice motive, whether it concerns procedures or distributions, seems to reside in an inclusive social identity that implies, and is implied by, the perceived boundaries of the justice problem. Hence, the social identity per-spective clarifies two features of people's fairness behaviors. First, it helps explain when people feel committed to a certain identity, and draw certain justice boundaries that exclude some individuals and groups from the proce-dures or distributions. Second, it helps us understand why people who iden-tify with a certain group do apply justice considerations to procedures and distributions that affect those included in their group, independent from or even counter to their own personal self-interest. Shared social identity is the basis of fairness motivation.

CONSIDERING THE PSYCHOLOGICAL BASIS OF FAIRNESS

Our contention that shared social identity is the basis of fairness motivation stands in contrast to earlier interpersonal analyses. Walster and Walster (1975), for example, proposed that we behave fairly to avoid experiences of personal distress. They argued that we experience retaliational distress upon being unfair because we are nervous of others' retaliation in response to our initial unfair behavior (cf., Reis & Gruzen, 1976; von Grumbkow, Deen, Steensma, & Wilke, 1976). If it is not material retaliation from others that keeps us fair, however, then symbolic retaliation (of sorts) from ourselves may obtain. This latter self-concept distress is said to occur when we are nervous because our own unfair-ness is contrary to our personal self-concepts of being fair people. With either form of distress, fair behavior is a form of distress reduction (or distress avoid-ance) and, especially in the latter case, maintenance and enhancement of per-sonal self-esteem (Kwun & Cummings, 1994; Schafer, 1988).

So, does fairness lead to enhanced positive evaluations of ourselves? It depends on the context. In interpersonal relations, it appears that Walster and Walster's (1975) hypothesis may be correct. We do often feel better about ourselves when we are fair interpersonally. However, in intergroup relations, this seems not to hold. Chin and McClintock (1993) showed, for example, that personal self-esteem was enhanced after people favored their own group in an unfair manner in intergroup allocations when this behavior was consistent with their personal values. Importantly, people expressed greater positive evaluations about their group memberships (i.e., they had enhanced "collective self-esteem") regardless of their personal values after being unfair between groups as compared to being fair between groups.

Within social identity theory, unfair in-group favoritism is understood as a means by which group members differentiate their group from other groups in a positive manner (Tajfel, Billig, Bundy, & Flament, 1971; Turner, 1975; Turner, Brown, & Tajfel, 1979). Such positive intergroup differentiation allows for people's own group to be relatively distinct, and such distinctiveness (in a positive manner) is assumed to lead to an enhancement of the sense of identity people derive from this group (Tajfel & Turner, 1986). Indeed, a long history of social identity research has shown us that, when making distributions between groups, people reliably act in a normatively unfair manner. In experimental situations in which no differences exist on which to determine differential resource allocations (e.g., need, input), people on average allocate resources in a manner that favors the relative advantage of their group over another (even at the expense of maximizing their own group's absolute profit). This pattern is not restricted to laboratories, as Brown (1978) observed it among employees' opinions about pay structures between different skill-level groups.

This research seriously brings into question the relative simplicity of the self-concept distress mechanism as the motivation for fairness. People seem to have increased self-esteem after being fair between individuals, but unfair (in-group favoring) between groups. This suggests that allocations have important meanings for self-definition beyond value consistency. In particular, allocations, as we argued above, provide people with important information about their group memberships. They have the function of clarifying and confirming salient self-categorizations, social categories that are important to people in any particular context. Platow (1997) showed, for example, that people actively infer shared group memberships among employees when resource allocations (in the form of payment for work) follow rules of distributive fairness; when allocations are unfair, however, people infer that the people receiving the money are from different groups.

Further research by Platow, Kuc, and Wilson (1998) showed that people will see themselves more as in-group members when resource allocations are fair within a group but unfair (in-group favoring) between groups. In this study, Australian participants read about an Australian granting agency distributing research money between two Australians, or between one Australian and one French national. Participants themselves were neither the allocators of the resource nor were they the recipients; they were, instead, passive observers.

The results were in line with the hypothesis that allocations provide important information about group memberships. The Australian participants saw themselves as more similar to Australians in general when the granting agency was fair rather than unfair between two Australians. In contrast, the participants saw themselves as more similar to Australians in general when the granting agency was unfair (in-group favoring) rather than fair between the Australian and the French national. To the degree that the similarity ratings are indicative of self-categorization as an Australian, these findings provide further evidence that resource allocations provide important information about group memberships.

Bringing us directly back to the work on self-concept distress is recent unpublished self-esteem data by Platow. In this study, college students observed a college student researcher distribute work tasks to two other students. The distribution was either fair or unfair within participants' own college (the salient group membership) or fair or unfair (in-group favoring) between the participants' own college and a college across town. As in the study presented above, participants were neither the resource allocator, nor were they recipients of the tasks being distributed. What Platow found was that college students' self-esteem was higher when the experimenter made a fair distribution within their university, but an unfair distribution (in-group favoring) between universities.

In all, this research again seriously brings into question the theoretical scope of interpersonal analyses of fairness. Fairness, and its psychological implications, are strongly rooted in our social categories, be they categories of workers, an organization, or a nation.

DEFINING RELEVANT FAIRNESS CRITERIA

Having established the moral community though the identification of social categorical boundaries, the question remains of how resources should be distributed and how potential recipients should be treated (Eckhoff, 1974). Shall we ignore differences between recipients, or shall we treat recipients according to some differentiating characteristics? Which characteristics are relevant? As outlined above, application of the equity distribution rule (Walster et al., 1978) relies heavily on such characteristics, calling them *inputs*, and a situation is considered fair in which the ratio of inputs to outcomes is equal for all interaction partners. Again, however, inputs can be anything from material contributions, work, abilities and efforts toward a common goal, to sex and ethnicity, to less quantifiable features like status. Because inputs are so variable and equity theory does not further specify which inputs would be considered relevant in certain situations, the theory has been criticized as relying on post hoc explanations and being tautological (Schwinger, 1980; Taylor et al.,

1987). In fact, Walster et al. (1978) contend that relevance of inputs is in the eye of the beholder. However, if that were absolutely true, how could justice function as a normative system that restricts individual selfishness, as equity theory maintains? How could one worker agree that another's skills deserve material acknowledgement and justify higher pay? How could any kind of differentiated salary system exist, as they obviously do, without being considered utterly unfair, leading to resentment, guilt, and disintegration among the workforce?

To help answer these questions, Wenzel (2001, Study 1) conducted a study in which he expected that, in a situation where two psychology graduates applied for a job as a psychologist, psychology student judges would prefer the job candidate who better represented what they would regard as essential qualities of psychologists (given that psychologists was the inclusive category). Moreover, the judges were told that their college's psychology education was better in theoretical training (vs. methodological training) but worse in methods (vs. theory) compared to a salient out-group college. When these judges strongly identified with their college, they considered the dimension on which their in-group was superior as more important for psychologists in general. Moreover, when their university was superior in theory, judges thought that the better theorist of the two job candidates was more deserving of the job. Thus, by declaring their own college's qualities as the more important and valuable ones of psychologists, strongly identified students claimed a higher status and positive identity for their own college. As it seems, they "projected" their subgroup's qualities onto the group of psychologists in general (Mummendey & Wenzel, 1999; Wenzel, Mummendey, Weber, & Waldzus, 2001). Importantly for our understanding of the equity rule, people's representation of psychologists determined their perception of relative entitlements of particular psychologists as job candidates.

The relevance of inputs thus derives from the representation of the inclusive category, which is influenced by norms and goals of relevant (sublevel) in-groups (see also Wenzel, 2001, in press). Conversely, an entitlement judgment implies or induces a certain representation of the inclusive category, from which the in-group may derive a positive distinctiveness and identity (Turner, 1987). Hence, from a social identity perspective, relevance of inputs is not merely in the eye of the beholder, but also determined by *social realities* of social groups and their norms, values, and goals. In this manner, a differentiated pay structure would be considered more legitimate and fair if it reflected the values of the inclusive group (e.g., organization, profession, or whatever fits the situation; cf. Haslam & Platow, 2001b). These are values on which employees would be more likely to agree if their views were less determined by partisan perspectives of subgroup identities but aligned through their shared identification with the inclusive category (Wenzel & Mikula, 2001).

THE SOCIAL IDENTITY ANALYSIS: FAIRNESS AND LIFE WITHIN GROUPS

We have discussed thoroughly the importance of shared group membership for understanding fairness.

Reconsidering the Impact of Fairness on Life within Groups

Shared group membership is accompanied by a variety of other factors such as liking for others, support of leaders, and the ability to influence fellow group members for a clearer and shared understanding of reality (Turner et al., 1987). Each of these has been examined within the social identity framework of fairness, taking as its starting point the assumption that distributive and procedural behaviors have meanings relevant for people's understandings of their own group memberships.

In initial research, Platow, O'Connell, Shave, and Hanning (1995) examined group members' liking of a fellow group member who distributed money in different ways. In one study, student participants rated a fellow student more favorably when he or she distributed money equally between two equally needy students than when he or she distributed money unequally. This is a completely reasonable finding, and one that is consistent with traditional analyses of fairness. The more interesting finding occurred, however, when the social context changed to one of intergroup relations. When student participants read about a fellow student giving money to a needy student and an equally needy police officer (out-group member), then participants rated the in-group allocator more favorably when he or she favored the student over the police officer than when he or she allocated equally. In other words, people liked fellow group members who were fair within their group, but who were unfair *in an in-group-favoring manner* between groups. Interestingly, the actual meaning of fairness also changed with the changes in the social context. While inequality in monetary allocation within the in-group (i.e., $300 to one person and nothing to the other) was seen as very unfair by participants, such inequality was seen as very fair between groups when it favored a fellow in-group member.

In their next series of studies, Platow, Hoar, Reid, Harley, and Morrison (1997; see also Platow & van Knippenberg, 2001) showed a similar pattern with group members' endorsements of in-group authorities. For example, New Zealand participants read a supposed memorandum written by the chief executive officer (CEO) of a local health authority. In it, the CEO outlined procedures for the distribution of time on a single kidney dialysis machine between two equally needy native-born New Zealand patients. The New Zealand participants supported the CEO more strongly when he or she suggested a fair rather than unfair distribution of the time between the two patients. However, when the memorandum was discussing how to distribute time between a native-born New Zealander and a recent immigrant to New Zealand, the New Zealand participants supported the CEO more strongly when he or she suggested an unfair distribution of time favoring the native-born New Zealander. Judgments of the CEO's fairness followed these endorsements, again suggesting that the actual meaning of fairness changes with changes in the social context.

Platow, Reid, and Andrew (1998) sought to learn whether a similar pattern of support for authorities would be observed with procedural fairness in addition to distributive fairness. In this study, laboratory participants were randomly assigned to ad hoc groups. Participants were then informed that a series of extra tasks needed to be completed by some of them, and that a leader (actually simulated by the computer) would be chosen from among them to make the distribution. Participants learned that two people other than themselves were to complete the extra tasks, and that the leader could canvass the opinions of one, both, or neither of the recipients about how to make the distribution. This was an explicit manipulation of process control (Thibaut & Walker, 1975). When the two recipients were fellow in-group members, participants supported the leader more when he or she canvased the opinions of both recipients (i.e., was procedurally fair) than when he or she canvased the opinions of only one recipient (i.e., was procedurally unfair). However, this difference in support disappeared when one of the recipients was a member of a different group, and the unfairness favored the fellow in-group member. As with the previous studies, judgments of procedural fairness followed the same pattern of leadership endorsement.

In a final series of studies, Platow, Hoar et al. (1997; Platow, Mills & Morrison, 2000) examined how influential fair and unfair people might be in guiding fellow group members' attitudes. Recall the New Zealand health authority CEO study described above. An additional feature of the memorandum was the CEO's expressed view that short memos should be used to inform hospital employees of new policies. After reading this, the New Zealand participants were asked their own personal views about the use of short memos to inform employees of new policies. As expected, participants aligned their own private views more closely with the CEO's when the CEO was fair within the in-group (i.e., between two life-long New Zealanders), but unfair between groups (i.e., favoring a life-long New Zealander over a recent immigrant to New Zealand), than participants' views.

The findings of this series of studies are simple and straightforward. We like people, support our leaders, and will be persuaded by our fellow in-group members when they are fair rather than unfair within our own groups. This pattern changes, however, when the social context changes. In intergroup situations, this difference disappears if not completely reverses. Although we have discussed these findings under the rubric of within-group dynamics, they are, of course, wholly consistent with our earlier analysis of *intergroup* fairness. This is highlighted by the changes in the meaning of otherwise identical forms of distributive and procedural behavior with shifts from intragroup to intergroup contexts.

COMING TO TERMS WITH CONSENSUS

The findings above on social influence are particularly noteworthy when we consider fairness rules as community-endorsed standards of how we ought to behave. "Community-endorsed" suggests some form of consensus, brought about by discussion and, indeed, persuasion and influence, as different parties negotiate over how best distributions ought to be made and procedures to unfold. In this section, we consider notions of consensus building by subgroups within broad political contexts that are psychologically similar to those of many organizations.

Moral communities have an inherent possibility for political division along subgroup lines when less abstract subgroup identities remain salient for those involved in what becomes intergroup conflict. Each subgroup within the moral community may use different *group*-based construals of appropriate rights and responsibilities when negotiating, for example, employment conditions. These differing construals will, in turn, shape group-based responses to perceived injustice and the associated justice claims. Accordingly, representations of justice may be shared by: (1) homogenous superordinate groups with no internal divisions; (2) subgroups happily coexisting within superordinate groups; and (3) subgroups in conflict within a larger, "superordinate" moral community.

One approach to achieving consensus about justice as a value of the moral community is to create conditions allowing for the recategorization of subgroups in terms of *one* common superordinate group (e.g., Gaertner, Dovidio, Anastasio, Bachman, & Rust, 1993). Earlier in this chapter, however, we discussed how "projection" processes could shape subgroups' representations of the superordinate category and lead to partisan notions of fairness (Mummendey & Wenzel, 1999; Wenzel et al., 2001). Thus, even a reference to the same one superordinate category can invoke disagreement and intergroup conflict about its relevant values as well as views about entitlement and justice that derive from them.

In many cases of conflict resolution in organizations and other political groups, subgroup projection process may be operative. Although complete recategorization to achieve consensus is thought possible by many theorists and managers (e.g., via organizational vision statements, strategic plans, organizationwide procedures, codes of conduct, and grievance procedures), it may be so only in relatively simple or ideal cases. In other cases, more *complex* and inherently disputed representations of justice will persist within the broader moral community defined by nominal superordinate category membership (e.g., Walzdus, Mummendey, Wenzel, & Weber, n.d.). Apparent consensus may thus be more the result of power imbalances and political tolerance rather than as a result only of sharedness flowing from complete recategorization of subgroup identity (cf. chapter 10, this volume). In these more complex cases, justice demands made by subgroups may reflect a desire for "organic" identities to be respected within diverse or pluralistic organizations or social groupings (e.g., Haslam, 2001). These complex representations of justice values cannot be understood fully by using a simple common in-group identity model. We consider some of these complex representations in the next section.

ORGANIZATIONAL JUSTICE AND HUMAN RIGHTS

One way that organizational group members aspire to build superordinate identities is through the use of a common language. This language is often the language of human rights (e.g., antidiscrimination policies and affirmative action), and is chosen because of its explicit use of an all-inclusive social category: humans. At first blush, this all-inclusiveness appears attractive for consensus building. Human rights, however, are justice-related concepts themselves and, hence, remain bounded by the social identity and self-categorization processes described above. As such, the use of human rights must be understood in the same way we argue for an intergroup analysis of all justice-related concepts.

Consider, for example, a study by Doise, Spini, and Clémence (1999). They observed apparent international consensus across 35 countries regarding rights-based justice values outlined in the United Nations Universal Declaration of Human Rights (1948). The apparent international consensus about human rights was evident when the inclusive category "human" defined the boundaries of the abstract problem of social justice maintenance. However, certain types of contextualizing information, historical experience, background knowledge, or, arguably, identity salience, led to systematic differences in how participants prioritized the value, meaning, and perceived efficacy of possible rights-based responses to injustices within their countries. This meant that Doise et al. (1999) could classify their participants as "advocates," "skeptics," "personalists," and "governmentalists," based not on their general representations of the abstract meaning of human rights, but on their contextualized, subgroup views about the justice demands of specific political situations.

Recent social identity work on human rights representations in Australia paints a similar picture (Nolan, in preparation). In at least three studies, apparent Australian national consensus is witnessed when both human rights activists and nonactivists are asked to construct a representation of the purpose of human rights law. Overwhelmingly, participants support an interpretation stating that the purpose of human rights is to protect every *individual* equally (an "equality-driven" construal of human rights), in preference to an interpretation suggesting that human rights should be used specifically to protect the needs of vulnerable *subgroups* (a "needs-based" construal of human rights). There is less support for the view that human rights be used to provide special treatment creating unique subgroup rights protecting indigenous Australians, refugees, or women as vulnerable subgroups.

However, explicit measures of social mobility and social change beliefs suggest that important differences exist between subgroup perspectives within the Australian community. Activist subgroups prefer to use social change beliefs to add meaning to violation contexts, whereas nonactivists use social mobility beliefs when responding to the same source of injustice. This pattern obtains even when both groups perceive the *same* violation to be unfair, and both groups support equality-driven construals of the purpose of human rights more than the needs-based construal of human rights presented.

We have recently found that activist subgroups within Australia (women's organizations arguing for liberal access to assisted reproductive technologies) strategically prefer inclusive and equality-driven justice campaigning in order to achieve maximum support for their subgroup claims within the broader moral community. This result accords with previous analyses of the processes and cognitions involved in political persuasion and mobilization (Simon & Klandermans, 2001). It may also be comforting for people to believe that justice, and rights, have an inherent moral basis, rather than only being used to support partisan perspectives evident during intergroup conflict. Along with this desire for inherent "truth" or moral basis may be a strategic perception by activists that there is rhetorical power to be exploited by appealing to a dialectic of "truth." In this sense, the preference for inclusive human rights rhetoric may relate to the perceived argumentative power of such inclusive rhetoric even in clearly defined conflicts within organizations or social groups.

CONCLUSION

We opened this chapter by highlighting shortcomings of fairness theory and research to date, and outlining various fairness rules. We then proposed that (1) fairness rules must be understood not simply in the abstract, but with reference to specific groups, the values of these groups, and, importantly, the broader social context—including intergroup relations—in which these groups exist; and (2) by understanding the broader social context in which these groups exist, there may very well be a rhetorical function of fairness in continuing political debate. So what conclusions can we draw from our analysis? We think there are three broad lessons that can be learned.

First, fairness rules are real. In any given context, group members know what is fair, and respond appropriately and systematically both to fairness and to unfairness. Employees know when they are being treated unfairly, and they will act accordingly to rectify that unfairness (Greenberg, 1993; Haslam, 2001). Second, the proviso "in any given context" is an integral part of understanding fairness. Actually, the phrase ought to read "in any given group, in any given intergroup context." Groups, including organizations, and our membership in them, are essential for a complete understanding of fairness. Groups allow fairness to be defined, and inform us of the values on which we should make our fairness judgments. Fairness also has the function of reflecting back, informing us of our membership in (or exclusion from) groups, and maintaining or advancing certain group values. As such, the application of specific distributive and procedural rules within and between groups has important meanings to us *as group members*. Moreover, the "in any given context" proviso means that specific distributive and procedural behaviors vary in their meanings from context to context. One form of distribution and one form of procedure for both interpersonal and intergroup relations is simply not a reality of either organizational or psychological life (Caddick, 1980; Diehl, 1989; Ng, 1984).

The third and final lesson, related closely to the second, is that fairness is not an individual, intrapsychic phenomenon. Fairness is negotiated between group members and between groups. It comes about through normal processes of protest, persuasion, and influence. To that degree, there are, indeed, times when fairness rules are employed more as rhetorical devices than absolute moral criteria. Recognizing this, however, is simply recognizing the reality of the resources over which the debate occurs. People and groups *are* engaged in struggles over material goods, and these struggles are often embedded in ongoing power differentials (Platow & Hunter, 2001). For this reason alone, management should never be surprised when unions reject employment offers as unfair. Although the ultimate goal of fairness is the resolution of conflict, the conflict itself is often over the building of a consensual agreement of what is fair. In this manner, management, for example, has no monopoly on fairness nor any greater insight into how to apply it than do workers. Fairness is negotiated between management and workers as they negotiate over their shared understanding of "us," of their common bond and identities as organizational members. The very fact that we do observe people applying fairness rules instead of pursuing their own personal self-interest is testament to their commitment to the social group in which their behavior is relevant (e.g., the organization, the state, the family). Fairness is, thus, real, as are the groups that allow fairness to be defined. So too, however, are the struggles between groups over the actual meaning of fairness and, hence, over the actual material resources for which individuals and groups strive.

ACKNOWLEDGMENTS

All authors contributed equally to this paper; Michael Platow simply coordinated the writing effort. The writing of this paper was supported in part by funds from the La Trobe University School of Psychological Science, making feasible the travel of the second and third authors to the school's 2000 Spring Workshop in Social Psychology on the topic of fairness and justice.

16

Perceiving and Responding to Gender Discrimination in Organizations

University of Kansas
NAOMI ELLEMERS
University of Leiden
NYLA R. BRANSCOMBE
University of Kansas

W omen continue to be disadvantaged in the labor force compared to men (Vasquez, 2001). Women have less power, status, and income than men, even when they have identical qualifications and perform the same jobs (Bartol, 1999; Jacobs, 1995; Reskin & Padavic, 1994; Stroh, Brett, & Reilly, 1992). Moreover, work is highly segregated according to gender (Reskin & Roos, 1990). The majority of working women are in clerical, nursing, or service occupations, all of which have less status and monetary compensation than comparable male-dominated occupations (Jacobs & Steinberg, 1990; Peterson & Runyan, 1993). Women who do attempt to achieve in predominantly male occupations tend to encounter discrimination and a "glass ceiling" beyond which achievement is difficult (Burn, 1996; Kanter, 1977), yet men in predominantly female occupations tend to be given a ride to the top on a "glass escalator" (Williams, 1992). Even women who have been successful in extremely competitive, male-dominated work environments encounter gender discrimination. This was the case with Ann Hopkins, who acquired multimillion dollar projects for Price Waterhouse, but was declined partnership, in part, because she was deemed insufficiently feminine (Hopkins, 1996). More recently, female professors at the highly prestigious Massachusetts

Institute of Technology discovered that they were systematically awarded less research support and lower salaries than their male colleagues (MIT, 1999).

In this chapter we consider a number of social–psychological factors that affect responses to the reality of gender inequality in the workplace. Taking a social identity approach, we argue that two general factors interact to determine responses to gender-based inequality: gender-group membership and beliefs about the social world (Tajfel & Turner, 1986). When group membership provides a subjectively meaningful way of understanding the social context, the self is categorized at the group level. This collective definition of the self creates the motivation to act in terms of group membership (Turner, Hogg, Oakes, Reicher, & Wetherell, 1987). When the social context facilitates the consideration of people in intergroup terms, individuals tend to act in ways that they perceive to be consistent with their in-group's norms and interests, and try to maintain a positively distinct in-group identity.

The social identity approach suggests that the existing state of gender-group relations and how people understand it are critical determinants of whether women and men will work to maintain or change the status quo. For this reason, we first address social and psychological factors that influence perceptions of discrimination against women. We argue that gender discrimination in many contemporary cultures occurs in ways that are difficult to see, and that identity-based motivations can discourage the perception of gender inequality among both women and men. Next, we explore the consequences of these perceptions for how people respond to inequality. In line with social identity theory, we argue that responses to inequality will depend on one's own gender-group membership, and the perceived pervasiveness, legitimacy, and stability of sexism. Finally, we outline the conditions that social identity theory suggests are necessary for reductions in inequality to occur.

PERCEPTIONS OF DISCRIMINATION

In general, both women and men are at least partially aware of their different positions within the social structure. Both women and men agree that women are afforded less status than are men (Eagly, 1987; Stewart, Vassar, Sanchez, & David, 2000), and women report more frequent and severe experiences as targets of discrimination than men do (Branscombe, 1998; Schmitt, Branscombe, Kobrynowicz, & Owen, in press; Swim, Cohen, & Hyers, 1998). Thus, women's and men's perceptions of their relative status are at least partially reflective of social reality. However, there are a number of social and motivational factors that are likely to lead both women and men to underestimate the likelihood or degree of gender inequality.

Social Factors

Because of the importance that the social identity approach places on people's subjective understanding of the social structure, it is necessary to consider the local, cultural, and historical context in which discrimination takes place. In many contemporary cultures, blatant sexism has generally gone out of style in favor of a more "modern," subtle variety (Swim, Aikin, Hall, & Hunter, 1995; Tougas, Brown, Beaton, & Joly, 1995). Modern sexism reflects the belief that gender discrimination is a thing of the past, rather than manifesting itself in explicit antiwomen sentiments. Sexist attitudes and discrimination are sometimes even framed in terms of benevolence toward women (Glick & Fiske, 1996; Jackson, 1994). While the shift away from "old-fashioned" discrimination might reflect a progressive change in social norms, the relative absence of explicit antiwomen sentiments may also make the occurrence of discrimination harder to detect (Jackman, 1994). At the same time, discrimination against women has become institutionalized, meaning that procedures, job expectations, and qualifications often privilege men relative to women (Benokraitis & Feagin, 1986). Such institutional discrimination where the exclusion of women is embedded in "standard rules and procedures" may be difficult to see as gender discrimination (Kappen & Branscombe, 2001). Nevertheless, individuals following the norms of the institution may unwittingly exclude women, even if they themselves are not motivated by sexist attitudes or beliefs.

When gender discrimination is not explicit, other information that would help to confirm or disconfirm that prejudicial treatment has taken place is often unavailable. For instance, individual workers have information about what has happened to them personally, but they often lack important social comparison information regarding the relative treatment of women and men. Without such intergroup comparative information, it is difficult to diagnose the extent to which gender has played a role in organizational outcomes. Sex segregation in the workforce may exacerbate this problem. Women working in positions where they are a numerical minority lack information about the fate of other women in the same job, making it difficult to determine whether gender bias or personal qualities are responsible for their negative outcomes (e.g., Hopkins, 1996). Conversely, women working in predominantly female occupations may rely solely on comparisons with other women in the local context, leading them to perceive their job outcomes as fair (Major, 1994). Even when comparative information is available, when it is presented on an individual case-by-case basis, personal attributions may still be made for the differential outcomes that occur. As Crosby, Clayton, Alksnis, and Hemker (1986) found, people fail to see a pattern of discrimination when work outcomes are learned individually. However, when information about outcomes is aggregated by gender, discrimination is more easily detected. In many organizations, where such social comparison data is lacking, people will often fail to see the intergroup nature of the outcomes received.

In a similar way, the success of individual women who have managed to break through the glass ceiling may make discrimination seem less plausible as an explanation for other women's relative lack of success. To the extent that the success of such token high-status women is taken as evidence that personal qualities matter rather than gender (Ely, 1994; Geis, 1993; Greenhaus & Parasuraman, 1993), people may infer that other women simply lack the necessary qualities to succeed. Thus, the success of token high-status women obscures the structural nature of the disadvantages that women face (see also Wright, Taylor, & Moghaddam, 1990). Indeed, those women who do not achieve similar success may come to believe that they only have themselves to blame.

Social contexts that encourage workers to think in individualistic terms may also deter perceptions of discrimination. Managerial practice and organizational theory have a long history of treating workers as individuals (e.g., Taylor, 1911). When managers focus workers' attention on their individual potential for advancement, they simultaneously discourage the examination of work outcomes in terms of social categories such as gender (Haslam, 2001). Organizational cultures that value individualism and place primacy on the individual self may therefore deter people from assessing work outcomes in group terms. At a broader level, cultural ideologies that value and justify individualism (e.g., beliefs in meritocracy) may mask the reality that group membership has real social and material consequences. Perceptions of discrimination require recognizing that social categories matter, and thus are inconsistent with the widely valued ideology of individualism (Hare-Mustin & Marecek, 1990). Consequently, discrimination may be less likely to be detected within cultures and organizations that stress the value of individual social mobility.

Similarly, individualistic explanations of prejudice and discrimination may also serve to reduce perceptions of discrimination. Psychologists and laypersons alike often explain discriminatory events in terms of prejudiced personalities. According to these theories, discrimination is carried out by a special type of person who tends to be prejudiced because of particular psychological attributes, attitude orientations, or intrapsychic conflicts (e.g., Adorno, Frenkel-Brunswik, Levinson, & Sanford, 1950; Altemeyer, 1996; Pratto, Sidanius, Stallworth, & Malle, 1994). By focusing attention on prejudiced individuals, such theories are likely to lead people away from examining the group-based nature of social outcomes (Billig, 1976; Oakes, Haslam, & Turner, 1994). Subscribing to such theories may lead to the underestimation of the pervasiveness and severity of discrimination to the extent that discrimination actually arises from the state of intergroup relations, not the personalities of individuals. Furthermore, collective resistance to discrimination is less likely when discrimination is seen as coming from a single individual rather than from the out-group as a whole (see Abelson, Dasgupta, Park, & Banaji, 1998).

Motivational Factors

Because encounters with sexism are often ambiguous (Crocker & Major, 1989), motivational pressures to minimize or exaggerate sexism can shape perceptions. Based on social identity theory, we argue that recognizing gender discrimination can be psychologically threatening for both women and men, albeit for different reasons. Such threats to identity may create motivational pressures to minimize perceptions of gender discrimination.

From a social identity perspective, we argue that women suffer psychological costs when they attribute their outcomes to discrimination. Recognizing that one's in-group is devalued, mistreated, or rejected by a privileged out-group has negative consequences for one's social identity (Tajfel, 1978; Tajfel & Turner, 1986). Discrimination attributions also imply a lack of control over one's life (Ruggiero & Taylor, 1997) and can have implications for future outcomes beyond the immediate situation. The negative psychological costs of perceiving discrimination against the in-group should be amplified the more that discrimination is seen as a pervasive phenomenon. Pervasive discrimination has greater implications for other situations and the status of the in-group compared to discrimination that is more isolated (Schmitt & Branscombe, in press-a).

Consistent with these hypotheses, the more that women perceive discrimination as a pervasive phenomenon, the worse their psychological well-being (Kobrynowicz & Branscombe, 1997; Klonoff, Landrine, & Campbell, 2000; Schmitt et al., in press). Recent experimental research (Schmitt, Branscombe, & Postmes, 2001b) has illustrated the importance of the perceived pervasiveness of discrimination for women's self-esteem. Women who read an essay suggesting that discrimination against women is pervasive reported lower personal and collective self-esteem than those who read an essay suggesting that discrimination is more isolated. Further research examined the effects of the perceived pervasiveness of discrimination when women were making attributions to prejudice following a single discriminatory experience. Women who were subjected to negative feedback following a mock job interview reported lower self-esteem and more negative affect when their outcome was seen as stemming from sexism that was pervasive compared to a situation in which the sexism of the evaluator was seen as isolated and not reflective of the attitudes of other possible evaluators.

Given the negative emotional consequences of perceiving discrimination as pervasive, women may prefer to attribute negative treatment to other plausible causes, especially under conditions of attributional ambiguity. This phenomenon was demonstrated in a number of studies in which Ruggiero and Taylor (1995, 1997) explicitly manipulated the probability of discrimination as an explanation for negative feedback. In these studies, women and members of other disadvantaged groups received negative feedback, and were presented with different base rates (0%, 25%, 50%, 75%, 100%) for the probability that the raters were biased against their group. Only when participants were told that 100% of the raters were biased and discrimination was a virtual certainty, did the disadvantaged attribute their failure to prejudice more than to their own performance. These findings suggest that women will tend to avoid perceptions of social reality that have negative implications for their social identity unless evidence for those perceptions is unambiguous. Because attributions to one's performance are likely to be less stable and more controllable than attributions to prejudice (Schmitt & Branscombe, 2002b), perceiving one's performance as the cause of a negative outcome incurs fewer psychological costs than perceiving discrimination as the cause (Ruggiero & Taylor, 1997).

Because perceptions of discrimination against women harm the psychological well-being of women, self-protection motives may encourage them to underestimate the likelihood that discrimination has occurred. Men may also have reasons to be reluctant to acknowledge gender inequality. Although men appear to suffer less than women when they perceive discrimination against their gender group (Schmitt & Branscombe, 2002b; Schmitt et al., 2002), they are threatened by perceptions of male privilege (Branscombe, 1998). Perceiving male privilege taints men's social identity because it implies that the status of their in-group is undeserved and that they may be more successful than women because of differential opportunities rather than because of their superior qualities. Such perceptions of the in-group's illegitimately obtained status can provoke feelings of collective guilt and threaten the value of the in-group's identity by suggesting that under conditions of truly equal opportunity, men might not enjoy the high status that they currently do. In addition, perceptions of male privilege can undermine internal attributions for their own personal accomplishments. As a result of these implications for their personal and social identities, men are likely to be motivated to avoid perceiving discrimination against women, especially when the social context makes their privilege hard to justify (see also Fajak & Haslam, 1998).

RESPONDING TO GENDER INEQUALITY

We have suggested a number of factors that will generally lead people away from perceiving the disadvantages that women face in the workplace. We have argued that discrimination against women is often difficult to see, and perceiving it can have negative consequences for the social identities of both women and men. Social identity theory suggests that these deterrents to perceiving gender inequality as a structural problem in the workplace encourage both women and men to endorse an individual mobility belief system. Under these conditions, women and men are likely to respond similarly, because their behavior reflects a generic motivation to climb the organizational hierarchy as individuals (see also Ellemers, van Knippenberg, de Vries, & Wilke, 1988; Ellemers, van Knippenberg, & Wilke, 1990). In this case, gender is not seen as relevant to social outcomes, and hence workers are likely to engage in attempts at individual mobility. However, when the social context facilitates the recognition of gender discrimination, it simultaneously fosters a definition of the self in gender-group terms. To explore this issue we start by considering the consequences of individual mobility attempts for gender-group relations. We then go on to examine how the perceptions of impermeable status boundaries between women and men lead to self-categorization at the gender-group level. We will argue that the consequences of categorization at the group level are moderated by the extent to which the state of gender-group relations is perceived to be illegitimate and unstable.

Individual Mobility Responses

When social and motivational deterrents to the perception of gender discrimination inhibit a definition of the self in gender-group terms, women and men will tend to engage in individual mobility as the primary route to improving their position at work (see Figure 16.1). When women and men act in their individual self-interests, intergroup conflict is unlikely. Indeed, a number of laboratory studies have demonstrated that intergroup conflict is less likely when members of different groups categorize themselves as individuals (Brewer & Miller, 1984), or as members of a common superordinate identity (Gaertner, Dovidio, Anastasio, Bachman, & Rust, 1993). While the avoidance of conflictual intergroup relations in itself may seem attractive, attempts at individual mobility do not challenge institutionalized forms of discrimination that also have their effect in the absence of the motivation to discriminate (Larwood, Szwajkowski, & Rose, 1988). Thus, beliefs in a social mobility structure are likely to deter social change because they encourage women to pursue individual upward mobility rather than acting collectively to resist gender inequality. In fact, organizational management may encourage perceptions of individual mobility opportunities precisely because this facilitates acceptance of current organizational policy, even in the face of continuing inequality (Haslam, 2001).

Individual women who have experienced relative success within a sexist system are more likely to believe that social mobility is possible compared to women who have encountered more gender barriers. After all, their own experiences provide them with evidence that individual success is possible. Hence, these women may help to maintain institutionalized forms of gender inequality by supporting the individual mobility belief system. Indeed, women at the managerial level tend to perceive themselves as different from "ordinary" women workers (Ellemers, 2001a). Instead, they primarily describe themselves and act in ways that are consistent with their high-status work role (e.g., dominant, ambitious, or competitive; see also Burwell & Sarkees, 1993), but may perceive other women in the organization in gender stereotypic terms (Ellemers, van den Heuvel, de Gilder, Maass, & Bonvini, 2001; see also Kanter, 1977).

Conforming to organizational norms and displaying masculine behavior may be necessary to avoid stereotypical performance expectations based on one's gender-group membership, but sometimes this strategy backfires when high status women who conform to their masculine work roles are sanctioned for not being "womanly enough" (e.g., Hopkins, 1996). The predicament of women who aim for individual success at work is further illustrated by empirical research showing that the devaluation of women leaders relative to men is more pronounced when women adopt stereotypically masculine leadership styles (Eagly, Makhijani, & Klonsky, 1992; Geis, 1993; Heilman, Block, Martell, & Simon, 1989). Finally, if such attempts at individual mobility fail, after having distanced the self from the in-group it may be rather difficult to turn back to other disadvantaged group members for support and acceptance (Branscombe & Ellemers, 1998).

Group-Based Responses

Although a number of social and motivational factors discourage the perception of discrimination, people will perceive it when evidence of group-based inequality is sufficiently clear. When group-based inequality is perceived, and status boundaries between women and men are seen as impermeable, individuals are likely to define themselves in terms of their gender-group identity. In other words, workers are more likely to categorize themselves as members of their gender-group the more that they understand that work outcomes are a function of gender-group membership. When women and men define themselves at the group level, they are likely to act in ways that they perceive as consistent with the maintenance of a positive gender-group identity. We now consider how beliefs about the legitimacy and stability of gender-group inequality moderate how women and men work to achieve a positive group identity, and the consequences of those identity protection strategies for changes to the status quo (see Figure 16.1).

Secure group relations. Perceptions of secure status relations between women and men are more likely when people accept ideologies that legitimate differential treatment according to gender, or suggest that men's dominance over women is inevitable. Such ideologies rely heavily on assumptions that women and men are essentially different, and that these differences are rooted in biology (Bem, 1993; Fausto-Sterling, 1985; Yzerbyt, Rocher, & Schadron, 1997). The stereotypes associated with the essentialist view of each gender are highly consistent with the positions of women and men in society and the different kinds of work that women and men generally do (Eagly,

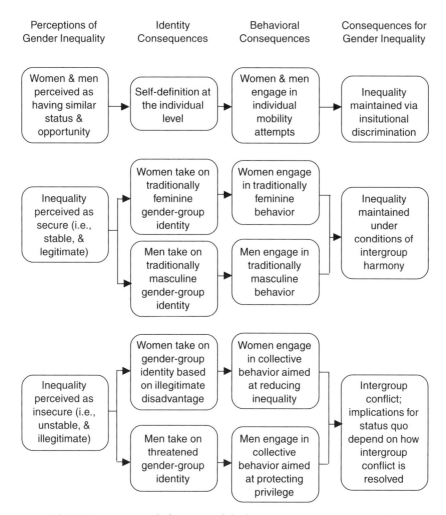

FIGURE 16.1. A social identity model of responses to gender inequality.

1987; Heilman et al., 1989). Essentialist notions of gender differences thus justify the perceived legitimacy of the sexual segregation of work (Hoffman & Hurst, 1990). Combined with assumptions that high-status positions in work organizations overlap with the masculine stereotype (see Burn, 1996 for a review), such ideologies become powerful justifications for men's overrepresentation in high-status jobs and women's overrepresentation in low-status jobs. In turn, because jobs typically held by women (e.g., in health care and education) require more stereotypically feminine behaviors, and jobs typically held by men require stereotypically masculine behaviors, gender segregation of the workforce tends to provide people with evidence that gender differences are real (Eagly, 1987).

Because essentialist ideologies of gender difference lead to the perception of women's and men's relative positions in society as legitimate and inevitable, they clearly have the potential for reinforcing gender inequality (Martin, 1986). Such ideologies maintain the status quo, at least in part, because of the way that they affect the social identities of women and men. Because such ideologies suggest that the status relations between genders are secure, women and men are likely to be motivated to achieve a positive group identity via social creativity—increasing the value assigned to the traits perceived to be associated with the in-group identity. When engaging in social creativity, women may focus on their superiority on stereotypically feminine attributes (e.g., warm and nurturing), but men may emphasize their stereotypically masculine traits (e.g., assertive and independent). Thus, under conditions of secure gender differences, women and men are likely to perceive themselves and behave in terms of traditional gender roles. Furthermore, under these conditions women will be relatively satisfied because they believe that they are being treated fairly, and can derive positive group-based esteem from women's perceived superiority on stereotypically feminine attributes. That is, they are likely to accept horizontal (according to job type) as well as vertical (according to job level) segregation of men and women at work, and only dispute the amount of value assigned to their in-group's defining attributes. In sum, social creativity of this sort is likely to lead to relatively harmonious gender-group relations, but simultaneously reinforce gender inequality.

Insecure group relations. When the status relations between women and men are clear, but the legitimacy and inevitability of current differences are called into question, this facilitates perceptions of conflictual intergroup relations. Given that insecure group relations represent potential gains for women, but represent potential losses for men, regarding current gender relations as insecure elicits different motivations and behavior for women than for men. When women consider gender inequality as pervasive, illegitimate, and potentially mutable, this encourages them to work together to improve their collective lot (Ellemers, 1993; Tajfel, 1978b). For men, however, those same perceptions of insecurity may motivate them to act collectively to protect their privileged status.

As suggested by social identity theory, the more women perceive discrimination against them as pervasive and illegitimate, the more likely they are to act collectively to resist it. For example, to the extent that women faculty at Massachusetts Institute of Technology were aware that their salaries, laboratory space, and research support were less favorable than those of their male colleagues, each of them initially attributed this to specific features of their personal situation, and was reluctant to raise the issue of gender inequality. Only when they discovered that there was a systematic difference between the way male and female faculty at their institution were treated did the women approach the dean to demand that these ongoing inequities be addressed (MIT, 1999). In view of the strong evidence they collectively put before him, the dean acknowledged that gender-based discrimination had occurred, and undertook action to redress the unjust allocations of rewards and facilities.

Self-categorization theory explains the effect of perceiving group-based disadvantage on collective behavior as being mediated by an emerging sense of collective identity (Turner et al., 1987). Experimental research confirms that perceiving prejudice against the in-group as pervasive encourages group identification relative to perceiving prejudice as less pervasive (Jetten, Branscombe, Schmitt, & Spears, 2001). Among women, perceiving gender discrimination is associated with higher levels of gender-group identification (Dion, 1975; Gurin & Townsend, 1986; Kelly & Breinlinger, 1996; Schmitt et al., in press). Furthermore, empirical studies have confirmed that gender-group identification is a strong predictor of collective action on the part of women. Tougas and Veilleux (1988) found that Canadian women's support for affirmative action for women was predicted by both identification with other women and the subjective sense of collective injustice. Kelly and Breinlinger (1996) found that identification with other women was highly predictive of participation in collective action for women as a group. Thus, resistance to gender inequality is most likely among women who subjectively experience the self as part of a collective that is illegitimately disadvantaged.

While challenges to the legitimacy and inevitability of gender inequality are likely to lead women to define themselves at the collective level and mobilize for social change, they are likely to have a different effect on men. Having higher status and more power than women can be a source of positive group identity and can encompass highly valued components of what it means to be a man (Kilmartin, 1994). Thus, men are likely to feel threatened when their privilege is challenged. To protect their in-group identity, men may then be motivated to convince themselves that their higher status is legitimate or that gender discrimination is rare. When women mobilize to improve their status through collective action, men may try to defuse such attempts at social change, and respond in ways that maintain the existing status relations. Men's collective opposition to women's challenges is likely to be most severe when men perceive their fortunes as declining relative to those of women's (Faludi, 1992).

One strategy that men in management can use to blur the status boundaries between gender groups and deemphasize intergroup differences in job opportunities is to allow token women to advance in the organization (Hogg & Abrams, 1988). By creating the illusion of fairness at an individual level, men can defend their social identity against the implication that their group's relatively high status is undeserved. Furthermore, tokenism protects men's status by undermining women's perceptions of group disadvantage and thus reduces their potential for collective action. A number of laboratory studies have confirmed that tokenism can be a highly effective strategy for deterring collective protest. For example, allowing even a small percentage (e.g., 2%) of low-status group members to advance into a higher status group deters collective resistance in favor of individual mobility strategies (Lalonde & Silverman, 1994; Wright et al., 1990).

To the extent that men are successful in convincing women that gender discrimination is rare or legitimate, they avoid intergroup conflict while maintaining the status quo (Jackman, 1994). If women adopt men's legitimizations for status differences, then they are likely to engage in social creativity and act in terms of traditional stereotypes of women. If men persuade women to perceive discrimination as rare, women may be encouraged to engage in individual mobility. If men's persuasion attempts fail, they may engage in covert discrimination that protects the status of men out of the eyesight of women. Finally, men can engage in outright intergroup conflict to protect their social position. This is typically the strategy of last resort because for men and other privileged groups, intergroup conflict may represent the greatest potential for loss because it strengthens collective resistance to the dominant group's privilege (Jackman, 1994).

CLAIMS OF GENDER DISCRIMINATION

While women's attempts to reduce gender inequality require making public claims of the illegitimacy of their lower status and negative treatment, social costs of bringing forth such an unpalatable message can be expected. Using racial discrimination claims as the example, Kaiser and Miller (2001) found that even when Whites agreed that a Black target was discriminated against, they disliked him more when he attributed his negative outcome to discrimination compared to when he blamed his own inadequacy. Similarly, Dijker (1987) found that Dutch participants listed "alluding to discrimination" as one of the factors that causes them negative emotions when interacting with members of disadvantaged immigrant groups.

Because women are likely to incur real social costs when they make public claims of discrimination, they may be wary of making such claims in the presence of those who are unlikely to endorse them. In a study by Stangor, Swim, Van Allen, and Sechrist (in press), women received negative feedback that was clearly attributable to gender discrimination, and then were asked to report whether or not they felt they had been discriminated against. Although women publicly reported discrimination in the presence of other women or when they responded privately on paper, women were much less likely to report that they had been discriminated against when they were asked to give their response publicly in the presence of men.

Research by Postmes, Branscombe, Spears, and Young (1999) suggests that this audience effect is diminished when group identification is sufficiently high. In their study, women responded to questions about the disadvantages or privileges they incur because of their gender-group membership. Women who were low in gender-group identification reported that women were more disadvantaged than privileged when they believed a female audience would see their responses, but described women as more privileged than disadvantaged when the audience was male. In contrast, women high in gender-group identification reported being more disadvantaged than privileged regardless of whether the audience was female or male (see also Ellemers, Van Dyck, Hinkle, & Jacobs, 2000). These findings suggest that when the self is defined and valued at the gender-group level, women may be willing to improve their collective lot, even if they risk a negative response from men by doing so.

When women do choose to risk personal costs and make public claims of discrimination, they may encourage other women to take similar risks and work for the good of the group. The knowledge that others have faced gender-based disadvantage can encourage women to reinterpret their own experience at the group level and internalize a sense of being collectively disadvantaged (Ruggiero, Taylor, & Lydon, 1997). In addition, women may be more likely to respond collectively to resist their disadvantage when other women make it clear that they have been discriminated against. Wright (1997) found that members of a disadvantaged group were more likely to support collective protest when an in-group member labeled the treatment of the ingroup as discrimination or responded with anger.

Recently, we conducted two studies to investigate how women and men respond differently to women who make claims of gender discrimination. All participants read about a concrete case of gender discrimination in the workplace in which a woman at a prestigious law firm competed with a male colleague for promotion to partnership. In all conditions, the woman was clearly described (and perceived by participants) as the better candidate. Nevertheless, she was turned down, while the male colleague was made partner. From the alleged comments provided by the men who had made this promotion decision, it was clear that gender discrimination had taken place. However, in different conditions of the study, we portrayed the female candidate as either *accepting* the outcome, or as *challenging* the outcome. After reading the case description, female and male participants were asked how much they liked the woman in question.

In line with social identity theory predictions, women and men responded differently to the vignettes. Women liked the target best when she protested, while men preferred her when she accepted the discriminatory decision. In the second study, participants were differentiated depending on how pervasive they believed gender discrimination to be. Perceptions about the pervasiveness of discrimination interacted with participant gender and how the target responded to the discrimination. Women and men who perceived discrimination as relatively infrequent did not like the target of discrimination differentially depending on whether she accepted or challenged the discrimination. In contrast, those who perceived gender discrimination as more pervasive rated the target in ways consistent with the interests of their gender in-group. When the target protested, women evaluated her more favorably than did men, but when she accepted the discriminatory outcome without protest, men evaluated her more favorably than women did. Consistent with social identity theory, women and men only responded differentially when they perceived the social context as being organized along group-based lines (i.e., when they perceived discrimination as pervasive).

CONCLUSIONS

We have attempted to outline a general social identity framework for understanding responses to gender inequality in the workplace. Two general points are central to this analysis. First, responses to gender inequality depend on whether the self is defined at the individual level or in gender-group terms. Second, and perhaps more importantly, the level and content of self-definition are shaped by perceptions and interpretations of the social structure. In particular, the perceived pervasiveness and legitimacy of sexism have important implications for self-definition and whether women and men accept or resist gender inequality.

Beliefs and attitudes about inequality do not arise in a social vacuum. Indeed, perceptions of gender discrimination are often effectively deterred by the values and beliefs promoted within the local, historical, and cultural context. Because men typically occupy the highest positions of power within organizations and society more generally, men have considerable power to promote beliefs and ideologies that protect their identity as men and deter women's collective mobilization. By promoting the belief that women and men have essentially different qualities, men legitimize gender segregation in the workforce and may lead women to accept their lower status as appropriate. Furthermore, men can make gender inequality more difficult to see by engaging in increasingly more subtle forms of discrimination, promoting individualistic ideologies, and allowing token women to succeed. To the extent that women believe that they are indeed treated based on their individual qualities rather than their gender-group membership, they are likely to act in there own personal interests rather than in the collective interests of women. Only when women reject these ideologies that legitimize and obscure gender inequality does social identity theory predict intergroup conflict, which can ultimately lead to social change. However, the same conditions that encourage women to work to reduce gender inequality are likely to encourage men to protect their privilege.

Extending this analysis, it becomes clear that what is good for men as individuals and good for men as a group are fairly consonant. For men, working to protect the status of men as a group helps to ensure that they have more opportunities to climb the organizational ladder as individuals. Furthermore, behavior consistent with the masculine stereotype is also consistent with the role expectations at higher levels in the organization (Wagner & Berger, 1997). When men act as individuals trying to succeed within the organization, they are likely to be acting in ways consistent with the norms of both their organizational and gender identities. Thus, men's personal and collective interests are simultaneously served regardless of whether they act as individuals or as group members.

In contrast, women's personal and collective interests can often be in conflict with one another. Unlike men, women are more likely to be forced to choose between acting in the interests of women as a group and acting in their own individual interests. Because women's efforts to challenge the status quo will incur costs, women who adopt social change beliefs and work to advance the position of women as a group may simultaneously limit their potential for individual advancement. Acting for reductions in inequality is especially likely to incur personal costs if women as a group are unsuccessful in their collective attempts at social change. Only when the number of collectively mobilized women reaches a critical mass and substantive improvement in women's positions is achieved are the personal and collective interests of women aligned (Kanter, 1977).

When women collectively organize for social change, they may adopt a variety of different goals depending on specific features of the local and historical context. Because women of different cultures, classes, and ethnicities often deal with qualitatively different forms of gender disadvantage, women organizing around their shared group membership in these other social categories may adopt goals specific to their particular situation. Having become aware of this, contemporary feminist movements have increasingly developed a more diverse and inclusive list of feminist goals (Pelak, Taylor, & Whittier, 1999). In addition, the collective demands of women's movements are likely to depend on prevailing theories of the roots of women's disadvantage (Pelak et al., 1999). For example, liberal feminist movements tend to work within the existing social structure because they believe that women's disadvantage can be eliminated through legally established rights. In contrast, feminists working from a more structuralist perspective are likely to focus on restructuring society rather that working within the existing structure. There is evidence that such structural changes can improve women's status. In Sweden, for example, women's and men's nearly identical participation in paid work is facilitated by providing long periods of paid leave for parents of infants, and allowing parents to reduce their workload for years while keeping their jobs (McLanahan & Kelly, 1999).

Throughout modern history women have collectively resisted their oppression in all regions of the world, often achieving at least some of their goals (Basu, 1995). Ultimately though, the elimination of gender inequality is only likely to be achieved when men also endorse feminist goals. Given that men are unlikely to embrace warmly changes in the status quo, convincing men to accept structural change is a difficult matter. To men, equality is likely to be perceived as a loss, and a serious threat to their identity as men. Convincing men to work for the total eradication of gender inequality may be especially difficult because men's gender-group identity is so closely tied to their privileged social position. Losing their privilege would require men to redefine completely their place in the world.

Under what conditions, then, will men support the elimination of gender inequality? We suggest that men are most likely to favor reductions in gender inequality when social conditions make it clear that giving up their privileges is the only way for them to maintain a positive group identity. Men may be most willing to give up their privilege when membership in a meaningful higher-order category creates the motivation to eliminate gender inequality. For instance, when an organization sincerely adopts the elimination of gender inequality as a goal, men in the organization cannot support male privilege and conform to organizational norms at the same time. However, organizational norms of equality that are framed in the rhetoric of individual opportunity may be counterproductive in this regard, as they render it more difficult to acknowledge the group-based inequality that exists. Thus, identification with the organization and its norms is most likely to lead to real changes when these norms involve (1) the recognition that gender does lead to differential outcomes (in rewards, resources, and opportunities), and (2) the belief that these differential outcomes cannot be justified.

Thus, only when men come to accept that they are illegitimately privileged as a group are they likely to feel morally compelled to advance the position of women and see reductions in inequality as something that benefits men by relieving them of the burden of their guilt. However, such goals are unlikely to originate from male-dominated positions of power within organizations and the social structure more generally. Rather, they are likely to arise when women promote such goals from a position of collective power, and make a convincing argument that gender discrimination is a pervasive and unjustifiable force. Thus, moving away from the individual mobility ideology, and acknowledging that gender-group categorization is an important determinant of people's outcomes, should constitute a first step toward redressing gender inequality in the workplace.

17

Why Consumers Rebel
Social Identity and the Etiology of Adverse Reactions to Service Failure

S. ALEXANDER HASLAM
University of Exeter
NYLA R. BRANSCOMBE
SEBASTIAN BACHMANN
University of Kansas

I was at Barcelona airport a few days ago, booked on the Debonair 18.30 flight to Luton. Turn up no later than 30 minutes before take-off they said. . . . At 21.15, the flight is announced—"but would the following four passengers wait at the gate until boarding is completed." The named four are Blank, Blank, Blank, and me. The three Blanks are by this time thoroughly cheesed off, and beginning to rage. "Why can't we go like everyone else?" "Because," says the re-appearing Blue Blazer, "you have been told to wait". . . . [Anyone] could guess what the eventual message would be. There were more plastic cards issued than there were seats on the plane. Confessing that later rather than earlier could only mean a smaller riot. (Peter Preston, The Guardian, *July 19, 1999, p. 3)*

If you believe everything you read in the newspapers, this is the age of rage. In general, this claim is seen to be causally linked to conditions peculiar to 21st century living. Some of these changes stem from technological and pharmaceutical developments (leading, for example, to road rage and 'roid rage), but a broader class of developments relate to the emergence of a consumer society in which the greater part of many Westerners' lives revolves around service transactions. When Wordsworth opined that "getting and spending we lay waste our powers" even he may not have been able to foresee that by the year 2000 approximately 50% of family income and nearly 10% of our waking hours would be devoted to acts of consumerism, covering activities such as traveling, shopping, vacationing, banking, and dining (Gutek, 1999; Schor, 1991).

Consistent with these patterns, in Western nations the service sector typically constitutes about three-quarters of the economy and has replaced manufacturing as the main realm of employment and economic growth (Gutek, 1995, 1999). And failure to satisfactorily deliver services appears to have contributed to one of the burgeoning forms of rage—consumer rage. This now encompasses phenomena as diverse as air rage, rail rage, bank rage, phone rage, and fan rage.

Rage, of course, represents only one form of consumer reaction to poor service. More moderate forms include anger, dissatisfaction, or disappointment (Schneider & Bowen, 1999), and each of these emotions can be translated into a gamut of behaviors that range from a passive withdrawal of custom to more active forms of protest (both legal and illegal). Predicting *which* of these responses will be selected and, more importantly, *why*, is an issue to which researchers have only recently turned their attention, as part of broader attempts to study and understand the psychology of service interactions. To date, though, such attempts have largely been based on theorizing in which the individual *as individual* is the primary unit of analysis and where the role of group memberships—in structuring both the perceptions of consumers and their behavioral reactions—is typically downplayed or neglected.

In an attempt to rectify this imbalance, the present chapter focuses on the role that social identity and self-categorization processes play in the experience and expression of consumer discontent. A key argument here is that precisely because so much consumer activity centers around psychologically important group memberships (e.g., where consumers seek out service, and are targeted as women, as students, as fans of a particular sport), those groups often have a major and distinct role to play in structuring the form and content of adverse reactions to poor service. Moreover, we suggest that service providers overlook this fact at their peril. For just as it is true that salient group memberships have a critical role to play in encouraging positive organizational outcomes (e.g., Ellemers, de Gilder, & van den Heuvel, 1998; Haslam, Powell & Turner, 2000; Ouwerkerk, Ellemers, & de Gilder, 1999; Tyler & Blader, 2000; van Knippenberg, 2000a), so too do they play a major role in facilitating consumer protest and revolt.

THE PSYCHOLOGY OF SERVICE INTERACTIONS

Two of the most substantial contributions to the service literature are pro-vided by the work of Gutek (e.g., 1995, 1999) and Schneider (e.g., Schneider & Bowen, 1999; Schneider, White, & Paul, 1998). A key element of Gutek's contribution is the development of a taxonomy that differentiates between three types of service interaction—the relationship, the pseudorelationship, and the encounter. Each of these is associated with distinct expectations on the part of customers and service providers, and each engenders different reactions to service failure and success.

Service relationships represent the most traditional form of interaction. In these, customers and providers have personal knowledge of each other and often have a history of prior interaction, as well as an anticipated future. More-over, such intimacy is reflected in a tendency to make relatively benign attri-butions about service delivery, helping to promote customer loyalty and commitment. This means that the customer is inclined to explain success in terms of the provider's internal characteristics (e.g., "He's a good hairdresser, mechanic, doctor, etc.") but failure in terms of external factors (e.g., "She must have been having a bad day," "The disease must have been too far advanced").

As Gutek (1999) argues, because they are expensive to develop and main-tain in contemporary society, relationships are the exception rather than the rule (as distinct from a century ago, say, when services were almost entirely interpersonal). More common today, then, is the *service encounter* which rep-resents the interaction of individuals who are treated as generic and inter-changeable representatives of the categories "customer" and "provider" (Gutek, Bhappu, Liao-Troth, & Cherry, 1999). The problem here, though, is that be-cause they are based on a lack of familiarity and intimacy, encounters lend themselves to relatively malign service-related attributions. Success is typi-cally dismissed as a product of factors external to the provider (e.g., "It was a hard job to mess up") but failure to internal factors (e.g., "The mechanics at that garage are useless"). Unlike relationships, encounters do little to encour-age customer allegiance, and are therefore seen as not particularly well-suited to the commercial interests of service organizations.

It is to deal with this problem, Gutek argues, that a hybrid form of inter-action—the *pseudorelationship*—has evolved. This combines the practicalities and economy of the service encounter with the loyalty-inducing features of the relationship. Rather than centering on personal knowledge and affinity between individual customer and provider, the pseudorelationship is based on creating and appealing to a more abstract relationship between a particular company and its customers. Companies develop customer knowledge by build-ing up databases. Customers, in turn, become familiar with the distinct practices and products of the company. Companies also provide rewards and incentives for loyal customers in a bid to recognize and encourage continued use of their services.

Gutek's taxonomy provides a useful way of classifying service encounters and generates attitudinal and behavioral predictions that fit with prominent social cognitive models of attribution (e.g., see Hewstone, 1989; Nisbett & Ross, 1980). However, it incorporates assumptions from familiarity- and exchange-based models of attraction and loyalty (cf. Linville, Fischer, & Salovey, 1989; Thibaut & Kelley, 1959) that have drawn criticism for being individualistic and lacking predictive value (e.g., see Oakes, Haslam, Morrison, & Grace, 1995; Tyler & Blader, 2000). Moreover, the taxonomy provides no broad theoretical model for *explaining* the cognitive and behavioral aspects of service interactions.

The two main models that have been presented as candidates for this task are based on the analysis of customer *expectations* and *needs*. As summarized by Schneider and Bowen (1999), the expectations model has traditionally dominated thinking in this area, essentially arguing that consumers' reactions to service are a linear function of the discrepancy between their expectations and the product they receive. To the extent that service exceeds expectations, customers experience satisfaction, but to the extent that it fails to meet expectations they experience dissatisfaction. Although it has some descriptive validity, Schneider and Bowen (1999, p. 37) critique the expectations model for failing to account for the extreme reactions of *delight* and *outrage* that can result when service is much better or much worse than expected. These reactions, they suggest, are the critical determinants of customers' willingness to use a particular providers' service in future and to act either as service *disciples* (e.g., recommending the provider to their friends) or as service *terrorists* (e.g., advising their friends to avoid the provider). To this problem we can add that the general process through which expectations are created is underspecified and seen largely to result from acontextual individual cognitions rather than context-dependent social processes. What consumers expect is not, we suspect, the result of fixed and personalized judgments of providers' claims, but something that is *negotiated* with the provider and other customers and that has the potential to change dramatically as those negotiations develop.

Schneider and Bowen (1999) respond to some of these issues by arguing that service reactions are dictated more by consumer *needs* than by their expectations. Along the lines of other theories in the organizational domain (e.g., Alderfer, 1972; Herzberg, Mausner, & Snyderman, 1959; Maslow, 1943), they argue that these needs are hierarchically organized. At the most basic level consumers are assumed to seek *security* (e.g., confidence that a plane won't crash, that a bank won't go bankrupt), at a more abstract level they are believed to seek *procedural* and *distributive justice* (e.g., to be treated fairly and to receive the product they paid for) and, at the most abstract level, they are assumed to seek positive *self-esteem* (e.g., to feel valued and special). For Schneider and Bowen (1999), the key to service delivery is an accurate assessment of which needs customers seek to have satisfied through provision of a given service, with delight resulting from an ability to cater effectively to those needs and outrage from an inability to do this (see also Blodgett, Granbois, & Walters, 1993; Goodwin & Ross, 1992; Oliver & Swan, 1989). Customers who buy a budget flight from Luton to Barcelona may only have security needs (and so may be happy so long as the plane doesn't crash), but those who have paid for a first-class ticket may have self-esteem needs (and so may be outraged if no one tells them that the flight is delayed).

This analysis is in many ways more sophisticated than that of the expectations model, partly because it suggests that expectations vary systematically as a function of the needs that particular consumers seek to satisfy through service interaction. Like the expectations model, though, it suffers from an assumption that needs do not change in response to ongoing features of the service interaction, and from a tendency to define needs in individualized terms. A group of people on a budget flight may well have bought their tickets individually with security needs uppermost in their mind, but on finding themselves waiting together for hours in a crowded airport terminal they may become sensitive to their need for procedural justice and *collective* self-esteem (e.g., to feel respected as a group; Haslam et al., 2000; Tyler & Blader, 2000). Indeed, their *discovery* of this shared need may lead them to express their outrage in a variety of novel ways (e.g., through creative forms of collective protest; cf. Reicher, 1982; Stott & Drury, 2000). While needs certainly play a key role in reactions to service, there remains a need for a theoretical analysis that explains how features of the service context make particular needs salient and raise demands for their satisfaction (cf. Landy, 1989, p. 379).

SOCIAL IDENTITY AND SERVICE

One of the distinct features of recent attempts to apply insights from social identity and self-categorization theories to the analysis of organizational behavior is that they provide a framework for understanding how and why individuals' needs change as a function of organizational context. In particular, Haslam et al. (2000; see also Haslam, 2001, pp. 98–106) draw on self-categorization theory (Turner, 1985; Turner, Hogg, Oakes, Reicher, & Wetherell, 1987) to suggest that needs are directly related to the salience of self-categories that are defined at different levels of abstraction. This means that, to the extent that individuals define themselves in terms of lower-level and noninclusive personal identities (i.e., as isolated individuals), their behavior will be motivated by needs related to the enhancement of the personal self (e.g., to increase or maintain personal self-esteem by improving one's own status), but to the extent that they define themselves in terms of a higher level and more inclusive social identity, needs will be more social in nature and related to the enhancement of the collective self (e.g., to increase collective self-esteem by improving the status of a relevant in-group). Following work by Tyler and colleagues (e.g., Huo, Smith, Tyler, & Lind, 1996; Tyler & Blader, 2000; Tyler, Degoey, & Smith, 1996; see chapter 9, this volume) we would also expect that when individuals define themselves in terms of a given social identity they will be particularly concerned to receive procedural justice from other members of that category (because fair treatment connotes respect), while they may be more concerned to receive distributive justice from members of non-self-categories (outgroups; but see chapter 15, this volume).

Based on work by Oakes and Turner (e.g., Oakes, 1987; Oakes, Haslam, & Turner, 1994; Turner, 1985), we propose that whether people define themselves in terms of a particular social identity will be an interactive function that derives from social self-categories *accessibility* and *fit*. This means that a social identity should be more salient to the extent (1) that it has prior meaning for perceivers and (2) that it serves to resolve subjectively perceived similarities and differences between people into meaningful in-group and out-group categories. Fit will be increased to the extent that within-category differences (e.g., between in-group members) are perceived to be smaller than between-category differences (the principle of *comparative fit*; Turner, 1985), and when those differences are consistent with expectations about category content (the principle of *normative fit*; Oakes, 1987). On this basis, we would expect, for example, that a group of disgruntled customers would be more likely to act in terms of a shared social identity and be attuned to needs and expectations that they collectively share (e.g., for security or justice) if they have a history of acting in terms of that identity (e.g., if they are friends or members of a organization) and if the differences between them (e.g., in opinions, knowledge, and treatment) appear to be much smaller than the differences between them and the service provider.

As well as helping us to understand issues of need salience, self-categorization principles also provide a framework for understanding the basis and impact of the various forms of service interaction outlined by Gutek (1999). Specifically, as Figure 17.1 illustrates, different types of interaction are predicated upon the social identities that are salient for customers and providers but these are defined differently in each case (e.g., at different levels of abstraction). In the case of the service relationship, provider and customer are aware of their distinct personal identities (e.g., John, Jane) but also define themselves as members of a distinct social category ("us") that defines their interpersonal relationship. They therefore act, and expect each other to act, in a way that promotes each others' interests (Turner, 1991). In the case of the pseudorelationship, provider and customer are aware of their distinct social

Relationship

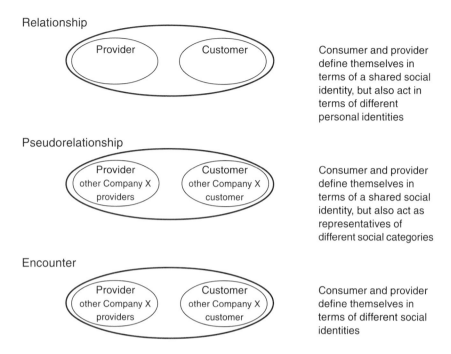

Pseudorelationship

Encounter

FIGURE 17.1. Schematic representation of the different social self-categories implicated in service relationships, encounters and pseudorelationships.

identities as a given company's employees or customers (and act as interchangeable representatives of these categories), but also have the capacity to define themselves in terms of a shared higher-order social identity (e.g., as "Toyota lovers," "Qantas people"). To the extent that this identity is salient and meaningful (which will not always be the case), they should act, and expect each other to act, in a manner that helps promote each others' interests. It is this capacity for a higher-order shared self-definition that differentiates the pseudorelationship from the encounter, for in the latter case no such capacity exists (beyond that provided by the shared norms that govern interaction in society as a whole). Accordingly, in service encounters provider and customer should be far less inclined to promote shared interests, and should not expect each other to do so either.

Amongst other things, this analysis helps to explain the differential pattern of attributions observed by Gutek and her colleagues across relationships and encounters (e.g., Gutek et al., 1999). In addition, it suggests that self-categorization and social identity processes (broadly speaking, who customers and providers "think they are" and how they define their relationship to each other), play a critical role both (1) in defining the needs and expectations of service participants and (2) in mediating between service experiences and outcomes. In the next section we outline some preliminary empirical work that attempts to test these assertions, and to flesh out some of their practical implications.

EMPIRICAL RESEARCH INTO THE ETIOLOGY OF ADVERSE REACTIONS TO SERVICE FAILURE

One of the most basic predictions of our analysis is that consumers will react more benignly to providers to the extent that they perceive themselves as sharing, and acting in terms of, a common social identity. This is one reason, we suspect, why providers often try to appeal to identities that they share with potential customers and seek to incorporate those identities into their company name or image (e.g., American Airlines, Aussie Home Loans, Student Travel Association; cf. Dutton, Dukerich, & Harquail, 1994). As well as having the obvious advantage of communicating what the core client base of the company is or is perceived to be (e.g., Americans, Australians, students), this strategy may serve to attract members of those categories to the company's services and help to retain them in the event of sub-optimal service delivery.

Study 1: When "We" Doesn't Cut It—Evidence that Low Identifiers Can Respond Negatively to Identity-Based Appeals

In order to investigate the above hypothesis empirically, we asked Australian students ($N = 152$) to imagine a situation where they had taken out a loan from a company called "Student Financial Services" (SFS). They were also given an advertising flier for the company which gave prominent mention to the fact that SFS charged no account-keeping or service fees. In one of four independent conditions, the flier (a) either emphasized or did not mention the fact that SFS was an Australian company and proud of that fact and (b) either emphasized or did not mention the fact that SFS was committed to the very highest standards of service. In this way, the company either appealed to the participants' social identity as Australian or did not, and either created a high expectation of service or did not.

Following this, the students were given information that, contrary to its advertised policy, SFS had in fact charged them an $86.00 account-keeping fee. They were also told that SFS had not replied to a letter in which they asked the company to explain and refund the fee, that another student like them had gone to SFS's office to enquire about the fee, but found the office closed, and that the same student had later gone to the office and found it open, but had been ushered out by staff who indicated that the office was closing (even though it was 15 minutes before the advertised closing time).

The purpose of this information was to maximize the likelihood that students would feel outraged by this treatment, with a view to seeing how they responded to the situation as a function of (a) their expectations of service; (b) the providers' appeal to a shared identity; and (c) their own level of identification with the category Australian (high vs. low). Accordingly, after receiving this information about SFS's service, measures were taken of the students' (a) anger; (b) willingness to use SFS services in future (a measure of passive protest); and (c) willingness to kick over a flower pot that was in the foyer of SFS's office (a measure of antinormative protest).

As expected, the results revealed a high level of indignation and outrage on the part of the students (on 7-point scales, the overall mean for the three dependent measures was 5.05). Analysis of variance also revealed a significant two-way interaction between service expectations and responses on the three dependent measures. While responses on the first two measures (anger and passive terrorism) were close to ceiling, antinormative protest was lower when SFS had not created high expectations compared to when it had. More importantly, across all three measures, the analysis also revealed a significant three-way interaction between expectations, appeal to shared identity, and level of participants' identification with Australia. The means for the three measures combined are presented in Figure 17.2. As can be seen, the interaction arose from the fact that adverse reactions to SFS's poor service were particularly pronounced when the company had created high expectations of service and appealed to an Australian identity, but the students did not identify strongly with that social category.

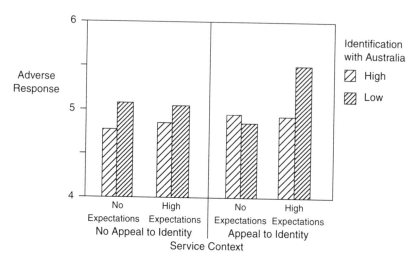

FIGURE 17.2. Study 1: Adverse responses to service failure as a function of service context and customers' identification with Australia.

This pattern is clearly consistent with our general argument that social categorization processes play an important role in structuring responses to service failure. In particular, it appears that identification with a shared category will determine how consumers respond to appeals to that identity in the event of poor service. In this case customers were particularly aggrieved when a service provider had broken promises of service and was seen to be appealing to a category membership that those customers did not themselves share. In contrast, customers who did share that identity were more forgiving under these circumstances (and no more outraged than those who had not been promised high service or had not been exposed to identity-based appeals).

Thus, there may be some dividends for providers that flow from invoking a social identity that is shared with clients (along lines suggested by Gutek's, 1999, analysis of pseudorelationships), but it also appears that there will be a downside to this strategy that is reflected in the adverse reaction of customers who are less committed to that identity. Appeals to identity may thus be something of a double-edged sword: helping to mollify the "true believers" but serving to aggravate the disaffected.

Study 2: When Saying Sorry Matters—Evidence that Identity-Based Service Relationships Demand Respect as Much as (if not more than) Material Restitution

Following on from Study 1, we conducted a second experiment to examine the impact of identity-related processes on attempts by providers to *recover* from the effects of delivering poor service (Dewar, 2000). In this study, students ($N = 120$) responded to a situation in which their car had broken down and they had taken it to be fixed either by a mechanic (Terry) that they had always used in the past (i.e., a provider with whom they had a service relationship), or by one that they had simply chosen because his garage was convenient (a service encounter). The participants were told that after the initial repairs, the car broke down again and that they took it back to the mechanic. The mechanic's response conveyed either high or low distributive justice and either high or low procedural justice. Distributive justice was manipulated by telling students that the mechanic had indicated he would (or would not) repair the car free of charge; procedural justice was manipulated by telling them that he had (or had not) also sincerely apologized for the fact that their car had not been repaired correctly. We then measured participants' (a) identification with the mechanic; (b) reluctance to use the mechanic in future (a measure of passive protest); and (c) willingness to discourage their friends from using his services (a measure of active protest).

Participants did indeed identify more with the mechanic in the service relationship than in the service encounter. Analysis of variance also revealed a three-way interaction on this measure, indicating that identification with the mechanic was highest in the context of a service relationship where he delivered both distributive and procedural justice. Examination of responses on the two protest measures also suggested that identification with the mechanic was translated into more positive responses to service failure. Participants were less likely to protest actively in a service relationship than in a service encounter.

This analysis also revealed a four-way interaction between form of response (active vs. passive terrorism), form of interaction (relationship vs. encounter), and procedural and distributive justice levels (high vs. low). Tests indicated that most of the variation in responses occurred when distributive justice was high. Relevant means are presented in Figure 17.3. From this it can be seen that there was a main effect for form of protest and for procedural justice. Generally, then, students were less likely to protest actively than passively and less likely to protest when they received an apology from the mechanic than when they didn't. However, a three-way interaction between relationship type, form of terrorism, and level of procedural justice arose from the fact that students indicated they would be much more inclined to engage in more active acts of consumer terrorism when they had a service relationship with the mechanic and he had displayed distributive but not procedural justice.

Consistent with work on the group-value model (e.g., Tyler et al., 1996; Smith & Tyler, 1997; see chapter 9, this volume), it thus appears that consumers were particularly vexed by service failure and were likely to respond to it in an actively adverse way when they believed that they and the mechanic shared

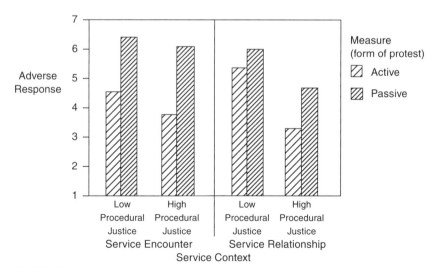

FIGURE 17.3. Study 2: Adverse responses to service failure (in the context of high distributive justice) as a function of response type, interaction type, and level of procedural justice.

an identity but he had failed to treat them with a level of respect commensurate with that identity. A shared social identity (realized here in the form of a service relationship) thus brings with it expectations of procedural justice and, if these are disregarded, consumers are more disposed actively to seek retribution. By the same token, these expectations were less relevant in the context of a service encounter. Here students were relatively content so long as they received distributive justice.

In this instance, then, the social identity approach advances understanding of responses to service failure by showing how different forms of service interaction make salient different needs and expectations—with different outcomes emerging in the two forms of interaction when particular needs and expectations are violated. As Study 1 had suggested, appeals to a shared social identity may encourage consumers to focus less on distributive outcomes, but this brings with it a requirement to satisfy procedural expectations. Indeed, the data from Study 2 imply that customers may be most disposed to commercially damaging forms of protest not when they fail to receive an expected service, but when they believe that sharing an identity-based relationship entitles them to be treated with respect and that respect is then not forthcoming.

Study 3: When Groups Rebel–Evidence that Social Identity Fit and Accessibility Interact to Encourage Collective Protest

The above studies indicate that consumer responses are affected by social identity-related concerns, even in one-on-one service interactions. However, social identity and self-categorization theories also lead us to predict that responses might be even more dramatic when individuals move from perceiving themselves as individual agents to perceiving themselves as part of a collective. To investigate this issue we conducted two studies modeled closely on previous work by Wright and his colleagues (e.g., Wright, 1997; Wright, Taylor, & Moghaddam, 1990; see also Lalonde & Silverman, 1994; Reynolds, Oakes, Haslam, Nolan, & Dolnik, 2000).

In the first of these studies, participants ($N = 84$) were presented with a scenario in which they had applied for tickets to a sporting event and were told to go to an office on a particular day to see if their application had been successful. On arrival at the office they learn that issue of the tickets has been delayed and they should return the following week. On that date, they turn up at the ticket office either with (a) nine *friends* or (b) nine *strangers* who are making the same application. All participants learn that they will not receive the desired tickets. They also learn that either (a) none of these nine people has been allocated tickets (a *closed* condition); (b) that three of the nine have been successful (a *quota* condition); or (c) that all nine of the other people have been successful in gaining the tickets (an *open* condition). In line with self-categorization theory (e.g., Turner, 1985; Oakes, 1987), the first of these manipulations was intended to impact on the *accessibility* of a social self-category—with perceivers being more ready to define themselves in terms of a shared social identity in the friends than in the strangers condition. The second manipulation was intended to impact upon the *fit* of a social-self category—with participants being least likely to define themselves as sharing an identity with the other applicants in the *open* condition and most likely to do so in the *closed* condition. Accordingly, we expected that participants would be most likely to behave collectively (as members of a common group) in the closed-friends condition, and most likely to behave as individuals in the open-strangers condition.

To examine the impact of these manipulations, participants were asked to indicate (a) their level of anger; (b) their willingness to share their grievances with the other applicants; and (c) their willingness to engage in collective protest by approaching the other participants to organize a petition of complaint. The results on these measures are presented in Figure 17.4. Analyses of variance revealed significant main effects for all three measures, a two-way interaction between fit and measure, and a three-way interaction between fit, accessibility, and measure.

The interaction between treatment and measure reflected the fact that participants were more likely to share their grievances with other applicants when access to the event was completely closed but most likely to get angry when they were the only applicant denied tickets. This pattern makes theoretical sense, but the clearest support for our predictions was provided through decomposition of the three-way interaction via separate two-way analyses on

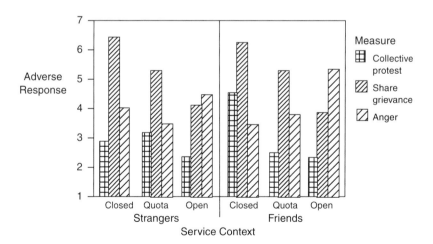

FIGURE 17.4. Study 3: Adverse responses to service failure as a function of response type, others seeking service and quota receiving service.

each measure. In particular, this analysis revealed a two-way interaction on the collective protest measure indicating that customers were most likely to seek to organize a petition in the condition where all applicants were denied tickets and all were friends of the participant. Interestingly too, this was the only condition in which desire to organize a collective protest exceeded participants' anger level. Indeed, in the study as a whole, there was evidence of a negative relationship between these two measures. Thus, while factors that made the group salient increased the likelihood of collective action (action that was in some sense adverse), that action also seemed to diffuse or creatively channel customers' sense of outrage.

At one level, our findings might encourage providers to engage in practices that undermine the entitativity of groups because these reduce the fit and accessibility of social self-categories and therefore reduce the likelihood of highly visible and publicly damaging collective action (Oakes, 1987; Reynolds, Oakes, Haslam, Turner, & Ryan, in press; Veenstra & Haslam, 2000). However, at another level they also suggest that such strategies might lead to more angry forms of displacement behavior. These behaviors may be less visible, but they may also be more idiosyncratic and more difficult to monitor. At the very least, it appears that the barring of avenues to collective protest is unlikely to make an organization's underlying problems disappear.

Study 4: When Tokenism Fails—Evidence that Violations of Identity-Based Interchangeability Lead to Antinormative Behavior

In order to explore the idea that the factors that lead to collective protest are not necessarily the same as those that lead to more antinormative (e.g., illegal) behavior, we conducted a final study. The design of this was modeled closely on that of Study 3, although here the scenario related to a domain in which issues of consumer rage have recently been much more topical—air travel. In this study, American students ($N = 134$) were asked to imagine that they had booked flights for an overseas vacation that they had been planning for some time. However, upon arriving at the check-in desk with nine other people (*friends* or *strangers*), they were told that there was only room on the plane for (a) the other nine people (*open*); (b) three of the other people (*quota*); or (c) none of the other people (*closed*). The study included two of the same measures as Study 3 (anger and collective protest: "Act collectively to make a special plea to the airport manager to be put on the flight"), as well as an aggregate measure of *vandalism*. The latter measure was constructed by asking participants how likely they would be to engage in five illegal and antisocial behaviors (e.g., sabotaging the airline's computers, ripping seats in the airport lounge, pouring soft drink on the carpet; $\alpha = .90$). Results are presented in Figure 17.5.

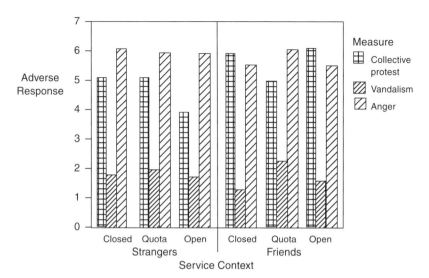

FIGURE 17.5. Study 4: Adverse responses to service failure as a function of response type, others seeking service and quota receiving service.

Overall, anger and willingness to engage in collective protest were much higher than in the previous study. Nonetheless, the pattern of results on the anger and collective protest measures was quite similar to that previously observed. So, although anger generally exceeded collective protest this was not the case under conditions of high accessibility (friends) and fit (closed). Interestingly too, and consistent with the arguments developed in relation to Study 3, this was also the condition in which there was least evidence of a willingness to engage in acts of vandalism.

Analysis of variance in fact suggested that vandalism was most likely to be countenanced in the condition where a social identity was accessible but the airline had imposed a quota on the number of people who could board the plane. Interpreted from the perspective of self-categorization theory, this may be because in this condition (a) the airline's action appeared to violate principles of procedural justice (by failing to treat members of a common category equivalently; see Platow, O'Connell, Shave, & Hanning, 1995) but (b) consumers were still in a position to respond collectively (with their other friends not placed on the flight) in order to exact some sort of retribution.

Again, then, these findings point to some of the dangers of tokenistic strategies that violate justice needs associated with a salient social identity. As our data and the work of Wright and colleagues (e.g., 1997; Wright & Taylor, 1998) suggests, tokenism may be an effective strategy for reducing collective protest, but it can also backfire by motivating behavior that is socially far less functional and, from an organization's perspective, far less manageable.

CONCLUSION

These studies give some indication of the significant role that social identity and self-categorization processes can play in the structuring of consumer responses to service failure. Consistent with the basic tenets of the social identity approach, the evidence here suggests that when made salient by features of social context, group memberships transform the psychology of the individual and make possible new forms of behavior (Haslam, 2001; Reicher, 1982; Turner, 1982, 1991, 2001). In the organizational domain, a great deal of this behavior is highly sought-after (e.g., compliance, loyalty, citizenship, discipleship), and this is probably one reason why providers often go out of their way to appeal to consumers' aspirations as group members (e.g., to be a better parent, a better wife, a better man). At the same time though, where groups are made salient through service interactions but service fails to satisfy needs and expectations, they can also be associated with novel forms of behavior that are very much *un*wanted (e.g., protest and terrorism). In this regard, the present research should sound warnings to providers of poor service who (a) appeal to social identities that are not shared with consumers (Study 1); (b) are procedurally unjust to those with whom they do share a social identity (Study 2); or (c) are distributively and procedurally unjust to all (Study 3) or some (Study 4) of the individuals in a group when those individuals define themselves in terms of a shared social identity.

But as a prelude to some final comments, let us return to Peter Preston, lamenting his horror experience at Barcelona airport with the three Blanks:

> I'll spare you the rest. The sting in the tail comes a few hours later, in the bleary morning, as the boss of the airport staff union beams across Breakfast Television, denouncing the spread of rage against his members and demanding formal staff training to counter it. Well, fine. Training, whether in karate or quick sprints to the exit, always helps. But sometimes—just sometimes—rage isn't an aberration, a mindless fury turned against innocent middle men or women. It is an absolutely rational response to absolutely crass performance. You don't feel better, suffering in bleak, introverted silence: you need to howl out loud. (1999, p. 3)

One important message of this chapter is that individuals who receive poor service are far more likely to "howl out loud" when they feel collectively affronted and are in a position to respond collectively (like the Blanks in Barcelona). And this is not because groups are any more irrational than individuals (indeed, evidence that it is isolated individuals who are responsible for many of the more bizarre forms of consumer rage suggests that, if anything, the opposite is true). Instead, it is because as members of a psychologically salient group, consumers are in a better position to challenge the source of any dissatisfaction and do something to improve their situation.

From the perspective of the service provider, the temptation is to see disaffected groups as problematic and to take steps to minimize their impact (e.g., by individualizing complainants; Haslam, 2001; Wright et al., 1990). However, from the broader perspective of society, it may be more appropriate to see the collective behavior of consumers—and the social identity salience that makes it possible—as an important and necessary social mechanism for keeping providers honest. Attempts to bypass this mechanism may therefore be counterproductive not only because they promote more idiosyncratic expressions of anger (as suggested by the results of Studies 3 and 4 and as witnessed in the headline-making antics of solo consumers), but also because they draw attention away from providers' primary responsibility: the delivery of service.

As psychologists it is often tempting to join our service provider clients in blaming those victims of poor service who act in antinormative ways. Although this is self-protective, it might be more productive instead to remind those providers of the benefits that can flow from living up to their distributive and procedural promises. Underlining the importance of social identities in the service domain—and of the distinctive needs they create and satisfy—seems like a good place to start.

References

Abelson, R. P., Dasgupta, N., Park, J., & Banaji, M. R. (1998). Perceptions of the collective other. *Personality and Social Psychology Review*, *2*, 243–250.

Abrams, D., & Hogg, M. A. (1990). Social identification, self-categorization and social influence. *European Review of Social Psychology*, *1*, 195–228.

Abrams, D., & Hogg, M. A. (1998). Prospects for research in group processes and intergroup relations. *Group Processes and Intergroup Relations*, *1*, 7–20.

Abrams, D., & Hogg, M. A. (2001). Collective identity: Group membership and self-conception. In M. A. Hogg & R. S. Tindale (Eds.), *Blackwell handbook of social psychology: Group processes* (pp. 425–460). Oxford, UK: Blackwell.

Abrams, D., Wetherell, M. A., Cochrane, S., Hogg, M. A., & Turner, J. C. (1990). Knowing what to think by knowing who you are: Self-categorization and the nature of norm formation, conformity and group polarization. *British Journal of Social Psychology*, *29*, 97–119.

Adams, J. S. (1965). Inequity in social exchange. In L. Berkowitz (Ed.), *Advances in experimental social psychology* (Vol.2, pp. 267–299). New York: Academic Press.

Adorno, T. W., Frenkel-Brunswik, E., Levinson, D. J., & Sanford, R. M. (1950). *The authoritarian personality*. New York: Harper.

Ajzen, I. (1991). The theory of planned behavior. *Organizational Behavior and Human Decision Processes*, *50*, 170–211.

Albert, S., Ashforth, B. E., & Dutton, J. E. (2000). Organizational identity and identi-fication: Charting new waters and building new bridges. *Academy of Management Review*, *25*, 13–17.

Albert, S., Ashforth, B. E., & Dutton, J. E. (2000). Organizational identity and identi-fication. *Academy of Management Review*. Special issue, vol. 25.

Albert, S., & Whetten, D. A. (1985). Organizational identity. In L. L. Cummings & B. M. Staw (Eds.), *Research in organizational behaviour* (Vol. 8, pp. 263–295). Greenwich, CT: JAI Press.

Aldag, R., & Fuller, S. R. (1993). Beyond fiasco: A reappraisal of the groupthink phenomenon and a new model of group decision processes. *Psychological Bulletin*, *113*, 552–553.

Alderfer, C. P. (1972). *Existence, relatedness and growth: Human needs in organizational settings*. New York: Free Press.

Allen, M. W., Gotcher, J. M., & Seibert, J. H. (1993). A decade of organizational communication research: Journal articles 1980–1991. *Communication Yearbook*, *16*, 252–330.

Altemeyer, B. (1996). *The authoritarian specter*. Cambridge, MA: Harvard University Press.

Anastasio, P., Bachman, B., Gaertner, S., & Dovidio, J. (1997). Categorization, recategorization and common ingroup identity. In R. Spears, P. J. Oakes, N. Ellemers, & S. A. Haslam (Eds.), *The social psychology of stereotyping and group life* (pp. 236–256). Oxford: Blackwell.

Argote, L., Turner, M. E., & Fichman, M. (1989). To centralize or not to centralize: The effects of uncertainty and threat on group structure and performance. *Organizational Behavior and Human Decision Processes, 43,* 58–74.

Argyle, M., & Dean, J. (1965). Eye-contact, distance and affiliation. *Sociometry, 28,* 289–304.

Armenakis, A. A., & Bedeian, A. G. (1999). Organizational change: A review of theory and research in the 1990s. *Journal of Management, 25,* 293–315.

Armenakis, A. A., Harris, S., & Feild, H. (2001). Paradigms in organizational change: Change agent and change target perspectives. In: R. Golembiewski (Ed.) *Handbook of organizational behavior* (pp. 631–658). New York: Marcel Dekker.

Ashforth, B. E., & Kreiner, G. (1999). "How can you do it?": Dirty work and the dilemma of identity. *Academy of Management Review, 24,* 413–434.

Ashforth, B. E., & Mael, F. (1989). Social identity theory and the organization. *Academy of Management Review, 17,* 20–39.

Augoustinos, M., & Reynolds, K. J. (2001). *Understanding prejudice, racism, and social conflict.* London: Sage.

Aune, R. K., & Basil, M. D. (1994). A relational obligations approach to the foot-in-the-mouth effect. *Journal of Applied Social Psychology, 24,* 546–556.

Azzi, A. E. (1992). Procedural justice and the allocation of power in intergroup relations: Studies in the United States and South Africa. *Personality and Social Psychology Bulletin, 18,* 736–747.

Azzi, A. E. (1993). Implicit and category-based allocations of decision-making power in majority-minority relations. *Journal of Experimental Social Psychology, 29,* 203–228.

Bales, R. F. (1950). *Interaction process analysis: A method for the study of small groups.* Reading, MA: Addison-Wesley.

Bandura, A. (1986). *Social foundations of thought and action: A social cognitive theory.* Englewood Cliffs, NJ: Prentice-Hall.

Bantel, K., & Jackson, S. (1989). Top management and innovations in banking: Does the composition of the team make a difference? *Strategic Management Journal, 10,* 107–124.

Barr, P. S., Stimert, J. L., & Huff, A. S. (1992). Cognitive change, strategic action, and organizational renewal. *Strategic Management Journal, 13,* 13–36.

Barreto, M. (2000). *Identity and strategy in pro-group behaviour.* Free University, Amsterdam: Doctoral dissertation.

Barreto, M., & Ellemers, N. (2000). You can't always do what you want: Social identity and self-presentational determinants of the choice to work for a low status group. *Personality and Social Psychology Bulletin, 26,* 891–906.

Bartol, K. M. (1999). Gender influences on performance evaluations. In G. N. Powell (Ed.), *Handbook of gender and work* (pp. 165–178). London: Sage.

Bass, B. M. (1985). *Leadership and performance beyond expectations.* New York: Free Press.

Bass, B. M. (1990a). *Bass and Stogdill's handbook of leadership: Theory, research and managerial applications.* New York: Free Press.

Bass, B. M. (1990b). From transactional to transformational leadership: Learning to share the vision. *Organizational Dynamics, 18,* 19–31.

Bass, B. M. (1998). *Transformational leadership: Industrial, military, and educational impact.* Mahwah, NJ: Erlbaum.

Bass, B. M., & Avolio, B. J. (1993). Transformational leadership: A response to critiques. In M. M. Chemers, & R. A. Ayman (Eds.), *Leadership theory and research: Perspectives and directions* (pp. 49–80). London: Academic Press.

Basu, A. (Ed.). (1995). *The challenge of local feminisms: Women's movements in global perspective.* Boulder, CO: Westview Press.

Baumeister, R. F., Smart, L., & Boden, J. M. (1996). Relation of threatened egotism to violence and aggression: The dark side of high self-esteem. *Psychology Review, 103,* 5–33.

Becker, T. E., & Billings, R. S. (1993). Profiles of commitment: An empirical test. *Journal of Organizational Behavior, 14,* 177–190.

Becker, T. E., Billings, R. S., Eveleth, D., & Gilbert, N. (1996). Foci and bases of employee commitment: Implications for job performance. *Academy of Management Journal, 39,* 464–482.

Bem, S. L. (1993). *The lenses of gender: Transforming the debate on sexual inequality.* New Haven, CT: Yale University Press.

Benokraitis, N. V., & Feagin, J. R. (1986). *Modern sexism: Blatant, subtle, and covert discrimination.* Englewood Cliffs, NJ: Prentice-Hall.

Berry, J. W. (1980). Social and cultural change. In H. C. Triandis & R. W. Brislin (Eds.), *Handbook of cross-cultural psychology* (vol. 5, pp. 211–279). Boston: Allyn & Bacon.

Berry, J. W. (1984). Cultural relations in plural societies: Alternatives to segregation and their sociopsychological implications. In N. Miller & M. B. Brewer (Eds.), *Groups in contact,* (pp. 11–27). Orlando, FL: Academic Press.

Berry, J. W. (1991). Understanding and managing multiculturalism: Some possible implications of research in Canada. *Psychology and Developing Societites, 3,* 17–49.

Berscheid, E., & Reis, H. T. (1998). Attraction and close relationships. In D. T. Gilbert, S. T. Fiske, & G. Lindzey (Eds.), *The handbook of social psychology* (4th ed., Vol. 2, pp. 193–281). New York: McGraw-Hill.

Bettencourt, B. A., Charlton, K., Dorr, N., & Hume, D. L. (2001). Status differences and ingroup bias: A meta-analytic examination of the effects of status stability, status legitimacy and group permeability. *Psychological Bulletin, 127,* 520–542.

Bhappu, A. D., Griffith, T. L., & Northcraft, G. B. (1997). Media effects and communication bias in diverse groups. *Organizational Behavior and Human Decision Processes, 70,* 199–205.

Bies, R. J., & Moag, J. S. (1986). Interactional justice: Communication criteria of fairness. In R. J. Lewicki & B. M. Straw (Eds.), *Research in organizational behavior* (Vol. 9, pp. 289–319). Greenwich, CT: JAI.

Bies, R. J., & Shapiro, D. L. (1987). Interactional fairness judgments: The influence of causal accounts. *Social Justice Research, 1,* 199–218.

Billig, M. (1976). *Social psychology and intergroup relations.* London: Academic Press.

Bizman, A., & Yinon, Y. (2000). Perceptions of dual identity and separate groups among secular and religious Israeli Jews. *Journal of Social Psychology, 140,* 589–596.

Blake, R. R., & Mouton, J. S. (1985). How to achieve integration on the human side of the merger. *Organizational Dynamics, 13,* 41–56.

Blau, P. M. (1964). *Exchange and power in social life.* New York: Wiley.

Blodgett, J. G., Granbois, D. H., & Walters, R. G. (1993). The effects of perceived justice on complainants' negative word-of-mouth behavior and repatronage intentions. *Journal of Retailing, 69,* 399–428.

Boekaerts, M., Pintrich, P. R., & Zeidner, M. (2000). *Handbook of self-regulation.* San Diego: Academic Press.

Borman, W. C., & Motowidlo, S. J. (1993). Expanding the criterion domain to include elements of contextual performance. In N. Schmitt & W. C. Borman (Eds.), *Personnel selection in organizations* (pp. 71–98). New York: Jossey-Bass.

Bornstein, G., Crum, L., Wittenbraker, J., Harring, K., Insko, C. A., & Thibaut, J. (1983). On the measurement of social orientation in the minimal group paradigm. *European Journal of Social Psychology, 13,* 321–350.

Botan, C. (1996). Communication work and electronic surveillance: A model for predicting panoptic effects. *Communication Monographs, 63,* 293–313.

Botticelli, P., Collis, D., & Pisano, G. (1997). *Intel Corporation: 1968–1997.* Harvard Business School, Harvard University, Case 9-787-137.

Bradberry, J. G., & Preston, J. C. (1992). Cultural diversity and organizational adaptivity in the face of global change. *Organization Development Journal, 10,* 67–73.

Branscombe, N. R. (1998). Thinking about one's gender-group's privileges or disadvantages: Consequences for well-being in women and men. *British Journal of Social Psychology, 37,* 167–184.

Branscombe, N. R., & Ellemers, N. (1998). Coping with group-based discrimination: Individualistic versus group-level strategies. In J. K. Swim & C. Stangor (Eds.), *Prejudice: The target's perspective* (pp. 243–266). New York: Academic Press.

Branscombe, N. R., Ellemers, N., Spears, R., & Doosje, B. (1999). The context and content of identity threat. In N. Ellemers, R. Spears, & B. Doosje (Eds.), *Social identity: Context, commitment, content* (pp. 35–58). Oxford: Blackwell.

Brewer, M. B. (1979). In-group bias in the minimal intergroup situation: A cognitive–motivational analysis. *Psychological Bulletin, 86*, 307–324.

Brewer, M. B. (1991). The social self: On being the same and different at the same time. *Personality and Social Psychology Bulletin, 17*, 475–482.

Brewer, M. B. (2000). Reducing prejudice through cross-categorization: Effects of multiple social identities. In S. Oskamp (Ed.), *Reducing prejudice and discrimination* (pp. 165–183). Mahwah, NJ: Lawrence Erlbaum.

Brewer, M. B., & Gardner, W. (1996). Who is this "We"? Levels of collective identity and self representation. *Journal of Personality and Social Psychology, 71*, 83–93.

Brewer, M. B., & Miller, N. (1984). Beyond the contact hypothesis: Theoretical perspectives on desegregation. In N. Miller & M. B. Brewer (Eds.), *Groups in contact: The psychology of desegregation* (pp. 281–302). New York: Academic Press.

Brewer, M. B., & Schneider, S. (1990). Social identity and social dilemmas: A double-edged sword. In D. Abrams & M. A. Hogg (Eds.), *Social identity theory: Constructive and critical advances* (pp. 169–184). London: Harvester Wheatsheaf.

Bronowski, J. (1974). *The ascent of man*. Boston, MA: Little, Brown.

Brown, A. D., & Starkey, K. (2000). Organizational identity and learning: A psychodynamic perspective. *Academy of Management Review, 25*, 102–120.

Brown, B. B., & Lohr, M. J. (1987). Peer-group affiliation and adolescent self-esteem: An integration of ego-identity and symbolic-interaction theories. *Journal of Personality and Social Psychology, 52*, 47–55.

Brown, R., & Wade, G. (1987). Superordinate goals and intergroup behaviour: The effect of role ambiguity and status on intergroup attitudes and task performance. *European Journal of Social Psychology, 17*, 131–142.

Brown, R. J. (1978). Divided we fall: Analysis of relations between different sections of a factory workforce. In H. Tajfel (Ed.), *Differentiation between social groups: Studies in the social psychology of intergroup relations* (pp. 395–427). London: Academic Press.

Brown, R. J. (1984). The role of similarity in intergroup relations. In H. Tajfel (Ed.), *The social dimension: European developments in social psychology* (pp. 603–623). Cambridge, UK: Cambridge University Press.

Brown, R. J., Condor, S., Mathews, A., Wade, G., & Williams, J. A. (1986). Explaining intergroup differentiation in an industrial organisation. *Journal of Occupational Psychology, 59*, 273–286.

Brush, T. H. (1996). Predicted change in operational synergy and post-acquisition performance of acquired businesses. *Strategic Management Journal, 17*, 1–24.

Bruins, J., Platow, M. J., & Ng, S. H. (1995). Distributive and procedural justice in interpersonal and intergroup situations: Issues, solutions and extensions. *Social Justice Research, 8*, 103–121.

Bryman, A. (1992). *Charisma and leadership in organizations*. London: Sage.

Buono, A. F., Bowditch, J. L., & Lewis, J. W. (1985). When cultures collide: The anatomy of a merger. *Human Relations, 38*, 477–500.

Buono, A. F., & Bowditch, J. L. (1989). *The human side of mergers and acquisitions: Managing collisions between people, cultures, and organizations*. San Francisco, CA: Jossey-Bass.

Burgelman, R. A. (1994). Fading memories: A process theory of strategic business exit in dynamic environments. *Administrative Science Quarterly, 39*, 24–56.

Burgelman, R. A., Carter, D. L., & Bamford, R. S. (1999). *Intel corporation: The evolution of an adaptive organization*. Stanford, CA: Stanford Graduate School of Business, case SM-65.

Burgelman, R. A. & Grove, A. S. (1996, Winter). Strategic dissonance. *California Management Review, 32*, 8–28.

Burke, K., & Chidambaram, L. (1996). Do mediated contexts differ in information richness? A comparison of collocated and dispersed meetings. *Proceedings of the Twenty Ninth Hawaii International Conference on System Sciences, 29,* 92-101.

Burn, S. M. (1996). *The social psychology of gender.* New York: McGraw-Hill.

Burns, J. M. (1978). *Leadership.* New York: Harper & Row.

Burwell, F. G., & Sarkees, M. R. (1993). Women and national security policy. In R. H. Howes & M. R. Stevenson (Eds.), *Women and the use of military force* (pp. 111–133). Boulder, CO: Lynne Rienner.

Bylinsky, G. (1981, December 14). Japan's ominous chip victory. *Fortune, 104,* 52–57.

Byrne, D. (1971). *The attraction paradigm.* New York, Academic Press.

Caddick, B. (1980). Equity theory, social identity, and intergroup relations. In L. Wheeler (Ed.), *Review of personality and social psychology* (Vol.1, pp. 219–245). Beverly Hills, CA: Sage.

Callaway, M. R., & Esser, J. K. (1984). Groupthink: Effects of cohesiveness and problem-solving procedures on group decision making. *Social Behavior and Personality, 12,* 157–164.

Callaway, M. R., Marriott, R. G., & Esser, J. K. (1985). Effects of dominance on group decision making: Toward a stress-reduction explanation of groupthink. *Journal of Personality and Social Psychology, 4,* 949–952.

Camacho, L. M., & Paulus, P. B. (1995). The role of social anxiousness in group brainstorming. *Journal of Personality and Social Psychology, 68,* 1071–1080.

Campbell, D. T. (1958). Common fate, similarity, and other indices of the status of aggregates of persons as social entities. *Behavioural Science, 3,* 14–25.

Campbell, D. T. (1965). Ethnocentrism and other altruistic motives. In David Levine (Ed.), *Nebraska Symposium on Motivation, 13,* 283–311. Lincoln: University of Nebraska Press.

Cartwright, D., & Zander, A. (1968). Groups and group membership: Introduction. In D. Cartwright & A. Zander (Eds.), *Group dynamics: Research and Theory* (3rd ed., pp. 45–62). London: Tavistock.

Cartwright, D., & Zander, A. (Eds.). (1968). *Group dynamics: Research and theory* (3rd ed.). London: Tavistock.

Cartwright, S., & Cooper, C. L. (1992). *Mergers and acquisitions: The human factor.* Oxford, UK: Butterworth/Heinemann.

Cartwright, S., & Cooper, C. L. (1993a). The role of culture compatibitilty in successful organizational marriage. *Academy of Management Executive, 7,* 57–69.

Cartwright, S., & Cooper, C. L. (1993b). The psychological impact of merger and acquisition on the individual: A study of building society managers. *Human Relations, 46,* 327–347.

Castells, M. (1996). *The information age: Economy society and culture:* Vol. 1. *The network society.* Oxford: Blackwell.

Castells, M. (1997). *The power of identity.* Oxford: Blackwell.

Chaiken, S. (1987). The heuristic model of persuasion. In M. P. Zanna, J. M. Olson, & C. P. Herman (Eds.), *Social influence: The Ontario symposium* (Vol. 5, pp. 3–39). Hillsdale, NJ: Erlbaum.

Champness, B. G. (1973). *The assessment of user reactions to confravision: II. Analysis and conclusions,* Unpublished ms., Communication Studies Group, University College, London.

Chemers, M. M. (2001). Leadership effectiveness: An integrative review. In M. A. Hogg & R. S. Tindale (Eds.), *Blackwell handbook of social psychology: Group processes* (pp. 376–399). Oxford, UK: Blackwell.

Chen, C. C., & Eastman, W. (1997). Toward a civic culture for multicultural organizations. *Journal of Applied Behavioral Science, 33,* 454–470.

Chin, M. G., & McClintock, C. G. (1993). The effects of intergroup discrimination and social values on level of self-esteem in the minimal group paradigm. *European Journal of Social Psychology, 23,* 63–75.

Cialdini, R. B. (1993). *Influence: Science and practice* (3rd ed.). New York: HarperCollins.

Clancy, H. (1997, June 1). Dynamic duos: Andrew Grove and Gordon Moore. *Computer Reseller News, 738,* 13–18.

Clark, R. D., & Maass, A. (1988). Social categorization in minority influence: The case of homosexuality. *European Journal of Social Psychology, 18,* 347–364.

Cogan, G. W., & Burgelman, R. A. (1989). *Intel Corporation (A): The DRAM decision.*

Stanford, CA: Graduate School of Business, Stanford University, Case BP-256.

Cogan, G. W., & Burgelman, R. A. (1991). *Intel Corporation (C): The DRAM decision*. Stanford, CA: Graduate School of Business, Stanford University, Case BP-256.

Cogliser, C. C., & Schriesheim, C. A. (2000). Exploring work unit context and leader-member exchange: A multi-level perspective. *Journal of Organizational Behavior, 21,* 487–511.

Cohen, R. L. (1986). Power and justice in intergroup relations. In H. W. Bierhoff, R. L. Cohen, & J. Greenberg (Eds.), *Justice in social relations* (pp. 65–84). New York: Plenum Press.

Cohen, R. L. (1987). Distributive justice: Theory and research. *Social Justice Research, 1,* 19–40.

Cohen, R. L. (1991). Membership, intergroup relations and justice. In R. Vermunt & H. Steensma (Eds.), *Social justice in human relations* (Vol. 1, pp. 239–277). New York: Plenum Press.

Conger, J. A., & Kanungo, R. N. (1987). Towards a behavioral theory of charismatic leadership in organizational settings. *Academy of Management Review, 12,* 637–647.

Conger, J. A., & Kanungo, R. N. (1988a). Behavioral dimensions of charismatic leadership. In J. A. Conger, & R. N. Kanungo (Eds.), *Charismatic leadership: The elusive factor on organizational effectiveness* (pp. 78–97). San Francisco, CA: Jossey-Bass.

Conger, J. A., & Kanungo, R. N. (1988b). The empowerment process: Integrating theory and practice. *Academy of Management Review, 13,* 91-112.

Constant, D., Sproull, L., & Kiesler, S. (1997). The kindness of strangers: The usefulness of electronic weak ties for technical advice. In S. Kiesler (Ed.), *Culture of the Internet* (pp. 303–322). Mahwah, NJ: Earlbaum.

Courtwright, J. A. (1978). A laboratory investigation of groupthink. *Communication Monographs, 45,* 229–246.

Crocker, J., & Luhtanen, R. (1990). Collective self-esteem and ingroup bias. *Journal of Personality and Social Psychology, 58,* 60–67.

Crocker, J., & Major, B. (1989). Social stigma and self-esteem: The self-protective properties of stigma. *Psychological Review, 96,* 608–630.

Cropanzano, R., Byrne, Z. S., Bobocel, D. R., & Rupp, D. E. (2001). Moral virtues, fairness heuristics, social entities, and other denizens of organizational justice. *Journal of Vocational Behavior, 58,* 164–209.

Crosby, F., Clayton, S., Alksnis, O., & Hemker, K. (1986). Cognitive biases in the perception of discrimination: The importance of format. *Sex Roles, 14,* 637–646.

Crown, D. F., & Rosse, J. G. (1995). Yours, mine and ours: Facilitating group productivity through the integration of individual and group goals. *Organizational Behavior and Human Decision Processes, 64,* 138–150.

Daft, R. L., & Lengel, R. H. (1984). Information richness: A new approach to managerial behavior and organizational design. *Research in Organizational Behavior, 6,* 191–233.

Daft, R. L., & Lengel, R. H. (1986). Organisational information requirements, media richness and structural design. *Management Science, 32,* 554–571.

D'Ambra, J., Rice, R. E., & O'Connor, M. (1998). Computer-mediated communication and media preference: An investigation of the dimensionality of perceived task equivocality and media richness. *Behaviour and Information Technology, 17,* 164–174.

Dansereau, F., Cashman, J., & Graen, G. (1973). Instrumentality theory and equity theory as complementary approaches in predicting the relationship of leadership and turnover amongst managers. *Organizational Behavior and Human Performance, 10,* 184–200.

Dansereau, F., Graen, G. B., & Haga, W. (1975). A vertical dyad linkage approach to leadership in formal organisations. *Organizational Behavior and Human Performance, 13,* 46–78.

Dasgupta, N., Banaji, M. R., & Abelson, R. P. (1999). Group entiativity and group perception: Association between physical features and psychological judgment. *Journal of Personality and Social Psychology, 77,* 991–1003.

David, B., & Turner, J. C. (1996). Studies in self-categorization and minority conversion:

Is being a member of the outgroup an advantage? *British Journal of Social Psychology, 35,* 179–199.

David, B., & Turner, J. C. (1999). Studies in self-categorization and minority conversion: The ingroup minority in intragroup and intergroup contexts. *British Journal of Social Psychology, 38,* 115–134.

Day, R. (1984, January 30). Intel seeks outside mfrs. To make its older devices. *Electronic News, 30,* 49.

Deaux, K. (1996). Social identification. In E. T. Higgins & A. W. Kruglanski (Eds.), Social psychology. *Handbook of basic principles.* New York: Guilford Press.

de Cremer, D. (in press). Charismatic leadership and cooperation in social dilemmas: A matter of transforming motives? *Journal of Applied Social Psychology.*

de Cremer, D., & van Knippenberg, D. (in press). How do leaders promote cooperation? The effects of charisma and procedural fairness. *Journal of Applied Psychology.*

de Cremer, D., & van Vugt, M. (1999). Social identification effects in social dilemmas: A transformation of motives. *European Journal of Social Psychology, 29,* 871–893.

De Dreu, C. K. W., Harinck, S., & van Vianen, A. E. M. (1999). Conflict and performance in groups and organizations. In C. L. Cooper & I. T. Robertson (Eds.), *International Review of Industrial and Organizational Psychology* (vol. 14, pp. 369–414). UK: Wiley.

De Dreu, C. K. W., & West, M. A. (2001). Minority dissent and team innovation: The importance of participation in decision making. *Journal of Applied Psychology, 86,* 1191–1201.

de la Garza, R. O., Falcon, A., & Garcia, F. C. (1996). Will the real Americans please stand up: Anglo and Mexican-American support of core American political values. *American Journal of Political Science, 40,* 335–351.

Deal, T. E., & Kennedy, A. A. (1982). *Corporate cultures: The rites and rituals of organizational life.* Reading, MA: Addison-Wesley.

Deery, S., Plowman, D., & Walsh, J., (1997). *Industrial relations: A contemporary analysis.* Sydney, Australia: McGraw-Hill.

Dennis, A. R., & Kinney, S. T. (1998). Testing media-richness theory in the new media: The effects of cues, feedback, and task equivocality. *Information Systems Research, 9,* 256–274.

Department of Trade and Industry (2000). *Business in the information age: International benchmarking study 2000.* http:// www.ukonlineforbusiness.gov.uk/Government/bench/ International/bench2000.pdf

Deutsch, M. (1968). The effects of cooperation and competition upon group processes. In D. Cartwright & A. Zander (Eds.), *Group dynamics: Research and theory* (3rd ed., pp. 461–482). London: Tavistock.

Deutsch, M. (1975). Equity, equality, and need: What determines which value will be used as the basis of distributive justice? *Journal of Social Issues, 31,* 137–149.

Deutsch, M. (1985). *Distributive justice: A social-psychological perspective.* New Haven, CT: Yale University Press.

Deutsch, M., & Gerard, H. B. (1955). A study of normative and informational influences upon individual judgment. *Journal of Abnormal and Social Psychology, 51,* 629–636.

Devine, P. G., Hamilton, D. L., & Ostrom, T. M. (Eds.). (1994). *Social cognition: Impact on social psychology.* San Diego, CA: Academic Press.

Dewar, S. (2000). *Can money buy love (or at least loyalty)? The role of distributive and procedural justice in service failure recovery.* Unpublished thesis: The Australian National University.

Diehl, M. (1988). Social identity and minimal groups: The effects of interpersonal and intergroup attitudinal similarity on intergroup discrimination. *British Journal of Social Psychology, 27,* 289–300.

Diehl, M. (1989). Justice and discrimination between minimal groups: The limits of equity. *British Journal of Social Psychology, 28,* 227–238.

Diehl, M. (1990). The minimal group paradigm: Theoretical explanations and empirical findings. *European Review of Social Psychology, 1,* 263–292.

Diener, E. (1980). Deindividuation: The absence of self-awareness and self-regulation in group members. In P. Paulus (Ed.), *The psychology of group influence* (pp. 209–242). Hillsdale, NJ: Erlbaum.

Dienesch, R. M., & Liden, R. C. (1986). Leader–member exchange model of leadership: A critique and further development. *Academy of Management Review, 11*, 618–634.

Dijker, A. J. (1987). Emotional reactions to ethnic minorities. *European Journal of Social Psychology, 17*, 305–325.

Dion, K. L. (1975). Women's reactions to discrimination from members of the same or opposite sex. *Journal of Research in Personality, 9*, 294–306.

Doise, W. (1986). *Levels of explanation in social psychology* (Elizabeth Mapstone, Trans.). Cambridge, UK: Cambridge University Press.

Doise, W., & Sinclair, A. (1973). The categorization process in intergroup relations. *European Journal of Social Psychology, 9*, 281–289.

Doise, W., Spini, D., & Clémence, A. (1999). Human rights studied as social representations in a cross-national context. *European Journal of Social Psychology, 29*, 1–29.

Donlon, J. P. (1997, July). Inside Andy Grove. *Chief Executive, 125*, 44–52.

Doosje, B., Ellemers, N., & Spears, R. (1995). Perceived intragroup variability as a function of group status and identification. *Journal of Experimental Social Psychology, 31*, 410–436.

Doosje, B., Ellemers, N., & Spears, R. (1999). Commitment and intergroup behavior. In N. Ellemers, R. Spears, & B. Doosje (Eds.), *Social identity: Context, commitment, content* (pp. 84–106). Oxford: Blackwell.

Doosje, B., Haslam, S. A., Spears, R., Oakes, P. J., & Koomen, W. (1998). The effect of comparative context on central tendency and variability judgements and the evaluation of group characteristics. *European Journal of Social Psychology, 28*, 173–184.

Doosje, B., Spears, R., & Ellemers, N. (2002). Social identity as both cause and effect: The development of group identification in response to anticipated and actual changes in the intergroup status hierarchy. *British Journal of Social Psychology, 41*, 57–76.

Douglas, A. (1957). The peaceful settlement of industrial and intergroup disputes. *Conflict Resolution 1*, 69–81.

Douglas, K. M. & McGarty, C. (2001). Identifiability and self-presentation: Computer-mediated communication and intergroup interaction. *European Journal of Social Psychology, 40*, 399–416.

Downs, C. W., & Adrian, A. (1997). *Communication audits*. Lawrence, KS: Communication Management.

Druckman, D., & Harris, R. (1990). Alternative models of responsiveness in international negotiation. *Journal of Conflict Resolution 34*, 234–251.

Dubrovsky, V. J., Kiesler, S., & Sethna, B. N. (1991). The equalization phenomenon: Status effects in computer-mediated and face-to-face decision making groups. *Human–Computer Interaction, 6*, 119–146.

Duck, J. M., & Fielding, K. S. (1999). Leaders and sub-groups: One of us or one of them? *Group Processes and Intergroup Relations, 2*, 203–230.

Dukerich, J. M., Kramer, R., & McLean Parks, J. (1998). The dark side of organizational identification. In D. A. Whetten, & P. C. Godfrey, P. C. (Eds.), *Identity in organizations: Building theory through conversations* (pp. 245–256). London: Sage.

Dunbar, K. (1995). How scientists really reason: Scientific reasoning in real-world laboratories. In R. J. Sternberg & J. E. Davidson (Eds.), *The nature of insight* (pp. 365–395). Cambridge, MA: MIT Press.

Dunphy, D., & Stace, D. (1990). *Under new management*. New York: McGraw-Hill.

Durham, C. C., Locke, E. A., Poon, J. M. L., & McLeod, P. L. (2000). Effects of group goals and time pressure on group efficacy, information seeking strategy and performance. *Human Performance, 13*, 115–138.

Dutton, J. E., & Dukerich, J. (1991). Keeping an eye on the mirror: Image and identity in organizaional adaptation. *Academy of Management Journal, 34*, 517–554.

Dutton, J. E., Dukerich, J. M., & Harquail, C. V. (1994). Organizational images and member identification. *Administrative Science Quarterly, 39*, 239–263.

Eagly, A. H. (1987). *Sex differences in social behavior: A social-role interpretation*. Hillsdale, NJ: Erlbaum.

Eagly, A. H., Makhijani, M. G., & Klonsky, B. G. (1992). Gender and the evaluation of leaders: A meta-analysis. *Psychological Bulletin, 111*, 3–22.

Eckhoff, T. (1974). *Justice: Its determinants*

in social interaction. Rotterdam, The Netherlands: Rotterdam University Press.

Eggins, R. A., Haslam, S. A., & Ryan, M. K. (2000). *Negotiation between groups in conflict: The importance of group representation and superordinate framing*. Manuscript submitted for publication.

Eggins, R. A., Haslam, S. A., & Reynolds, K. J. (2002). Social identity and negotiation: Subgroup representation and superordinate consensus. *Personality and Social Psychology Bulletin, 28*, 887–899.

Eggins, R. A., & Ryan, M. K. (2000). *Negotiation at work: "Old" vs. "new" models of managing the workplace and the people in it*. Paper presented at the EAESP small group meeting on Social Identity Processes in Organizations. University of Amsterdam, The Netherlands.

Ellemers, N. (1993). The influence of sociostructural variables on identity enhancement strategies. *European Review of Social Psychology, 4*, 27–57.

Ellemers, N. (2001a). Individual upward mobility and the perceived legitimacy of intergroup relations. In J.T. Jost & B. Major (Eds.), *The psychology of legitimacy: Emerging perspectives on ideology, justice, and intergroup relations* (pp. 205–222). New York: Cambridge University Press.

Ellemers, N. (2001b). Social identity, commitment, and work behavior. In M. A. Hogg & D. J. Terry (Eds.), *Social identity processes in organizational contexts* (pp. 101–114). Philadelphia: Psychology Press.

Ellemers, N. (2001c). Social identity and group norms. In van Horskamp & B. Musschenga (Eds.), *The many faces of individualism* (pp. 225–237). Belgium: Peeters.

Ellemers, N., & Barreto, M. (2000). The impact of relative group status: Affective, perceptual and behavioural consequences. In R. Brown & S. Gaertner (Eds.), *The Blackwell handbook of social psychology: Vol 4. Intergroup processes* (pp. 324–343). Oxford: Basil Blackwell.

Ellemers, N., Barreto, M., & Spears, R. (1999). Commitment and strategic responses to social context. In N. Ellemers, R. Spears, & B. Doosje. (Eds.), *Social identity: Context, content, commitment* (pp. 59–83). Oxford: Blackwell,

Ellemers, N., de Gilder, D., & van den Heuvel, H. (1998). Career-oriented versus team-oriented commitment and behaviour at work. *Journal of Applied Psychology, 83*, 717–730.

Ellemers, N., Doosje, B. & Spears, R. (2001). *Sources of respect: The effects of being liked by ingroups and outgroups*. Unpublished manuscript. Leiden University.

Ellemers, N., Doosje, B., van Knippenberg, A., & Wilke, H. (1992). Status protection in high status minorities. *European Journal of Social Psychology, 22*, 123–140.

Ellemers, N., Kortekaas P., & Ouwerkerk, J. W. (1999). Self-categorization, commitment to the group and group self-esteem as related but distinct aspects of social identity. *European Journal of Social Psychology, 29*, 371–389.

Ellemers, N., Németh, E., & Mlicki, P. (2000). *Social identity threat and resistance to organizational change: The case of the Hungarian Police Force*. Paper presented at the EAESP small-group meeting on Social Identity Processes in Organizations, Amsterdam.

Ellemers, N., Spears, R., & Doosje, B. (1997). Sticking together or falling apart: Ingroup identification as a psychological determinant of group commitment versus individual mobility. *Journal of Personality and Social Psychology, 72*, 617–626.

Ellemers, N., Spears, R., & Doosje, B. (Eds.). (1999). *Social identity: Context, content, commitment*. Oxford, UK: Blackwell.

Ellemers, N., Spears, R., & Doosje, B. (2002). Self and social identity. *Annual Review of Psychology, 53*, 161–186.

Ellemers, N., van den Heuvel, H., de Gilder, D., Maass, A., & Bonvini, A. (2001). *The underrepresentation of women in science: Differential commitment or the Queen-bee syndrome?* Manuscript submitted for publication.

Ellemers, N., van Dyck, C., Hinkle, S., & Jacobs, A. (2000). Intergroup differentiation in social context: Identity needs versus audience constraints. *Social Psychology Quarterly, 63*, 60–74.

Ellemers, N., & van Knippenberg, A. (1997). Stereotyping in social context. In R. Spears, P. J. Oakes, N. Ellemers, & S. A. Haslam (Eds.), *The social psychology of stereotyp-*

ing and group life (pp. 119–143). Oxford, UK: Blackwell.

Ellemers, N., van Knippenberg, A., de Vries, N. K., & Wilke, H. (1988). Social identification and permeability of group boundaries. *European Journal of Social Psychology, 18*, 497–513.

Ellemers, N., van Knippenberg, A., & Wilke, H. (1990). The influence of permeability of group boundaries and stability of group status on strategies of individual mobility and social change. *British Journal of Social Psychology, 29*, 233–246.

Ellemers, N., van Rijswijk, W., Bruins, J., & de Gilder, D. (1998). Group commitment as a moderator of attributional and behavioural responses to power use. *European Journal of Social Psychology, 28*, 555–573.

Ellemers, N., van Rijswijk, W., Roefs, M., & Simons, C. (1997). Bias in intergroup perceptions: Balancing group identity with social reality. *Personality and Social Psychology Bulletin, 23*, 186–198.

Ellemers, N., Wilke, H., & van Knippenberg, A. (1993). Effects of the legitimacy of low group or individual status on individual and collective identity enhancement strategies. *Journal of Personality and Social Psychology, 64*, 766–778.

Elsbach, K. D. (1999). An expanded model of organizational identification. *Research in Organizational Behavior, 21*, 163–200.

Elsbach, K. D. (2000). Coping with hybrid organizational identities: Evidence from California Legislative Staff. In J. Wagner (Ed.), *Advances in qualitative organizational research* (Vol. 3, pp. 59–90). Amsterdam: Elsevier Science.

Elsbach, K. D., & Bhattacharya, C. B. (2001). Defining who you are by what you're not: Organizational disidentification and the National Rifle Association. *Organization Science, 12*, 393–413.

Elsbach, K. D., & Kramer, R. M. (1996). Members' responses to organizational identity threats: Encountering and countering the Business Week rankings. *Administrative Science Quarterly, 41*, 442–476.

Ely, R. J. (1994). The effects of organizational demographics and social identity on relationships among professional women. *Administrative Science Quarterly, 39*, 203–238.

Emerson, R. H. (1962). Power-dependence relations. *American Sociological Review, 27*, 31–41.

Emler, N., & Reicher, S. (1995). *Adolescence and delinquency*. Oxford, UK: Blackwell.

Epitropaki, O., & Martin, R. (1999). The impact of relational demography on the quality of leader-member exchanges (LMX) and employees' work attitudes and well being. *Journal of Occupational and Organizational Psychology, 72*, 237–240.

Erber, R., & Fiske, S. T. (1984). Outcome dependency and attention to inconsistent information. *Journal of Personality and Social Psychology, 47*, 709–726.

Esser, J. K., & Lindoerfer, J. S. (1989). Groupthink and the space shuttle Challenger accident: Toward a quantitative case analysis. *Journal of Behavioral Decision Making, 2*, 167–177.

Fajak, A., & Haslam, S.A. (1998). Gender solidarity in hierarchical organizations. *British Journal of Social Psychology, 37*, 73–94.

Faludi, S. (1992). *Backlash: The undeclared war against American women*. New York: Doubleday.

Fausto-Sterling, A. (1985). *Myths of gender: Biological theories about women and men*. New York: Basic Books.

Feibus, M. (1987, July 14). Intel, AMD are back in the black. *San Jose Mercury News*, p. 1F.

Feldman, D. C. (1984). The development and enforcement of group norms. *Academy of Management Review, 9*, 47–53.

Festinger, L. (1950). Informal social communication. *Psychological Review, 57*, 271–282.

Festinger, L. (1953). An analysis of complaint behavior. In M. Sherif, & M. O. Wilson (Eds.), *Group relations at the cross-roads* (pp. 232–256). New York: Harper.

Festinger, L. (1957). *A theory of cognitive dissonance*. Stanford, CA: Stanford University Press.

Festinger, L. (1987). A personal memory. In N. E. Gruenberg, R. E. Nisbett, J. Rodin, & J. E. Singer (Eds.), *A distinctive approach to psychological research: The influence of Stanley Schachter* (pp. 1–9). Hillsdale, NJ: Erlbaum.

Festinger, L., Schachter, S., & Back, K. W.

(1950). *Social pressures in informal groups: A study of human factors in housing.* New York: Harper.

Fiedler, F. E. (1965). A contingency model of leadership effectiveness. In L. Berkowitz (Ed.), *Advances in experimental social psychology* (Vol.1, pp. 149–190) New York: Academic Press.

Fiedler, F. E. (1971). *Leadership.* Morristown, NJ: General Learning Press.

Fielding, K. S., & Hogg, M. A. (1997). Social identity, self-categorization, and leadership: A field study of small interactive groups. *Group Dynamics: Theory, Research, and Practice, 1,* 39–51.

Fielding, K. S., & Hogg, M. A. (2000). Working hard to achieve self-defining group goals: A social identity analysis. *Zeitschrift für Sozialpsychologie, 31,* 191–203.

Fiol, C. M. (1995). Managing culture as a competitive resource. *Journal of Management, 17,* 191–211.

Fiol, C. M., Hatch, M. J., & Golden-Biddle, K. (1998). Organizational culture and identity: What's the difference anyway? In D. A. Whetten & P. C. Godfrey, P.C. (Eds.), *Identity in organizations: Building theory through conversations* (pp. 56–59). London: Sage.

Fishbein, M., & Ajzen, I. (1975). *Belief, attitude, intention, and behavior: An introduction to theory and research.* Reading, MA: Addison-Wesley.

Fisher, F., Kopelman, E., & Schneider, A. K. (1996). *Beyond Machiavelli: Tools for coping with conflict.* New York: Penguin.

Fiske, S. T., Bersoff, D. N., Borgida, E., Deaux, K., & Heilman, M. E. (1991). Social science research on trial: The use of sex stereotyping research in *Price Waterhouse v. Hopkins. American Psychologist, 46,* 1049–1060.

Fiske, S. T., & Dépret, E. (1996). Control, interdependence and power: Understanding social cognition in its social context. In W. Stroebe & M. Hewstone, (Eds.), *European Review of Social Psychology, 7,* 31–61.

Fiske, S. T., & Taylor, S. E. (1984). *Social cognition.* Reading, MA: Addison Wesley.

Fiske, S. T., & Taylor, S. E. (1991). *Social cognition* (2nd ed.). New York: McGraw-Hill.

Fitzgerald, T. H. (1988). Can change in organizational culture really be managed? *Organizational Dynamics, 17,* 5-15.

Fleishman, E. A., & Peters, D. A. (1962). Interpersonal values, leadership attitudes, and managerial success. *Personnel Psychology, 15,* 43–56.

Flowers, M. L. (1977). A laboratory test of some implications of Janis's groupthink hypothesis. *Journal of Personality and Social Psychology, 35,* 888–896.

Foa, E. B., & Foa, U. G. (1980). Resource theory: Interpersonal behavior as exchange. In K. J. Gergen, M. S. Greenberg, & R. H. Willis (Eds.), *Social exchange: Advances in theory and research* (pp. 77–94). New York: Plenum Press.

Foddy, M., & Hogg M. A. (1999). Impact of leaders on resource consumption in social dilemmas: The intergroup context. In M. Foddy, M. Smithson, S. Schneider, & M. A. Hogg (Eds.), *Resolving social dilemmas: Dynamic, structural, and intergroup aspects* (pp. 309–330). Philadelphia, PA: Psychology Press.

Foddy, M., Platow, M. J., & Yamagishi, T. (2001). *Group-based trust in strangers: Evaluations or expectations?* Unpublished manuscript, La Trobe University, Australia.

Fodor, E. M., & Smith, T. (1982). The power motive as an influence on group decision making. *Journal of Personality and Social Psychology, 42,* 178–185.

Folger, R., & Cropanzano, R. (1998). *Organizational justice and human resource management.* Thousand Oaks, CA: Sage.

Folger, R. & Konofsky, M. (1989). Effects of procedural and distributive justice on reactions to pay raise decisions. *Academy of Management Journal, 32,* 115–130.

Foschi, M. (1997). On scope conditions. *Small Group Research, 28,* 535–555.

Fox-Wolfgramm, S. J., Boal, K. B., & Hunt, J. G. (1998). Organizational adaptation to institutional change: A comparative study of first-order change in prospector and defender banks. *Administrative Science Quarterly, 43,* 87–126.

Foy, N. (1994). *Empowering people at work.* Aldershot, UK: Gower.

French, J. R. P., Jr., & Raven, B. (1968). The bases of social power. In D. Cartwright &

A. Zander (Eds.), *Group dynamics: Research and theory* (3rd ed., pp. 259–269). London: Tavistock.

Fulk, J., & Boyd, B. (1991). Emerging theories of communication in organizations. *Journal of Management, 17,* 407–446.

Gaertner, S. L., & Dovidio, J. F. (2000). *Reducing intergroup bias. The common ingroup identity model.* Philadelphia, PA: Psychology Press.

Gaertner, S. L., Dovidio, J. F., Anastasio, P., Bachman, B., & Rust, M. (1993). The common ingroup identity model: Recategorization and the reduction of intergroup bias. *European Review of Social Psychology, 4,* 1–26.

Gaertner, S. L., Dovidio, J. F., & Bachmann, B. A. (1996). Revisiting the contact hypothesis: The induction of a common ingroup identity. *International Journal of Intercultural Relations, 20,* 271–290.

Gaertner, S. L., Dovidio, J. F., Mann, J., Murrell, A., & Pomare, M. (1990). How does cooperation reduce intergroup bias? *Journal of Personality and Social Psychology 59,* 692–704.

Gaertner, S. L., Dovidio, J. F., Rust, M. C., Nier, J. A., Banker, B. S., Ward, C. M., Mottola, G. R., & Houlette, M. (1999). Reducing intergroup bias: Elements of intergroup cooperation. *Journal of Personality and Social Psychology, 76,* 388–402.

Gaertner, S. L., Mann, J., Murrell, A., & Dovidio, J. F. (1989). Reducing intergroup bias: The benefits of recategorization. *Journal of Personality and Social Psychology, 57,* 239–249.

Gaertner, S. L., Rust, M. C., Dovidio, J. F., Bachman, B. A., & Anastasio, P. A. (1994). The contact hypothesis: The role of a common ingroup identity on reducing intergroup bias. *Small Group Research, 25,* 224–249.

Gaertner, S. L., Rust, M. C., Dovidio, J. F., Bachman, B. A., & Anastasio, P. A. (1996). The contact hypothesis: The role of a common ingroup identity on reducing intergroup bias among minority and majority group members. In J. Nye & A. Brower (Eds.), *What's social about social cognition? Research on socially shared cognition in small groups* (pp. 230–260). Newbury Park, CA: Sage.

Gagliardi, P. (1986). The creation and change of organizational cultures. *Organization Studies, 7,* 117–134.

Galinsky, A. D., Hugenberg, K., Groom, C., & Bodenhausen, G. (in press). The reappropriation of stigmatizing labels: Implications for social identity. In M. A. Neale, E. A. Mannix, & J. Polzer (Ed.), *Research on managing groups and teams* (Vol. 5). Greenwich, CT: Elsevier Science Press.

Galpin, T. (1996). *The human side of change: A practical guide to organization redesign.* San Francisco: Jossey-Bass.

Gardner, J., Paulsen, N., Gallois, C., Callan, V., & Monaghan, P. (2001). Communication in organizations: An intergroup perspective. In H. Giles & P. Robinson (Eds.), *New handbook of language and social psychology* (2nd ed., pp. 561–584). Chichester, UK: Wiley.

Geis, F. L. (1993). Self-fulfilling prophecies: A social psychological view of gender. In A. E. Beall & R. J. Sternberg (Eds.), *The psychology of gender* (pp. 9–54). New York: Guilford Press.

Gerstner, C. R., & Day, D. V. (1997). Meta-analytic review of Leader–Member Exchange theory: Correlates and construct issues. *Journal of Applied Psychology, 82,* 827–844.

Ghoshal, S., & Bartlett, C. A. (1997). *The individualized corporation: A fundamentally new approach to management.* New York: HarperCollins Business.

Giddens, A. (1984). *The consititution of society: Outline of the theory of structuration.* Cambridge, UK: Polity.

Gilbert, D. T., Fiske, S. T., & Lindzey, G. (Eds.) (1998). *The handbook of social psychology* (4th ed.). New York: McGraw-Hill.

Gilbert, D. T., & Malone, P. S. (1995). The correspondence bias. *Psychological Bulletin, 117,* 21–38.

Gilbreth, L. M. (1914/1971). *The psychology of management: The function of the mind in determining, teaching and installing methods of least waste.* Ann Arbor, MI: University Microfilms.

Giles, H., & Coupland, N. (1991). *Language: Contexts and consequences.* Pacific Grove, CA: Brooks/Cole.

Giles, H., Wilson, P., & Conway, A. (1981). Accent and lexical diversity as determinants of impression formation and employment selection. *Lanuage Sciences*, *3*, 92–103.

Gillmor, D. (2000, January 23). Exploring leadership: Andy Grove. *San Jose Mercury News*, 1A, 21A.

Gioia, D. A. (1998). From individual to organizational identity. In D. A. Whetten & P. C. Godfrey (Eds.), *Identity in organizations: Building theory through conversations* (pp. 17–32). London: Sage.

Gioia, D. A., Schultz, M., & Corley, K. G. (2000). Organizational identity, image, and adaptive instability. *Academy of Management Review*, *25*, 63–81.

Gioia, D. A., & Thomas, J. B. (1996). Identity image and issue interpretation: Sensemaking during strategic change in academia. *Administrative Science Quarterly*, *40*, 370–403.

Glick, P., & Fiske, S. T. (1996). The Ambivalent Sexism Inventory: Differentiating hostile and benevolent sexism. *Journal of Personality and Social Psychology*, *70*, 491–512.

Goethals, G. R., & Darley, J. M. (1987). Social comparison theory: Self-evaluation and group life. In B. Mullen & G. R. Goethals (Eds.), *Theories of group behavior* (pp. 21–47). Berlin: Springer.

Goldhaber, G. M. (1993). *Organizational communication* (6th ed.). Dubuque, IA: Brown.

Gonzalez, R., & Brown, R. J. (1999). *Maintaining the salience of subgroup and superordinate group identities during intergroup contact*. Paper presented at the Small Groups Preconference to the Annual Meeting of the Society of Experimental Social Psychology, St Louis, MO, October 14–16.

Goodwin, C., & Ross, I. (1992). Consumer responses to service failures: Influences of procedural and interactional fairness perceptions. *Journal of Business Research*, *25*, 149–163.

Graen, G. B., Novak, M., & Sommerkamp, P. (1982). The effects of leader-member exchange and job design on productivity and satisfaction: Testing a dual attachment model. *Organizational Behavior and Human Performance*, *30*, 109–131.

Graen, G. B., & Scandura, T. (1987). Toward a psychology of dyadic organizing. In B. Staw & L. L. Cummings (Eds.), *Research in organizational behavior* (Vol. 9, pp. 175–208). Greenwich, CT: JAI press.

Graen, G. B., Scandura, T., & Graen, M. R. (1986). A field experimental test of the moderating effects of growth need strength on productivity. *Journal of Applied Psychology*, *71*, 484–491.

Graen, G. B., & Uhl-Bien, M. (1991). Partnership-making applies equally well to team mate–sponsor team mate–competence network, and team mate–team mate relationships. *Journal of Managerial Systems*, *3*, 33–48.

Graen, G. B., & Uhl-Bien, M. (1995). Relationship-based approach to leadership: Development of leader-member exchange (LMX) theory of leadership over 25 years: Applying a multi-level multi-domain approach. *Leadership Quarterly*, *6*, 219–247.

Graham, B., & Burgelman, R. A. (1991). *Intel Corporation (B): Implementing the DRAM decision*. Graduate School of Business, Stanford University, case BP-256B.

Graves, D. (1981). Individual reactions to a merger of two small firms of brokers in the re-insurance industry: A total population survey. *Journal of Management Studies*, *18*, 89–113.

Greenbaum, H. H. (1974). The audit of organizational communication. *Academy of Management Journal*, *17*, 739–754.

Greenberg, G. (1993). Stealing in the name of justice: Information and interpersonal moderators of theft reactions to underpayment inequity. *Organizational Behavior and Human Decision Making Processes*, *54*, 81–103.

Greenberg, G., & Baron, R. (2000). *Behavior in Organizations* (6th ed.). Upper Saddle River, NJ: Prentice-Hall.

Greenberg, J. (1987). A taxonomy of organizational justice theories. *Academy of Management Review*, *12*, 9–22.

Greenberg, J. (1993). Stealing in the name of justice: Informational and interpersonal moderators of theft reactions to underpayment inequity. *Organizational Behavior and Human Decision Processes*, *54*, 81–103.

Greenberg, J., & Cropanzano, R. (Eds.). (2001). *Advances in organizational justice*. Stanford, CA: Stanford University Press.

Greenhaus, J. H., & Parasuraman, S. (1993). Job performance attributions and career advancement prospects: An examination of gender and race effects. *Organizational Behavior and Human Decision Processes, 55*, 273–297.

Greer, J. (1985, July 16). Intel posts first operating loss in 15 years. *San Jose Mercury News*, p. 1F.

Grove, A. S. (1984, July 23). How to make confrontation work for you. *Fortune, 110*, 73–76.

Grove, A. S. (1996). *Only the paranoid survive: How to exploit the crisis points that challenge every company.* New York: Doubleday.

Gurin, P., & Townsend, A. (1986). Properties of gender identity and their implications for gender consciousness. *British Journal of Social Psychology, 25*, 139–148.

Gustavsen, B. (1985). Workplace reform and democratic dialogue. *Economic and Industrial Democracy, 6*, 461–479.

Gustavsen, B. (1986). The design of conferences and the evolving role of democratic dialogue in changing working life. *Human Relations, 39*(2), 101–116.

Gutek, B. A. (1995). *The dynamic of service: Reflections on the changing nature of the service industry.* San Francisco: Jossey-Bass.

Gutek, B. A. (1999). The social psychology of service interactions. *Journal of Social Issues, 55*, 603–617.

Gutek, B. A., Bhappu, A., Liao-Troth, M., & Cherry, B. (1999). Distinguishing between service relationships and encounters. *Journal of Applied Psychology, 84*, 218–233.

Guzzo, R. A., & Dickson, M. W. (1996). Teams in organizations: Recent research on performance and effectiveness. *Annual Review of Psychology, 47*, 307–338.

Guzzo, R. A., Yost, P. R., Campbell, R. J., & Shea, G. P. (1993). Potency in groups: Articulating a construct. *British Journal of Social Psychology, 32*, 87–105.

Hackman, J. R., & Morris, C. G. (1975). Group tasks, group interaction process, and group performance effectiveness: A review and proposed integration. *Advances in Experimental Social Psychology, 8*, 45–99.

Hains, S. C., Hogg, M. A., & Duck, J. M. (1997). Self-categorization and leadership: Effects of group prototypicality and leader

stereotypicality. *Personality and Social Psychology Bulletin, 23*, 1087–1100.

Hall, D., & Mansfield, R. (1971). Organizational and individual response to stress. *Administrative Science Quarterly, 16*, 533–547.

Hall, R. J., & Lord, R. G. (1995). Multi-level information processing explanations of followers' leadership perceptions. *Leadership Quarterly, 6*, 265–287.

Hamilton, D. L., & Sherman, S. J. (1996). Perceiving persons and groups. *Psychological Review, 103*, 336–355.

Haney, C. (1991). The Fourteenth Amendment and symbolic legality: Let them eat due process. *Law and Human Behavior, 15*, 193–204.

Hare-Mustin, R., & Marecek, J. (1990). *Making a difference: Psychology and the construction of gender.* New Haven, CT: Yale University Press.

Harkins, S. G., & Szymanski, K. (1989). Social loafing and group evaluation. *Journal of Personality and Social Psychology, 56*, 934–941.

Harley, B. (1999). The myth of empowerment: Work organization, hierarchy and employee autonomy in contemporary Australian workplaces. *Work, Employment and Society, 13*, 41–66.

Hartley, J. F. (1992). Joining a trade union. In J. F. Hartley & G. M Stephenson (Eds.), *Employment relations* (pp. 163–183). Oxford, UK: Blackwell.

Haslam, S. A. (1997). Stereotyping and social influence: Foundations of stereotype consensus. In R. Spears, P. J. Oakes, N. Ellemers, & S. A. Haslam (Eds.), *The social psychology of stereotyping and group life* (pp. 119–143). Oxford, UK: Blackwell.

Haslam, S. A. (2001). *Psychology in organizations: The social identity approach.* London: Sage.

Haslam, S. A., Eggins, R. A., & Reynolds, K. J. (2001). The ASPIRe model: Actualizing Social and Personal Identity Resources to improve strategic planning and encourage sustainable productivity in organizations. Manuscript submitted for publication.

Haslam, S. A., Eggins, R. A., & Reynolds, K. J. (in press). The ASPIRe model: Actualizing Social and Personal Identity Resources to enhance organizational outcomes. *Jour-*

nal of Organizational and Occupational Psychology.

Haslam, S. A., & McGarty, C. (2001). A 100 years of certitude? Social psychology, the experimental method and the management of scientific uncertainty. British Journal of Social Psychology, 40, 1–21.

Haslam, S. A., McGarty, C., Brown, P. M., Eggins, R. A., Morrison, B. E., & Reynolds, K. J. (1998). Inspecting the emperor's clothes: Evience that random selection of leaders can enhance group performance. Group Dynamics: Theory, Research, and Practice, 2, 168–184.

Haslam, S. A., Oakes, P. J., McGarty, C., Turner, J. C., & Onorato, S. (1995). Contextual changes in the prototypicality of extreme and moderate outgroup members. European Journal of Social Psychology, 25, 509–530.

Haslam, S. A., Oakes, P. J., Reynolds, K. J., & Turner, J. C. (1999). Social identity salience and the emergence of stereotype consensus. Personality and Social Psychology Bulletin, 25, 809–818.

Haslam, S. A., & Platow, M. J. (2001a). The link between leadership and followership: How affirming a social identity translates vision into action. Personality and Social Psychology Bulletin, 27, 1469–1479.

Haslam, S. A., & Platow, M. J. (2001b). Your wish is our command: The role of shared social identity in translating a leader's vision into followers' action. In M. A. Hogg & D. J. Terry (Eds.), Social identity processes in organizational contexts (pp. 213–228). Philadelphia, PA: Psychology Press.

Haslam, S. A., Powell, C., & Turner, J. C. (2000). Social identity, self-categorization and work motivation: Rethinking the contribution of the group to positive and sustainable organizational outcomes. Applied Psychology: An International Review, 49, 319–339.

Haslam, S. A., & Turner, J. C. (1992). Context-dependent variation in social stereotyping 2: The relationship between frame of reference, self-categorization and accentuation. European Journal of Social Psychology, 22, 251–278.

Haslam, S. A., & van Knippenberg, D. (2000). The positive impact of workplace diversity:

A product of ideology-based identification rather than demography. Unpublished manuscript, University of Exeter.

Haslam, S. A., Ryan, M. K., Postmes, T., Spears, R., Webley, P., & Smithson, M. (2001). Rethinking groupthink: Social identity salience as a basis for the maintenance of commitment to faltering organizational projects. Manuscript submitted for publication.

Haslam, S. A., Turner, J. C., Oakes, P. J., McGarty, C., & Hayes, B. K. (1992). Context-dependent variation in social stereotyping 1: The effects of intergroup relations as mediated by social change and frame of reference. European Journal of Social Psychology, 22, 3–20.

Haslam, S. A., Turner, J. C., Oakes, P. J., McGarty, C., & Reynolds, K. J. (1998). The group as a basis for emergent stereotype consensus. European Review of Social Psychology, 9, 203–239.

Haslam, S. A., Turner, J. C., Oakes, P. J., Reynolds, K. J., & Doosje, B. (in press). From personal pictures in the head to collective tools in the world: How shared stereotypes allow groups to represent and change social reality. In C. McGarty, V. Y. Yzerbyt, & R. Spears (Eds.), Stereotypes as explanation: The formation of meaningful beliefs about social groups. Cambridge, UK: Cambridge University Press.

Haslam, S. A., Turner, J. C., Oakes, P. J., Reynolds, K. J., Eggins, R. A., Nolan, M., & Tweedie, J. (1998). When do stereotypes become really consensual? Investigating the group-based dynamics of the concensualization process. European Journal of Social Psychology, 28, 755–776.

Haslam, S. A., Veenstra, K., & Wegge, J. (2001). The advantages of collective empowerment: Evidence that participative group goal setting improves performance when the going gets tough. Unpublished manuscript, University of Exeter.

Hatch, M. J. (1993). The dynamics of organizational culture. Academy of Management Review, 18, 657–693.

Haunschild, P. R., Moreland, R. L., & Murrell, A. J. (1994). Sources of resistance to mergers between groups. Journal of Applied Social Psychology, 24, 1150–1178.

Hayashi, A. M. (1987, November 15). The new Intel: Moore mature, Moore competitive. *Electronic Business, 33,* 54–64.

Hegtvedt, K. (2001, October). *Doing justice to the group: Examining the role of the group in justice research.* Paper presented at the 9th Annual Preconference on Small Groups, Spokane, Washington.

Heilman, M. E., Block, C. J., Martell, R. F., & Simon, M. C. (1989). Has anything changed? Current conceptions of men, women, and managers. *Journal of Applied Psychology, 74,* 935–942.

Henderson, L. S. (1987). The contextual nature of interpersonal communication in management theory and research. *Management Communication Quarterly, 1,* 7–31.

Herring, S. (1996). Posting in a different voice: Gender and ethics in computer-mediated communication. In C. Ess (Ed.), *Philosophical perspectives on computer-mediated communication* (pp. 115–146). New York: State University of New York Press.

Hertel, G. (2000). Motivation gains in groups: A brief review of the state of the art. *Zeitschrift für Sozialpsychologie, 31,* 169–175.

Herzberg, F. (1987). One more time: How do you motivate employees? *Harvard Business Review, 65,* 109–120.

Herzberg, F., Mausner, B., & Snyderman, B. (1959). *The motivation to work.* New York: Wiley.

Hewstone, M. (1989). *Causal attribution: From cognitive process to collective beliefs.* Oxford, UK: Blackwell.

Hewstone, M. (1996). Contact and categorization: Social psychological interventions to change intergroup relations. In C. N. Macrae, C. Stangor, & M. Hewstone (Eds.), *Stereotypes and stereotyping* (pp. 323–368). New York: Guilford.

Hewstone, M., & Brown, R. J. (1986a). Contact is not enough: An intergroup perspective on the "contact hypothesis." In M. Hewstone & R. J. Brown (Eds.), *Contact and conflict in intergroup encounters* (pp. 1–44). Oxford, UK: Blackwell.

Hewstone, M., & Brown, R. J. (Eds.) (1986b). *Contact and conflict in intergroup encounters. Social psychology and society.* Oxford, UK: Basil Blackwell.

Hewstone, M., Fincham, F., & Jaspars, J. (1981). Social categorization and similarity in intergroup behaviour: A replication with "penalties." *European Journal of Social Psychology, 11,* 101–107.

Hewstone, M., Martin, R., Hammer-Hewstone, C., Crisp, R. J., & Voci, A. (2001). Majority–minority relations in organizations: Challenges and opportunities. In M. A. Hogg & D. J. Terry (Eds.), *Social identity processes in organizational contexts* (pp. 67–87). Philadelphia, PA: Psychology Press.

Hiemstra, G. (1982). Teleconferencing, concern for face, and organizational culture. *Communication Yearbook, 6,* 874–904.

Hiltz, S. R., Turoff, M., & Johnson, K. (1989). Experiments in group decision making, 3: disinhibition, deindividuation, and group process in pen name and real name computer conferences. *Decision Support Systems, 5,* 217–232.

Hinkle, S., & Brown, R. J. (1990). Intergroup comparisons and social identity: Some links and lacunae. In D. Abrams & M. A. Hogg (Eds.), *Social identity theory: Constructive and critical advances* (pp. 48–70). Hemel Hempstead, UK: Harvester Wheatsheaf.

Hinsz, V. B. (1995). Goal setting by groups performing an additive task: A comparison with individual goal setting. *Journal of Applied Social Psychology, 25,* 965–990.

Hirschman, A. O. (1970). *Exit, voice and loyalty.* Cambridge, MA: Harvard University Press.

Hoffman, C., & Hurst, N. (1990). Gender stereotypes: Perception or rationalization? *Journal of Personality and Social Psychology, 58,* 197–208.

Hofstede, G. (1980). *Culture's consequences.* Beverly Hills, CA: Sage.

Hogan, E. A., & Overmyer-Day, L. (1994). The psychology of mergers and acquisitions. In C. L. Cooper & L. T. Robertson (Eds.), *International review of industrial and organizational psychology* (vol. 9, pp. 247–281). New York: Wiley.

Hogg, M. A. (1987). Social identity and group cohesiveness. In J. C. Turner, M. A. Hogg, P. J. Oakes, S. D. Reicher, & M. S. Wetherell (Eds.), *Rediscovering the social group: A self-categorization theory* (pp. 89–116). Oxford, UK: Blackwell.

Hogg, M. A. (1992). *The social psychology of group cohesiveness: From attraction to social identity*. Hemel Hempstead, UK: Harvester Wheatsheaf.

Hogg, M. A. (1993). Group cohesiveness: A critical review and some new directions. *European Review of Social Psychology, 4*, 85–111.

Hogg, M. A. (1996). Intragroup processes, group structure and social identity. In W. P. Robinson (Ed.), *Social groups and identities: Developing the legacy of Henri Tajfel* (pp. 65–93). Oxford, UK: Butterworth-Heinemann.

Hogg, M. A. (2000). Subjective uncertainty reduction through self-categorization: A motivational theory of social identity processes. In W. Stroebe & M. Hewstone (Eds.), *European Review of Social Psychology* (vol. 11, pp. 232–255). Chichester, UK: Wiley.

Hogg, M. A. (2001a). A social identity theory of leadership. *Personality and Social Psychology Review, 5*, 184–200.

Hogg, M. A. (2001b). From prototypicality to power: A social identity analysis of leadership. In S. R. Thye, E. J. Lawler, M. W. Macy, & H. A. Walker (Eds.), *Advances in group processes* (Vol.18, pp. 1–30). Oxford, UK: Elsevier.

Hogg, M. A. (2001c). Social identification, group prototypicality, and emergent leadership. In M. A. Hogg & D. J. Terry (Eds.), *Social identity processes in organizational contexts* (pp. 197–212). Philadelphia, PA: Psychology Press.

Hogg, M. A. (2001d). Social categorization, depersonalization, and group behavior. In M. A. Hogg & R. S. Tindale (Eds.), *Blackwell handbook of social psychology: Group processes* (pp. 56–85). Oxford, UK: Blackwell.

Hogg, M. A. (2002). Social identity. In M. Leary & J. Tangney (Eds.), *Handbook of self and identity* (pp. 462–479). New York: Guilford.

Hogg, M. A., & Abrams, D. (1988). *Social identifications: A social psychology of intergroup relations and group processes*. London: Routledge.

Hogg, M. A., & Abrams, D. (1990). Social motivation, self-esteem and social identity. In D. Abrams & M. A. Hogg (Eds.), *Social identity theory: Constructive and critical advances* (pp. 28–47). London: Harvester-Wheatsheaf.

Hogg, M. A., & Hains, S. C. (1996). Intergroup relations and group solidarity: Effects of group identification and social beliefs on depersonalized attraction. *Journal of Personality and Social Psychology, 70*, 295–309.

Hogg, M. A., Hains, S. C., & Mason, I. (1998). Identification and leadership in small groups: Salience, frame of reference, and leader stereotypicality effects on leader evaluations. *Journal of Personality and Social Psychology, 75*, 1248–1263.

Hogg, M. A., Martin, R., Weeden, K., & Epitropaki, O. (2001). *Effective leadership in salient groups: Revisiting leader-member exchange theory from the perspective of the social identity theory of leadership*. Manuscript submitted for publication.

Hogg, M. A., & Reid, S. A. (2001). Social identity, leadership, and power. In A. Y. Lee-Chai & J. A. Bargh (Eds.), *The use and abuse of power: Multiple perspectives on the causes of corruption* (pp. 159–180). Philadelphia, PA: Psychology Press.

Hogg, M. A., & Terry, D. J. (2000). Social identity and self-categorization processes in organizational contexts. *Academy of Management Review, 25*, 121–140.

Hogg, M. A., & Terry, D. J. (Eds.) (2001). *Social identity processes in organizational contexts*. Philadelphia, PA: Psychology Press.

Hogg, M. A., Terry, D. J., & White, K.M. (1995). A tale of two theories: Critical comparison of identity theory and social identity theory. *Social Psychology Quarterly, 58*, 255–269.

Hollander, E. P. (1958). Conformity, status, and idiosyncracy credit. *Psychological Review, 65*, 117–127.

Hollander, E. P. (1985). Leadership and power. In G. Lindzey & E. Aronson (Eds.), *The handbook of social psychology* (3rd ed., Vol. 2, pp. 485–537). New York: Random House.

Holson, L. M. (1999, January 4). After 2.5 trillion in combinations in 1998, the sky's the limit in 1999. *New York Times*.

Hopkins, A. B. (1996). *So ordered: Making partner the hard way*. Amherst, MA: University of Massachusetts Press.

Hopkins, N., Reicher S., & Levine M. (1997). On the parallels between social cognition and the "new racism". *British Journal of Social Psychology, 36,* 305–329.

Hornsey, M. J., & Hogg, M. A. (1999). Subgroup differentiation as a response to an overly-inclusive group: A test of optimal distinctiveness theory. *European Journal of Social Psychology, 29,* 543–550.

Hornsey, M. J., & Hogg, M. A. (2000). Assimilation and diversity: An integrative model of subgroup relations. *Personality and Social Psychology Review, 4,* 143–156.

Hornsey, M. J., & Hogg, M. A. (2000a). Subgroup relations: A comparison of mutual intergroup differentiation and common ingroup identity models of prejudice reduction. *Personality and Social Psychology Bulletin, 26,* 242–256.

Hornsey, M. J., & Hogg, M. A. (2000b). Intergroup similarity and subgroup relations: Some implications for assimilations. *Personality and Social Psychology Bulletin, 26,* 948–958.

Hornsey, M. J., & Hogg, M. A. (2000c). Assimilation and diversity: An integrative model of subgroup relations. *Personality and Social Psychology Bulletin, 4,* 143–156.

House, R. J. (1971). A path–goal theory of leader effectiveness. *Administrative Science Quarterly, 16,* 321–339.

Huber, G. P., & Glick, W. H. (1993). *Organizational change and redesign: Ideas and insights for improving performance.* Oxford: Oxford University Press.

Hunter, J. A., Platow, M. J., Howard, M. L., & Stringer, M. (1996). Social identity and intergroup evaluative bias: Realistic categories and domain specific self-esteem in a conflict setting. *European Journal of Social Psychology, 26,* 631–647.

Huo, Y. J., Smith, H. J., Tyler, T. R. & Lind, E. A. (1996). Superordinate identification, subgroup identification, and justice concerns: Is separatism the problem, is assimilation the answer? *Psychological Science, 7,* 40–45.

Huo, Y. J., & Tyler, T. R. (2001a). Ethnic diversity and the viability of organizations: The role of procedural justice in bridging differences. In J. Greenberg & R. Cropanzano (Eds.), *Advances in organiza-* tional justice (pp. 213–244). Palo Alto, CA: Stanford University Press.

Huo, Y. J. & Tyler, T. R. (2001b). *Procedural justice, identity and social regulation across Group boundaries: Does subgroup loyalty undermine relationship-based governance?* Unpublished manuscript, University of California, Los Angeles.

Huxtable, R. D. (1998). *A social sense of justice: The power of relationships in the interaction of procedural and distributive justice.* Unpublished Ph.D. thesis, University of Victoria, Canada.

Isabella, L. (1990). Evolving interpretations as a change unfolds: How managers construe key organizational events. *Academy of Management Journal, 33,* 7–41.

Ivancevich, J. M., Schweiger, D. M., & Power, F. R. (1987). Strategies for managing human resources during mergers and acquisitions. *Human Resource Planning, 10,* 18–35.

Jackman, M.R. (1994). *The velvet glove: Paternalism and conflict in gender, class, and race relations.* Berkeley, CA: University of California Press.

Jackson, S. E. (1992). Team composition in organizational settings: Issues in managing an increasingly diverse workforce. In S. Worchel, W. Wood & J. A. Simpson (Eds.), *Group processes and productivity* (pp. 136–180). Newbury Park, CA: Sage.

Jackson, T. (1997). *Inside Intel: Andy Grove and the rise of the world's most powerful chip company.* New York: Plume/Putnam.

Jacobs, J.A. (Ed.). (1995). *Gender inequality at work.* London: Sage.

Jacobs, J.A., & Steinberg, R. (1990). Compensating differentials and the male-female wage gap: Evidence from the New York state comparable worth study. *Social Forces, 69,* 439–468.

Jaffe, D., Scott, C., & Tobe, G. (1994). *Rekindling commitment: How to revitalize yourself, your work, and your organization.* San Francisco: Jossey-Bass.

James, K., & Greenberg, J. (1989). Ingroup salience, intergroup comparison and individual performance and self-esteem. *Personality and Social Psychology Bulletin, 15,* 604–616.

Janis, I. L. (1972). *Victims of groupthink.* Boston: Houghton Mifflin.

Janis, I. L. (1982). *Groupthink: Psychological studies of policy decisions and fiascoes* (2nd ed.). Boston: Houghton Mifflin.

Janis, I. L. (1989). *Crucial decisions: Leadership in policymaking and crisis management*. New York: Free Press.

Janis, I. L., & Mann, F. (1977). *Decision making*. New York: Free Press.

Jasso, G. (1993). Analyzing conflict severity: Prediction of distributive justice theory for the two sub-group case. *Social Justice Research, 6*, 357–382.

Jasso, G. (1994). Assessing individual and group differences in the sense of justice: Framework and application to gender differences in the justice of earnings. *Social Science Research, 23*, 368-406.

Jehn, K. A. (1995). A multimethod examination of the benefits and detriments of intragroup conflict. *Administrative Science Quarterly, 40*, 256–282.

Jehn, K. A., Northcraft, G. B., & Neale, M. A. (1999). Why differences make a difference: A field study of diversity, conflict, and performance in workgroups. *Administrative Science Quarterly, 44*, 741–763.

Jemison, D. B., & Sitkin, S. B. (1986). Corporate acquisitions: A process perspective. *Academy of Management Review, 11*, 145–163.

Jessup, L. M., Connolly, T., & Tansik, D. A. (1990). Toward a theory of automated group work: The deindividuating effects of anonymity. *Small Group Research, 21*, 333–348.

Jetten, J., Branscombe, N. R., Schmitt, M. T., & Spears, R. (2001). Rebels with a cause: Group identification as a response to perceived discrimination from the mainstream. *Personality and Social Psychology Bulletin, 27*, 1204–1213.

Jetten, J., O'Brien, A. & Trindall, N. (2002). Changing identity: Predicting adjustment to organizational restructure as a function of subgroup and superordinate identification. *British Journal of Social Psychology, 41*, 281–297.

Jetten, J., Postmes, T., & McAuliffe, B. J. (1997). "We're *all* individuals": Group norms of individualism and collectivism: Levels of identification and identity threat. *European Journal of Social Psychology, 32*, 189–207.

Jetten, J., Spears, R., & Manstead, A. R. (1997). Strength of identification and intergroup differentiation: The influence of group norms. *European Journal of Social Psychology, 27*, 603–609.

Jetten, J., Spears, R., & Manstead, A. R. (1999). Group distinctiveness and intergroup discrimination. In N. Ellemers, R. Spears, & B. Doosje (Eds.), *Social identity: Context mommitment, content* (pp. 107–126). Oxford, UK: Blackwell.

Johansen, R. (1977). Social evaluations of teleconferencing. *Telecommunications Policy, 1*, 395–419.

Johansen, R., Vallee, J., & Collins, K. (1978). Learning the limits of teleconferencing: Design of a teleconference tutorial. In M. C. J. Elton, W. A. Lucas, & D. W. Conrath (Eds.), *Evaluating new telecommunications systems* (pp. 385–398). New York: Plenum.

Johnson, B. M. (1977). *Communication: The process of organizing*. Boston, MA: Allyn & Bacon.

Johnson, T., & Graen, G. B. (1973). Organizational assimilation and role rejection. *Organizational Behavior and Human Performance, 10*, 72–78.

Jones, E., Gallois, C., Barker, M., & Callan, V. (1994). Evaluations of interactions between students and academic staff: Influence of language accommodation, ethnic group, and status. *Journal of Language and Social Psychology, 13*, 158–191.

Jost, J. T., & Elsbach, K.D. (2001). How status and power differences erode personal and social identities at work: A system justification critique of organizational applications of social identity theory. In M. A. Hogg & D. J. Terry (Eds.), *Social identity processes in organizational contexts* (pp. 181–196). Philadelphia: Psychology Press.

Judson, A. (1991). *Changing behavior in organizations: Minimizing resistance to change*. Cambridge, UK: Basil Blackwell.

Kahneman, D. (1973). *Attention and effort*. Englewood Cliffs, NJ: Prentice-Hall.

Kaiser, C. R., & Miller, C. T. (2001). Stop complaining!: The social costs of making attributions to discrimination. *Personality and Social Psychology Bulletin, 27*, 254–263.

Kanter, R. M. (1977). *Men and women of the corporation*. New York: Basic Books.

Kappen, D. M., & Branscombe, N. R. (2001). The effects of reasons given for ineligibility on perceived gender discrimination and feelings of injustice. *British Journal of Social Psychology, 40,* 295–313.

Karasawa, M. (1991). Toward an assessment of social identity: The structure of group identification and its effects on in-group evaluations. *British Journal of Social Psychology, 30,* 293–307.

Karau, S. J., & Hart, J. W. (1998). Group cohesiveness and social loafing: Effects of a social interaction manipulation on individual motivation within groups. *Group Dynamics: Theory, Research and Practice, 2,* 185–191.

Karau, S. J., & Williams, K. D. (1993). Social loafing: A meta-analytic review and theoretical integration. *Journal of Personality and Social Psychology, 65,* 681–706.

Karau, S. J., & Williams, K. D. (1997). The effects of group cohesiveness on social loafing and social compensation. *Group Dynamics: Theory, Research and Practice, 1,* 156–168.

Katz, D. (1964). The motivational basis of organizational behavior. *Behavioral Science, 9,* 131–146.

Katz, D., & Braly, K. (1933). Racial stereotypes of one hundred college students. *Journal of Abnormal and Social Psychology, 28,* 280–290.

Katz, D., & Kahn, R. L. (1972). *The social psychology of organizations* (2nd ed.). New York: Wiley.

Kayany, J. M. (1998). Contexts of uninhibited online behavior: Flaming in social newsgroups on Usenet. *Journal of the American Society for Information Science, 49,* 1135–1141.

Keenoy, T. (1992). Constructing control. In J. F. Hartley & G. M Stephenson (Eds.), *Employment relations* (pp. 91–110). Oxford, UK: Blackwell.

Keller, T., & Dansereau, F. (2000). The effects of adding items to scales: An illustrative case of LMX. *Organizational Research Methods, 4,* 131–143.

Kelley, H. H., & Thibaut, J. (1978). *Interpersonal relations: A theory of interdependence.* New York: Wiley.

Kelly, C. (1993). Group identification, intergroup perceptions and collective action. *European Review of Social Psychology, 4,* 59–83.

Kelly, C., & Breinlinger, S. (1995). Identity and justice: Exploring women's participation in collective action. *Journal of Community and Applied Psychology, 5,* 41–57.

Kelly, C., & Breinlinger, S. (1996). *The social psychology of collective action: Identity, injustice and gender.* London: Taylor & Francis.

Kelly, C., & Kelly, J. (1991). "Them and us": Social psychology and "the new industrial relations." *British Journal of Industrial Relations, 29,* 25–48.

Kelly, C., & Kelly, J. (1994). Who gets involved in collective action? Social psychological determinents of individual participation in trade unions. *Human Relations, 47,* 63–88.

Kelly, J., & Kelly, C. (1992). Industrial action. In J. F. Hartley & G. M Stephenson (Eds.), *Employment relations* (pp. 246–268). Oxford, UK: Blackwell.

Kelman, H. C. (1961). Processes of opinion change. *Public Opinion Quarterly, 25,* 57–78.

Kerr, N. L. (1983). Motivation losses in small groups: A social dilemma analysis. *Journal of Personality and Social Psychology, 45,* 819–828.

Kerr, S. (1995). On the folly of rewarding A, while hoping for B. *Academy of Management Executive, 9,* 7–14.

Kiesler, S. (1986). The hidden messages in computer networks. *Harvard Business Review, 64,* 46–60.

Kiesler, S., Siegel, J., & McGuire, T. (1984). Social psychological aspects of computer-mediated communications. *American Psychologist, 39,* 1123–1134.

Kiesler, S., & Sproull, L. (1992). Group decision making and communication technology. *Organizational Behavior and Human Decision Processes, 52,* 96–123.

Kilmartin, C. T. (1994). *The masculine self.* New York: Macmillan.

Kinicki, A. J., & Vecchio, R. P. (1994). Influences on the quality of supervisor–subordinate relations: The role of time-pressure, organizational commitment, and locus of control. *Journal of Organizational Behavior, 15,* 75–82.

Kirkbride, P. S. (1992). Power. In J. F. Hartley & G. M Stephenson (Eds.), *Employment relations* (pp. 67–88). Oxford, UK: Blackwell.

Kleinbeck, U., & Fuhrmann, H. (2000). Effects of a psychologically based management system on work motivation and productivity. *Applied Psychology: An International Review, 49*, 596–610.

Klonoff, E. A., Landrine, H., & Campbell, R. (2000). Sexist discrimination may account for well-known gender differences in psychiatric symptoms. *Psychology of Women Quarterly, 24*, 93–99.

Knight, D., Durham, C. C., & Locke, E. A. (2001). The relationship of team goals, incentives, and efficacy to strategic risk, tactical implication, and performance. *Academy of Management Journal, 44*, 326–339.

Kobrynowicz, D., & Branscombe, N. R. (1997). Who considers themselves victims of discrimination? Individual difference predictors of perceived gender discrimination in women and men. *Psychology of Women Quarterly, 21*, 347–363.

Kohn, A. (1993). Why incentive plans cannot work. *Harvard Business Review, 73*, 59–67.

Koper, G., Van Knippenberg, D., Bouhuijs, F., Vermunt, R., & Wilke, H. (1993). Procedural fairness and self-esteem. *European Journal of Social Psychology, 23*, 313–325.

Kotter, J. (1995). Leading change: Why transformation efforts fail. *Harvard Business Review, 73*, 59–67.

Kramer, R. M. (1991a). Intergroup relations and organizational dilemmas. *Research in Organizational Behavior, 13*, 191–228.

Kramer, R. M. (1991b). Intergoup relations and organizational dilemmas: The role of categorization processes. In L. L. Cummings & B. M. Staw (Eds.), *Research in orgainzational behavior* (Vol. 13, pp. 191–228). Greenwich CT: JAI Press.

Kramer, R. M. (1998). Revisiting the Bay of Pigs and Vietnam decisions twenty-five years later: How well has the groupthink hypothesis stood the test of time? *Organizational Behavior and Human Decision Processes, 2/3*, 236–271.

Kraut, R., Patterson, M., Lundmark, V., Kiesler, S., Mukopadhyay, T., & Scherlis, W. (1998). Internet paradox: A social technology that reduces social involvement and psychological well-being? *American Psychologist, 53*, 1017–1031.

Kreps, G. L. (1990). *Organizational communication.* (2nd ed.). White Plains, NY: Longman.

Krishman, H. A., Miller, A., & Judge, W. Q. (1997). Diversification and top management team complementarity: Is performance improved by merging similar or dissimilar teams? *Strategic Management Journal, 18*, 361–374.

Kroon, M. B. R., 't Hart, P., & van Kreveld, D. (1991). Managing group decision making processes: Individual versus collective accountability and groupthink. *International Journal of Conflict Management, 2*, 91–116.

Kropotkin, P. (1972). *Mutual aid: A factor of evolution.* London: Allen Lane. (Original work published 1902)

Kuhn, T. (1962). *The structure of scientific revolutions.* Chicago: University of Chicago Press.

Kwan, J. L. (2001, June 20). Robert Noyce: The genius behind Intel. *San Jose Mercury News*, p. S35.

Kwun, S. K., & Cummings, L. L. (1994). Role of self-esteem in resolving inequity. *Psychological Reports, 75*, 95–111.

LaFromboise, T., Coleman, H. L. K., & Gerton, J. (1993). Psychological impact of biculturalism: Evidence and theory. *Psychological Bulletin, 114*, 395–412.

Lalonde, R. N. (1992). The dynamics of group differentiation in the face of defeat. *Personality and Social Psychology Bulletin, 18*, 336–342.

Lalonde, R. N., & Silverman, R. A. (1994). Behavioral preferences in response to social injustice: The effects of group permeability and social identity salience. *Journal of Personality and Social Psychology, 66*, 78–85.

Landy, F. J. (1989). *Psychology of work behavior* (4th ed.). Pacific Grove, CA: Brooks Cole.

Langfred, C. W. (1998). Is group cohesiveness a double-edged sword? An investigation of the effects of cohesiveness on performance. *Small Group Research, 29*, 124–143.

Larwood, L., Szwajkowski, E., & Rose, S. (1988). Sex and race discrimination resulting from manager–client relationships: Applying the rational bias theory of managerial discrimination. *Sex Roles, 18*, 9–29.

Lawler, E. E. (1986). *High involvement man-*

agement: Participation strategies for improving organizational performance. San Francisco: Jossey-Bass.

Lawler, E. E. (1992). The ultimate advantage: Creating the high-involvement organization. San Franciso: Jossey-Bass.

Lawler, E. E. III (1968). Equity theory as a predictor of productivity and work quality. Psychological Bulletin, 70, 596–610.

Lawler, E. E., III. (1973). Motivation in work organizations. Monterey, CA: Brooks/Cole.

Lawler, E. E., III, Mohrman, S. A., & Ledford, G. E., Jr. (1995). Creating high performance organizations: Practices and results of employee involvement and total quality management. San Francisco: Jossey-Bass.

Lazarus, R. S., & Folkman, S. (1984). Stress, appraisal, and coping. New York: Springer Publishing.

Lea, M. (1991). Rationalist assumptions in cross-media comparisons of computer-mediated communication. Behaviour and Information Technology, 10, 153–172.

Lea, M., & Giordano, R. (1997). Representations of the group and group processes in CSCW research: A case of premature closure? In G. C. Bowker, S. L. Star, W. Turner, & L. Gasser, (Eds.), Social science, technical systems and cooperative work: Beyond the great divide (pp 5–26). Mahwah, NJ: Erlbaum.

Lea, M., O'Shea, T., & Fung, P. (1995). Constructing the networked organization: Content and context in the development of electronic communications. Organization Science, 6, 462–478.

Lea, M., O'Shea, T., Fung, P., & Spears, R. (1992). "Flaming" in computer-mediated communication: Observations, explanations, implications. In M. Lea (Ed.), Contexts of computer-mediated communication (pp. 89–112). Hemel Hempstead, UK: Harvester-Wheatsheaf.

Lea, M., Postmes, T., & Rogers, P. (1999). SIDE-VIEW: An interactive web environment to support group collaborative learning. Educational Technology and Society, 2, 33–34.

Lea, M., & Rogers, P. (2001a, April 25). SIDE-VIEW: Development and evaluation of a system for Internet collaborative learning groups. Invited seminar to the Teaching, Research and Development Network, Manchester Federal Business School.

Lea, M., & Rogers, P. (2001b). Anonymity effects on group consensus: the role of self-categorization, accountability and duty to the group. Manuscript in preparation, University of Manchester.

Lea, M., Rogers, P. & Postmes, T. (2002). SIDE-VIEW: Evaluation of a system to develop team players and improve productivity in Internet collaborative learning groups. British Journal of Educational Technology, 33, 53–64.

Lea, M., & Spears, R. (1991). Computer-mediated communication, de-individuation and group decision making. International Journal of Man–Machine Studies, 39, 283–301.

Lea, M., & Spears, R. (1992). Paralanguage and social perception in computer-mediated communication. Journal of Organizational Computing, 2, 321–342.

Lea, M., & Spears, R. (1995). Love at first byte? Building personal relationships over computer networks. In J. T. Wood & S. Duck (Eds.), Understudied relationships: Off the beaten track (pp. 197–233). Thousand Oaks, CA: Sage.

Lea, M., Spears, R., & De Groot, D. (2001). Knowing me, knowing you: Anonymity effects on social identity processes within groups. Personality and Social Psychology Bulletin 27, 526–537.

Lea, M., Spears, R., Watt, S. E., Berg, M., & Te Haar, W. (2001). Visibility and anonymity effects on identification and stereotyping: Influence of category cues. Manuscript in preparation, University of Manchester.

Lea, M., Spears, R., Watt, S. E., & Rogers, P. (2000). The InSIDE story: Social psychological processes affecting on-line groups. In T. Postmes, R. Spears, M. Lea, & S. D. Reicher (Eds.), SIDE-issues centre-stage: Recent developments in studies of de-individuation in groups (pp. 47–62). Amsterdam: KNAW.

Leana, C. R. (1985). A partial test of Janis' groupthink model: Effects of group cohesiveness and leader behavior on defective decision making. Journal of Management, 11, 5–17.

Leary M. R., & Baumeister R. F. (2000). The

nature and function of self-esteem: Socio-meter theory. *Advances in Experimental Social Psychology, 32,* 1–62.

Leavitt, H. J. (1972). *Managerial psychology: An introduction to individuals, pairs, and groups in organizations.* (3rd ed.). Chicago: University of Chicago Press.

Ledford, G. E. (1993). Employee involvement: Lessons and predictions. In J. R. Galbraith & E. E. Lawler (Eds.), *Organizing for the future: The new logic for managing complex organizations* (pp. 143–169). San Francisco: Jossey-Bass.

Leeke, J. (1984, October 16). Intel carves out influential market niche. *PC Week, 41,* 75.

Lemaine, G. (1974). Social differentiation and social originality. *European Journal of Social Psychology, 4,* 17–52.

Lenzner, R. (1995, September 11). The reluctant entrepreneur. *Forbes, 156,* 162–167.

Lerner, M. J. (1977). The justice motive: Some hypotheses as to its origins and forms. *Journal of Personality, 45,* 1–52.

Leung, K., Chiu, W. H., & Au, Y. F. (1993). Sympathy and support for industrial actions: A justice analysis. *Journal of Applied Psychology, 78,* 781–787.

Leventhal, G. S. (1980). What should be done with equity theory? New approaches to the study of fairness in social relationships. In K. J. Gergen, M. S. Greenberg & R. H. Willis (Eds.), *Social exchange: Advances in theory and research* (pp. 27–55). New York: Plenum.

Levine, J. M., & Moreland, R. L. (1990). Progress in small group research. *Annual Review of Psychology, 41,* 585–634.

Levine, J. M., & Moreland, R. L. (1995). Group processes. In A. Tesser (Ed.), *Advanced social psychology* (pp. 419–465). New York: McGraw-Hill.

Lewin, K. (1947). Group decision and social change. In T. M. Newcomb & E. L. Hartley (Eds.), *Readings in social psychology* (pp. 330–344). New York: Holt, Rinehart & Winston.

Lickel, B., Hamilton, D. L., Wieczorkowska, G., Lewis, A., Sherman, S. J., & Uhles, A. N. (2000). Varieties of groups and the perception of group entitativity. *Journal of Personality and Social Psychology, 78,* 223–246.

Liden, R. C., & Graen, G. B. (1980). Generalizability of the Vertical Dyad Linkage model of leadership. *Academy of Management Journal, 23,* 451–465.

Liden, R. C., Sparrowe, R. T., & Wayne, S. J. (1997). Leader–member exchange theory: The past and potential for the future. *Research in Personnel and Human Resources Management, 15,* 47–119.

Likert, R. (1961). *New patterns of management.* New York: McGraw-Hill.

Lind, E. A., & Earley, P. C. (1992). Procedural justice and culture. *International Journal of Psychology, 27,* 227–242.

Lind, E. A. & Tyler, T. R. (1988). *The social psychology of procedural justice.* New York: Plenum.

Linville, P. W., Fischer, G. W., & Salovey, P. (1989). Perceived distributions of the characteristics of in-group and out-group members: Empirical evidence and a computer simulation. *Journal of Personality and Social Psychology, 57,* 165–188.

Lippitt, R., & White, R. (1943). The "social climate" of children's groups. In R. G. Barker, J. Kounin, & H. Wright (Eds.), *Child behavior and development* (pp. 485–508). New York: McGraw-Hill.

Locke, E. A. (2000). Motivation, cognition and action: An analysis of studies on task goals and knowledge. *Applied Psychology: An International Review, 49,* 408–429.

Locke, E. A., Alavi, M., & Wagner III, J. A. (1997). Participation in decision making: An information exchange perspective. *Research in Personnel and Human Resource Management, 15,* 293–331.

Locke, E. A., & Latham, G. P. (1990a). Work motivation and satisfaction: Light at the end of the tunnel. *Psychological Science, 1,* 240–246.

Locke, E. A., & Latham, G. P. (1990b). *A theory of goal setting and task performance.* Englewood Cliffs, NJ: Prentice-Hall.

Locke, J. (1764/1952). *The second treatise of government.* New York: Macmillan.

Long, K. M., & Spears, R. (1997). The self-esteem hypothesis revisited: Differentiation and the disaffected. In R. Spears, P.J. Oakes, N. Ellemers, & S. A. Haslam (Eds.), *The social psychology of stereotyping and group life* (pp. 296–317). Oxford, UK: Blackwell.

Long, K. M., & Spears, R. (1998). Opposing effects of personal and collective self-esteem on interpersonal and intergroup comparisons. *European Journal of Social Psychology, 28*, 913–930.

Longley, J., & Pruitt, D. G. (1980). Groupthink: A critique of Janis's theory. In L. Wheeler (Ed.). *Review of Personality and Social Psychology* (Vol.1, pp. 507–513). Beverly Hills, CA: Sage.

Lord, R. G., Brown, D. J., & Harvey, J. L. (2001). System constraints on leadership perceptions, behavior and influence: An example of connectionist level processes. In M. A. Hogg & R. S. Tindale (Eds.), *Blackwell handbook of social psychology: Group processes* (pp. 283–310). Oxford, UK: Blackwell.

Lord, R. G., Foti, R. J., & DeVader, C. L. (1984). A test of leadership categorization theory: Internal structure, information processing, and leadership perceptions. *Organizational Behavior and Human Performance, 34*, 343–378.

Lott, A. J., & Lott, B. E. (1965). Group cohesiveness as interpersonal attraction: A review of relationships with antecedent and consequent variables. *Psychological Bulletin, 64*, 259–309.

Lubatkin, M. (1983). Mergers and the performance of the acquiring firm. *Academy of Management Review, 8*, 218–225.

Ludwig, T. D., & Geller, E. S. (1997). Assigned versus participative goal setting and response generalization: Managing injury control among professional pizza deliverers. *Journal of Applied Psychology, 82*, 253–261.

Luhtanen, R., & Crocker, J. (1992). A collective self-esteem scale: Self-evaluation of one's social identity. *Personality and Social Psychology Bulletin, 18*, 302–318.

Maass, A., Salvi, D., Arcuri, L., & Semin, G. (1989). Language use in intergroup contexts: The linguistic intergroup bias. *Journal of Personality and Social Psychology, 57*, 981–993.

MacKenzie, S. B., Podsakoff, P. M., & Fetter, R. (1991). Organizational citizenship behavior and objective productivity as determinants of managerial evaluations of salespersons' performance. *Organizational Behavior and Human Decision Processes, 50*, 123–150.

Mackie, D. M. (1986). Social identification effects in group polarization. *Journal of Personality and Social Psychology, 50*, 720–728.

Mackie, D. M., & Cooper, J. (1984). Attitude polarization: Effects of group membership. *Journal of Personality and Social Psychology, 46*, 575–585.

Mackie, D. M., Worth, L. T., & Asuncion, A. G. (1990). Processing of persuasive ingroup messages. *Journal of Personality and Social Psychology, 58*, 812–822.

Mael, F., & Ashforth, B. E. (1992). Alumni and their alma mater: A partial test of the reformulated model of organizational identification. *Journal of Organizational Behavior, 13*, 103–123.

Mael, F., & Tetrick, L. E. (1992). Identifying organizational identification. *Educational and Psychological Measurement, 52*, 813–824.

Maier, N. R. F. (1952). *Principles of human relations*. New York: Wiley.

Major, B. (1994). From social inequality to personal entitlement: The role of social comparisons, legitimacy appraisals, and group membership. In M.P. Zanna (Ed.), *Advances in experimental social psychology* (Vol. 26, pp. 293–348). San Diego, CA: Academic Press.

Major, D. A., Kozlowski, S. W. J., Chao, G. T., & Gardner, P. D. (1995). A longitudinal investigation of newcomer expectations, early socialization outcomes, and the moderating effects of role development factors. *Journal of Applied Psychology, 80*, 418–431.

Markovsky, B. (1985). Toward a multilevel distributive justice theory. *American Sociological Review, 50*, 822–839.

Markovsky, B. (1991). Prospects for a cognitive-structural justice theory. In R. Vermunt & H. Steensma (Eds.), *Social justice in human relations: Societal and psychological origins of justice* (Vol.2, pp. 33–58). New York: Plenum.

Markus, H., & Kitayama, S. (1991). Culture and the self: Implications for cognition, emotion, and motivation. *Psychological Review, 98*, 224–253.

Marques, J. M., Abrams, D., Páez, D., &

Hogg, M. A. (2001). Social categorization, social identification, and rejection of deviant group members. In M. A. Hogg & R. S. Tindale, (Eds.), *Blackwell handbook of social psychology: Group processes* (pp. 400–424). Oxford, UK: Blackwell.

Martin, J. (1971). *Future developments in telecommunications*. Englewood Cliffs, NJ: Prentice-Hall.

Martin, J. (1986). The tolerance of injustice. In J. M. Olson, C. P. Herman, & M. P. Zanna (Eds.), *Relative deprivation and social comparison: The Ontario symposium*, (Vol. 4, pp. 217–242). Hillsdale, NJ: Erlbaum.

Martin, J. (1993). *Cultures in organizations*. New York: Oxford University Press.

Martin, J., & Harder, J.W. (1994). Bread and roses: Justice and the distribution of financial and socioemotional rewards in organizations. *Social Justice Research, 7*, 484–496.

Marvin, C. (1988). *When old technologies were new: Thinking about electric communication in the late nineteenth century*. Oxford: Oxford, UK: University Press.

Marx, K. (1906). *Capital: A critique of political economy*. (S. Moore & E. Aveling, Trans.). New York: Modern Library. (Original work published 1867)

Marx, K., & Engels, F. (1986). *The communist manifesto* (S. Moore, Trans.). Harmondsworth, UK: Penguin Books. (Original work published 1848)

Maslach, C., Schaufeli, W. B., & Leiter, M. P. (2001). Job burnout. *Annual Review of Psychology, 52*, 397–422.

Maslow, A. H. (1943). A theory of motivation. *Psychological Review, 50*, 370–396.

Massachusetts Institute of Technology. (1999). *A study on the status of women faculty in science at MIT*. Cambridge, MA: Author.

Matheson, K., & Zanna, M. P. (1988). The impact of computer-mediated communication on self-awareness. *Computers in Human Behavior, 4*, 221–233.

Matheson, K., & Zanna, M. P. (1989). Persuasion as a function of self-awareness in computer-mediated communication. *Social Behaviour, 4*, 99–111.

Mathieu, J. E., & Zajac, D. (1990). A review and meta-analysis of the antecedents, correlates, and consequences of organizational commitment. *Psychological Bulletin, 108*, 171–194.

Matsui, T., Kakuyama, T., & Onglatco, M. L. U. (1987). Effects of goals and feedback on performance in groups. *Journal of Applied Psychology, 72*, 407–415.

Mayo, E. (1933). *The human problems of an industrial civilisation*. Cambridge, MA: Macmillan.

Mayo, E. (1949). *The social problems of an industrial civilisation*. London: Routledge & Kegan Paul.

McGarty, C. (1999). *The categorization process in social psychology*. London: Sage.

McGarty, C. (2001). Social identity theory does not maintain that identification produces bias and self-categorization theory does not maintain that salience is identification. *British Journal of Social Psychology, 40*, 173–176.

McGarty, C., Haslam, S. A., Hutchinson, K. J., & Turner, J. C. (1994). The effects of salient group membership on persuasion. *Small Group Research, 25*, 267–293.

McGrath, J. E. (1997). Small group research, that once and future field: An interpretation of the past with an eye to the future. *Group Dynamics: Theory, Research, and Practice, 1*, 7–27.

McLanahan, S. S., & Kelly, E. L. (1999). The feminization of poverty: Past and future. In J. S. Chafetz (Ed.), *Handbook of the sociology of gender* (pp. 127–145). New York: Plenum.

McQuail, D. (1994). *Mass communication theory. An introduction*. London: Sage.

Messick, D. M., Bloom, S., Boldizar, J. P., & Samuelson, C. D. (1985). Why we are fairer than others. *Journal of Experimental Social Psychology, 21*, 480–500.

Messick, D., & Kramer, R. M. (Eds.). (2003). *New thinking about the psychology of leadership*. Mahwah, NJ: Erlbaum.

Messick, D. M., & Kramer, R. (Eds.). (in press). *The psychology of leadership: Some new approaches*. Mahwah, NJ: Erlbaum.

Messick, D. M., & McClintock, C. G. (1968). Motivational bases of choice in experimental games. *Journal of Experimental Social Psychology, 4*, 1–25.

Meyer, J. P., & Allen, N. J. (1984). Testing the "side-bet theory" of organizational commitment: Some methodological considerations. *Journal of Applied Psychology, 69,* 372–378.

Meyer, J. P., & Allen, N. J. (1997). *Commitment in the workplace.* Thousand Oaks, CA: Sage.

Mikula, G., Petri, B., & Tanzer, N. (1990). What people regard as unjust: Types and structures of everyday experiences of injustice. *European Journal of Social Psychology, 20,* 133–149.

Miller, D. T. (2001). Disrespect and the experience of injustice. *American Review of Psychology, 52,* 527–553.

Miller, D. T., & Ratner, R. K. (1998). The disparity between the actual and assumed power of self-interest. *Journal of Personality and Social Psychology, 74,* 53–62.

Milliken, F., & Martins, L. (1996). Searching for common threads: Understanding the multiple effects of diversity in organizational groups. *Academy of Management Review, 21,* 402–433.

Mintzberg, H. (1983a). *Power in and around organizations.* Englewood Cliffs, NJ: Prentice-Hall.

Mintzberg, H. (1983b). *Structure in fives: Designing effective organizations.* Englewood Cliffs: Prentice-Hall.

Mirvis, P., & Marks, M. L. (1986, January/Feburary). Merger syndrome: Management by crisis. *Mergers and Acquisitions,* 70–76.

Mitchell, T. R., & Silver, W. S. (1990). Individual and group goals when workers are interdependent: Effects on task strategies and performance. *Journal of Applied Psychology, 75,* 185–193.

Mlicki, P., & Ellemers, N., (1996). Being different or being better? National stereotypes and identifications of Polish and Dutch students. *European Journal of Social Psychology, 26,* 97–114.

Moad, J. (1984, November 5). Intel systems operations cut back: Growth lag cited. *Electronic Business, 30,* 1.

Monge, P. R., & Fulk, J. (1999). Communication technology for global network organizations. In G. DeSanctis & J. Fulk (Eds.), *Shaping organization form: Communication, connection, and community* (pp. 71–100). Thousand Oaks, CA: Sage.

Monge, P. R., & Contractor, N. S. (2001). Emergence of communication networks. In

L. L. Putnam & F. M. Jablin (Eds.), *New handbook of organizational communication* (2nd ed., pp. 440–502). Newbury Park, CA: Sage.

Moorhead, A., Steel, M., Alexander, M., Stephen, K., & Duffin, L. (1997). *Changes at work: The 1995 Australian Workplace Industrial Relations Survey.* South Melbourne, Australia: Longman.

Moorhead, G., Ference, R., & Neck, C. P. (1991). Group decision fiascoes continue: Space shuttle Challenger and a revised groupthink framework. *Human Relations, 44,* 539–550.

Moreland, R. L., Argote, L., & Krishnan, R. (1996). Socially shared cognition at work: Transactive memory and group performance. In J. Nye & A. Brower (Eds.), *What's social about social cognition? Research on socially shared cognition in small groups* (pp. 57–84). Newbury Park, CA: Sage.

Moreland, R. L., Hogg, M. A., & Hains, S. C. (1994). Back to the future: Social psychological research on groups. *Journal of Experimental Social Psychology, 30,* 527–555.

Moreland, R. L., & Levine, J. M. (1982). Group socialization: Temporal changes in individual–group relations. In L. Berkowitz (Ed.), *Advances in experimental social psychology* (Vol. 15, pp. 137–192). New York: Academic Press.

Moreland, R. L., & Levine, J. M. (2001). Socialization in organizations and work groups. In M. Turner (Ed.), *Groups at work: Theory and research* (pp. 69–112). Mahwah, NJ: Erlbaum.

Morgenson, G. (1997). *Forbes' great minds of business.* New York: Wiley.

Morkes, J. (1993, July). Success likes to follow Intel's Gordon Moore. *R&D, 35,* 32.

Morley, I. E., & Stephenson, G. M. (1969). Interpersonal and interparty exchange: A laboratory simulation of an industrial negotiation at the plant level. *British Journal of Psychology, 60,* 543–545.

Morrison, B. E. (1997). *Redefining the self in self-interest.* Unpublished Ph.D. Thesis, Division of Psychology. Australian National University, Canberra.

Moscovici, S. (1976). *Social influence and social change.* London: Academic Press.

Moscovici, S. (1985). Social influence and

conformity. In G. Lindzey & E. Aronson (Eds.), *The handbook of social psychology* (3rd ed., Vol.2, pp. 347–412). New York: Random House.

Mottola, G. R., Bachman, B. A., Gaertner, S. L., & Dovidio, J. F. (1997). How groups merge: The effects of merger integration patterns on anticipated commitment to the merged organization. *Journal of Applied Social Psychology, 27,* 1335–1358.

Mowday, R. T., Porter, L. W., & Steers, R. M. (1982). *Employee-organization linkages.* New York: Academic Press.

Mowday, R. T., & Sutton, R. I. (1993). Organizational behavior: Linking individuals and groups to organizational contexts. *Annual Review of Psychology, 44,* 195–229.

Mullen, B., Brown, R., & Smith, C. (1992). Ingroup bias as a function of salience, relevance, and status: A integration. *European Journal of Social Psychology, 22,* 103–123.

Mummendey, A., & Schreiber, H. J. (1983). Better or different? Positive social identity by discrimination against or differentiation from outgroups. *European Journal of Social Psychology, 13,* 389–397.

Mummendey, A., & Schreiber H. J. (1984). "Different" just means "better": Some obvious and some hidden pathways to ingroup favoritism. *British Journal of Social Psychology, 23,* 363–368.

Mummendey, A., & Simon, B. (1989). Better or different? III. The impact of importance of comparison dimension and relative ingroup size upon intergroup discrimination. *British Journal of Social Psychology, 28,* 1–16.

Mummendey, A., & Wenzel, M. (1999). Social discrimination and tolerance in intergroup relations: Reactions to intergroup difference. *Personality and Social Psychology Review, 3,* 158–174.

Nahavandi, A., & Malekzadeh, A. R. (1988). Acculturation in mergers and acquisitions. *Academy of Management Review, 13,* 79–90.

Neale, M. A., Mannix, E. A., & Polzer, J. (Eds.). (in press). *Research on managing groups and teams* (Vol. 5). Greenwich, CT: Elsevier Science Press.

Neale, M. A., Mannix, E. A., & Polzer, J. (in press). Identification, salience and diversity: Social identity and self-categorization theo-

ries' contribution to innovation and creativity within teams. In J. Polzer (Ed.), *Research on managing groups and teams* (Vol. 5). Greenwich, CT: JAI Press.

Neck, C. P., & Moorhead, G. (1992). Jury deliberations in the Trial of U. S. v. John DeLorean: A case analysis of groupthink avoidance and an enhanced framework. *Human Relations, 45,* 1077–1091.

Newcomb, T. M. (1943). *Personality and social change.* New York: Holt, Rinehart, & Winston.

Ng, S. H. (1980). *The social psychology of power.* London: Academic Press.

Ng, S. H. (1984). Equity and social categorization effects on intergroup allocation of rewards. *British Journal of Social Psychology, 23,* 165–172.

Ng, S. H., & Bradac, J. J. (1993). *Power in language: Verbal communication and social influence.* Newbury Park, CA: Sage.

Nicholas, S., & Semmartino, A. (2000). Corporate awareness of diversity in the Australian workplace: The mind of the CEO. In *21st century business delivering the diversity dividend: Research reports of the productive diversity partnership program* (p. 148). Canberra: Department of Immigration and Multi-Cultural Affairs.

Nisbett, R. E., & Ross, L. (1980). *Human inference: Strategies and shortcomings of social judgement.* Engelwood Cliffs, NJ: Prentice-Hall.

Nkomo, S. M., & Cox, T., Jr. (1996). Diverse identities in organizations. In S. R. Clegg, C. Hardy, & W. R. Nord (Eds.), *Handbook of organizational studies* (pp. 338–356). Thousand Oaks, CA: Sage.

Noel, J. G., Branscombe, N. R., & Wann, D. L. (1995). Peripheral ingroup membership status and public negativity toward outgroups. *Journal of Personality and Social Psychology, 68,* 127–137.

Nolan, M. A. (2002). *Perception of intergroup injustice, collective rights and international human rights law.* Unpublished Ph.D. thesis, School of Psychology, The Australian National University, Canberra.

Nolan, M. A., & Oakes, P. J. (2000, November). *The selection of justice norms in the human rights context: Social beliefs, justice norms and activist identity.* Paper presented at the Spring Workshop in Social

Psychology on Justice and Fairness, School of Psychological Science, La Trobe University, Melbourne, Australia.

Nunamaker, J. F. Jr., Applegate, L. M., & Konsynski, B. R. (1987). Facilitating group creativity: Experience with a group-decision support system. *Journal of Management Information Systems, 3*, 5–19.

Nunamaker, J. F., Jr., Briggs, R. O., Mittleman, D. D., Vogel, D. R. & Balthazard, P. A. (1997). Lessons from a dozen years of group support systems research: A discussion of lab and field findings. *Journal of Management Information Systems, 13*, 163–207.

Nunamaker, J. F., Jr., Dennis, A. R., Valacich, J. S., Vogel, D. R. & George, J. F. (1993). Group support systems research: experience from lab and field, in L. M. Jessup & J. S. Valacich (Eds.), *Group support systems: New perspectives* (pp. 123–145). New York: Macmillan.

Nykodym, N. (1988). Organizational communication theory: Interpersonal and non-interpersonal perspectives. *Communications, 14*, 7–18.

O'Connor, K. M., Gruenfeld, D. H., & McGrath, J. E. (1993). The experience and effects of conflict in continuing workgroups. *Small Group Research, 24*, 362–382.

O'Leary-Kelly, A. M., Martocchio, J. J., & Frink, D. D. (1994). A review of the influence of group goals on group performance. *Academy of Management Journal, 37*, 1285–1301.

Oakes, P. J. (1987). The salience of social categories. In J. C. Turner, M. A. Hogg, P. J. Oakes, S. D. Reicher, & M. S. Wetherell (Eds.), *Rediscovering the social group: A self-categorization theory* (pp. 117–141). Oxford, UK: Blackwell.

Oakes, P. J., & Haslam, S. A. (2001). Distortion v. meaning: Categorization on trial for inciting intergroup hatred. In M. Augoustinos & K. J. Reynolds (Eds.), *Understanding prejudice, racism, and social conflict* (pp. 179–194). London: Sage.

Oakes, P. J., Haslam, S. A., Morrison, B., & Grace, D. (1995). Becoming an ingroup: Reexamining the impact of familiarity on perceptions of group homogeneity. *Social Psychology Quarterly, 58*, 52–61.

Oakes, P. J., Haslam, S. A., & Turner, J. C. (1994). *Stereotyping and social reality*. Oxford, UK: Blackwell.

Oakes, P. J., Haslam, S. A., & Turner, J. C. (1998). The role of prototypicality in group influence and cohesion: Contextual variation in the graded structure of social categories. In S. Worchel, J. F. Morales, D. Paez, & J.-C. Deschamps (Eds.), *Social identity: International perspectives* (pp. 75–92). London: Sage.

Oakes, P. J., Turner, J. C., & Haslam, S. A. (1991). Perceiving people as group members: The role of fit in the salience of social categorizations. *British Journal of Social Psychology, 30*, 125–144.

Oliver, R. L., & Swan, J. E. (1989). Consumer perceptions of interpersonal equity and satisfaction in transactions: A field study approach. *Journal of Marketing, 53*, 21–35.

Opotow, S. (1990). Moral exclusion and injustice: An introduction. *Journal of Social Issues, 46*, 1–20.

Opotow, S. (1995). Drawing the line: Social categorization and moral exclusion. In J. Z. Rubin & B. B. Bunker (Eds.), *Conflict, cooperation, and justice* (pp. 347–369). San Francisco: Jossey-Bass.

Opotow, S. (1996). Is justice finite? The case of environmental inclusion. In L. Montada & M. J. Lerner (Eds.), *Current societal concerns about justice* (pp. 213–218). New York: Plenum.

Organ, D. W. (1988). *Organizational citizenship behavior: The good soldier syndrome*. Lexington, MA: Lexington Books.

Organ, D. W. (1997). Organizational citizenship behavior: Its construct clean-up time. *Human Performance, 10*, 85–97.

Organ, D. W., & Moorman, R. H. (1993). Fairness and organizational citizenship behavior: What are the connections? *Social Justice Research, 6*, 5–18.

Organ, D. W., & Ryan, K. (1995). A meta-analytic review of attitudinal and dispositional predictors of organizational citizenship behavior. *Personnel Psychology, 48*, 775–802.

Ouwerkerk, J. W., de Gilder, D., & de Vries, N. K. (2000). When the going gets tough the tough get going: Social identification and individual effort in intergroup competition. *Personality and Social Psychology Bulletin, 26*, 1550–1559.

Ouwerkerk, J. W., Ellemers, N., & de Gilder, D. (1999). Social identification, affective commitment and individual effort on behalf of the group. In N. Ellemers, R. Spears, & B. J. Doosje (Eds.), *Social identity: Context, commitment, content* (pp. 184–204). Oxford, UK: Blackwell.

Ouwerkerk, J., Ellemers, N., Smith, H., & Van Knippenberg, A. (in press). Giving groups a past and a future: Affective and motivational consequences of intergroup comparisons in a dynamic situation. *British Journal of Social Psychology*.

Parker, M. (1993). Industrial relations myth and shop floor reality: The team concept in the auto industry. In N. Lichtenstein & J. H. Howell (Eds.), *Industrial democracy in America* (pp. 249–272). Cambridge: Cambridge University Press.

Parker, M., & Slaughter, J. (1988). *Choosing sides: Unions and the team concept.* Boston: South End Press.

Pasmore, W., & Fagans, M. (1992). Participation, individual development, and organizational change: A review and synthesis. *Journal of Management, 18,* 375–397.

Paulus, P. B., & Dzindolet, M. T. (1993). Social influence processes in group brainstorming. *Journal of Personality and Social Psychology, 64,* 575–586.

Paulus, P. B., Larey, T. S., Putman, V. L., Leggett, K. L., & Roland, E. J. (1996). Social influence processes in computer brainstorming. *Basic and Applied Social Psychology, 18,* 3–14.

Pawar, B. S., & Eastman, K. (1997). The nature and implications of contextual influences on transformational leadership. *Academy of Management Review, 22,* 80–109.

Pearce, J. L. (1987). Why merit pay doesn't work: Implications from organizational theory. In D. B. Balkin & L. R. Gomez-Meija (Eds.), *New perspectives on compensation* (pp. 169–178). Englewood Cliffs, NJ: Prentice-Hall.

Pelak, C.F., Taylor, V., & Whittier, N. (1999). Gender movements. In J. S. Chafetz (Ed.), *Handbook of the sociology of gender* (pp. 147–175). New York: Plenum.

Pelled, L. H. (1996). Relational demography and perceptions of group conflict and performance: A field investigation. *International Journal of Conflict Management, 7,* 230–246.

Pelled, L. H., Eisenhardt, K. M., & Xin, K. R. (1999). Exploring the black box: An analysis of work group diversity, conflict, and performance. *Administrative Science Quarterly, 44,* 1–28.

Perelman, C. (1963). *The idea of justice and the problem of argument.* London: Routledge & Kegan Paul.

Perry, T. S. (1992). E-mail at work. Special report/electronic mail. *IEEE Spectrum* (October, 24–28).

Peters, T., & Waterman, R. H. (1982). *In search of excellence.* New York: Harper & Row.

Peterson, V. S., & Runyan, A. S. (1993). *Global gender issues.* Boulder, CO: Westview Press.

Pettigrew, A. M., Woodman, R. W., & Cameron, K. S. (2001). Studying organizational change and development: Challenges for future research. *Academy of Management Journal, 44,* 697–713.

Pettigrew, A. M., Woodman, R. W., & Cameron, K. S. (Eds.). (2001). Organizational change. *Academy of Management Journal.* Special issue, 44.

Petty, R. E., & Cacioppo, J. T. (1986). The elaboration likelihood model of persuasion. In L. Berkowitz (Ed.), *Advances in experimental social psychology* (Vol. 19, pp. 123–205). New York: Academic Press.

Pfeffer, J. (1981). *Power in organizations.* Boston, MA: Pitman.

Pfeffer, J. (1992). *Understanding power in organizations.* Marchfield, MA: Pitman.

Phinney, J. S. (1990). Ethnic identity in adolescents and adults: Review of research. *Psychological Bulletin, 108,* 499–514.

Pickering, J. M., & King, J. L. (1995). Hardwiring weak ties: Interorganizational computer-mediated communication, occupational communities and organizational change. *Organization Science, 6,* 479–486.

Pilegge, A. J., & Holtz, R. (1997). The effects of social identity on the self-set goals and task performance of high and low self-esteem individuals. *Organizational Behavior and Human Decision Processes, 70,* 17–26.

Pinsonneault, A., & Heppel, N. (1998). Anonymity in group support systems research:

A new conceptualization, measure, and contingency framework. *Journal of Management Information Systems, 14*, 89–108.

Platow, M. J. (1997, April). *On the psychological meaning of distributive behavior*. Paper presented at the 5th Brisbane Symposium on Social Identity Theory, The University of Queensland, Brisbane, Queensland, Australia.

Platow, M. J. (1999). *Distributive and procedural justice: Acceptability as solutions to social dilemmas*. Paper presented at the La Trobe University School of Psychological Science Spring Workshop in Social Psychology, Solutions to Real World Dilemmas, Melbourne, Australia.

Platow, M. J., & Brodie, M. (1999). The effects of linguistic voice on evaluations and attributions of ingroup and outgroup members. *Asian Journal of Social Psychology, 2*, 187–200.

Platow, M. J., Durante, M., Williams, N., Garrett, M., Walshe, J., Cincotta, S., Lianos, G., & Barutchu, A. (1999). The contribution of sport fan identity to the production of prosocial behavior. *Group Dynamics, 3*, 161–169.

Platow, M. J., Haslam, S. A., Both, A., Chew, I., Cuddon, M.., Goharpey, N., Maurer, J., Rosini, S., Tsekouras, A., & Grace, D. M. (2002). *"It's not funny when they're laughing": A self-categorization social-influence analysis of canned laughter*. Unpublished manuscript, La Trobe University, Australia.

Platow, M. J., Hoar, S., Reid, S. A., Harley, K., & Morrison, D. (1997). Endorsement of distributively fair and unfair leaders in interpersonal and intergroup situations. *European Journal of Social Psychology, 27*, 465–494.

Platow, M. J., & Hunter, J. A. (2001). Realistic intergroup conflict: Prejudice, power, and protest. In M. Augoustinos & K. J. Reynolds (Eds.), *Understanding prejudice, racism, and social conflict* (pp. 195–212). London: Sage.

Platow, M. J., Kuc, B., & Wilson, N. A. (1998, August). *Distributive behavior as a self-categorization cue*. Paper presented at the 1998 Annual Convention of the American Psychological Association, San Francisco, CA.

Platow, M. J., Mills, D., & Morrison, D.

(2000). The effects of social context, source fairness, and perceived self-source similarity on social influence: A self-categorization analysis. *European Journal of Social Psychology, 30*, 69–81.

Platow, M. J., O'Connell, A., Shave, R., & Hanning, P. (1995). Social evaluations of fair and unfair allocators in interpersonal and intergroup situations. *British Journal of Social Psychology, 34*, 363–381.

Platow, M. J., Reid, S. A., & Andrew, S. (1998). Leadership endorsement: The role of distributive and procedural behavior in interpersonal and intergroup contexts. *Group Processes and Intergroup Relations, 1*, 35–47.

Platow, M. J., & van Knippenberg, D. (2001). A social identity analysis of leadership endorsement: The effects of leader ingroup prototypicality and distributive intergroup fairness. *Personality and Social Psychology Bulletin, 27*, 1508–1519.

Podsakoff, P. M., Ahearne, M., & MacKenzie, S. B. (1997). Organizational citizenship behavior and the quantity and quality of work group performance. *Journal of Applied Psychology, 82*, 262–270.

Podsakoff, P. M., MacKenzie, S. B., & Ahearne, M. (1997). Moderating effects of goal acceptance on the relationship between group cohesiveness and productivity. *Journal of Applied Psychology, 82*, 974–983.

Podsakoff, P. M., MacKenzie, S. B., Paine, J. B., & Bachrach, D. G. (2000). Organizational citizenship behaviors: A critical review of the theoretical and empirical literature and suggestions for future research. *Journal of Management, 26*, 513–563.

Pollack, A. (1985, October 11). Intel posts loss; ends RAM line. *New York Times*, p. D1.

Postmes, T., Branscombe, N. R., Spears, R., & Young, H. (1999). Comparative processes in personal and group judgments: Resolving the discrepancy. *Journal of Personality and Social Psychology, 76*, 320–338.

Postmes, T., & Lea, M. (2000). Social processes and group decision making: Anonymity in group decision support systems. *Ergonomics, 43*, 1152–1174.

Postmes, T. & Spears, R. (1998). Deindividuation and antinormative behavior: A meta-analysis. *Psychological Bulletin, 123*, 238–259.

Postmes, T., & Spears, R. (1999). *When boys will be boys, and it's all girl's talk: Status differences in computer-mediated group discussions*. Manuscript submitted for publication.

Postmes, T., & Spears, R. (2001). Quality of decision making and group norms. *Journal of Personality and Social Psychology, 80*, 918–930.

Postmes, T., Spears, R., & Lea, M. (1998). Breaching or building social boundaries? SIDE-effects of computer mediated communication. *Communication Research, 25*, 689–715.

Postmes, T., Spears, R., & Lea, M. (2000). The formation of group norms in computer-mediated communication. *Human Communication Research, 26*, 341–371.

Postmes, T., Spears, R., Sakhel, K., & De Groot, D. (2001). Social influence in computer-mediated groups: The effects of anonymity on social behavior. *Personality and Social psychology Bulletin, 27*, 1243–1254.

Postmes, T., Tanis, M., & DeWit, B. (2001). Communication and commitment in organizations: A social identity approach. *Group Processes and Intergroup Relations, 4*, 227–246.

Pratkanis, A. R., & Turner, M. E. (1994). Nine principles of successful affirmative action: II. Branch Rickey, Jackie Robinson, and the integration of baseball. *Nine: The Journal of Baseball History and Social Policy Perspectives 3*, 36–65.

Pratkanis, A. R., & Turner, M. E. (1999). Groupthink and preparedness for the Loma Prieta earthquake: A social identity maintenance analysis of causes and preventions. In E. A. Mannix & M. A. Neale (Series Eds.) & R. Wageman (Vol. Ed.), *Research on managing groups and teams: Vol.2. Groups in Context* (pp. 115–136). Stamford, CT: JAI Press.

Pratt, M. G. (1998). To be or not to be? Central questions in organizational identification. In D. A. Whetten & P. C. Godfrey (Eds.), *Identity in organizations: Building theory through conversations* (pp. 171–207). Thousand Oakes, CA: Sage.

Pratt, M. G. (2000, July). *Learning to work and learning to identify: Lessons from a lon-gitudinal study of medical residents*. Paper presented at the EAESP Small Group Meeting on Social Identity Processes in Organizations, Amsterdam.

Pratto, F., Sidanius, J., Stallworth, L. M., & Malle, B. F. (1994). Social dominance orientation: A personality variable predicting social and political attitudes. *Journal of Personality and Social Psychology, 67*, 741–763.

Preston, P. (1999, July 19). It's time the airlines told us the truth: Flying is an endurance test. *The Guardian, 92*, 3.

Pruijt, H. (2000). Repainting, modifying, smashing Taylorism. *Journal of Organizational Change Management, 13*, 439–451.

Pruitt, D. G., Peirce, R. S., Zubek, J. M., McGillicuddy, N. B., & Welton, G. L. (1993). Determinants of short-term and long-term success in mediation. In S. Worchel & J. A. Simpson (Eds.), *Conflict between people and groups: Causes, processes, and resolutions. Nelson Hall series in psychology* (pp. 60–75). Chicago: Nelson-Hall.

Rabbie, J. M., Schot, J. C., & Visser, L. (1989). Social identity theory: A conceptual and empirical critique from the perspective of a behavioral interaction model. *European Journal of Social Psychology, 19*, 171–202.

Raven, B. H. (1974). The Nixon group. *Journal of Social Issues, 30*, 297–320.

Redding, W. C. (1973). *Communications within the organziation*. New York: Industrial Communication Council.

Reicher, S. D. (1982). The determination of collective action. In H. Tajfel (Ed.), *Social identity and intergroup relations* (pp. 41–84). Cambridge: Cambridge University Press.

Reicher, S. D. (1984). Social influence in the crowd: Attitudinal and behavioural effects of deindividuation in conditions of high and low group salience. *British Journal of Social Psychology, 23*, 341–350.

Reicher, S. D. (1987). Crowd behaviour as social action. In J. C. Turner, M. A. Hogg, P. J. Oakes, S. D. Reicher, & M. S. Wetherell, *Rediscovering the social group: A self-categorization theory* (pp. 171–202). Oxford, UK: Blackwell.

Reicher, S. D., Drury, J., Hopkins, N., & Stott, C. (2001). A model of crowd prototypes and crowd leaders. In C. Barker (Ed.), *Leadership and social movements* (pp. 178–195). Manchester, UK: Manchester University Press.

Reicher, S. D., & Hopkins, N. (1996). Seeking influence through characterising self-categories: An analysis of anti-abortionist rhetoric. *British Journal of Social Psychology, 35,* 297–311.

Reicher, S. D., Hopkins, N., & Condor, S. (1997). Stereotype construction as social influence. In R. Spears, P. J. Oakes, N. Ellemers, & S. A. Haslam (Eds.), *The social psychology of stereotyping and group life* (pp. 94–118). Oxford, UK: Blackwell.

Reicher, S. D., & Levine, M. (1994). Deindividuation, power relations between groups and the expression of social identity: The effects of visibility to the outgroup. *British Journal of Social Psychology, 33,* 145–163.

Reicher, S. D., Levine, M., & Gordijn, E. (1998). More on deindividuation, power relations between people and the expression of social identity: Three studies on the effects of visibility to the in-group. *British Journal of Social Psychology, 37,* 15–40.

Reicher, S. D., Spears, R., & Postmes, T. (1995). A social identity model of deindividuation phenomena. *European Review of Social Psychology, 6,* 161–198.

Reichers, A. E. (1985). A review and reconceptualization of organizational commitment. *Academy of Management Review, 10,* 465–476.

Reichheld, A. E. (1996). *The loyalty effect.* Cambridge, MA: Harvard Business School Press.

Reid, S. A., & Ng, S. H. (2000). Conversation as a resource for influence: Evidence for prototypical arguments and social identification processes. *European Journal of Social Psychology, 30,* 83–100.

Reis, H. T., & Gruzen, J. (1976). On mediating equity, equality, and self-interest: The role of self-presentation in social exchange. *Journal of Experimental Social Psychology, 12,* 487–503.

Reskin, B., & Padavic, I. (1994). *Women and men at work.* Thousand Oaks, CA: Pine Forge.

Reskin, B., & Roos, P. (1990). *Job queues, gender queues: Explaining women's inroads into male occupations.* Philadelphia, PA: Temple University Press.

Reynolds, K. J., Eggins, R. A., & Haslam, S. A (2001). *Uncovering diverse identities in organizations: AIRing versus auditing.* Unpublished manuscript, The Australian National University.

Reynolds, K. J., Oakes, P. J., Haslam, S. A., Nolan, M., & Dolnik, L. (2000). Responses to powerlessness: Stereotypes as an instrument of social conflict. *Group Dynamics: Theory, Research and Practice, 4,* 275–290.

Reynolds, K. J., Oakes, P. J, Haslam, S. A., Turner, J. C., & Ryan, M. K. (in press). Social identity as the basis of group entiativity: Elaborating the case for the "science of social groups per se." In V. Yzerbyt, C. M. Judd, & O. Corneille (Eds.), *The psychology of group perception: Contributions to the study of homogeneity, entitativity, and essentialism.* Philadelphia: Psychology Press.

Reynolds, K. J., Ryan, M., & Turner, J. C. (2002). *The effects of group membership and resource power on individual productivity.* Unpublished manuscript: The Australian National University.

Reynolds, K. J., Turner, J. C., & Haslam, S. A. (2000). When are we better than them and they worse than us? A closer look at social discrimination in positive and negative domains. *Journal of Personality and Social Psychology, 78,* 64–80.

Reynolds, K. J., & Uzubalis, M. (2000, April 27–30). *Being a good organisational citizen: Is identity the answer?* Paper presented at the 6th meeting of the Australasian Association of Social Psychologists, Perth, Australia.

Rice, R. E. (1984). *The new media: Communication, research and technology.* Beverly Hills, CA: Sage.

Rice, R. E. (1987). Computer-mediated communication and organizational innovation. *Journal of Communication, 37,* 65–94.

Rice, R. E. (1992). Task analyzability, use of new media, and effectiveness: A multi-site exploration of media richness. *Organization Science, 3,* 475–500.

Rice, R. E. (1993). Media appropriateness: Using social presence theory to compare traditional and new organizational media. *Human Communication Research, 19,* 451–484.

Rice, R. E., & Love, G. (1987). Electronic emotion: Socio-emotional content in a computer-mediated communication network. *Communication Research, 14*, 85–108.

Riordan, C., & Shore, L. (1997). Demographic diversity and employee attitudes: Examination of relational demography within work units. *Journal of Applied Psychology, 82*, 342–358.

Robbins, S. P. (1998). *Organizational behavior*. Upper Saddle River, NJ: Simon & Schuster.

Roccas, S., Horenczyk, G., & Schwartz, S. H. (2000). Acculturation discrepancies and well-being: The moderating role of conformity. *European Journal of Social Psychology, 30*, 323–334.

Roccas, S., & Schwartz, S. H. (1993). Effects of intergroup similarity on intergroup relations. *European Journal of Social Psychology, 23*, 581–595.

Rocker, R. (1938/1981). *The methods of anarcho-syndicalism*. Sydney, Australia: Monty Miller Press.

Roethlisberger, F. J., & Dickson, W. J. (1939). *Management and the worker*. Cambridge, MA: Harvard University Press.

Rosenberg, M. (1965). *Society and the adolescent self-image*. Princeton, NJ: Princeton University Press.

Ross, L. (1977). The intuitive psychologist and his shortcomings. In L. Berkowitz (Ed.), *Advances in experimental social psychology* (Vol.10, pp. 174–220). New York: Academic Press.

Rothbart, M. (1993). Intergroup perception and social conflict. In S. Worchel & J. A. Simpson. (Eds.), *Conflict between people and groups: Causes, processes, and resolutions. Nelson Hall series in psychology* (pp. 93–109). Chicago: Nelson-Hall.

Rothbart, M., & John, O. P. (1993). Intergroup relations and stereotype change: A social–cognitive analysis and some longitudinal findings. In P. M. Sniderman & P. E. Tetlock. (Eds.), *Prejudice, politics, and the American dilemma* (pp. 32–59). Stanford, CA: Stanford University Press.

Rousseau, D. M. (1998). Why workers still identify with organizations. *Journal of Organizational Behavior, 19*, 217–233.

Rousseau, J. J. (1967). The social contract. In L. G. Crocker (Ed.), *Jean-Jacques Rousseau: The social contract and discourse on the origin of inequality* (H. J. Tozer, Trans.). New York: Washington Square Press. (Original work published 1762)

Rubin, M., & Hewstone, M. (1998). Social identity theory's self-esteem hypothesis: A review and some suggestions for clarification. *Personality and Social Psychology Review, 2*, 40–62.

Ruggiero, K. M., & Taylor, D. M. (1995). Coping with discrimination: How minority group members perceive the discrimination that confronts them. *Journal of Personality and Social Psychology, 68*, 826–838.

Ruggiero, K. M., & Taylor, D. M. (1997). Why minority group members perceive or do not perceive the discrimination that confronts them: The role of self-esteem and perceived control. *Journal of Personality and Social Psychology, 72*, 373–389.

Ruggiero, K. M., Taylor, D. M., & Lydon, J. E. (1997). How disadvantaged group members cope with discrimination when they perceive that social support is available. *Journal of Applied Social Psychology, 27*, 1581–1600.

Rusbult, C. E., Farrell, D., Rogers, G., & Mainous, A. G. (1988). Impact of exchange variables on exit, voice, loyalty, and neglect: An integrative model of responses to declining job satisfaction. *Academy of Management Journal, 31*, 599–627.

Sachdev, I., & Bourhis, R. Y. (1987). Status differentials and intergroup behaviour. *European Journal of Social Psychology, 17*, 277–293.

Sachdev, I., & Bourhis, R. Y. (1991). Power and status differentials in minority and majority group relations. *European Journal of Social Psychology, 21*, 1–24.

Salerno, L. (1980, May/June). Creativity by the numbers. *Harvard Business Review, 58*, 122–132.

Sanna, L. J., & Parks, C. D. (1997). Group research trends in social and organizational psychology: Whatever happened to intragroup research? *Psychological Science, 8*, 261–267.

Sashkin, M., & Burke, W. (1987). Organization development in te nineteen-eighties. *Journal of Management, 13*, 393–417.

Scandura, T. A. (1999). Rethinking leader–member exchange: An organizational justice perspective. *Leadership Quarterly, 10,* 25–40.

Scandura, T. A., & Graen, G. B. (1984). Moderating effects of initial leaders-member exchange status on the effects of a leadership intervention. *Journal of Applied Psychology, 69,* 428–436.

Schafer, R. B. (1988). Equity/inequity, and self-esteem: A reassessment. *Psychological Reports, 63,* 637–638.

Schmitt, C. H. (1986, May 26). At work with the valley's toughest boss: Andy Grove keeps a forceful grip at chip giant Intel. *San Jose Mercury News,* p. 1F.

Schmitt, M. T. & Branscombe, N. R. (2002). The good, the bad, and the manly: Threats to one's prototypicality and evaluations of fellow in-group members. *Journal of Experimental Social Psychology, 37,* 510–517.

Schmitt, M. T., & Branscombe, N. R. (2001). The meaning and consequences of perceived discrimination in disadvantaged and privileged social groups. *European Review of Social Psychology 12,* 166–199.

Schmitt, M. T., & Branscombe, N. R. (2002). The internal and external causal loci of attributions to prejudice. *Personality and Social Psychology Bulletin, 28,* 484–492.

Schmitt, M. T., Branscombe, N. R., & Kobrynowicz, D., & Owen, S. (2002). Perceiving discrimination against one's gendergroup has different implications for well-being in women and men. *Personality and Social Psychology Bulletin, 28,* 197–210.

Schmitt, M. T., Branscombe, N. R., & Postmes, T. (2001). Women's emotional responses to the perception of pervasive gender discrimination. *European Journal of Social Psychology.*

Schneider, B., & Bowen, D. E. (1999). Understanding customer delight and outrage. *Sloan Management Review, Fall,* 35–45.

Schneider, B., White, S. S., & Paul, M. C. (1998). Linking service climate and customer perceptions of service quality: Test of a causal model. *Journal of Applied Psychology, 83,* 150–163.

Schoennauer, A. W. (1967). Behavior patterns of executives in business acquisitions. *Personal Administration, 30,* 27–31.

Schor, J. B. (1991). *The overworked American: The unexpected decline of leisure.* New York: Basic Books.

Schriesheim, C. A., Castro, S. L., & Cogliser, C. C. (1999). Leader–member exchange (LMX) research: A comprehensive review of theory, measurement, and data-analytic practices. *Leadership Quarterly, 10,* 63–113.

Schriesheim, C. A., Castro, S. L., & Yammarino, F. J. (2000). Investigating contingencies: An examination of the impact of span of supervision and upward controllingness on leader-member exchange using traditional and multivariate within- and between-entities analysis. *Journal of Applied Psychology, 85,* 659–677.

Schweiger, D. L., & Ivancevich, J. M. (1985). Human resources: The forgotten factor in mergers and acquisitions. *Personnel Administrator, 30,* 47–61.

Schwinger, T. (1980). Just allocations of goods: Decisions among three principles. In G. Mikula (Ed.), *Justice and social interaction* (pp. 95–125). New York: Springer.

Schwinger, T., & Lamm, H. (1981). Justice norms in allocation decisions: Need consideration as a function of resource adequacy for complete needs satisfaction, recipients' contributions, self-presentation in social exchange. *Journal of Experimental Social Psychology, 12,* 487–503.

Sears, D. O., Citrin, J., Cheleden, S. V., & van Laar, C. (1999). Cultural diversity and multicultural politics: Is ethnic balkanization psychologically inevitable? In D. A. Prentice & D. T. Miller (Eds.), *Cultural divides: Understanding and overcoming group conflict* (pp. 35–79). New York: Russell Sage Foundation.

Sedikides, C., & Brewer, M. B. (Eds.) (2001). *Individual self, relational self, collective self* (pp. 123–143). Philadelphia, PA: Psychology Press.

Sewell, G (1998). The discipline of teams: The control of team-based industrial work through electronic and peer surveillance. *Administrative Science Quarterly, 43,* 397–428.

Shamir, B., House, R. J., & Arthur, M. B. (1993). The motivational effects of charismatic leadership: A self-concept based concept. *Organizational Science, 4,* 577–594.

Shaw, M. E. (1981). *Group dynamics: The psychology of small group behavior* (2nd ed.). New York: McGraw-Hill.

Shepard, C. A., Giles, H., & LePoire, B. A. (2001). Communication accomodation theory. In H. Giles & P. Robinson (Eds.), *New Handbook of Language and Social Psychology* (2nd ed., pp. 33–56). Chichester, UK: Wiley.

Sheridan, J. (1997, December 15). Andy Grove: Building an information age legacy. *Industry Week, 23,* 64–76.

Sherif, M. (1936). *The psychology of social norms.* New York: Harper.

Sherif, M. (1966). *In common predicament: Social psychology of intergroup conflict and cooperation.* Boston, MA: Houghton-Mifflin.

Sherif, M., & Sherif, C. (1953). *Groups in harmony and tension: An integration of studies in intergroup relations.* New York: Harper.

Sherman, S. (1993, February 22). Andy Grove: How Intel makes spending pay off. *Fortune, 127,* 56–61.

Sherman, S. J., Hamilton, D. L., & Lewis, A. C. (1999). Perceived entitativity and the social identity value of group memberships. In D. Abrams & M. A. Hogg (Eds.), *Social identity and social cognition* (pp. 80–110). Malden, MA: Blackwell.

Short, J., Williams, E., & Christie, B. (1976). *The social psychology of telecommunications.* Chichester, UK: Wiley.

Shrivastava, P. (1986). Postmerger integration. *Journal of Business Staregy, 7,* 65–76.

Sidanius, J. & Pratto, F. (1999). *Social dominance: An intergroup theory of social hierarchy and oppression.* New York: Cambridge University Press.

Siegel, J., Dubrovsky, V., Kiesler, S., & McGuire, T. (1986). Group processes in computer-mediated communication. *Organizational Behaviour and Human Decision Processes, 37,* 157–187.

Simon, B., Hastedt, C., & Aufderheide, B. (1997). When self-categorization makes sense: The role of meaningful social categorization in minority and majority members' self-perception. *Journal of Personality and Social Psychology, 73,* 310–320.

Simon, B., & Klandermans, B. (2001). Politicized collective identity: A social psychological analysis. *American Psychologist, 56,* 319–331.

Simon, B., Loewy, M., Stürmer, S., Weber, U.,

Freytag, P., Habig, C., Kaupmeier, C., & Spahlinger, D. (1998). Collective identification and social movement participation. *Journal of Personality and Social Psychology, 74,* 646–658.

Simon, B., & Sturmer, S. (2001). *Respect for group members: Intragroup determinants of collective identification and group-serving behavior.* Unpublished manuscript: University of Kiel.

Singh, J. (1988). Consumer complaint intentions and behavior: Definitional and taxonomical issues. *Journal of Marketing, 52,* 93–107.

Smith, E. R., & Henry, S. (1996). An in-group becomes part of the self: Response time evidence. *Personality and Social Psychology Bulletin, 22,* 635–642.

Smith, H. J., & Tyler, T. R. (1996). Justice and power: When will justice concerns encourage the advantaged to support policies which redistribute economic resources and the disadvantaged to willingly obey the law? *European Journal of Social Psychology, 26,* 171–200.

Smith, H. J., & Tyler, T. R. (1997). Choosing the right pond: The influence of the status of one's group and one's status in that group on self-esteem and group-oriented behaviours. *Journal of Experimental Social Psychology, 33,* 146–170.

Smith, H. J., Tyler, T. R. & Daubenmeir, J. (2002). *Co-op members and construction workers: When does procedural fairness shape self-evaluations?* Unpublished manuscript, Sonoma State University.

Smith, H. J., Tyler, T. R., Huo, Y. J., Ortiz, D. J., & Lind, E. A. (1998). The self-relevant implications of the group-value model: Group membership, self-worth and procedural justice. *Journal of Experimental Social Psychology, 34,* 480–493.

Smith, V. (1997). New forms of work organization. *Annual Review of Sociology, 23,* 315–339.

Sparrowe, R. T., & Liden, R. C. (1997). Process and structure in leader–member exchange. *Academy of Management Review, 22,* 522–552.

Spears, R., Doosje, B., & Ellemers, N. (1997). Self-stereotyping in the face of threats to group status and distinctiveness: The role of group identification. *Personality and*

Social Psychology Bulletin, 23, 538–553.

Spears, R., & Haslam, S. A. (1997). Stereotyping and the burden of cognitive load. In R. Spears, P. J. Oakes, N. Ellemers, & S. A. Haslam (Eds.), *The social psychology of stereotyping and group life* (pp. 171–207). Oxford, UK: Blackwell.

Spears, R., & Lea, M. (1992). Social influence and the influence of the "social" in computer-mediated communication. In M. Lea (Ed.) *Contexts of computer-mediated communication* (pp. 30–65). Hemel Hempstead, UK: Harvester-Wheatsheaf.

Spears, R., & Lea, M. (1994). Panacea or panopticon? The hidden power in computer-mediated communication. *Communication Research, 21,* 427–459.

Spears, R., Lea, M., & Lee, S. (1990). De-individuation and group polarization in computer-mediated communication. *British Journal of Social Psychology, 29,* 121–134.

Spears, R., Lea, M., & Postmes, T. (2000). On Side: Purview, problems and prospects. In T. Postmes, R. Spears, M. Lea, & S. D Reicher (Eds.), *SIDE issues centre stage: Recent developments in studies of de-individuation in groups* (pp. 1–16). Amsterdam: KNAW.

Spears, R., Lea, M., & Postmes, T. (2001). Social psychological theories of computer-mediated communication: Social pain or social gain? In W. P. Robinson & H. Giles (Eds.), *The new handbook of language and social psychology* (pp. 601–623). Chichester, UK: Wiley.

Spears, R., & Manstead, A. S. R. (1989). The social context of stereotyping and differentiation. *European Journal of Social Psychology, 19,* 101–121.

Spears, R., Oakes, P. J., Ellemers, N., & Haslam, S. A. (Eds.). (1997). *The social psychology of stereotyping and group life.* Oxford, UK: Blackwell.

Spears, R., Postmes, T., Lea, M., & Wolbert, A. (2002). The power of influence and the influence of power in virtual groups: A SIDE look at CMC and the Internet. *Journal of Social Issues, 58,* 91–107.

Sproull, L., & Kiesler, S. (1986). Reducing social context cues: Electronic mail in organizational communication. *Management Science, 32,* 1492–1512.

Sproull, L., & Kiesler, S. (1991). *Connections: New ways of working in the networked organization.* Cambridge, MA: MIT Press.

Stangor, C., Swim, J. K., Van Allen, K. L., & Sechrist, G. B. (2002). Reporting discrimination in public and private contexts. *Journal of Personality and Social Psychology, 82,* 69–74.

Starbuck, W. H., Greve, A., & Hedberg, B. L. T. (1978). Responding to crises. *Journal of Business Administration, 9,* 111-137.

Stasser, G., Vaughan, S. I., & Stewart, D. D. (2000). Pooling unshared information: The benefits of knowing how access to information is distributed among group members. *Organizational Behavior and Human Decision Processes, 82,* 102–116.

Steiner, I. D. (1972). *Group process and productivity.* New York: Academic Press.

Steiner, I. D. (1974). Whatever happened to the group in social psychology? *Journal of Experimental Social Psychology, 10,* 94–108.

Steiner, I. D. (1986). Paradigms and groups. *Advances in Experimental Social Psychology, 19,* 251–289.

Steinfield, C. W. (1986). Computer-mediated communication in an organizational setting: explaining task-related and socioemotional uses. *Communication Yearbook, 9,* 777–804.

Stephan, W. G., & Stephan, C. W. (1985). Intergroup anxiety. *Journal of Social Issues, 41,* 157–175.

Stephenson, G. M. (1981). Intergroup bargaining and negotiation. In J. C. Turner & H. Giles (Eds.), *Intergroup behaviour* (pp. 168–198). Oxford, UK: Blackwell.

Stephenson, G. M. (1984). Intergroup and interpersonal dimensions of bargaining and negotiation. In H. Tajfel. (Ed.), *The social dimension* (pp.646-667). Cambridge: Cambridge University Press.

Stewart, T. L., Vassar, P. M., Sanchez, D. T., & David, S. E. (2000). Attitudes toward women's societal roles moderates the effect of gender cues on target individuation. *Journal of Personality and Social Psychology, 79,* 143–157.

Stogdill, R. (1974). *Handbook of leadership.* New York: Free Press.

Stott, C. J., & Drury, J. (2000). Crowds, context and identity: Dynamic categorization processes in the "poll tax riot." *Human Relations, 53,* 247–273.

Street, R. L., Jr. (1984). Speech convergence and speech evaluation in fact-finding interviews. *Human Communication Research, 11*, 139–169.

Stroebe, W., & Diehl, M. (1994). Why groups are less effective than their members: On productivity losses in idea-generating groups. *European Review of Social Psychology, 5*, 271–303.

Stroh, L. K., Brett, J. M., & Reilly, A. H. (1992). All the right stuff: A comparison of female and male managers' career progression. *Journal of Applied Psychology, 77*, 251–260.

Suls, J., & Wheeler, L. (Eds.) (2000). *Handbook of social comparison: Theory and research*. New York: Kluwer/Plenum.

Sumner, M. (1988). The impact of electronic mail on managerial and organizational communications. In P. B. Allen (Ed.), *Proceedings of the IFIP conference on office information systems. Palo Alto, CA. March* (pp. 96–109). New York: ACM.

Susskind, L., & Cruikshank, J. (1987). *Breaking the impasse*. New York: Basic Books.

Sutcliffe, K. M. (2001). Organizational environments and organizational information processing. In L. L. Putnam & F. M. Jablin (Eds.), *New handbook of organizational communication* (2nd ed., pp. 199–230). Newbury Park, CA: Sage.

Swann Jnr., W. B., Milton, L. P., & Polzer, J. T. (2000). Should we create a niche or fall in line? Identity negotiation and small group effectiveness. *Journal of Personality and Social Psychology, 79*, 238–250.

Swim, J. K., Aikin, K. J., Hall, W. S., & Hunter, B. A. (1995). Sexism and racism: Old-fashioned and modern prejudices. *Journal of Personality and Social Psychology, 68*, 199–214.

Swim, J. K., Cohen, L. L., & Hyers, L. L. (1998). Experiencing everyday prejudice and discrimination. In J. K. Swim & C. Stangor (Eds.), *Prejudice: The target's perspective* (pp. 37–60). New York: Academic Press.

Syroit, J. E. M. M. (1991). Interpersonal and intergroup injustice: Some theoretical considerations. In R. Vermunt & H. Steensma (Eds.), *Social justice in human relations: Societal and psychological origins of justice* (pp. 259–277). New York: Plenum.

Tajfel, H. (1970). Experiments in intergroup discrimination. *Scientific American, 223*, 96–102.

Tajfel, H. (1974). Social identity and intergroup behaviour. *Social Science Information, 14*, 101–118.

Tajfel, H. (1975). The exit of social mobility and the voice of social change. *Social Science Information, 14*, 101–118.

Tajfel, H. (Ed.) (1978a). *Differentiation between social groups: Studies in the social psychology of intergroup relations*. London: Academic Press.

Tajfel, H. (1978b). *The social psychology of the minority*. London: Minority Rights Group.

Tajfel, H. (1978c). Interindividual behaviour and intergroup behaviour. In H. Tajfel (Ed.), *Differentiation between groups: Studies in the social psychology of intergroup relations* (pp. 27–60). London: Academic Press.

Tajfel, H. (1979). Individuals and groups in social psychology. *British Journal of Social and Clinical Psychology, 18*, 183–190.

Tajfel, H. (1981a). *Human groups and social categories*. Cambridge: Cambridge University Press.

Tajfel, H. (1981b). Social stereotypes and social groups. In J. C. Turner & H. Giles (Eds.), *Intergroup behaviour* (pp. 144–167). Oxford, UK: Blackwell.

Tajfel, H. (1982). Psychological conceptions of equity: The present and the future. In P. Fraisse (Ed.), *Psychologie de demain* (pp. 149–166). Paris: Presses Universitaires de France.

Tajfel, H. (1984). Intergroup relations, social myths and social justice in social psychology. In H. Tajfel (Ed.), *The social dimension: European developments in social psychology* (Vol. 2, pp. 695–715). Cambridge: Cambridge University Press.

Tajfel, H., Billig, M. G., Bundy, R. F., & Flament, C. (1971). Social categorization and intergroup behaviour. *European Journal of Social Psychology, 1*, 149–177.

Tajfel, H., Flament, C., Billig, M. G., & Bundy, R. F. (1971). Social categorization and intergroup behavior. *European Journal of Social Psychology, 1*, 149–177.

Tajfel, H., & Turner, J. C. (1979). An integrative theory of intergroup conflict. In W. G. Austin & S. Worschel (Eds.), *The social psy-*

chology of intergroup relations (pp. 33–47). Monterey, CA: Brooks/Cole.

Tajfel, H., & Turner, J. C. (1986). The social identity theory of intergroup behaviour. In S. Worchel & W. G. Austin (Eds.), *Psychology of intergroup relations* (2nd ed., pp. 7–24). Chicago: Nelson-Hall.

Taylor, D. M., & McKirnan, D. J. (1984). A five-stage model of intergroup relations. *British Journal of Social Psychology, 23,* 291–300.

Taylor, D. M., & Moghaddam, F. M. (1987). *Theories of intergroup relations: International social psychological perspectives.* New York: Praeger.

Taylor, D. M., & Moghaddam, F. M. (1994). *Theories of intergroup relations: International social psychological perspectives* (2nd ed.). New York: Praeger.

Taylor, D. M., Moghaddam, F. M., Gamble, I., & Zellerer, E. (1987). Disadvantaged group responses to perceived inequality: From passive acceptance to collective action. *Journal of Social Psychology, 127,* 259–272.

Taylor, F. W. (1911). *Principles of scientific management.* New York: Harper.

Taylor, S. E., & Fiske, S. T. (1975). Point-of-view and perceptions of causality. *Journal of Personality and Social Psychology, 32,* 439–445.

Taylor, S. E., & Fiske, S. T. (1978). Salience, attention, and attribution: Top of the head phenomena. In L. Berkowitz (Ed.), *Advances in experimental social psychology* (Vol. 11, pp. 249–288). New York: Academic Press.

Terry, D. J. (2001). Intergroup relations and organizational mergers. In M. A. Hogg & D. J. Terry (Eds.), *Social identity processes in organizational contexts* (pp. 229–248). Philadelphia, PA: Psychology Press.

Terry, D. J., & Callan, V. J. (1998). Ingroup bias in response to an organizational merger. *Group Dynamics: Theory, Research and Practice, 2,* 67–81.

Terry, D. J., Carey, C. J., & Callan, V. J. (2001). Employee adjustment to an organizational merger: An intergroup perspective. *Personality and Social Psychology Bulletin, 27,* 267–290.

Terry, D. J., Hogg, M. A., & Blackwood, L. (2001). Attitudes, behavior, and social con-

text: The role of norms and group membership in social influence processes. In J. Forgas & K. Williams (Eds.), *Social influence* (pp. 253–270). Philadelphia: Taylor & Francis.

Terry, D. J., & O'Brien, A. T. (2001). Status, legitimacy, and ingroup bias in the context of an organizational merger. *Group Processes and Intergroup Relations, 4,* 271–289.

Tetlock, P. E. (1979) Identifying victims of groupthink from public statements of decision makers. *Journal of Personality and Social Psychology, 37,* 1314–1324.

Tetlock, P. E., Peterson, R. S., McGuire, C., Chang, S., & Feld, P. (1992). Assessing political group dynamics: A test of the groupthink model. *Journal of Personality and Social Psychology, 63,* 403–425.

't Hart, P. (1990). *Groupthink in government.* Amsterdam: Swets & Zeitlinger.

Thayer, L. (1968). *Communication and communication systems.* Homewood, IL: Irwin.

Thibaut, J. W., & Kelley, H. H. (1959). *The social psychology of groups.* New York: Wiley.

Thibaut, J., & Walker, L. (1975). *Procedural justice: A psychological analysis.* New York: Erlbaum.

Thibaut, J., & Walker, L. (1978). A theory of procedure. *California Law Review, 66,* 541–566.

Thibaut, J. W. & Kelly, H. H. (1959). *The social psychology of groups.* New York: Wiley.

Thierry, H. (1998). Compensating work. In P. J. D. Drenth, H. Thierry, & C. J. de Wolff (Eds.), *Handbook of work and organizational psychology* (Vol. 4, pp. 291–319). Philadelphia, PA: Psychology Press.

Thompson, J. E., & Carsrud, A. L. (1976). The effects of experimentally induced illusions of invulnerability and vulnerability on decisional risk taking in triads. *Journal of Social Psychology, 100,* 263–267.

Thye, S. R., Lawler, E. J., Macy, M. W., & Walker, H. A. (Eds.) (2001). *Advances in group processes* (Vol. 18). Oxford, UK: Elsevier.

Tindale, R. S., & Anderson, E. M. (1998). Small group research and applied social psychology: An introduction. In R. S. Tindale, L. Heath, J. Edwards, E. J. Posavac, F. B. Bryant, Y. Suarez-Balcazar,

E. Henderson-King, & J. Myer (Eds.), *Social psychological applications to social issues: Theory and research on small groups* (Vol. 4, pp. 1–8). New York: Plenum.

Tjosvold, D. (1995). Cooperation theory, constructive controversy, and effectiveness: Learning from crisis. In R. A. Guzzo & E. Salas (Eds.), *Team effectiveness and decision making in organizations* (pp. 79–112). San Francisco: Jossey-Bass.

Tjosvold, D. (1998). Cooperative and competitive goal approach to conflict: Accomplishments and challenges. *Applied Psychology: An International Review*, 47, 285–313.

Tompkins, P. K., & Redding, W. C. (1988). Organizational communication: Past and present tenses. In G. M. Goldhaber & G. A. Barnett (Eds.), *Handbook of organizational communication* (pp. 5–34). Norwood, NJ: Ablex.

Tornblom, K. Y., & Foa, U. G. (1983). Choice of a distribution principle: Cross-cultural effects of the effects of resources. *Acta Sociologica*, 26, 161–173.

Tougas, F., Brown, R., Beaton, A. M., & Joly, S. (1995). Neosexism: Plus ca change, plus c'est pareil. *Personality and Social Psychology Bulletin*, 21, 842–849.

Tougas, F., & Veilleux, F. (1988). The influence of identification, collective relative deprivation, and procedure of implementation on women's response to affirmative action: A causal modelling approach. *Canadian Journal of Behavioural Science*, 20, 15–28.

Townsend, J., Phillips, J. S., & Elkins, T. J. (2000). Employee retaliation: The neglected consequence of poor leader-member exchange relations. *Journal of Occupational Health Psychology*; 5, 457–463.

Trevino, L. K., Daft, R. L., & Lengel, R. H. (1990). Understanding managers' media choices: A symbolic interactionist perspective. In J. Fulk & C. Steinfield (Eds.), *Organizations and communication technology* (pp. 71–94). Newbury Park, CA: Sage.

Trew, T. (1979). Theory and ideology at work. In R. Fowler, B. Hodge, G. Kress, & T. Trew (Eds.), *Language and control* (pp. 94–116). London: Routledge & Kegan Paul.

Triandis, H. C. (1989). The self and social behavior in differing cultural contexts. *Psychological Review*, 96, 506–520.

Tsui, A., Egan, T., & O'Reilly, C. (1992). Being different: Relational demography and organizational attachment. *Administrative Science Quarterly*, 37, 549–579.

Turner, J. C. (1975). Social comparison and social identity: Some prospects for intergroup behaviour. *European Journal of Social Psychology*, 5, 5–34.

Turner, J. C. (1981). The experimental social psychology of intergroup behavior. In J. C. Turner & H. Giles (Eds.), *Intergroup behavior* (pp. 66-101). Chicago: University of Chicago Press.

Turner, J. C. (1982). Towards a cognitive redefinition of the social group. In H. Tajfel (Ed.), *Social identity and intergroup relations* (pp. 15–40). Cambridge: Cambridge University Press.

Turner, J. C. (1985). Social categorization and the self-concept: A social cognitive theory of group behaviour. In E. J. Lawler (Ed.), *Advances in Group Processes* (Vol. 2, pp. 77–122) Greenwich, CT: JAI Press.

Turner, J. C. (1987). A self-categorization theory. In J. C. Turner, M. A. Hogg, P. J. Oakes, S. D. Reicher, & M. S. Wetherell (Eds.), *Rediscovering the social group: A self-categorization theory* (pp. 42–67). Oxford, UK: Blackwell.

Turner, J. C. (1991). *Social influence*. Buckingham, UK: Open University Press.

Turner, J. C. (1999). Some current themes in research on social identity and self-categorization theories. In N. Ellemers, R. Spears, & B. Doosje (Eds.), *Social identity: Context, commitment, content* (pp. 6–34). Oxford, UK: Blackwell.

Turner, J. C. (2001). Foreword. In S. A. Haslam, *Psychology in organizations: The social identity approach* (pp. x–xiii). London: Sage.

Turner J. C., & Brown R. J. (1978). Social status, cognitive alternatives and intergroup relations. In H. Tajfel (Ed.), *Differentiation between social groups: Studies in the social psychology of intergroup relations* (pp. 171–199). London: Academic Press.

Turner, J. C., Brown, R. J., & Tajfel, H. (1979). Social comparison and group interest in ingroup favouritism. *European Journal of Social Psychology*, 9, 187–204.

Turner, J. C., & Haslam, S. A. (2001). Social identity, organizations, and leadership. In M. E. Turner (Ed.), *Groups at work: Theory and research* (pp. 25–65). Mahwah, NJ: Erlbaum.

Turner, J. C., Hogg, M. A., Oakes, P. J., Reicher, S. D., & Wetherell, M. S. (1987). *Rediscovering the social group: A self-categorization theory.* Oxford, UK: Blackwell.

Turner, J. C., & Oakes, P. J. (1989). Self-categorization and social influence. In P. B. Paulus (Ed.), *The psychology of group influence* (2nd ed., pp. 233–275). Hillsdale, NJ: Erlbaum.

Turner, J. C., Oakes, P. J., Haslam, S. A., & McGarty, C. A. (1994). Self and collective: Cognition and social context. *Personality and Social Psychology Bulletin, 20,* 454–463.

Turner, J. C., & Onorato, R. S. (1999). Social identity, personality and the self-concept: A self-categorization perspective. In T. R. Tyler, R. Kramer, & O. John (Eds.), *The psychology of the social self* (pp. 11–46). Hillsdale, NJ: Erlbaum.

Turner, M. E. (1992). Group effectiveness under threat: The impact of structural centrality and performance set. *Journal of Social Behavior and Personality, 7,* 511–528.

Turner, M. E., & Horvitz, T. (2000). The dilemma of threat: Group effectiveness and ineffectiveness in crisis. In M. E. Turner (Ed.), *Groups at Work: Theory and research.* (pp. 445–470). Mahwah, NJ: Erlbaum.

Turner, M. E., & Pratkanis, A. R. (1994a). [Effects of structured decision aids on decision effectiveness under groupthink]. Unpublished raw data. San Jose State University.

Turner, M. E., & Pratkanis, A. R. (1994b). Social identity maintenance prescriptions for preventing groupthink: Reducing identity protection and enhancing intellectual conflict. [Special issue]. *International Journal of Conflict Management, 5,* 254–270.

Turner, M. E., & Pratkanis, A. R. (1997). Mitigating groupthink by stimulating constructive conflict. In C. K. de Dreu & E. van de Vliert (Eds.), *Using conflict in organizations* (pp. 53–71). London: Sage.

Turner, M. E., & Pratkanis, A. R. (1998a). A social identity maintenance theory of groupthink. *Organizational Behavior and Human Decision Processes, 73,* 210–235.

Turner, M. E., & Pratkanis, A. R. (1998b). Twenty-five years of groupthink research: Lessons in the development of a theory. *Organizational Behavior and Human Decision Processes, 73,* 105–115.

Turner, M. E., Pratkanis, A. R., Probasco, P., & Leve, C. (1992). Threat, cohesion, and group effectiveness: Testing a social identity maintenance perspective on groupthink. *Journal of Personality and Social Psychology, 63,* 781–796.

Tyler, T. R. (1989). The psychology of procedural justice: A test of the group value model. *Journal of Personality and Social Psychology, 57,* 830–838.

Tyler, T. R. (1997). The psychology of legitimacy: A relational perspective on voluntary deference to authorities. *Personality and Social Psychology Review, 1,* 323–345.

Tyler, T. R. (1998). The psychology of authority relations: A relational perspective on influence and power in groups. In R. M. Kramer & M. A. Neale (Eds.), *Power and influence in organizations* (pp. 251–260). London: Sage.

Tyler, T. R. (1999). Why people cooperate with organizations: An identity-based perspective. *Research in Organizational Behavior, 21,* 201–246.

Tyler, T. R., & Blader, S. L. (2000). *Cooperation in groups. Procedural justice, social identity, and behavioral engagement.* Philadelphia, PA: Psychology Press.

Tyler, T. R., Boeckmann, R. J., Smith, H. J., & Huo, Y. J. (1997). *Social justice in a diverse society.* Boulder, CO: Westview Press.

Tyler, T. R., & Degoey, P. (1995). Collective restraint in social dilemmas: Procedural justice and social identification effects on support for authorities. *Journal of Personality and Social Psychology, 69,* 482–497.

Tyler, T. R., Degoey, P., & Smith, H. (1996). Understanding why the justice of group procedures matters: A test of the psychological dynamics of the group-value model. *Journal of Personality and Social Psychology, 70,* 913–930.

Tyler, T. R., Huo, Y. J., & Lind, E. A. (1999). The two psychologies of conflict resolution:

Differing antecedents of pre-experience choices and post-experience evaluations. *Group Processes and Intergroup Relations*, 2, 99–118.

Tyler, T. R., & Lind, E. A. (1992). A relational model of authority in groups. In M. Zanna (Ed.), *Advances in Experimental Social Psychology*, 25, 115–191.

Tyler, T. R., Lind, E. A., & Huo, Y. J. (1995). *Social categorization and social orientation effects on the psychology of procedural justice.* Unpublished manuscript, University of California, Berkeley.

Tyler, T. R., Lind, E. A., Ohbuchi, K., Sugawara, I., & Huo, Y. J. (1998). Conflict with outsiders: Disputing within and across cultural boundaries. *Personality and Social Psychology Bulletin, 24*, 137–146.

Tyler, T. R., & Smith, H. J. (1998). Social justice and social movements. In D. Gilbert, S. Fiske, & G. Lindzey (Eds.), *The handbook of social psychology* (4th ed., pp. 595–629). Boston: McGraw-Hill.

Tyler, T. R., & Smith, H. J. (1999). Justice, social identity and group processes. In T. R. Tyler, R. Kramer, & O. John (Eds.), *The psychology of the social self* (pp. 223–264). Mahwah, NJ: Erlbaum.

Uhl-Bien, M., & Graen, G. B. (1993). Leadership-making in self-managing professional work teams: An empirical investigation. In K. E. Clark, M. B. Clark & D. P. Campbell (Eds.), *The impact of leadership* (pp. 379–387). West Orange, NJ: Leadership Library of America.

Uzubalis, M. (1999). *For the good of the organization: The role of social identity salience and influence in employees' performance of organizational citizenship behaviour.* Unpublished thesis: The Australian National University.

Valacich, J. S., Dennis, A. R., & Nunamaker, J. F. (1991). Electronic meeting support: The Group Systems concept [Special issue]. *International Journal of Man Machine Studies, 34*, 261–282.

Valacich, J. S., Jessup, L. M., Dennis, A. R., & Nunamaker, J. F. (1992). A conceptual framework of anonymity in group support systems. *Group Decision and Negotiation, 1*, 219–241.

Valacich, J. S., Paranka, D., George, J. F., &

Nunamaker, J. F. (1993). Communication concurrency and the new media: A new dimension for media richness. *Communication Research, 20*, 249–276.

van den Bos, K., Vermunt, R., & Wilke, H. A. M. (1996). The consistency rule and the voice effect: The influence of expectations on procedural fairness judgments and performance. *European Journal of Social Psychology, 26*, 411–428.

van der Weijden, B., & Ellemers, N. (2000). *Onderzoek naar de mening van medewerkers over de invoering van kostprijzen.* Unpublished research report. Leiden University.

van Dyne, L., Cummings, L. L., & Parks, J. M. (1995). Extra-role behaviors: In pursuit of construct and definitional clarity (a bridge over muddied waters). *Research in Organizational Behavior, 117*, 215–285.

van Dyne, L., Graham, J. W., & Dienesch, R. M. (1994). Organizational citizenship behaviour: Construct redefinition, measurement, and validation. *Academy of Management Journal, 37*, 765–802.

van Knippenberg, A., & Ellemers, N. (1990). Social identity and intergroup differentiation processes. *European Review of Social Psychology, 1*, 137–169.

van Knippenberg, A., & Ellemers, N. (1993). Strategies in intergroup relations. In M. A. Hogg & D. Abrams (Eds.), *Group motivation: Social psychological perspectives* (pp. 17–23). New York: Prentice-Hall.

van Knippenberg, A., & van Oers, H. (1984). Social identity and equity concerns in intergroup perceptions. *British Journal of Social Psychology, 23*, 351–361.

van Knippenberg, D. (1999). Social identity and persuasion: Reconsidering the role of group membership. In D. Abrams & M. A. Hogg (Eds.), *Social identity and social cognition* (pp. 315–331). Oxford, UK: Blackwell.

van Knippenberg, D. (2000a). Work motivation and performance: A social identity perspective. *Applied Psychology: An International Review, 49*, 357–371.

van Knippenberg, D. (2000b). Group norms, prototypicality, and persuasion. In D. J. Terry & M. A. Hogg (Eds.), *Attitudes, behavior, and social context: The role of norms* and group membership, (pp. 157–170). Mahwah, NJ: Erlbaum.

van Knippenberg, D. (2002). *Social identification, what it is and is not. A theoretical note on the nature of identification and the need for clear conceptualizations.* Unpublished manuscript, University of Amsterdam.

van Knippenberg, D. (in press). Intergroup relations in organizations. In M. West, D. Tjosvold, & K. G. Smith (Eds.), *International handbook of organizational teamwork and cooperative working.* Chichester, UK: Wiley.

van Knippenberg, D., De Dreu, C. K. W., & Homan, A. C. (2001). *Towards an integrative theory of organizational diversity and group performance: The Categorization-Elaboration Model.* Unpublished manuscript, University of Amsterdam.

van Knippenberg, D., Haslam, S. A., & Platow, M. J. (2000, July). *A social identity perspective on organizational diversity. When is being different not a problem?* Paper presented at the EAESP Small Group Meeting on Social Identity Processes in Organizations, Amsterdam.

van Knippenberg, D., & Hogg, M. A. (Eds.) (2001). Social identity processes in organizations. [Special issue]. *Group Processes and Intergroup Relations*, Vol. 4.

van Knippenberg, D., & Hogg, M. A. (Eds.) (in press). *Identity, leadership, and power.* London: Sage.

van Knippenberg, D., Platow, M. J., & Haslam, S. A. (2001). *Group composition and group identification: Diversity as an aspect of identity.* Unpublished manuscript, University of Amsterdam.

van Knippenberg, D., & Sleebos, E. (2001). *Further explorations of the organizational identification concept: Identification versus commitment.* Unpublished manuscript, University of Amsterdam.

van Knippenberg, D., van Knippenberg, B., Monden, L., de Lima, F. (2002). Organizational identification after a merger: A social identity perspective. *British Journal of Psychology, 41*, 233–252.

van Knippenberg, D., van Knippenberg, B., & van Dijk, E. (2000). Who takes the lead in risky decision making? Effects of group members' individual riskiness and proto-

typicality. *Organizational Behavior and Human Decision Processes, 83*, 213–234.

van Knippenberg, D., & van Leeuwen, E. (2001). Organizational identity after a merger: Sense of continuity as the key to postmerger identification. In M.A. Hogg & D.J. Terry (Eds.), *Social identity processes in organizational contexts* (pp. 249–264). Philadelphia, PA: Psychology Press.

van Knippenberg, D., & van Schie, E. C. M. (2000). Foci and correlates of organizational identification. *Journal of Occupational and Organizational Psychology, 73*, 137–147.

van Leeuwen, E., & van Knippenberg, D. (1999). *Social value orientations and group performance: The role of expectations of other group members' effort.* Unpublished manuscript, Leiden University.

van Leeuwen, E., van Knippenberg, D., & Ellemers, N. (2001a). *The merits of a merger mismatch: Shifts in identification from pre- to post-merger group membership.* Unpublished manuscript, Leiden University.

van Leeuwen, E., van Knippenberg, D., & Ellemers, N. (2001b, May). *Continuing and changing group identities: The effects of merging on social identification and ingroup bias.* Paper presented at the Tenth European Congress on Work and Organizational Psychology, Prague.

van Maanen, B., & Ellemers, N. (1999). *Organisatieverandering: identiteitsverandering? Een sociaal psychologische verklaring voor weerstand tegen organisatieverandering, onderzocht in het onderwijs.* Unpublished research report. Amsterdam: Free University.

Van Oudenhoven, J. P., & deBoer, T. (1995). Complementarity and similarity of partners in international mergers. *Basic and Applied Social Psychology, 17*, 343–356.

van Vugt, M., & de Cremer, D. (1999). Leadership in social dilemmas: The effects of group identification on collective actions to provide public goods. *Journal of Personality and Social Psychology, 76*, 587–599.

Vasquez, M. J. T. (2001). Leveling the playing field—Toward the emancipation of women. *Psychology of Women Quarterly, 25*, 89–97.

Vecchio, R. P. (1982). A further test of leadership effects due to between-group and within-group variation. *Journal of Applied Psychology, 67,* 200–208.

Vecchio, R. P. (1998). Leader-member exchange, objective performance, employment duration, and supervisor ratings: Testing for moderation and mediation. *Journal of Business and Psychology, 12,* 327–341.

Veenstra, K., & Haslam, S. A. (2000). Willingness to participate in industrial protest: Exploring social identification in context. *British Journal of Social Psychology, 39,* 153–172.

Veugelers, W. (1998). Werken aan de vernieuwing van de Tweede Fase Voortgezet Onderwijs. In: W. Veugelers & H. Zijlstra (Eds.), *Lesgeven in het studiehuis* (pp. 11–18). Netherlands: Garant.

Vollman, T. (1996). *The transformation imperative.* Boston, MA: Harvard Business School Press.

von Grumbkow, J., Deen, E., Steensma, H., & Wilke, H. (1976). The effect of future interaction on the distribution of rewards. *European Journal of Social Psychology, 6,* 119–123.

Vroom, V. H. (1964). *Work and motivation.* New York: Wiley.

Wagner, D. G., & Berger, J. (1997). Gender and interpersonal task behaviors: Status expectation accounts. *Sociological perspectives, 40,* 1–32.

Wagner, J. A. (1994). Participation's effects on performance and satisfaction: A reconsideration of research evidence. *Academy of Management Review, 19,* 312–330.

Wagner, J. A. (1995). Studies of individualism–collectivism: Effects on cooperation in groups. *Academy of Management Journal, 38,* 152–172.

Wagner, W., Pfeffer, J., & O'Reilly, C. (1984). Organizational demography and turnover in top management groups. *Administrative Science Quarterly, 29,* 74–92.

Walker, I., & Crogan, M. (1998). Academic performance, prejudice, and the jigsaw classroom: New pieces to the puzzle. *Journal of Community and Applied Social Psychology, 8,* 381–393.

Walter, G. A. (1985). Culture collision in mergers and acquisitions. In P. J. Frost, L.

F. Moore, M. R. Louis, C. C. Lundberg, & J. Martin (Eds.), *Organizational culture.* Beverly Hills, CA: Sage.

Wallace, N. (1998). *Soldiering reassessed: Congruity between self-categorization, task condition and goals as a determinant of social loafing, labouring and facilitation.* Unpublished thesis. The Australian National University.

Walster, E., & Walster, G. W. (1975). Equity and social justice. *Journal of Social Issues, 31,* 21–43.

Walster, E., Walster, G. W., & Berscheid, E. (1978). *Equity: Theory and research.* Boston: Allyn & Bacon.

Walther, J. B. (1992). Interpersonal effects in computer-mediated interaction: A relational perspective. *Communication Research, 19,* 52–90.

Walther, J. B. (1994). Anticipated ongoing interaction versus channel effects on relational communication in computer-mediated interaction. *Human Communication Research, 20,* 473–501.

Walther, J. B. (1995). Relational aspects of computer-mediated communication: Experimental observations over time. *Organizational Science, 6,* 186–203.

Walther, J. B. (1997). Group and interpersonal effects in international computer-mediated collaboration. *Human Communication Research, 24,* 186–203.

Walther, J. B. & Burgoon, J. K. (1992). Relational communication in computer-mediated interaction. *Human Communication Research, 19,* 50–88.

Walzdus, S., Mummendey, A., Wenzel, M., & Weber, U. (in press). Towards tolerance: Representations of superordinate categories and perceived ingroup prototypicality. *Journal of Exerimental Social Psychology.*

Walzer, M. (1983). *Spheres of justice: A defense of pluralism and equality.* New York: Basic Books.

Watson, W., Kumar, K., & Michaelsen, L. (1993). Cultural diversity's impact on interaction processes and performance: Comparing homogeneous and diverse task groups. *Academy of Management Journal, 36,* 590–602.

Wayne, S. J., Shore, L. M., & Liden, R. C. (1997). Perceived organizational support and leader-member exchange: A social exchange perspective. *Academy of Management Journal, 40,* 82–111.

Weber, M. (1947). *The theory of social and economic organization.* (A. M. Henderson & T. Parsons, Trans.). Glencoe, IL: Free Press.

Weber, Y., Shenkar, O., & Raveh, A. (1996). National and corporate cutlural fit in merger/acquisitions: An exploratory study. *Management Science, 42,* 1215–1227.

Wegge, J. (1999, June 22–24). *Participation in goal-setting: Some novel findings and a comprehensive theory as a new ending to an old story.* Paper presented at the 4th International Work Motivation conference. Sydney, Australia.

Wegge, J. (2000). Participation in group goal setting: Some novel findings and a comprehensive model as a new ending to an old story. *Applied Psychology: An International Review, 49,* 498–516.

Wegge, J. (2001). Zusammensetzung von Arbeitsgruppen. In E. Witte (Ed.), *Leistungsverbesserungen in aufgabenorientierten Kleingruppen* (pp. 35–94). Lengerich: Pabst.

Wegge, J. (2001a). Gruppenarbeit Group work. In H. Schuler (Ed.), *Lehrbuch der Personalpsychologie* (pp. 483–507). Göttingen, Germany: Hogrefe.

Wegge, J. (2001b). Motivation, information processing and performance: Effects of goal setting on basic cognitive processes. In A. Efklides, J. Kuhl, & R. Sorrentino (Eds.), *Trends and prospects in motivational research* (pp. 271–298). Dordrecht: Kluwer.

Wegge, J. (2001c). Participative and directive group goal setting: Two equivalent leadership techniques promoting motivation gains in groups? Manuscript submitted for publication.

Wegge, J. (2002). Emotionen in Organisationen [Emotions in organizations]. In H. Schuler (Ed.), *Enzyklopädie der Psychologie. Organisationspsychologie* (5.1-89). Göttingen: Hogrefe.

Wegge, J., & Haslam, S. A. (2001). *Motivation gains and motivation losses in teams.* Unpublished manuscript, University of Dortmund.

Wegge, J., & Kleinbeck, U. (1996). Goal setting and group performance: Impact of

achievement and affiliation motives, participation in goal setting, and task interdependence of group members. In T. Gjesme & R. Nygard (Eds.), *Advances in motivation* (pp. 145–177). Oslo: Scandinavian University Press.

Wegner, D. (1986). Transactive memory: A contemporary analysis of the group mind. In B. Mullen & G. R. Goethals (Eds.), *Theories of group behavior* (pp. 185–208). New York: Springer-Verlag.

Weick, K. E. (1969). *The social psychology of organizing.* Reading, MA: Addison Wesley.

Weick, K. E., & Roberts, K. H. (1993). Collective mind in organizations: Heedful interrelating on flight decks. *Administrative Science Quarterly, 38,* 357–381.

Weingart, L. R. (1992). Impact of group goals, task component complexity, effort, and planning on group performance. *Journal of Applied Psychology, 77,* 682–293.

Weisband, S. P. (1992). Group discussion and first advocacy effects in computer-mediated and face-to-face decision making groups. *Organizational Behavior and Human Decision Processes, 53,* 352–380.

Weisband, S. P., Scheider, S. K., & Connolly, T. (1995). Computer-mediated communication and social information: Status salience and status differences. *Academy of Management Journal, 38,* 1124–1151.

Weldon, E., Jehn, K. A., & Pradhan, P. (1991). Processes that mediate the relationship between a group goal and improved group performance. *Journal of Personality and Social Psychology, 61,* 555–569.

Weldon, E., & Weingart, L. R. (1993). Group goals and group performance. *British Journal of Social Psychology, 32,* 307–334.

Wenzel, M. (1997). *Soziale Kategorisierungen im Bereich distributiver Gerechtigkeit.* Münster: Waxmann.

Wenzel, M. (2000). Justice and identity: The significance of inclusion for perceptions of entitlement and the justice motive. *Personality and Social Psychology Bulletin, 26,* 157–176.

Wenzel, M. (2001). A social categorization approach to distributive justice: Social identity as the link between relevance of inputs and need for justice. *British Journal of Social Psychology, 40,* 315–335.

Wenzel, M. (2002). What is social about justice? Inclusive identity and group values as the basis of the justice motive. *Journal of Experimental Social Psychology, 38,* 205–218.

Wenzel, M., & Mikula, G. (2001). Conflicts, diplomacy and the psychology of justice. Unpublished manuscript: Australian National University.

Wenzel, M., Mummendey, A., Weber, U., & Waldzus, S. (in press). The ingroup as pars pro toto: Projection from the ingroup onto the inclusive category as a precursor to social discrimination. *Personality and Social Psychology Bulletin.*

West, M. A. (1990). The social psychology of innovation in groups. In M. A. West & J. L. Farr (Eds.), *Innovation and creativity at work: Psychological and organizational strategies* (pp. 309–333). Chichester, UK: Wiley.

Whetten, D. A., & Godfrey, P.C. (Eds.) (1998). *Identity inorganizations: Building theory through conversations.* London: Sage.

Whyte, G. (1989). Groupthink reconsidered. *Academy of Management Journal, 14,* 40–56.

Widmeyer, W. N., & Ducharme, K. (1997). Team building through team goal setting. *Journal of Applied Sport Psychology, 9,* 97–113.

Wiener, M., & Mehrabian, A. (1968). *Language within language: Immediacy, a channel in verbal communication.* New York: Appleton-Century-Crofts.

Wigboldus, D. H. J., Semin, G., & Spears, R. (2000). How do we communicate stereotypes? Linguistic bases and inferential consequences. *Journal of Personality and Social Psychology, 78,* 5–18.

Wilder, C. (1985, October 14). Intel to exit dynamic RAM chip mart: Company posts $3.6 million loss in third-quarter 1985. *Computerworld,*

Wilder, D. A. (1990). Some determinants of the persuasive power of in-groups and out-groups: Organization of information and attribution of independence. *Journal of Personality and Social Psychology, 59,* 1202–1213.

Williams, C. L. (1992). The glass escalator: Hidden advantages for men in the "female" professions. *Social Problems, 39,* 253–267.

Williams, K. D., & Karau, S. J. (1991). Social loafing and social compensation: The effects of expectations of co-worker performance. *Journal of Personality and Social Psychology, 61,* 570–581.

Williams, K. Y., & O'Reilly, C. A. (1998). Demography and diversity in organizations: A review of 40 years of research. *Research in Organizational Behavior, 20,* 77–140.

Williams, L. J., & Anderson, S. E. (1991). Job satisfaction and organizational commitment as predictors of organizational citizenship and in-role behaviors. *Journal of Management, 17,* 601–617.

Winter, S. J., & Taylor, S. L. (1999). The role of information technology in the transformation of work: A comparison of post-industrial, industrial, and protoindustrial organization. In G. DeSanctis & J. Fulk (Eds.), *Shaping organization form: Communication, connection, and community* (pp. 101–128). Thousand Oaks, CA: Sage.

Wirbel, L. & Ristelhueber, R. (1984, October 14). Intel phases out DRAM: Motorola dropping 64K units as price pressure mounts. *Electronic News, 31,* 1.

Woodman, R. (1989). Organization change and development: New arenas for inquiry and action. *Journal of Management, 15,* 205–228.

Worchel, S., Rothgerber, H., Day, E. A., Hart, D., & Butemeyer, J. (1998). Social identity and individual productivity within groups. *British Journal of Social Psychology, 37,* 389–413.

Wright, P. M., George, J. M., Farnsworth, S. R., & McMahan, G. C. (1993). Productivity and extra-role behavior: The effects of goals and incentives on spontaneous helping. *Journal of Applied Psychology, 78,* 374–381.

Wright, S. C. (1997). Ambiguity, social influence, and collective action: Generating collective protest in response to tokenism. *Personality and Social Psychology Bulletin, 23,* 1277–1290.

Wright, S. C., & Taylor, D. M. (1998). Responding to tokenism: Individual action in the face of collective injustice. *European Journal of Social Psychology, 28,* 647–667.

Wright, S. C., Taylor, D. M., & Moghaddam, F. M. (1990). Responding to membership in a disadvantaged group: From acceptance to collective protest. *Journal of Personality and Social Psychology, 58,* 994–1003.

Yu, A. (1998). *Creating the digital future: The secrets of consistent innovation at Intel.* New York: Free Press.

Yukl, G. (1998). *Leadership in organizations.* New York: Prentice-Hall.

Yzerbyt, V., Rocher, S., & Schadron, G. (1997). Stereotypes as explanations: A subjective essentialistic view of group perception. In R. Spears, P.J. Oakes, N. Ellemers, & S.A. Haslam (Eds.), *The social psychology of stereotyping and group life* (pp. 20–50). Oxford, UK: Blackwell.

Zaccaro, S. J., & Dobbins, G. H. (1989). Contrasting group and organizational commitment: Evidence for differences among multilevel attachments. *Journal of Organizational Behavior, 10,* 267–273.

Zimbardo, P. G. (1969). The human choice: individuation reason and order versus deindividuation impulse and chaos. In W. J. Arnold & D. Levine, (Eds.), *Nebraska Symposium on Motivation* (Vol.17, pp. 237–307). Lincoln: University of Nebraska Press.

Zmud, R. (1990). Opportunities for strategic information manipulation through new information technology. In J. Fulk & C. Steinfield (Eds.), *Organizations and communication technology* (pp. 95–116). Newbury Park, CA: Sage.

Zuboff, S. (1988). *In the age of the smart machine: The future of work and power.* New York: Basic Books.

Zuckerman, M. (1979). Attribution of success and failure revisited, or the motivational bias is alive and well in attributional theory. *Journal of Personality, 47,* 245–287.

Author Index

LIVERPOOL
JOHN MOORES UNIVERSITY
AVRIL ROBARTS LRC
TEL. 0151 231 4022

Subject Index

Books are to be returned on or before

LIVERPOOL JMU LIBRARY

3 1111 01177 5929

LIVERPOOL
JOHN MOORES UNIVERSITY
AVRIL ROBARTS LRC
TITHEBARN STREET
LIVERPOOL L2 2ER
TEL. 0151 231 4022